AMERICAN WINE

AMERICAN WINE

A COMING-OF-AGE STORY

TOM ACITELLI

CHICAGO
REVIEW
PRESS

Copyright © 2015 by Tom Acitelli
All rights reserved
First edition
Published by Chicago Review Press Incorporated
814 North Franklin Street
Chicago, Illinois 60610
ISBN 978-1-56976-167-0

Library of Congress Cataloguing-in-Publication Data
Acitelli, Tom.
  American wine : a coming-of-age story / Tom Acitelli. — First edition.
    pages cm
  Includes bibliographical references and index.
  ISBN 978-1-56976-167-0 (cloth)
  1. Wine and wine making—United States—History. 2. Wine industry—
United States—History. 3. Vintners—United States—Biography. I. Title.

  TP557.A235 2015
  338.4'766320973—dc23

                    2015012582

Interior design: Jonathan Hahn
Interior layout: Nord Compo

Printed in the United States of America
5 4 3 2 1

To my sister Nan

CONTENTS

PART II

PART III

Prologue

THE WORLD'S BIGGEST WINE MARKET

2010 | Brooklyn

It was 2010, and my wife and I were in a classic red-sauce joint in Brooklyn, one that had thus far mercifully escaped the waves of gentrification sweeping the borough. The elderly waiter asked us what sort of wine we would like with our pastas. Being a worldly Manhattan transplant (via North Carolina), I asked for a wine list—the usual pages and columns listing grape types and vintages, the sorts chockablock adjectivally redolent descriptions of what I might taste and smell; and, of course, containing the prices. Those prices! Banes of first dates, always scaling upward in what seemed like a maddeningly arbitrary manner that you never, ever encountered with beer.

The waiter frowned.

"The wine list, please," I repeated.

"Wine, yes," he said in a heavy Italian accent, smiling as he seemed to understand. "We have red, white, and rosé—you know, pink-a."

Poor man. I knew better, didn't I? Wine, especially the sort you ordered in restaurants, was and always had been infinitely more complex. Everyone knew that. Where were the grapes, the vintages, the prices? Where were *oaky* and *jammy* and their battalions of descriptive chums? Here, in this red-sauce throwback, where the menu, too, was simple, we were being offered three generic choices.

Not until I started researching this book, the first history of American fine wine since its rise in the early 1960s, did I realize that that elderly waiter was on to something—and that I and other consumers had been woefully misled.

About three years after that Brooklyn encounter, just as I commenced my research in earnest, the *New York Times* published an article about what the writer called "the 'wine-ification' of beer, the push by many brewers to make their product as respectable to pair with braised short ribs as is a nice Chateauneuf-du-Pape, and at a price to match." The article cited the many

American craft breweries packaging their beers in twenty-two-ounce, wine-like bottles and the rash of restaurants sporting such bottles along with those of wine.

All hell broke loose among the craft beer commentariat. Fans and producers inundated the article's online version with comments and soon took the debate to beer blogs and trade websites. I knew enough from my last book, *The Audacity of Hops: The History of America's Craft Beer Revolution*, to know that beer in twenty-two-ounce bottles was nothing new; it dated from at least the early 1990s, when newer breweries resorted to the packaging to save money (bigger bottles meant fewer bottles to fill). I also knew that beer aficionados had been pairing their brews with food since at least the 1970s in the United States, and that restaurants had begun introducing the practice about ten years later.

What I did not know—even after a couple of years immersed in food and drink research—was what rankled some in the American craft beer movement: that wine, however fine, was the wrong measure for beer, however crafted. Why? Because fine wine in the United States, like craft beer, was still coming into its own in the second decade of the twenty-first century, and it was still trying to overcome the consuming public's decades-old perception of it as either fortified hooch or the stuff Europeans (or their American children) drank. "The old American term for an alcoholic was 'wino,' and there's a reason for that," thundered Garrett Oliver, the well-respected brewmaster of the Brooklyn Brewery, in a statement responding to the *Times* article. Until fairly recently, the concept of American-made fine wine, or fine wine in general, was simply foreign to many in this nation (as was, for that matter, the concept of craft beer, the sort made with traditional ingredients in small batches by independent brewers).

Still the perception held all the way into the pages of the national newspaper of record that wine in America was the beverage—was the foodstuff, period—against which all others were, and should be, measured in terms of quality, value, and desirability; and, more important, that American consumers had always taken this for granted. No popular history book, I soon discovered, had drawn that relatively straight (though still revolutionary) line from about the late 1960s—when fine wine, especially American-made fine wine, was as exotic in the United States as a beer from a brewery not called Anheuser-Busch—to our current cornucopia of grape expectations. None, either, had paid much attention to the rise of tangential fields, such as wine bars and sommeliers, or the intersection of pop culture and American fine wine; those tended to be explained away as inevitable offshoots, a kind of build-it-and-they-will-come by-product of fine wine, when, in fact, their growth was no more assured than fine wine's in general. Indeed, I was surprised to learn that even those working decades in the industry were unfamiliar with some of the events, turning points, and personalities I will recount (though American wine professionals can be forgiven for mixing up their names and dates—they've been awfully busy lately). Finally, no book until now has yet to accurately explain why Americans have largely come to prefer lusher, stronger wines. Contrary to near-canonical myth, it is not because of the opinions of one particular critic from suburban Baltimore.

This book is the first of its kind: a popular history of American fine wine that draws a clear line from the late 1960s through today, connecting the dots—the people, the places, the events, the trends, and the simple twists of fate.

From the end of Prohibition in 1933 through the 1960s, Americans really did face essentially only three choices, the same ones the waiter in Brooklyn annunciated: red, white, and rosé (a.k.a. pink), the latter open to all sorts of syrupy sweet interpretations. It is a difficult thing to believe in our era of wine-laden supermarket aisles, wine critics at most major newspapers, entire magazines dedicated solely to wine and its wonders, and even television shows and movies hinging on fine wine. If US consumers wanted something better, they usually had to turn to France or, in a pinch, Italy. American-made wines were generic, nondescript, made cheaply to be sold cheaply in screwtop jugs or straight from the tap in whatever vessel would hold them; and they weren't that popular, even with Americans themselves and especially with foreigners, who knew better.

Moreover, if Americans drank wine at all, they drank fortified varieties, those designed to wallop rather than to wow. In the first three decades-plus after the end of Prohibition, no new wineries of note opened in California's Napa Valley, which would become the nation's leading wine-making region; only a handful throughout the land crafted what this book will call fine wine. I was surprised to learn of grapes such as Alicante Bouschet and Carignan, cheaper varieties that undergirded most of the wine made and sold in the United States before the 1960s.

Things such as corkscrews and bulbous stemmed glasses—staples of many American households today—were uncommon and difficult to find into the 1960s; guides to pairing food and wine were equally so. The typical grocery store wine selection, even in larger, more cosmopolitan cities such as New York or Chicago, was dominated by generic, fortified brands, with the only fine wine selections coming invariably from France. Giant metropolitan areas such as Washington, DC–Baltimore and Los Angeles might have but one or two places that sold American-made fine wine.

Then, starting in the 1960s, things happened that changed everything forever. This book tells the story of what happened and why.

It's a story of underdog triumph, of beating not only formidable technological and agricultural odds but, more importantly of overcoming a huge societal deficit. Simply put, Americans by and large didn't *get* fine wine, and they didn't care to understand it, either. Frank Prial, the first regular wine critic for the *New York Times* (a job created in 1972, owing to the changes starting in the 1960s), summed it up beautifully: fine wine "came in at the top" in terms of perception, and it has confronted that sense of exoticness ever since.

Unless they grew up as part of immigrant families from southern Europe or traveled to certain overseas locales, most American consumers first experienced fine wine before the 1960s, if they did at all, through the gobbledygook of British critics, the leading wine writers in the English language, or through bottles from France, which had dominated the field for as long as anyone alive could remember—a dominance that allowed France to mask serious shortcomings in its wine.

A few events, the coverage they engendered, and a surprisingly few individuals changed all that. (Again, contrary to what has become received wisdom in American fine wine, it was *individuals*, plural, rather than one particular individual from suburban Baltimore.) Now America is the single biggest wine marketplace on earth, and some of the most enviable fine wine ever made dominates the US marketplace.

What do I mean by "fine wine"? Any drier, nonfortified wine, at any price point, made primarily from higher-end grape types, most of which originated in Europe. You know the names: Merlot, Chardonnay, Cabernet Sauvignon, Pinot Noir, Nebbiolo, Riesling, and more. These wines may be parts of blends; their grapes may have at times been grafted with lower-end grapes to further their cultivation; or they may stand alone, as what are called varietals, strong and independent in their bottles. They are, however they reach consumers, decidedly different from their fortified, sweeter forebears that once dominated domestic wine production. Also, I think "fine wine" should once and for all replace the term "table wine" as an acknowledgment of just how far wine has come in the United States in the last fifty-odd years. People, including many in the industry, have generally dispatched "table wine" to refer to those wines neither sparkling nor fortified; given the frenetic growth and unprecedented diversification of wine, such a definition is extremely limiting now. It's time to retire it in favor of a broader tent. Plus

I would wager that relatively few Americans actually sit at the kitchen or dining-room table to drink their wine.

While it will cover the rise of fine wine in America and the coming of age of certain styles in the United States, this book is neither a style guide nor a food-pairing guide. Oceans of real and virtual ink have been spilled in service of both of those pursuits. This book instead traces in large part how we got to the shores of that ocean of wine writing. Readers will not have to be intimately versed in wine terminology; where necessary, it will be explained. Nor will readers need to be schooled in wine-making. Wine is fermented grape juice. Yeast, whether added by the winemaker or from the skins of grapes themselves, breaks down the sugar of the juice to produce ethyl alcohol, the intoxicating element in wine. There are two major types of wine: red and white. Within those are myriad styles, varietals, blends, and so on. Certain of these will feature prominently in our story and will be explained then.

One last note for the reader perhaps wary of the often verbosely flabby subject of wine. Early craft beer critics, I quickly discovered in the research for my last book, took their subject very seriously but strove to make it accessible to the reading—and drinking—public. In fact, that accessibility was key to the growth of American craft beer, as the vast majority of smaller breweries did not advertise and instead leaned on media coverage to spread the hoppy word. I realized in pursuing this book, however, that wine critics, until fairly recently, often presented American fine wine as an opaque subject akin in difficulty to string theory; it demanded of readers a handy thesaurus, a flush credit line, and a genuflecting humility before the often self-appointed arbiters of taste. I don't know why the early critics, most of them European, presented their subject like that (and, thankfully, the trend is reversing itself). I think Prial's observation that fine wine "came in at the top" goes a long way to explaining the clubby verbosity surrounding a lot of wine criticism all the way into the twenty-first century; people—and critics are people—felt they had to sound particularly sophisticated when discussing Merlot, Chardonnay, et al., or they would not be taken seriously. Also, fine wine was commoditized, and quickly so, on a scale other drinks throughout American history could only dream of matching. No Ivy League economist has ever, after all, penned a treatise called "On Soda Pop Bullshit."

For now, put aside the critics (though they will come to play an outsized role, for good and ill in our story). Just know this going in: the *history* of American fine wine needn't be boring. The nation stood on the brink of something wonderful at the start of the 1960s, an underdog story little assured of a happy ending but one with all the makings of a gripping, good yarn. It has turned out to be a tale of rakes and rebels, characters and charismatics, the villainous and the virtuous, the world's worst bosses and the world's cleverest workers; of deflated egos and inflated prices, of naked ambition and cloaked deception; it is a story that transcends international boundaries, that celebrates American entrepreneurialism and its embrace of immigration; a story that could not have unfolded anywhere else. It is a story of sudden shifts as well as changes a long time coming.

And it all begins once upon a time with a pair of lovers stopping for lunch in France.

PART I

FRENCH CONNECTIONS
1948 | Rouen

"**W**ine at lunch?" **Julia Child's cheerful,** chirpy incredulity rended the restaurant's silence.

It was November 3, 1948, a Wednesday, and she and her husband of nearly two years, Paul Child, had stopped for lunch in Rouen, the town in northern France infamous as the site where the English burned Joan of Arc at the stake in the fifteenth century. The motoring couple—who were traveling from the North Atlantic ferry dock at Le Havre to Paris so Paul could take up a new position in the US Foreign Service—stopped en route at a restaurant recommended by the *Guide Michelin* called La Couronne, off Rouen's Place du Vieux Marché. The restaurant was warm, with a brown-and-white dining room that struck Julia Child as charmingly old-fashioned, if a little too cozy. A waiter was talking to other diners. Paul, fluent in French, whispered a translation: "The waiter is telling them about the chicken they ordered—how it was raised, how it will be cooked, what side dishes they can have with it, and which wines would go best."

Julia was amazed at the prospect. Wine for lunch? Even an American of her upbringing and opportunity could be forgiven for thinking it wholly inappropriate, scandalous even, to tipple the fruit of the vine in the early afternoon (in this particular case, a crisp, white Pouilly Fumé from the Loire region). Not so in France: wine made from higher-end grapes such as Chardonnay, Merlot, and Cabernet Sauvignon had been a staple of the afternoon table for decades, even centuries, by the time Paul and Julia drove their way into the heart of Gaul. The France they drove through still very much showed the shocks of World War II, which had traversed it for nearly five years, from the quick German invasion in May 1940 to the Allied liberation that began with D-day in June 1944. Bombed-out buildings shadowed the roads they passed, and desperate, economically decimated towns welcomed whatever business travelers might bestow. Americans in general were hailed as heroes, the US military and its attendant groups, including the foreign service, very much a presence in a France still dazed by cataclysm in 1948.

The Childs could not have known this—for the story had yet to be told—but World War II had also damaged the French wine industry, an integral part not only of the nation's economy but of its very identity as well. France for ages had been the world's leading wine producer and arbiter of taste; no one alive in 1948 could remember a time when France was not the global beacon of enology, the study of wine, and the producer of its most sought-after styles and vintages (*vintages* refer to the years the grapes were harvested). The Germans knew this. The Nazis looted what they wanted from French cellars and châteaus upon their conquest. Though Adolf Hitler was said to have declared French wine "nothing but vulgar vinegar," his top deputies were fans. Hermann Göring, the Third Reich's air chief, preferred wines from France's famed Bordeaux area, and the especially odious propaganda minister, Joseph Goebbels, was partial to ones from Bourgogne. They and others amassed vast collections of French wines throughout the war, spiriting them to their own cellars in Germany or inhaling them nightly in France.

Postwar efforts to recover wine that the Nazis purloined took years and sometimes proved fruitless. In one of the Nazis' last acts of barbarism toward France, as French resistance leader Charles de Gaulle made his triumphant entry into Paris on August 26, 1944, the Germans bombed the city's nearly four-hundred-year-old wholesale wine center, the Halle aux Vins. The attack destroyed thousands of valuable bottles and "sent shivers down the spines of wine merchants" in other parts of France, including Bordeaux and Bourgogne, the nation's two most highly regarded wine regions. As it turned out, heavy fighting largely spared the vineyards in both of those prime wine-making locales. Enough expertise survived as well to allow perhaps France's most spirited industry to toddle forth from the war and quickly assume its place once again at the pinnacle of world wine. As we will see in our story of the rise of American fine wine, that position was due almost as much to French expertise and effort after World War II as to the reactions of consumers, including Julia Child, to French wine.

By 1948 thirty-six-year-old Julia Child (née McWilliams) was what was commonly called a housewife, though by then she had already lived a peripatetic life that would have been the envy of most adventurous men. The oldest child of well-to-do parents in Pasadena, California, she was courted by the heir to the *Los Angeles Times*, but she eschewed a life of prominent leisure as the spouse of the most influential newspaper publisher in the Golden State, as well as the position of advertising manager for a Beverly Hills furniture store, for more stirring fare. This included stints in Ceylon, present-day Sri Lanka, and China while serving in the Office of Strategic Services, the precursor to the Central Intelligence Agency, during World War II.

It was in Ceylon that Julia McWilliams met Paul Child. The pair circled each other for a while, caught up in clandestine work amid the wartime tumult, with neither sure about the other's intentions. Julia undoubtedly had a crush on Paul, while Paul, a worldly New Jersey native ten years her senior, saw Julia as a "grown-up little girl" for whom he felt sorry and wanted to guide. The two married shortly after the war's end, and Julia Child spent the next fifteen years traveling with her husband to Paul's different posts in the foreign service: Marseille, Bonn, Oslo, and, for five years starting in 1948, Paris. It was during this time that Paul, in a move momentous for the American fine wine movement, introduced Julia to French cuisine. Within four years of that pleasant shock in Rouen, Julia Child would start putting her thoughts on the subject down on paper.

THE MAN WHO DREW A LINE IN FRENCH WINE

1945–1960 | Bordeaux

Around the time Julia Child was enjoying her revelation in Rouen, Émile Peynaud was ramping up a career as a winemaker and consultant that would change wine-making globally and forever. Born in 1912 in a town several miles south of the port city of Bordeaux in the region of the same name, Peynaud got his first job in the wine business at age fifteen, as a cellar worker. Captured by the Germans early during World War II, he spent much of the war in a prison camp, emerging to continue his training with persistent gusto. He was the proverbial young man in a hurry, brimming with fixes for the flaws he saw in the way his countrymen made wine.

Starting in the late 1940s, Peynaud served as a consultant to several wineries, a business that would flourish in the coming decades. It was his research, however, including while as a faculty member at the University of Bordeaux, that made Peynaud a legend. "There was really one world for winemakers before Émile Peynaud, and another world after," the managing director of the French First Growth Château Margaux told the *New York Times* after Peynaud's death in 2004. In the same article, the newspaper's chief wine critic, Eric Asimov, put it this way: "More than any other individual, Dr. Peynaud helped to bring winemakers into the modern world."

Peynaud's reputation grew so formidable that it was said that if his white Citroën simply slowed in front of a particular winery, that winery's standing would rise, as people in the industry understood it had hired Peynaud as a consultant. His ideas and techniques were exported to the United States in the century's latter decades, sometimes by his university students but often enough simply through imitation—winemakers the world over, and their customers, wanted the lusher, heavier wines he and his clientele ended up producing. By the time he retired in 1990, the genial winemaker with a wide face dominated by a prominent Gallic nose and bushy eyebrows had consulted for hundreds of wineries, including in the United States.

Peynaud's efforts to improve wine-making ran in tandem with his approach to enjoying wine. By all accounts unpretentious in a business noted for asseverations on the subject of wine-making, Peynaud, ever the Frenchman, saw wine as a natural accoutrement to food, to living itself; he rejected the notion that a fine wine could only be appreciated after cellaring for years. He wholeheartedly ascribed to the notion that wines could be enjoyed sooner after bottling, provided they were made and bottled correctly. This belief in the viability of younger fine wines made them all the more appealing to consumers not intent on shelling out money only to wait years to enjoy the product.

What were his earth-rattling innovations? In particular, Peynaud convinced French wineries, those in Bordeaux especially, to pick their higher-end grapes—in Bordeaux, principally the red ones: Cabernet Sauvignon, Cabernet Franc, and Merlot—later in the year and to keep their cellars cleaner, not to mention replace their superannuated, often irreversibly dirty oak aging barrels more regularly. He also convinced winemakers to use the finest-quality grapes they could find or grow, a triumphant effort he would deem "the crowning achievement" of his long career. Crucially, Peynaud was able to marry the sound science behind his beliefs about wine-making with a clear, concise way of explaining them.

The practices he championed, the cellar hygiene in particular, seem obvious in hindsight, but they were startling in the 1940s and 1950s. Part of this was the novelty of Peynaud's advice; the other was the legacy of history. The French wine industry that Peynaud preached to had very little reason to fret its norms, no matter the often uneven, even vinegary results. "The greatest wines on earth come from France," declared Alexis Lichine, a famed vintner and critic from Bordeaux, in his 1951 guide, *Wines of France*. No one argued. Even a generation later, Hugh Johnson, then the greatest chronicler of wine in the British Isles, and perhaps the world, expended 30 percent of his groundbreaking 247-page *The World Atlas of Wine* on French wines. American fine wine, by contrast, took up 3 percent of the tome, a little more than Australian wine and less than Spanish.

And critics mattered hugely in this particular culinary realm. Wineries, then as now, often swaddled their fare in lush vocabulary and perspicacious labeling. To get their wine into the hands of distributors and consumers, especially American ones who might be averse to buying it in the first place, they needed interlocutors: critics like Johnson—who became editor of *Wine & Food* magazine, an organ of the International Wine & Food Society, shortly after plunging into fine wine as a Cambridge University student—and fellow Englishman Harry Waugh, the longtime export director of major liquor concern Harvey's of Bristol, who emerged as "the man with the million-dollar palate" through books and columns starting in the 1960s. Such critics, before Peynaud and especially after, came to prefer French wine—to evangelize it, even. Waugh, for one, cofounded the Bordeaux Club in the late 1940s, its increasingly posh dinners a well-covered showcase for the wines of that French region. Around the time his *World Atlas of Wine* was published, Johnson crowned France "the undisputed mistress of the vine"—and as with Alexis Lichine twenty years earlier, no one argued.

Yes, French fine wine even before Peynaud could be quite good, due to fortuitous geography and an agrarian relationship with the grape stretching back to ancient times. But the French also knew how to market it, starting with a legendary classification carved out of whole cloth nearly a century before Peynaud started to build a reputation. As part of the 1855 Exposition Universelle in Paris, a grand industrial and agricultural showcase, Emperor Napoleon III decreed that wine merchants rank the best operations in Bordeaux. This they did, first creating a classification for red wines that started with five châteaus—Haut-Brion, Lafite, Latour, Margaux, and Mouton—called First Growths (or *Premier Cru* in French). After these came Second, Third, Fourth, and Fifth Growths—each, in the merchants' estimation, less desirable than those preceding it. A similar classification broke down white wines from Bordeaux; for that, the merchants named eleven First Growths and one so-called Superior First Growth, Château d'Yquem.

The 1855 classifications helped spin an enduring mystique about French wine. The classifications also set a precedent of government involvement and protection in the labeling of wine, which proved especially fortuitous shortly after Napoleon III's exposition. In the late nineteenth century, a tiny vineyard-devouring bug called phylloxera struck France, decimating the stocks of some of the nation's choicest wineries. Eventually, the blight was eradicated by grafting French vines with phylloxera-resistant American ones, but not before some unscrupulous merchants began blending First and Second Growths with inferior wines—without, of course, telling consumers. The French government stepped in, laying down a revolutionary labeling system called Appellation d'Origine Contrôlée (or AOC) in 1935.

To this day, French wines bear AOC designations to strictly certify that they are what they say they are and come from where they say they come from. The designations, which soon spread to other French foodstuffs, such as meat and cheese, as well as to other countries, added a fresh varnish of exclusivity to French wines, as did the widespread French practice of identifying the grape type of most wines, which was not widely adopted in the United States until the 1960s. The French cared, and showed they cared, where their wine came from; this furthered the idea of terroir, a word derived from the French word *terre*, for "land," and meaning that the geography of a foodstuff—including the climate it was cultivated in and the culture that nurtured it—defined it in major ways.

Never mind that most French could care less. As much as Julia Child found the idea of wine at lunch novel in the 1940s (as most of her fellow Americans would), the average French wine consumer was perfectly happy with his or her glass of plonk. Seemingly sophisticated terms such as *terroir*, *Premier Cru*, and *Haut-Brion* meant little to French drinkers from Dunkirk to Marseille, Brest to Strasbourg. Wine, to the masses, was a simple accompaniment to food, no more exotic than any seasoning or a glass of water. While this relationship went a long way toward explaining the numbers behind French wine—by the mid-1900s, France supported perhaps a thousand wineries for around forty-five million citizens—it also camouflaged its waning reach domestically. Although the trend would not be all that obvious until the 1970s, the French were drinking less and less wine, less and less regularly (though those French who *were* drinking were drinking quite a bit). Besides, France's centuries-old oenophile aura tended to mask what was, until Peynaud came along, an uneven product of obvious flaws and shortcomings. French wines might taste like the nectar of the gods, or they might taste like spoiled fruit juice. Consistent quality was no more a virtue than uniform cleanliness.

Peynaud's pioneering work on grape harvesting and equipment mainte-
nance—as well as in malolactic fermentation, which converted a tart-tasting
grape by-product called malic acid into milder-tasting lactic acid—created
rounder, clearer, more drinkable wines, and uniformly so. By the 1950s, Bordeaux winemakers were turning out consistently fantastic wines. Just in time,
too: the industry was recovering not only from the ravages of World War II
but from the aftershocks of the phylloxera blight of the late nineteenth century
and the unscrupulous practices that arose to compensate for that, including blending inferior wine with First and Second Growths. More important
than the consistency of French wine by the 1950s was its *taste* by the same
period. The post-Peynaud vintages in Bordeaux in particular tended to taste
heavier and richer than their tarter and thinner forebears, marked even in
their infancies by a delicate though unmistakable fruitiness. Yes, a lusher,
fuller, fruitier taste was a defining hallmark of all-powerful French fine wine
as the 1960s dawned.

"SO YOU'D LIKE TO KNOW WINES!"
1962 | Chicago

The titles of Ruth Ellen Church's columns throughout 1962 said it all: "Wines
Can Be Divided Into Five Classes," "Let's Learn About Wines: Today's Lesson Is on Sauternes," "Our Wine Columnist Visits Home of Famed Sherry,"
or, even more simply, "So You'd Like to Know Wines!"

That last headline loomed above Church's initial foray into what became
the first weekly wine column in a major American newspaper, in this case
the *Chicago Tribune*, the largest daily newspaper in the Midwest, then with
a readership of more than three million. Born in Humboldt, Iowa, in 1910,
Church graduated from Iowa State University with degrees in journalism and
food and nutrition the same year that Prohibition was repealed; she worked
briefly as the society editor for a small Iowa newspaper before landing at
the *Tribune* as its cooking editor in 1936. Along with her pioneering wine
column, she spearheaded what was likely the first test kitchen at a major US
newspaper, the sort of place where *Tribune* writers could create dishes and
photographers could snap shots of them.

That first wine column was published on February 16, 1962, a Friday, in a section of the newspaper that, in those sexist times, was reserved for supposed womanly interests such as cooking and entertaining in the home (something Church *did* love to do); indeed, Church's column shared a page with recipes for curried shrimp and onion pie. Still, its style—conversational, shorn of the loquaciousness typical of the European wine writing of the age—was as notable as its timing. No other newspaper in the nation, at a time when most Americans got their news from newspapers, would tackle wine quite like Church and the *Tribune* for years to come. The advice she gave in her columns, as indicated by the straightforward headlines, assumed very little expertise or interest on the part of readers, suggesting that publishers and editors felt no great demand for wine writing. Even if people did care, the subject seemed so daunting, so impenetrable, as Church's lead for that first column also suggested:

Many Americans are eager to learn more about wines and their uses, but the subject is tangled in so much nonsense about vintages and varietals, tastings and temperatures, rules and ritual (wine drinking is almost a ritual with some connoisseurs) that most of us are confused. We are almost afraid to serve wine in our homes for fear of choosing an inferior product or making some blunder in serving it.

Just how might Americans avoid such pitfalls? Church offered no-nonsense advice: "[I]f you plan to invest in an assortment of wines, you'd better make or buy a wine rack. A shelf in your basement or a cool spot in the house may do."

Where Church's wine writing oozed common sense and conversation, the writing of Robert Lawrence Balzer smelled of an Anglican High Mass. His wine criticism bordered on baroque, and by the 1960s it made him the most notable published American voice on the subject. Here is the lead of his inaugural wine column for the *Los Angeles Times'* weekend magazine on November 22, 1964, the Sunday before Thanksgiving:

Fine wines, like beautiful women, invite comparison, but no one expects them to be identical. Their compelling attraction lies in their difference and individuality. The question of the relative merits of California and European wines is often asked. It dwells like a ferment in the minds of the uncertain whose wine-tasting experience is limited. To the expert, the question is not a riddle; the answer lies in the history of both California and European wines to the present moment and a full awareness of what Samuel Johnson called "the wild vicissitudes of taste."

A defense of California's fine wines followed. It included more aphorisms—"Glory, the grape, love, gold . . . in these are sunk the hopes of all men and of every nation" from Lord Byron—and generous helpings of history: wines from what is now Austria's South Tyrol were prized by Roman emperors, those chasing the California gold rush in the 1840s were the state's first big consumers of wine, a Frenchman from Bordeaux brought and planted the first French grapevines in the Los Angeles area in the 1830s on the site of what became Union Station in downtown. Taken together, these explanations of history and location tell us quite a bit: namely that readers of the largest newspaper west of the Mississippi, in what was then the nation's third-largest city, needed the explanations. If a Los Angeleno bought wine in 1964, it was likely to be a generic from a large producer such as E. & J. Gallo or Italian Swiss Colony, or if it were of the fine wines that Balzer's column talked about, its labels said little, if anything, about origins, history, or even the grape type. Balzer could anticipate that American consumers simply would not know to ask, and wouldn't generally care, where their wine came from—or even that it *mattered* where it came from in the first place.

Finally, Balzer reveled in European comparisons: "There *are* California wines as fine as the best in Europe," the column baldly declared in the second paragraph [emphasis in the original]. The wines of Europe were clearly the wines for California winemakers, and consumers, to aspire to, and not the other way around. In the end, Balzer all but pleaded with his readers to learn more about California wine:

> It is simultaneously one of the most sophisticated yet simple taste experiences born of thirst and nourishment, and perhaps the most provocative beverage known to man. The challenge to make better wine never ends, nor, in the experience of the wine-lover, does the search to find it. The story of wine in California is the story of the state's history, continuing until this moment.

Robert Lawrence Balzer was in a unique position to beg. He knew from experience what kinds of wines Los Angelenos bought, and he knew from living overseas how good wine could be. Born in 1912 in Des Moines, Iowa, he migrated westward with his family, who opened a gourmet grocery store on North Larchmont Boulevard in Hollywood, just south of the Studios at Paramount. After earning a degree in English literature from Stanford University and studying at the Royal Academy of Dramatic Art in London, and despite knowing very little about the subject, Balzer's father put him in charge of the fine wine at the family store, one of the few retailers in all of North America that carried such a selection. At twenty-four, Balzer found himself advising customers such as Cecil B. DeMille, Alfred Hitchcock, Ingrid Bergman, and Marlon Brando on what bottles to buy. To spur sales, Balzer also put out what was quite possibly the first regular newsletter about California wines, touting wines the store carried from such Prohibition survivors as Almaden and Inglenook.

Almaden—founded near San Jose in 1852 by Frenchman Etienne Theé, who planted vines from his home country—proclaimed itself the Golden State's first winery. And Inglenook had roots in the 1880s, when a Finnish immigrant named Gustave Ferdinand Niebaum, who made a fortune in the fur trade, built a château in Napa Valley, that lush, thirty-mile-long dip an hour's drive northeast of San Francisco, between the Mayacamas Mountains to the west and the Vaca Mountains to the east. Together, this pair of wineries represented a significant portion of the California wineries still crafting wines from higher-end varietals such as Chardonnay, Cabernet Sauvignon, and Merlot; and because they represented a significant portion of *California* wineries doing so, they represented a significant portion of *American* ones doing so as well.

Were one to spread out a map of the nation from the early 1960s, including the then-recently admitted states of Alaska and Hawaii, one would see the majority of the country's wineries, 237 out of about 420, clustered in the Golden State; and most of those would be clustered in Northern California. New York and Ohio followed distantly with 46 and 39, respectively, and huge expanses of the United States, including the Rocky Mountains and Great Plains, held barely any; there was one in Texas. Most of these American wineries, too, made sweeter, fortified wines from generic grapes; and if what they made was then commonly known as table wine, they generally did not make it well. American know-how sorely lagged Europe's; wines could emerge cloudy, or rife with bacteria, easily spoiled and little worth aging for sharper taste. Nor did those making table wines often label them as Chardonnay, Merlot, Cabernet, and so forth. The federal government, so keen a generation before to erase much of the wine-making industry, did not require those labels, and besides, most Americans would not have understood the specialized names. Balzer seemed to recognize that a sea change in how

Americans perceived fine wine would have to precede any changes in the industry. It would be a slow, probably circuitous process, much like Balzer's own route to writing about wine in a major newspaper.

Before starting his *Times* column, Balzer served as a flight instructor in the US Army during World War II. He wrote his first book on wine, called *California's Best Wines*, in 1948; managed restaurants in Southern California while collecting awards for his writing and cooking; and, in a move that seemed not to surprise those who knew him, became an ordained Buddhist monk while working as a photographer for United Press International in Southeast Asia. Balzer lived for a time in Cambodia, in a thatch-roof hut with bamboo floors, gathering material for another book, this one about his new religion. While he lived in Cambodia, he abstained from sex and, ironically, alcohol—a fast he would, of course, break upon his return to California.

The blond-haired, blue-eyed Balzer, slender and nattily dressed, was what one might call a Renaissance man; his family's affluence afforded him the ease to dabble in such disparate passions as photography, mysticism, and wine—and his wealth also garnered him the notoriety to have his conversion to Buddhism covered in the local press. His contribution to American fine wine, however, should not be understated: his writing inaugurated modern American fine wine criticism, for good or bad. Balzer achieved such a milestone not through writing for the *Los Angeles Times* but through writing about wine for an old Stanford classmate, Will Rogers Jr. Rogers, a future congressman and the son of the famous humorist, suggested Balzer write a wine column for the newspaper that Rogers published and edited called the *Beverly Hills Citizen*, then one of the largest weekly newspapers in the West. Balzer obliged, and on January 27, 1939, Rogers's *Citizen* published Balzer's first column under the tagline, "Concerning Wines and Foods," and with Balzer's autograph as the byline. Though the columns would sometimes be separated by months—the next one doesn't seem to have appeared until September 1940—Balzer's missives in the *Citizen* represented the first regular wine column in any American publication following Prohibition.

The second recurring wine column came from Robert Mayock, scion of a local wine-making family, whose first column appeared in the *San Jose Evening News* on May 28, 1942, under the humorless headline, "A Man's Column About Wining and Dining," and next to an ad imploring readers to buy war bonds, complete with a cartoon mocking Hitler. The column was little more than a chatty, name-dropping rundown of an annual barbecue hosted by the Wine & Food Society of San Francisco. Mayock wrote barely anything about wine, and his column appears to have died on the vine fairly fast. Balzer's romped onward, however, an anomaly on the American media landscape. The topic of wine was simply verboten, even for magazines with cosmopolitan readerships; *House & Garden*, for instance, was the only magazine that tackled fine wine in the 1930s—and in the rare instances it did, it tackled European, not American, ones.

Balzer clearly used the *Citizen* columns to hone the sort of flowery, felicitous prose he employed for a much wider audience when writing for the *Times* nearly twenty-five years later. Also in that very first column in January 1939, not even six years since the repeal of Prohibition, he wrote about a challenge that would continue to confound critics, retailers, marketers, and consumers for decades, and that would come to define much of the American fine wine movement: which wines to buy and how to drink them. In this, Balzer belied the choice in wines that American consumers might already face:

> With the lifting of the shroud, in 1933, a flood of information on the use of wine issued forth from both public and private presses. My lady hostess was told that she must serve wine only in a glass with a stem so many inches high, the diameter of the aperture so wide; that she must never commit the social error of serving red wine in champagne glasses; that she must serve this wine at so many degrees, and that wine at another temperature; that she must serve red wine with red meat and white wine with white meat, and so on ad infinitum. Small wonder that she became confused, and the most natural consequence in the world was that she should think twice before serving wine to guests, for who is there today who wishes to lay before the world his supposed inadequacies or lack of information?

Who, indeed? Frank Schoonmaker, Balzer's only real competition as an American wine writer in the first couple of decades after Prohibition, voiced the same lament. A South Dakota native who grew into a preference for bow ties, Schoonmaker studied at Princeton University for a couple of years before dropping out in 1925 to travel Europe, becoming one of the pioneers in budget-travel writing with guides such as *Through Europe on Two Dollars a Day*. He would eventually serve during World War II in the Office of Strategic Services, the same branch that brought together Paul and Julia Child. It was during his travels in a Europe hurtling toward the precipice of that war, however, that Schoonmaker immersed himself in French wines. Armed with that know-how, Schoonmaker and Tom Marvel, a New York City journalist and a wine expert, produced *The Complete Wine Book* in 1934. It was just what its title implied but was also a sharp critique of the state of American wine a year after Prohibition: namely that it was a shame that so much of it was merely grape juice with a kick—with wineries and, by extension, consumers, clearly not caring if it was labeled properly or produced with any special care.

Their *American Wines*, published seven years later, painted a similarly depressing, if humorous, picture of the nation's relationship with the fermented grape nearly a decade after Repeal. The first chapter of *American Wines* was titled "Wine Hokum," and it seemed to presage the immense importance, positive or not, that critics would come to play in one of the then-saddest worldwide corners of wine:

> No sooner had legalized wines appeared than a flock of etiquette oracles, wine-wise savants, and pundits in the Art of Gracious Living sprang up, eager to tell us how to behave. Grave warnings against the iniquitous cocktail, advice on the "smart" wine to accompany each course, counsel on temperature and hints on the correct glasses and service of wines flooded the land. It was the worst possible start wine could have had.

It would be many years before any other formidable American wine critic would want to cut so ruthlessly to the chase. As it was, Schoonmaker's transition from writing about wine to selling it left a vacuum. It was soon filled, first with practicality by Ruth Ellen Church at the *Chicago Tribune* and then with panache by Robert Lawrence Balzer, when he kicked off his stint at the *Los Angeles Times* in November 1964 with that inaugural column brazenly insisting there were "California wines as fine as the best in Europe."

PINK CHABLIS VS. PREMIER CRU

1965 | Modesto, California

Ernest Gallo would call the 1965 television spot for his California winery's Pink Chablis its "most effective commercial . . . ever." It started with the medieval mellifluousness of lutes sounding and then faded to two actors done up in gossamer garb worthy of a high school musical set in medieval

Tuscany. A male announcer intoned over the scene of the standing male actor pouring some Pink Chablis for the seated female one: "Once upon a time, a handsome prince poured a goblet of wine for a beautiful princess. It was a white wine. White as the waters in the crystal fountain. White as the diamonds in her crown. It was called Chablis."

Cut to the smiling princess, clearly beguiled by the contents of her glass: "It's the finest wine in all the realm." Back to the announcer and the image of the white wine turning pink, a stunning enough trick given the infancy of color TV:

> And so great was her praise that the wine blushed pink. Now this legendary wine is re-created for you by Ernest and Julio Gallo. Pink like rosé, drinks like Chablis. Gallo Pink Chablis. The first really new table wine in years. The smart wine for young, modern tastes. Pink like rosé, drinks like Chablis. Pink Chablis.

This was American wine as the rest of the world knew it circa 1965. It was phenomenally popular. E. & J. Gallo Winery's sales share of the domestic market crested one-third by the end of the decade. Because of this reach, and the reach of other giants peddling in generic wines sourced from lower-end grapes, critics, including Ruth Ellen Church, often overlooked what little American-made fine wine there was, the nation noteworthy solely for its bulk production, screwtop jugs, and remarkably corny commercials. The French had First Growth Bordeaux; America had Pink Chablis. (And the public, even had it wanted to know, had no idea what Pink Chablis was; a Gallo print advertisement from 1974 vaguely described it as the product of "the finest premium grapes from California," apparently "tender white" and "lusty red" ones.) Decades after Prohibition by that point, and more than halfway done with the twentieth century, it seemed it would be forever thus—America an underdog, France the champ.

Nothing seemed to foretell this more strongly than that bounding success of Gallo, which brothers Ernest and Julio started out of Modesto, California, in 1933, the year of Repeal. The business really got going after World War II, when Gallo's annual sales jumped from four million gallons to sixteen million gallons; in the mid-1950s, Gallo sold 10 percent of the wine in the United States. At the start of the 1960s, right before the debut of Pink Chablis, Gallo was the biggest winery in America, creator of the nation's most ubiquitous brands. They made their wines in wineries that grew to "the size of oil refineries," in an operation that became so large it was more cost-effective to make their own bottles than to deal with an outside vendor.

These oceans of wine initially came from nondescript, utilitarian grapes, not the higher-end grapes such as Cabernet Sauvignon and Merlot on which French wineries hung their reputations. Gallo slapped generic-sounding names on their wines, too, with labels that told little of the grapes used to make the foodstuff inside. "Grape wine with natural pure flavors" adorned the label of Gallo's Thunderbird aperitif wine—that and the admonition to "serve cold." Its Spanada was composed of "grape wine & natural fruit flavors." Its Vine Rosé aimed a tad higher: "Light, Pink Wine/Fragrant, Provocative, Delicious." The brothers Gallo sold these concoctions to an undiscerning American public through forceful marketing campaigns, including television commercials.

As noted, Gallo was merely the largest of the generic kingpins. Others, including Italian Swiss Colony winery of Asti, California, duked it out with Gallo in the late 1950s for sales hegemony, and contributed to sweeter, fortified wines smoking fine wines sales-wise well into the 1960s. In California, the nation's premier wine-making state, three-quarters of all cases produced from the end of Prohibition in 1933 through the early 1960s were of the generic variety, often sealed with screwtops and designed to wallop, not wow. By the end of that decade, fewer than two dozen California wineries were competing in the fine wine market, with most of the state's roughly 230 wineries opting for the more reliably lucrative generic sector. This added to the perception of fine wine as the purview of the wealthy—or perhaps of the French, the Italians, the Other—that kept it from the tables of most American households.

The government had been doing its part, too, starting almost in tandem with the rise of the brothers Gallo. Spooked by the illegal alcohol trade that Prohibition had sparked, government at all levels had thrown up warrens of laws and regulations following Repeal. These legalities and their enforcement turned what had been an everyday foodstuff for millions into the stuff of wonderment, if not embarrassment—the kind of thing you were loath to admit you enjoyed unless you knew your listener well.

The American wine industry, in California as well as in areas as far-flung as the Finger Lakes district of New York and the Ohio River Valley, had been especially vibrant before the Eighteenth Amendment and its enforcing agent, the Volstead Act, turned most of wine's manufacture and sale into crimes in 1920. The industry's vibrancy came from a unique American mixture of entrepreneurial pluck and the climatology of a rapidly expanding continental empire. Simply put, there were a lot of opportunities for people to take their vineyard-growing chances. European immigrants, particularly from Italy, and their descendants took these chances mostly in Northern California. In southern Ohio, it was arrivals from the Eastern Seaboard who saw the opportunity for grape cultivation in what would become known, for a while at least, as America's Rhineland. The pre-Prohibition wine they produced, too, was recognized for its quality: at the Exposition Universelle in Paris in 1900, a veritable Olympics of territorial swagger that drew goods from fifty-eight nations as well as more than fifty million visitors, forty dif ferent American wines won medals, not only from California but from New Jersey, Virginia, New York, and Ohio.

More important than this reputation for quality was the perception of American wine among its domestic consumers: wine, from higher-end grapes or otherwise, was seen as just another foodstuff that had its place at the table alongside meat and bread. America's millions of recent immigrants, especially from Southern Europe, drank it from the same glasses they might use for juice, coffee, or water; most of it was sold in bulk, too, poured from barrels into secondhand jugs or bottles lugged back and forth from home, rendering wine, as historian Thomas Pinney put it, all the more "unpretentious, accessible, familiar, and cheap." It was used in the central sacrament of Roman Catholicism, the religion of many recent immigrants, as well as in the rites of other faiths. There was nothing odd about wine as part of a meal, lunch or otherwise, and certainly nothing illicit—at least not to most Americans.

Prohibition changed all that. It forever lumped wine in with liquor, turning it into just another form of booze, with all the negative connotations that go along with that. Worse, to dam the tide of criminality governments were sure would wash over the wine trade post-Repeal (just as it had during Prohibition, after all), Washington, the various states, and even local officials ensnared wine-making and sales in a web of regulation that persists to this day and that was largely absent before 1920, all in the name of, as one observer noted, placing "an article formerly contraband in the bastard category of things legally allowed but morally reprehensible." Prohibition lived on in varying degrees. Some states, for instance Florida and Alabama, levied high taxes on wine; others, like Pennsylvania, got into wine distribution, putting themselves between the winemaker and the consumer. Crucially, every state, including California in 1945, outlawed the sale of wine in bulk; it had to be bottled, no matter the added cost to wineries.

These laws, too, made little distinction between fine wines from higher-end grapes and the fortified wines that dominated the market. As this legal web spread, the perception of what little American fine wine existed, both at home and abroad, declined. Even an American like Julia Child, raised in privilege and exposed to the wider world, could be pleasantly stunned to see decent-tasting wine accompanying a midday meal. Wine had already become a novel thing for most Americans by 1948, tossed from the everyday realm into one of unfamiliarity, even exoticness. American-made fine wine was especially exotic—and not in the good way. Rather, for those dwindling few who might be paying attention, it was an international also-ran, largely overlooked in its homeland and dismissed abroad, its production and sales far behind that of its generic screwtop brethren, its bouquets and tastes unworthy of the adjectival redolence that critics heaped upon its European counterparts.

It was this huge societal deficit, this seeming inevitability of American inferiority, that had to be overcome; before more fine wineries could open, before more fine wine could be sold, before there would ever be demand for the services of those schooled in the ways of Émile Peynaud, before an entire industry and way of life could blossom and pollinate, Americans had to be retaught the enjoyment and appreciation of fine wine. Improbably, Julia Child, the spy-turned-housewife, turned on to fine wine in France, would play a major role.

SERVE WITH FISH, POULTRY, AND VEAL

1961–1967 | Boston—Washington, DC

Ten days after Ruth Ellen Church commenced the nation's first weekly wine column in the *Chicago Tribune*, Julia Child stepped in front of the WGBH-TV cameras a little after 9:30 PM on Monday, February 26, 1962. Her host that evening, P. Albert Duhamel, was barely past forty years old, but he was already the star of Boston College's English faculty and the book editor of the old *Boston Herald*. His weekly *I've Been Reading* television program was an erudite forum for the public network's audience, which, though regional, was influential enough to have a national reach. In those still early days of television, other hubs of power throughout the land, especially in Washington, DC, and New York City, paid attention to what WGBH broadcast in Boston.

As it was, Duhamel usually culled *I've Been Reading*'s guests from his Rolodex of fellow academics, who in turn caught a bit of buzz for their books. The particular book to be featured February 26, however, was different. *Mastering the Art of French Cooking* began as a "big jumble of recipes" crafted in the 1940s by Simone Beck, a Parisian friend of Julia's, who, like Paul Child, had helped expand the culinary horizons of the arriviste from California. Beck, her friend Louisette Bertholle, and Julia had even gone in on a successful English-language cooking school in Paris that charged the princely sum of 7,000 francs (or about $20) for three classes, but their collaboration really flowered when the trio turned to crafting Beck's recipes into a groundbreaker of a guide to French cooking for Americans. Child took the lead, working from 1952 onward not only to add some conversational spice that would make the recipes go down easier for an American audience, but to tinker with the plans to make sure the recipes were correct. The task involved repeated trials and repeated errors, sometimes due simply to the differences in French and US measurements, though often because of Beck's glib approach to what appeared, to her French mind, to be obvious dishes. With the manuscript tightened, the three authors sent it off to publishers, only to see it come back repeatedly rejected. Finally, eight years after Child entered the picture, Alfred A. Knopf—then a family-run independent publisher in New York—said yes.

On Thursday, September 28, 1961, a postman delivered one of the first copies of *Mastering the Art of French Cooking* to the Childs' new house on Irving Street, a leafy throughway just to the east of Harvard's main campus in Cambridge. Paul had resigned from the foreign service the year before, ending the couple's fifteen-year run of idyllic international postings and landing them near Paul's more sedate childhood haunts in the Boston area, where his family had moved after his New Jersey birth. Both around the half-century mark, Paul and Julia could be forgiven for thinking their most exciting days were behind them.

Then Knopf published the book to rapturous praise. Craig Claiborne, the *New York Times'* food writer, called it "the most comprehensive, laudable and monumental work" on French cooking, one that would likely "remain as the definitive work for non-professionals." James Beard, perhaps the nation's most influential food writer, declared "I love your cookbook—I just wish I had written it myself" at a luncheon he had organized for Child and Beck with top food editors. Child even made an appearance on NBC's *Today Show*, which reached four million viewers, and Beck and Child gave heavily attended cooking demonstrations at places such as Bloomingdale's in Manhattan. The unknown authors of an oft-rejected manuscript became minor celebrities virtually overnight. *Mastering the Art of French Cooking* sold ten thousand copies in its first four months, a more than respectable number for first-time authors and all the more impressive for the book's sheer size: 732 pages, thicker than the Boston phone directory.

But it was the appearance on humble WGBH in Boston, facilitated by an old Paris friend of the Childs who worked at the station, that really did it for *Mastering the Art of French Cooking*—and for Julia Child. Even before the cameras started rolling, there were signs that this particular *I've Been Reading* episode would be special, or at least different. Child had phoned producer Russell Morash shortly before the taping, requesting a particular piece of equipment.

"You want—what?" Morash asked incredulously.

"A hot plate, dearie, so I can make an omelet," Child replied.

Morash had heard all sorts of requests during his nearly four years at WGBH. They were usually of the mundane sort: an orchestra needed an instrument replaced, someone had broken a beaker during a scientific experiment. A hot plate, and the on-air cooking that it implied, was totally novel to the twenty-seven-year-old out of Boston University. Still, he told Child he would see what he could do.

As it turned out, Child got her hot plate. She, with Paul in tow, also showed up with a giant whisk, an omelet pan, and eggs. WGBH filmed in temporary studio space in Boston, the station's Cambridge facilities just across the Charles River having burned down in October 1961. The Harris tweed–wearing P. Albert Duhamel played his role as host unwittingly well, fading gradually into the psychological and physical background after effusively praising Child and her book in his introduction. Then it was over to Child and her hot plate.

"I thought it would be nice if we made an omelet," Child said directly into the camera. It was, according to one biographer, as if she'd said, "I thought it'd be nice to create nuclear fission." Omelets were surely unknown to most Americans, an exotic French foodstuff like Cabernet Sauvignon; yet here was a very tall woman with an impossibly high-pitched voice moving the culinary goalposts that much further on live TV. "They're so delicious," she continued, "and so easy to make." Child grabbed a small copper bowl and the giant whisk, cracking two eggs into the bowl with one hand and beating them into yellow pulp with the other. Child then lifted the omelet pan, explaining matter-of-factly that viewers were not likely to find one of their own, even in a cosmopolitan city like Boston. Still, they needed an omelet pan—that and butter, generous helpings of butter—to make the dish work.

Child was explaining how an omelet had to be "exciting" in the mouth when Duhamel interjected, "This is going to work on that little burner?"

"Oh, yes! And it's going to be delicious, just you wait." Child knew she was taking a risk; the hot plate that NBC had provided her and Beck for a similar feat on the *Today Show* barely reached the requisite temperature in time.

This time things went off without a hitch. Through a flurry of flourishes, the whisked eggs crackling in the sizzling butter, her six-foot-three frame moving up and down, side to side, in a strangely casual rhythm, and her conversation with the camera rarely ceasing, Child created an omelet. She proceeded to fork off a little bit for a clearly reluctant Duhamel; he ate it, his face lighting up, his mouth clearly excited.

"There, you see," Child said, "just as I said: delicious."

Morash saw the potential in what had just happened on an otherwise staid show on an otherwise predictable Monday evening in 1962 America. WGBH did, too; the network received twenty-seven letters from viewers praising the show, an extraordinary number at the time. WGBH soon commissioned from Child three pilot episodes of a French cooking show called *The French Chef*. Taped during a single week in June 1962, with two cameras in a basement auditorium of the Boston Gas Company headquarters a few blocks south of Boston Common, the three pilots—"The French Omelet," "Coq au Vin," and "Soufflés"—aired the following month, drawing more praise, enough for WGBH to commit to twenty-six additional episodes, starting with one on beef bourguignon and ending with Child crafting crêpe suzette. Crucially, and unlike cooking shows that had come before, they were broadcast during prime time, at 8:00 PM, not during the day. By 1967 roughly one hundred public television stations across the United States were carrying *The French Chef*, and Julia Child was on the cover of *Time* magazine, the nation's largest newsweekly.

The success of the series was not inevitable. Other cooking shows had failed where *The French Chef* took hold. James Beard, a trained actor before he became a noted food writer, saw his *I Love to Eat* series flop on NBC in the 1940s; Beard seemed to simply seize up in front of the cameras. Another national cooking show focused on French cuisine, hosted by English chef Dione Lucas on CBS, had failed to catch fire shortly after Beard's unsuccessful television run. Myriad other local cooking shows had come and gone between then and *The French Chef*'s 1962 debut.

Then something clicked; some tipping point was scaled. A big part of it was the inimitable Julia Child: her carefree approach to complicated dishes disarmed viewers and made them think that they, too, could cook like the Parisians cooked. Another reason may have been the show's simple production value, necessitated by WGBH's shoestring budget. Paul and Julia bought the ingredients for the show's recipes themselves, and the set was simple—a demonstration kitchen at the Cambridge Electric Light Company on the other side of the Charles River from Boston. This simplicity kept the focus on the cooking—and on Child, who continued to speak in a conversational, even conspiratorial, tone with her growing legion of viewers. Patching together a potato fritter that had come apart during an early show, she told the camera, "You can always pick it up. If you are alone in the kitchen, who's going to see?" She used a blowtorch to caramelize the top of a crème brûlée, a bow saw to slice a tuna into steaks. Finally, *The French Chef* seemed to gel karmically with the interest of the nation's young First Couple in all things French, including food. In 1961 thirty-one-year-old Jackie Kennedy had hired French chef René Verdon to head the White House Mess, long notorious for functional meals without flair or fuss. Verdon's first official White House meal, a lunch for British prime minister Harold Macmillan and sixteen guests in April 1961, included trout in Chablis and sauce Vincent, beef filet au jus, and artichoke bottoms Beaucaire, and a dessert of meringue shell filled with raspberries and chocolate.

Whatever its causes and however long it took for the larger public to realize it, *The French Chef* with Julia Child was a Culinary Event in America—one that included, importantly for our story, fine wine. Her relationship with fine wine and food stretched back at least to that 1948 lunch in Rouen, of course, and found its way into *Mastering the Art of French Cooking* in an entire six-page section devoted not only to what wines to use in cooking what foods, but what wines to *drink* with what foods. It was penned in the same conversational, approachable way as the prose for the recipes. Here is the entry under "Full-Bodied Dry, White Wines":

> *White Burgundy, Côtes du Rhône, and the dry Graves are examples.* Serve with fish, poultry, and veal in cream sauces. White Burgundy can also be drunk with foie gras, and it is not unheard of to serve a Meursault with Roquefort cheese.

Child herself saw wine in the pre-Prohibition sense: she could not imagine eating a delicious meal, of her own concoction or not, without a glass of fine wine. Paul Child kept a wine cellar, and wine was a part of their dinner parties in Cambridge; in 1975, a *New York Times* critic would drop by the house on Irving Street to profile Paul's cellar. Shockingly, Julia Child drank in front of the cameras, capping her show on soufflés, for instance, with sips of white wine. In the early 1960s, drinking on live television was taboo;

colored water usually filled the role should a host or an actor absolutely have to mimic wine-drinking on camera. Moreover, in keeping with the show's strict no-endorsements policy, Child often obscured with her hands the labels of the wines she drank on air, rendering the bottles no more exotic than the next eggshell she would crack.

In the end, it may have been this sort of holistic approach to French cuisine that explained not only the success of *The French Chef* but also its profound influence on American food and drink, in particular fine wine. In correspondence with WGBH about the format and audience in spring 1962, Child wrote of doing shows "on French cooking," not "in French cooking." The prepositional choice appeared to be no accident: Child wanted to get across not only how to make different dishes but how to enjoy those dishes. Her creations were deliberately intended to be a part of a wider approach to food (and drink) and its enjoyment. In this, she showed a certain brazen-ness—or at least the lingering effects of having lived abroad so long.

To hang a television show on the notion that Americans would like not only to learn how to cook French recipes but also to spend time enjoying them during languorous repasts was absurd in the early 1960s (the Kennedy White House notwithstanding). When it came to eating in the 1960s, it looked like Americans by and large wanted sameness and speed. Swanson had introduced the first TV dinners in 1954; the plastic-wrapped meals-in-minutes could be zapped to warmth in kitchen microwaves, which outsold gas-range stovetops by the mid-1970s. Americans could scarf these microwaved meals just beyond the glowing penumbra of another sea-changing home technology: by the end of the 1960s, more than sixty million households (out of sixty-three million total) would own at least one television set.

TV dinners and other similar developments irrevocably sundered certain eating habits. The sort of conversational sit-down dining before freshly pre-pared plates that so blew Julia Child's mind in Rouen quickly became a thing of the past for many, if not most, Americans. It was an America of fast food (the first McDonald's franchises opened in the early 1950s) and supermarkets (a word that entered the national lexicon shortly before the Kennedy years), of consolidation and homogeneity in American food production perhaps best evidenced by the sharp drop in the number of farms servicing the nation's stomachs: from more than 5.3 million in 1950 to far fewer than 4 million in 1960, on its way to fewer than 3 million by 1970. Things started tasting the same—produced as they were in a dwindling number of places, and regard-less of how far they were shipped over the new Interstate Highway System, which rolled out in the 1950s.

Such an arctic environment for good food and drink made Julia Child's from-the-get-go success all the more remarkable. Whether that success would translate into success for the food and drink she championed, including fine wine, remained to be seen—though the omens were not good. E. & J. Gallo still dominated domestic wine production; its Pink Chablis waited in the wings, prepared to wash over the nation like so much syrup. If Americans, including American critics, thought of fine wine, they generally thought of France. Americans were a hesitant bunch food-wise, the marketplace an unforgiving terrain.

Then, in California, as if on cue, in the same year as Gallo's runaway success with Pink Chablis, the first hero of the American fine wine movement emerged. He was not a particularly likeable hero. Born into affluence, a perfectionist with boundless energy—some would say arrogance—he had all the trappings of the world's worst boss. Those who worked for him chafed until they could stand no more and left, his sons buckled under his constant nit-picking, and even his own mother stood coldly by as he was forced out of the family business. As successful as he seemed to be on the outside, as ubiquitous as his brands would become, our hero was not all that good at business—he nearly ruined himself early on and then flirted with disaster for decades—but no individual in American fine wine up to that point had possessed what our hero did: vision and the moxie to execute it on a grand scale.

FATHERS AND SONS AND BROTHERS

1906–1965 | Sassoferrato, Italy—Virginia, Minnesota— Lodi, California—St. Helena, California

"Say that again and I'll hit you," Robert Mondavi warned his younger brother Peter.

The two were at the family winery in Napa Valley on a crisp autumn morning in 1965. Peter had again accused Robert of spending too much of the company's money. This time it was over funds he had used years before to buy his wife a mink coat for a state dinner honoring the Italian prime minister at the Kennedy White House.

Peter repeated the accusation. Robert gave his brother another chance: "Take it back."

"No."

Robert beat his brother so hard that he left purple marks on Peter's throat.

That the two came to blows surprised few in their volatile family's orbit. Robert and Peter Mondavi, both in their early fifties by the time of the fight, were the sons of Cesare and Rosa Mondavi, owners of the Charles Krug Winery. It was the oldest winery in Napa Valley, started by a Prussian immigrant in 1861. The Mondavis acquired Charles Krug in 1943 in a $75,000 deal pushed by Robert and Rosa and financed by Bank of America, the future financial giant started in San Francisco in 1904 by the son of another Italian immigrant. The Mondavis quickly folded their existing winery, Sunny St. Helena (which mostly made generic wines for bulk or jug sales) into the Charles Krug brand, which had a reputation as one of the few fine wine makers in the valley, America's premier wine-making region. It was a savvy marketing move, whatever the other business considerations, to allow the Charles Krug luster to rub off a bit on the rest of the family's cheaper stuff.

Rosa and Robert may have pushed the deal, but it had to go by Cesare first. He was the family's undisputed head and would become a compelling example of the southern European immigrants who would help change the perception of American fine wine through a mixture of luck and risk. Cesare had emigrated to America in early 1906 from the village of Sassoferrato, in the swampy Marche region of Italy northeast of Rome. He passed through Ellis Island in March, heading immediately westward to labor in the ore mines of Minnesota. After two years, he returned to Sassoferrato, where he met Rosa, a sometime domestic servant with a reputation for hardheadedness. The two married in 1908 in the village square and together embarked for America. Things would be different there, Cesare told his bride: easier, not like in central Italy, with its often hand-to-mouth existence amid unforgiving terrain. They traveled across the Atlantic Ocean in steerage class, with a hundred or so berths sharing a single bathroom. A cold, pelting rain greeted them in New York Harbor on their way back to Minnesota. Recalling her husband's promise of a better life in the States, Rosa Mondavi thought to herself, What an ugly joke.

The couple found salvation, however, in small business. First, they partnered with another Italian family in a grocery store in Virginia, Minnesota. The store catered to other immigrants by selling foodstuffs like fresh pasta, sausage, olive oil, and wine. Eventually the Mondavis sold their stake in the grocery store in order to open a bar that also targeted Italians. At the same time as both the store and the bar, the family took in boarders in their small three-bedroom house, their only source of heat a wood-burning stove in the kitchen. Finally, the Mondavis turned to wine—or, more specifically, to grapes.

In 1919, as Prohibition dawned, the local Italian American club asked Cesare to head to Lodi, California, near Sacramento, to buy wine grapes. California's Central Valley proved a powerful draw for the young father of four, with his neatly trimmed handlebar mustache, dark brown hair, and piercing almond-colored eyes. Not only did its climate and terrain remind him of central Italy, but as Robert Mondavi biographer Julia Flynn Siler noted, "class and cultural prejudices against Italian immigrants in California were less corrosive than in the Midwest." One of the things that did separate the Mondavis and their fellow Italian immigrants from the longer-established Minnesotans was wine itself. Immigrant families, particularly on Sundays as well as myriad Catholic feast days throughout the year, drank wine from squat, unassuming glasses. The wine itself was usually of their own making, and they poured it strong and unfiltered from wooden barrels in cellars and garages, even backyards. The Mondavis also drank their own wine at nearly every meal, albeit watered-down versions for the children—Robert, Peter, Mary, and Helen—while Cesare and Rosa might even pour a dram in their morning coffee.

Prohibition turned out to be kind to Cesare and Rosa Mondavi. The grape wholesale business they started shortly after arriving in Lodi in 1923 thrived, even surviving a grape-market plunge in 1926, due to overplanting, and the general economic plunge in 1929, which sent the world into the Great Depression. California's unemployment rate shot into the double digits seemingly overnight and stayed there, year after year. But it was during the 1930s that Cesare and Rosa were able to send their sons to Stanford, perhaps the most expensive university west of the Mississippi—what *Time* magazine described in 1931, Robert's freshman year, as "predominantly a rich man's college." It was within this bastion of privilege, galaxies away from ancestral Sassoferrato, that Robert Mondavi studied economics and business. His plans for a career as a businessman or lawyer, however, were interrupted by his father's jump from grapes to *fermented* grapes; when Prohibition ended in 1933, Cesare Mondavi saw the potential in California sooner than most.

Though Prohibition had hurt the state's wine industry, it did not destroy it. Several vineyards and wholesalers, including Cesare Mondavi, stayed in business through the 1920s and early 1930s providing grapes under a laughable quirk of the National Prohibition Act, nicknamed the Volstead Act. It allowed households to make two hundred gallons a year of "nonintoxicating" fruit juice—enough for roughly two and a half bottles a day of what invariably turned out to be intoxicating wine. Several wineries also stayed in business providing wine for religious rites, allowing them to pivot out of Prohibition with much of their production capacity intact. Compared with the decimation the liquor and beer trades experienced, wine commercially emerged after Repeal relatively unscathed.

Privately, too, it fared better because of the Volstead quirk and the very nature of wine. One did not need various ingredients to make it at home as a would-be home brewer did to make beer—grape juice alone would suffice, with the yeast that occurs naturally on the grape skins (not to mention in the air) doing the work of fermentation. Instead, it was the perception of wine that Prohibition pummeled. To southern European immigrants like the Mondavis and their children, however, that perception had never really wavered: wine was still an everyday staple, nothing exotic about it. Whatever the quality of the wine they made at home, and much of it was said to be barely drinkable, they and millions like them carried a candle for it throughout the darkest days of government proscription.

At this point in our story of the American fine wine movement, it is important to step back and examine the role of grapes, as they will come to play an outsized role. Most California wines were unexotic in their taste. The vast majority of California's grape-growing acres turned out the sorts of grapes prized for their utilitarianism: they grew pretty much anywhere, under all sorts of conditions, could ship well to all those households making two hundred gallons of nonintoxicating fruit juice yearly, and could be converted quickly into de facto alcoholic punch. The grape names that dominated during and right after Prohibition are virtually unknown to most consumers today, and serious critics disdained them back then.

Take Alicante Bouschet, a grape conceived in southern France in the 1860s by crossing the Grenache and Petit Bouschet grapes. Its thick skin helped it travel well, including on trains from California vineyards to wholesalers and bootleggers as far afield as New York City. Its dark red juice was so pulpy and sugary that Alicante Bouschet could also be pressed two or three times to yield twice the normal amount of fermentable juice as other grapes. In short, Alicante Bouschet was an alcoholic workhorse—and that voluminous output propelled Alicante Bouschet to become the second-most-planted grape in California by the early 1930s, eventually spreading to cover around ten thousand acres. How was it, though, beyond its alcoholic one-two? *Los Angeles Times* critic Robert Lawrence Balzer pronounced Alicante Bouschet to have "vulgar virtues" and wrote it was popular solely because "it afforded California vineyardists an appealing money crop during the dry era."

The critic-turned-merchant Frank Schoonmaker went even further. To him, a grape like Alicante Bouschet, with its strictly utilitarian function—including the speed at which it could ferment and the ease with which it could grow—was just another lamentable example of American wine's lack of time and place. Schoonmaker declared that the grape could serve a purpose as a coloring aide; otherwise, it should be avoided. The wines that Alicante Bouschet produced invariably tasted and smelled bitter and big—tannic concoctions difficult to get into and easy to forget; bland and leathery, if not chalky. US vintners could overlook such characteristics. Why? While the French emphasized terroir, the Americans emphasized getting drunk fast. The Alicante Bouschet was "common and coarse" to Schoonmaker, used in only the cheapest blends wrongly "baptized 'Burgundy' or 'claret.'" Again, time and place meant little to American vintners—a fact that the popularity of Alicante Bouschet only illustrated. According to Schoonmaker, the grape had "no place in any respectable vineyard and should be eliminated."

Critics witheringly scorned other post-Prohibition grapes that growers and wholesalers prized. Schoonmaker found that Carignan, another deep red grape that seemed to grow everywhere, might produce "sound, agreeable wine," but such wine was "never distinguished." The Salvador grape, a hybrid from California's Central Valley and unknown in Europe, had, Schoonmaker wrote in the early 1960s, "no possible value except as a coloring agent, or dye; can hardly be called a wine grape." Yet these grapes blanketed hundreds of thousands of prime grape-growing acres in the decades following Prohibition, gobbling up not only natural resources like soil and water but the resources of a wine industry bent on slaking the American public's demand for sweet, strong wines of origins immaterial.

This proliferation of Salvador, Carignan, Alicante Bouschet, and their utilitarian ilk of course meant less space for the choicer grape types, those native to Europe and to France in particular. While Alicante Bouschet, for instance, grew "practically everywhere" in California, according to one researcher, Cabernet Franc grew "hardly anywhere, unfortunately." It is staggering now—given more than eight decades of hindsight since Repeal in 1933—that Merlot grapes covered barely fifty acres of California wine country by 1961, while Carignan covered twenty-five thousand.

Schoonmaker, Balzer, and other well-traveled sorts knew the qualities of finer, drier wines made from grapes such as Chardonnay, Cabernet Franc, Cabernet Sauvignon, Malbec, Merlot, Nebbiolo, and Pinot Noir. These wine writers wondered aloud when better-quality grapes might be grown widely in America for American vintners to craft into fine wine. "Certainly deserves a try," Schoonmaker wrote of Nebbiolo in his formidable *Encyclopedia of Wine* in the early 1960s. "Hardly anywhere, unfortunately," he noted of Cabernet Franc's infinitesimal share of California's soil. Schoonmaker and a few others saw around the corners of contemporary American wine-making to the potential that might be realized, critically and commercially, in cultivating these higher-end grapes and letting consumers know clearly where the wines these grapes spawned came from and when. In a booming echo of Émile Peynaud's work in Bordeaux, the story of American fine wine can be told largely in the growing acceptance, literally and figuratively, of these higher-end grapes and how to use them.

In those first decades after Repeal, however, such grapes were seen as the provenance of the well-heeled and the well-traveled, the sort of tipple of those who could afford trips to the First Growth châteaus themselves or, at the very least, to the relatively small number of fine-dining restaurants in America's biggest cities. The industry and wine consumers regarded the likes of Balzer and Schoonmaker as, if not ignorable eccentrics lucky enough to have traveled and to have dined so finely, then as insufferable scolds. Schoonmaker, in particular, was singled out for derision by California vintners who saw his calls for clear labeling by varietal and vineyard location as the stuff of snobbery, an East Coast elitist's pretensions to French trappings. Most Americans who drank wine wanted it cheap, sweet, and strong; never mind the grape or the vintner's address.

A HIGHER CALLING

1965 | St. Helena, California

S unny St. Helena, the Napa Valley winery Cesare Mondavi controlled, focused on bulk wines, which were exactly what they sound like: punchy jug wines made from grapes like Carignan, not aged much, and then shipped quickly to retailers in railroad tanks (thus its nickname, "tank wine"). Sunny St. Helena, about two hours' drive northwest of the Mondavi home in Lodi, did a respectable trade. By the late 1930s, the winery was churning out five hundred thousand gallons annually, enough to place it comfortably toward the top, production-wise, of the more than forty wineries in the storied valley between Sacramento and San Francisco. Napa had been one of the most prolific wine-making areas in the United States before Prohibition, its grape-friendly climate a fortuitous accident of ancient history, its acreage increasingly cultivated by southern European immigrants like the Mondavis, who saw wine as an everyday beverage and not as a freak cousin to beer or liquor.

Robert Mondavi, however, wanted more than simply solid production numbers. After graduating from Stanford, he had taken what he would describe as a "crash course" in grape-growing and wine-making at the University of California, Berkeley, and joined his father's business with a head full of ideas and a passionate streak of perfectionism. This crash course put him on a collision course with his younger brother Peter, who also graduated from Stanford and studied wine-making at Berkeley—as well as serving in the air force during World War II, a crucible Robert avoided through exemptions for growers of grapes and tomatoes, both foodstuffs vital to the war effort.

The reserved and meticulous Peter headed production at Sunny St. Helena and, later, the combined Charles Krug operation after he returned from the war in 1943. Crucially, before he shipped out, he had introduced cold fermentation to Sunny St. Helena. By keeping temperatures low to preserve freshness, the winery was able to craft exceptionally crisp, clear white wines, something then still novel in the United States. It was Robert who put this cold fermentation into practice while Peter was away; the wines he produced this way sold well, being lighter and fruitier than not only most of the competition but most of Sunny St. Helena's own products.

Robert's success with cold fermentation, and his success in persuading Cesare to buy control of the more prestigious Charles Krug in the first place, sparked friction between the brothers, who were temperamentally polar opposites to begin with. Where Robert was handsome and gregarious, Peter was smaller in stature and more reserved, even shy (his childhood nickname, Babe—as in the baby of the four Mondavi siblings—stuck into adulthood). An ambitious workaholic who believed in his ideas about wine with "an evangelical fervor," Robert always seemed to be upgrading the family business. He built a lab in an old water tower behind his St. Helena home, spent a chunk of his 1940 honeymoon visiting the winery's sales accounts, and was never at a loss when it came to suggesting how to improve the quality of the family's products.

Peter wanted little of Robert's alleged improvements—production was *his* wheelhouse, not Robert's. Besides, the sorts of quality enhancements that Robert was pushing made little marketplace sense. Was not most of the wine produced and bought in the United States on the sweeter, stronger side? Moreover, the sort of wine drinking he and Robert had grown up on at the elbows of their immigrant parents, the very notion of that kind of relationship to the grape, was anathema to most of their countrymen. Finally, Charles Krug, including the old Sunny St. Helena, was chugging along nicely financially. Why fix what wasn't broken? Besides, Charles Krug's output in terms of what would one day be uniformly called premium wine was nothing to sneeze at stylistically: decent, quality-controlled fine wine that might not wow the critics but that was certainly lush and rounded enough to pass for a decent imitation of the French.

Still, Robert pushed. Emboldened by his success with cold fermentation, he bubbled over almost daily from the 1940s into the 1960s with ideas for how to further refine Charles Krug's wine and place the Mondavis on the same enological footing as the great wine-making houses of Europe. The idea seemed preposterous to Peter and others, if not counterproductive as well. Robert, though, felt he was on to something. It wasn't just technological changes such as cold fermentation that spurred him; he was very much aware, too, by the early 1960s of Frank Schoonmaker's push for varietal labeling of American wine and of Julia Child's recent cookbook and television success. Like Child, Robert ate a particularly revelatory lunch during his first trip to France—in his case at the La Pyramide restaurant in the small village of Vienne outside of Lyon in 1962.

"This is the kind of wine I want to create," he told his wife, Marge, after sampling one of the bottles complementing their repast. "Wines that have grace and style, harmony and balance."

More portentously for the American fine wine movement, Robert himself lived within an idyllic Northern California bubble of good, local food topped off by good, local wine in that European tradition; he was, as Child might have put it in a letter to her television show's producers, "*in* the European tradition" rather than simply around it. Mondavi might while away an evening eating in the kitchen of the Hotel St. Helena, which was run by an elderly Italian, or at one of a number of solid Italian restaurants in Napa Valley, the meals invariably accompanied by one of the handful of locally produced fine wines. He might spend a chunk of a workday in San Francisco at a meeting of the Wine Institute, which dozens of wineries started less than a year after Repeal not only to lobby the government on behalf of wine but to educate a skeptical public. At the Wine Institute, Robert could bounce ideas off generic wine kingpins such as Ernest Gallo, whose family business dominated American-made wine sales. Robert also met vintners such as John Daniel, the scion of an old San Francisco clan who owned Inglenook. The winery—started in the late nineteenth century by Daniel's granduncle, Finnish fur kingpin Gustave Ferdinand Niebaum—was one of the most esteemed producers of American fine wines. Inglenook and a few other wineries, including Beaulieu (established at the turn of the century by a French couple named Georges and Fernande de Latour), focused on fine wines sourced from higher-end grapes such as Cabernet Sauvignon; these fine wineries did not try to compete with Gallo, nor with Charles Krug and its Sunny St. Helena lines, for that matter. Instead, they made fine wine because, like the storied wineries of France, that's what they wanted to make. Daniel's Inglenook wines tasted fuller and richer than most anything American vintners produced—or were seemingly able to produce. As Daniel explained to Robert at one point, such wines took nothing away from the wider American wine industry as a whole; they only enhanced it.

Robert desperately wanted to put Daniel's lesson into wider action. He took to telling his Napa compatriots, "One bad wine in the valley is bad for every winery in the valley. One good wine in the valley is good for everyone." He saw the potential in his own dining and drinking habits, as well as in those represented by the sudden and wide appeal of Julia Child. Moreover, in 1963, he turned fifty; he was restless, worried his opportunities in wine were passing him by, his potential going unrealized. Cesare Mondavi's death in 1959 at age seventy-six left control of Charles Krug in Rosa's hands. Robert thought his mother didn't have the business acumen to steer the winery where he wanted it to go. "We needed a great dream, a defining mission, a higher calling," he later remembered. His frustration deepened, as did his estrangement from his family, including from Peter, who, during Robert's time of dreaming and scheming, had been keeping Charles Krug on a steady financial path that bulk wine ballasted.

The fight over the mink coat Robert allegedly bought with company money settled everything. Within a few weeks of the argument, on November 11, 1965, the Charles Krug board of directors met in the twenty-seat dining room of Rosa's house on the winery's lands. Peter was made general manager of Charles Krug and Robert was forced into a six-month leave of absence; the only two dissenting votes came from nonrelatives. Cut adrift at age fifty-two, Cesare Mondavi's eldest son felt tremendously insulted, even betrayed. The rift between Robert and his brother was Shakespearean, biblical, Cain versus

Abel, though Abel was not killed but left to stagger on, dazed and wounded, an object of gossip throughout Napa Valley. When Robert found out that Rosa had even frozen out his son Michael, about to graduate college, from the family business, he confronted his mother. She held firm; her son, and *his* son, had to go.

"If that's the case, Mother," Robert said, "I'm going to build a winery."

OPTIMISM

1921–1966 | The Crimea, Russia—Paris—Davis, California

The Cossack lifted the spiritless body of the young lieutenant from the frozen hedgerow on the battlefield and threw it over the back of his horse. For at least the second time in his twenty years, Andre Tchelistcheff had escaped death.

Tchelistcheff's first brush with death had been shortly after he was born in 1901, on lands 140 miles west of Moscow that his family had lived on for eight centuries. He suffered from an abdominal inflammation and had to endure rudimentary treatments in an era before penicillin: the doctors routinely extracted fluid from his stomach with a syringe, and his diet consisted of buckwheat, milk, and so much raw beef that Tchelistcheff never in his long life forgot the taste of blood.

There were other painful episodes along the way. Tchelistcheff was raised in that prelapsarian era of European aristocracy, one of country estates and earnest leisure interrupted by noblesse oblige, usually in the form of government service or a military commission—an era swept abruptly away by World War I, the Spanish Flu, and the Russian Revolution. Tchelistcheff's father was a jurist who sided with the White Russians, advocating for a Western-style republic to replace the czarist monarchy overthrown in 1917; his politics were more than enough to have him and his family marked for death by Lenin and the Red Russians. So the family fled south using forged passports, abandoning their ancestral lands to the depravity of the Communists; they linked up with the White Russians and their army, which the younger Tchelistcheff joined in his late teens. He fought in the bitter, confused cold of the Crimea, suffering his knockout blow while assaulting Red machine-gun nests, his last bits of strength expended crawling to the relative safety of the hedgerow. Officials told his family in nearby Yalta that he was dead, and they held a funeral for him the same day the Cossack retrieved Tchelistcheff's limp body from the battlefield.

From there, Tchelistcheff's life accelerated. He studied agriculture and animal science at a university in Czechoslovakia, met up with his exiled family in the newly formed Yugoslavia shortly after, married the daughter of a fellow exile in Belgrade, and then in 1930 moved to Paris, where he got momentously acquainted with wine. He studied at the Pasteur Institute and elsewhere, and worked for storied French wineries like Moët & Chandon in Champagne. Tchelistcheff's immersion in wine, following a failed attempt at poultry farming with a fellow Russian expat, would have far-reaching effects for the American fine wine movement.

In Paris in 1938, as US winemakers were rubbing their eyes after the long darkness of Prohibition, Tchelistcheff met a Frenchman who had been living in California. A member of a French wine-making family, Georges de Latour had bought and quickly expanded the Beaulieu winery in Rutherford, California, in Napa Valley, at the turn of the twentieth century. Latour and his wife, Fernande, were from Dordogne, in Bordeaux, but rather than sink their monies into fine wines to rival those of their homeland, they quickly fell into churning out the generic fare common to most American wineries. When Prohibition struck in 1920, the Latours struck a deal with the Catholic archdiocese of San Francisco to produce its sacramental wines; not only that, but Beaulieu gobbled up another winery renowned for its whites—and promptly added white wines to its repertoire of altar offerings. By Repeal, the Latours and Beaulieu were among the most financially stable of America's wineries, the future rolling lucratively out before them in waves of the same nondescript wines they'd specialized in before Prohibition.

Then, during Tchelistcheff's 1938 trip to Paris, just as an incalculably more menacing darkness descended on Europe, Georges de Latour pivoted. Would Tchelistcheff like to come to California to create an enological rival to France?

Latour had intended during his trip to Paris to recruit a fellow Frenchman for the task, but instead he picked the White Russian refugee, with his high cheekbones and courtly manners (women were "madam" and men "my dear sir" to Tchelistcheff). Thus started one of the most impactful collaborations in American fine wine, though it lasted only until Latour's death in 1940. Their most celebrated production was the Georges de Latour Private Reserve Cabernet Sauvignon, renowned not only for its quality (born of Tchelistcheff's crucial decision to age it in American oak barrels) but for its reliance on higher-end grapes, a reliance spelled out clearly on the label. The varietal, or wine style made from one grape, became a gold standard in California reds, though it was largely ignored, and unavailable, in France where Latour wanted to impress.

Tchelistcheff remained with Beaulieu for thirty-three years after Latour's death, pioneering techniques that included barrel-aging, protecting vineyards from frost, and cold and malolactic fermentation (the conversion of malic acid into lactic to create softer, rounder wines). Perhaps most crucially, Tchelistcheff also preached and practiced cleanliness in wine-making, a tenet not uniformly embraced, even by aspirational wineries like Beaulieu (shortly after his September 1938 arrival, Tchelistcheff found a rat floating in a vat of Sauvignon Blanc). Over many decades, myriad wineries in the United States and Italy hired the winemaker as a consultant. Had America already enjoyed the universal acclaim of France when it came to fine wine, it's possible Tchelistcheff would have enjoyed even wider influence; he was as close to an Émile Peynaud as the United States produced.

And while much of Tchelistcheff's training originated in France, some of the research he drew on for his California know-how came locally, from the University of California, Davis. There, in the college town fifteen miles west of Sacramento, two doctoral candidates spent the years after Repeal codifying where in California certain higher-end grapes could grow. Maynard Amerine—a native of Modesto, California, whose expertise was in plant physiology—and Texas native Albert Winkler, who went to Berkeley to study horticulture, collaborated at UC Davis to devise what came to be known as the Winkler Scale. Published in 1944, it classified the five most desirable wine-grape-growing areas in California using degree days—or, how many days during the April–October growing season each region registered the best temperatures for maturing vines.

Like everything in wine, the Winkler Scale's five regions were often measured against regions in France. For instance, Region I, the best in California for growing higher-end grapes, included part of Napa Valley around Oakville, where Robert Mondavi happened to be looking for land in 1965 and 1966, and was comparable to the French region of Burgundy. It would, Winkler and Amerine concluded, be good for growing the likes of Pinot Noir, Chardonnay, and Sauvignon Blanc. Region II, the next-best, covered most of the rest of Napa as well as much of Sonoma County and was comparable to Bordeaux, with its Merlot and Cabernet Sauvignon grapes.

The work of Amerine, Winkler, and their colleagues in UC Davis's Department of Viticulture and Enology, founded in the 1880s and reestablished in

1935 after Repeal, was exacting and thorough—though also not without its fun: the researchers made thousands of five-gallon sample batches of wine, with vineyards often donating the grapes to offset the department's dearth of funds; and these batches, naturally, had to be tasted. The scale, the end result of this and other research, was meant to provide winemakers with a framework for growing higher-end grapes that Winkler thought would lead to higher-end wines and make California—and, by extension, America—a bigger player in world wine.

There were other promising signs pointing to a new attitude toward American fine wine. Competitive wine judging returned in 1934 to the California State Fair, which more than forty thousand people attended. In the late 1940s, Tchelistcheff formed the Napa Valley Technical Group, a sort of roving bull session for winemakers intent on crafting better wines; its roster included the Mondavi brothers and Robert Mondavi's inspiration, John Daniel. Around the same time, too, a San Francisco businessman named Martin Stelling Jr. cobbled together what was reputed to be the single-biggest fine wine vineyard in the world in Napa Valley, some five thousand acres. In 1950 a group of winemakers formed the American Society for Enology and Viticulture, another clearinghouse of information and, perhaps more important, a way to boost the professional prestige of the winemaker, until then seen largely as a technical tradesman as utilitarian as the majority of grapes he worked with. Why shouldn't Winkler have been optimistic?

Paul Garrett, a pre-Prohibition pioneer in bottled American wines through his Virginia Dare brand, spoke for the optimists in 1934, when he surveyed the possibilities from his Manhattan apartment: "There is no reason why our industry should be a small industry. It ought to be—it can be—bigger than the automobile industry, bigger than the steel industry, if wine makers will seize the opportunity that lies before them," the seventy-one-year-old told a reporter from *Fortune* magazine. "Who knows that if wine were properly presented to the American people they might not accept it for what it is—a wholesome, health-giving accompaniment of good food?"

Forget the optimism. Despite the increasing organization and enthusiasm within the industry, California's future in fine wine seemed shaky at best. First, most of California's grape-growing acreage continued to be covered, season in and season out, by lower-end grapes such as Carignan, Salvador, and Alicante Bouschet, ensuring one vintage after another of the sorts of sweeter generics Americans had come to prefer coming out of Prohibition. Most of the sixteen thousand acres of new wine grapes planted in the five years after Repeal were composed of this lot, with higher-end grapes making up relatively infinitesimal additions. By 1940, for instance, fewer than five hundred acres of Pinot Noir grapes were growing in all of California—a state roughly fifty thousand square miles bigger than Italy. As Winkler himself noted, the situation improved little in the following decade; the acreage share of the lower-end grapes continued to balloon, as did the production of the wines they produced. Wineries were unwilling to pay a premium for the higher-end grapes; it simply didn't make economic sense—such grapes yielded less and made the types of wines Americans *didn't* prefer.

Despite the groundbreaking efforts of Latour, Tchelistcheff, Winkler, Amerine, and a handful of others since Repeal, never mind the verbal exertions of Ruth Ellen Church, Frank Schoonmaker, and Robert Lawrence Balzer, the American wine industry entered the 1960s dominated by the punchier generic products from the likes of E. & J. Gallo; these generics accounted for more than 60 percent of the wine that Americans consumed in 1965. Pink Chablis appeared to have a commercial future as rosy as its hue and the French a hegemonic dominance that no American(s) could ever hope to wrest.

Robert Mondavi was aware of all this. As the 1960s got under way, Mondavi continued to lead a dual enological life. On the one hand, he was the frenetic perfectionist of a family winery largely dedicated to the safe path of ever more tank wine. On the other, he was immersed not only within culinary routines that fit fine wine nicely into the mix but also within the more stylistically ambitious faction of the California wine industry, including as a member of Tchelistcheff's Napa Valley Technical Group and the wider Wine Institute out of San Francisco. Mondavi knew the trends and the trade-offs—and could therefore see the immense difficulties he faced in making good on his boast to his mother that he was "going to build a winery." And not just any winery, either: Mondavi planned one dedicated to producing fine wine, a clean and sobering break not only with his family's past but with much of the industry; the trends would be bucked and there would be as few trade-offs as possible.

Maybe there was no market yet for fine wine in America, Mondavi thought in 1966, as he cobbled together financing and manpower. *But so what?*

"IT'S BEAUTIFUL"

1966 | Oakville, California

The Roman Catholic priest in the long, black robe layered with a white cassock faced the gondola that held the Pinot Noir grapes. He had been invited from the nearby Carmelite monastery in St. Helena to dedicate the opening of the first major new winery in Napa Valley since Prohibition ended in 1933. The priest intoned a benediction in English and Latin, and a mechanical lift hoisted the gondola, tipping its contents onto a hopper that sent the grapes—there would be twenty tons that day—on their way toward becoming wine.

Shortly after 10:00 AM on September 6, 1966, the Tuesday after Labor Day, Robert Mondavi's winery was officially off the ground. Mondavi himself said a few words after the benediction—words about new beginnings, words that attempted to summarize the last several months of frantic fundraising and manufacturing, the work and the worry that went into what the small but growing Northern California fine wine world sensed was a turning point in their—and, by extension, America's—wine industry.

Yet it was not to be. The dedication of the Robert Mondavi Winery in Oakville, California, on that sunny September morning does not appear to have been covered in the media beyond tiny St. Helena and its surroundings. It was likely little noted beyond the Mondavi family and the families of Robert's partners, who comprised the bulk of the few-dozen-strong audience at the dedication (though, in a sign of the marketing that would become part of his legend, Mondavi also invited James Beard, perhaps the nation's most famous food writer). For all the import that would be heaped upon the winery in the next fifty years, at the time you would have been hard-pressed to see its impact coming. From the outside—and, as we'll see, from the inside—it seemed another earnest attempt that would resonate little in the wider wine marketplace, which in 1966 was still dominated by the sorts of wines Robert Mondavi was specifically committed to *not* making.

What had he committed to making? In his own words, written decades later, Mondavi modestly declared his intentions: "The winery I envisioned was to be a showcase for the most advanced wine-making techniques and equipment in America, if not the world." It would be an aesthetic triumph, too, one to rival the First Growth châteaus of France, with their charm adding to the mystique, and price tag, of their bottles. The Robert Mondavi Winery, its namesake envisioned, would be a destination spot unlike any that any vintner had ever consciously created in the United States. It was that consciousness that would set Mondavi apart from the winemakers who had come before in America—and would mean so much to the many, many who came afterward. One simply did not, on either side of the Atlantic, make too much of a fuss about the aesthetic and—gasp!—tourist potential of a winery.

Such an ambitious reach, of course, far exceeded Mondavi's grasp, evidenced early on by his financial scrounging. He relied personally on consultancy work following his dismissal from the family winery in November 1965, which quickly shed the pretense of being temporary (though his brother Peter and mother Rosa saw to it that Robert received a $9,000-a-year consultancy fee, despite the fact that he never actually advised Charles Krug in any formal capacity). As for the new winery, Robert cobbled together funding from myriad sources inside and outside of wine. Bill and Ina Hart, old friends of his who were longtime Napa Valley boosters, loaned him $50,000, as did Bank of America, which had underwritten much of the Mondavis' 1943 takeover of Charles Krug. Then there was the $100,000 from Fred Holmes and Ivan Shoch, two prominent Napa Valley vineyard owners who had a feeling about Mondavi—and who took stakes in the new winery in exchange for their six figures of funding.

Cliff May also came on board after Bill Lane, a mutual acquaintance and publisher of lifestyle magazine *Sunset*, introduced the two. May was a San Diego native, who during the Great Depression designed the first examples of what would become that staple of post–World War II suburban living: the California ranch house. He was part architect, part interior designer, part landscape guru, and he turned out to be just what Mondavi needed and wanted.

"Bob," May asked the vintner during an early 1966 meeting in May's West Los Angeles office, "how big are you going to have this winery?"

Mondavi hedged. Aware that May charged more than the average designer and also aware of his precarious finances, Mondavi haggled with May for about half an hour. Then he threw up his hands. "You know," he said, "if you draw this up for what we want in the future, maybe fifty thousand or a hundred thousand cases, all my money will be going toward your fee. We won't have any money left over!"

"Bob, I'll make a deal with you," May said. "If you agree to go ahead and retain me, I'll design this for you to handle twenty-five thousand cases. But I'll also design it so that you can expand it."

That was all Mondavi needed to hear. Soon after the West Los Angeles meeting, May flew to Napa on a private plane, landing at John Daniel's small private airstrip next to the Inglenook winery. He, Mondavi, Shoch, Holmes, and Michael Mondavi, Robert's eldest son—and the one whom Peter Mondavi, and grandmother Rosa, did not want at Charles Krug—visited potential winery sites around the valley. At a site along Highway 29 in the tiny burg of Oakville, May stopped dead in his tracks. The group was standing in a vineyard dating from the mid-nineteenth century and legendary for fostering superb Cabernet Sauvignon grapes in particular—unusual in a California teeming with the vines of lower-end grapes. It was called To Kalon, or roughly "It's Beautiful" in Greek.

"This is the site," May told his companions.

He took out an old nine-by-twelve-inch manila envelope and a pencil, and began sketching his conception of what the Robert Mondavi Winery could look like. "This will be the entrance," he said, drawing a large archway. "For a mission style, you'll need a tower, like a bell tower." So May drew a modest, though distinctive, tower to the archway's right. Then he penciled in a *V* spreading back from the archway in what looked to the elder Mondavi like the wings of a graceful bird in flight.

Robert Mondavi was as rapturous over the location of To Kalon as his designer; Charles Krug had actually purchased a parcel of the land in 1958, and Ivan Shoch owned part of it as well, having bought in through Martin Stelling Jr., the would-be fine wine pioneer whose vision for Napa Valley was cut short by a fatal car accident in 1950. Mondavi liked To Kalon's proximity to Highway 29 in Oakville, which was about six miles south of St. Helena and twelve miles north of the city of Napa; he also liked its exposure to the sun, its natural drainage, the annual rainfall it drew, even the fact that nothing man-made intruded upon it: no shed, no electrical pole, no winery buildings. Mondavi saw it as unspoiled California countryside, the sort of site perfect not only for higher-end grapes but also for people to visit. With Shoch acting as the middleman, Mondavi purchased twelve acres of To Kalon, and after filing incorporation papers with the State of California on Valentine's Day, he and his partners broke ground on the winery on July 16, 1966.

It was May's design and Mondavi's long-term plans that separated the Robert Mondavi Winery from the wineries that had come before and those that would come immediately after; his cageless panache was what made the winery the most significant new one in Napa Valley since Prohibition, though it wasn't the first. That distinction belonged to Joe Heitz.

Joe Heitz, like Robert Mondavi, came from the wine world—something that would increasingly prove to be an anomaly. Born and raised on an Illinois farm about one hundred miles west of Chicago, Heitz joined the US Army Air Corps after two years of junior college. He served during World War II as a mechanic at an air base in Fresno, California, going door-to-door looking for part-time work "to pick up beer money." One of the doors he knocked on belonged to bulk wine behemoth Italian Swiss Colony, which hired Heitz and changed the course of his life. He went on to earn bachelor's and master's degrees in enology from UC Davis, worked various other jobs in wine (including for E. & J. Gallo in Modesto), before settling into a long run as an assistant winemaker under Andre Tchelistcheff at Beaulieu, making $325 a month. After a stint teaching enology at Fresno State University, he and his wife, Alice, settled again in Napa Valley. There they filed incorporation papers for their Heitz Wine Cellars on May 15, 1964. Heitz originally bought an eight-acre parcel south of St. Helena for $5,000 in 1961, relocating three years later to a 160-acre tract just east of the town in an area called Spring Valley.

After dabbling in blends, including one for a respectable Chardonnay, Heitz released his Martha's Vineyard Cabernet Sauvignon in 1966. (It was named for the Oakville vineyard where Heitz got the grapes, not for the resort enclave in Massachusetts.) Critics ecstatically received the wine: Martha's Vineyard Cabernet Sauvignon became one of the iconic American fine wines of the mid-twentieth century, right up there with the Georges de Latour Private Reserve Cabernet Sauvignon. Not only was its complexity and quality praised, but its "distinctive expression of terroir" was hailed as well. Heitz's Cabernet Sauvignon was the first Napa wine since Prohibition to slap the vineyard's name on the label—a simple yet bold statement in that era of Pink Chablis, when place seemed to matter so little in American wine. Myriad other wineries would imitate the move in the coming decades, but Heitz Wine Cellars stood out in the mid-1960s for its emphasis on recording and championing the exact origins of its grapes. As for the tall, intense, sometimes irascible Heitz himself, who always went by Joe and who disdained the flowery language often used to describe wine, his peers recognized him not merely as a winemaker but, as one contemporary put it, Napa Valley's "first artisan."

Its first *star*, however, seemed far off.

ON ROUTE 66

1964–1966 | Chicago

Born in November 1928 and raised in the Polish American enclave of Bucktown in Chicago, Warren Winiarski seemed etymologically destined for a career in wine—his surname means "son of a winemaker" in Polish. Winiarski's father, Stephen, however, was a livery driver whose wine-making was solely a hobby. Winiarski would press his ear to his father's bubbling barrels of fruit, honey, and dandelion wines, occasionally helping the batches along by picking the dandelions from farms on the metropolis's outskirts. He also took over the family garden by age ten and grew, as he remembered it, some "fantastic tomatoes," carrots, lettuce, and beets. The wine-making and gardening notwithstanding, Winiarski's future seemed to lie in his voracious reading, first at the local public library and then, when he had exhausted its stable, at the used bookstores of Chicago's Old Town.

One book in particular, Mortimer J. Adler's 1940 national bestseller *How to Read a Book: The Art of Getting a Liberal Education*, seemed to set Winiarski on his life's path. Intrigued by Adler's everyman approach to comprehending the Western intellectual canon, Winiarski dropped his forestry major at Colorado A&M—he didn't really like the technical curriculum anyway—and decamped for St. John's College in Annapolis, Maryland, where Adler was a visiting lecturer. In 1952 Winiarski started graduate school in political philosophy at the University of Chicago, another Adler stomping ground, and spent the following year in Italy researching the Rosetta stone for political strategists, Nicolo Machiavelli, in Naples and Florence. It was during this period abroad that Winiarski's life pivoted again.

This time the lynchpin for change was no book; it was the simple act of having wine with meals. In the Winiarski household back in Chicago, wine was trotted out on special occasions; in Italy, it was an everyday foodstuff, devoid of exoticism. The experience stuck with Winiarski, though it eventually receded toward the back of his mind. Instead, he focused his energies on lecturing in the University of Chicago's liberal arts curriculum, based partly on Mortimer Adler's work, and continuing to pursue his own master's. Winiarski settled into a life of academia, and he and his wife, Barbara, a painter, started a family in his hometown. Then a friend brought a bottle of passable American wine to lunch one day, and Winiarski's life was upended again. The lunchtime wine was an epiphany, a simple accoutrement that brought his year in Italy flooding back: "Wine revealed itself in a stunning way," he later remembered.

Winiarski then leveled his formidable literary capabilities at wine, reading everything he could on the subject, including Frank Schoonmaker and Tom Marvel's *American Wines* and the 1941 follow-up, *The Complete Wine Book*. He visited local wine shops and honed his palate; he made wine at his home in faculty housing in a crock he'd found in an antique store in Baltimore (the crock birthed wine that tasted salty, suggesting a previous life as a pickle mixer); he even drove to New Mexico to see grape harvesting up close, living out of the family station wagon and bringing grapes back home for another round of (non-pickled) wine-making. When Winiarski finally finished his master's degree in 1962, instead of plunging into a doctorate that might have kept him in the Windy City for several more years, he turned to wine full-time. I've said all I have to say about Machiavelli, he thought.

He and his family split for California in August 1964, in a white Chevrolet station wagon, pulling a U-Haul trailer along Route 66 from Chicago.

ROBERT'S FOLLY

1966–1968 | Oakville, California

"**H**ow the hell do you know** about that?" Lee Stewart asked his younger charge. Warren Winiarski had taken a short wine-making class at the University of California, Davis, and wanted to know if Stewart's wines were suffering from tournee, a microbial spoilage. Stewart, a man so often dyspeptic that his contemporaries nicknamed him the Stone, didn't know if his wines had tournee—nor did he care. He told Winiarski as much, and the two got on with their work that day making wine.

Winiarski's second full-time job in American wine, after arriving in California in 1964, was as an assistant winemaker at the Robert Mondavi Winery in Oakville. Before that, the thirty-six-year-old who sported black-framed glasses spent two years at Stewart's Souverain Winery on Howell Mountain, about sixteen miles northeast of Mondavi and May's epiphany at To Kalon.

Souverain, like Inglenook and Beaulieu, was among a handful of Northern California wineries feeling their way along the fine wine path, ferreting out a niche that barely existed. Stewart himself, starting shortly after his first harvest in 1944, blazed trails in American Zinfandels and Pinot Noirs, before turning to similar critical success in Cabernet Sauvignons in the 1960s; he also fermented his Chardonnay like the French, in wooden barrels rather than stainless steel, and many credit him with introducing Petite Sirah as a varietal in the United States, complete with a clearly demarcated label stating the grape type and the winery. The consultant he hired, Andre Tchelistcheff (the White Russian émigré who made Beaulieu's name in post-Prohibition wine), spurred many of Stewart's innovations. Tchelistcheff imparted his experience with controlled malolactic and cold fermentations, making Stewart's wines cleaner, yet more complex.

Much as he had from wine books in Chicago, Winiarski soaked up all he could from Stewart in Howell Mountain. It was a two-man operation, from the vine to the bottling, with Stewart showing Winiarski not only the basics of wine-making, such as pruning and racking, but also strategies like adding bentonite to the whites to rid them of unwanted proteins, and how to safely stack cases of wine fourteen high. The pair often kept up a running dialogue throughout the working day, with the pupil peppering the teacher with so many questions that Stewart worried Winiarski was only using his Souverain for a quick springboard to his own Napa Valley winery.

That was not the case: for two years, through the 1965 harvest, Winiarski and his family endured a rustic existence, worlds away from Chicago. Winiarski and wife Barbara, with their son and daughter, rented an aged cabin off Crystal Springs Road, farther down the mountain than Stewart's winery, in a valley where you might not see another light on at night. The cabin had a wood-burning stove and secondhand furniture (some of the family's clothes came secondhand, too), and entertainment arrived in the form of opera on the radio on Saturdays. The family grew vegetables and Winiarski shot deer, in and out of season. All the while, along with the tutorials from his gruff employer, he read and read about wine. Albert Winkler's and Maynard Amerine's classifications were his bible; it was Amerine, in fact, who recommended he connect with Lee Stewart, who didn't have enough money to hire a proper technician and therefore might be willing to play ball with an arriviste looking to learn the ropes.

It was only in 1966 that Winiarski segued to the new, ground-up winery everyone in the valley was talking about—and not necessarily in glowing terms. The Robert Mondavi Winery was rushing to put out its first bottles in 1967, which meant a frenzied 1966, the peaceful dedication in September notwithstanding. It was all hands on deck, with Mondavi and wife Marge, as well as their children, working alongside Winiarski, Ivan Shoch, and Bill Hart amid sawdust, pipe dope, and electrician's tape, the hours often frustrating, the worry always there.

Crucially, the weather cooperated. There were no frosts, and the spring and summer of 1966 were particularly warm, though not too warm, with cool evenings and mornings shrouded in dense fog. This weather pushed the Napa grape harvest—for Mondavi and everyone else—back a couple of weeks, giving the new operation that much more time to build and be honed. The final Cabernet grapes, for instance, were harvested on November 11, weeks after the usual time. Also, though Peter Mondavi and his older brother weren't on speaking terms, Charles Krug helped with the crush since the Robert Mondavi Winery's brand-new crusher was not up to the task by itself. Such support from Krug, five miles up Highway 29, belied the novelty of Mondavi's brand-new ground-up winery: Robert Mondavi was intent on solely producing fine wines, so why fear the competition when such bottles composed so little of the marketplace? A little help for what some wags were calling "Robert's Folly" couldn't hurt Krug's bottom line in generic wines.

Nor, it looked like, was Krug intimidated by the construction site that the new winery's slice of To Kalon had quickly become. Work continued apace on Cliff May's V, its point facing Highway 29, its arms opening around the vineyard flanked by the Mayacamas Mountains—visitors would see both landmarks as they passed through the winery's broad, inviting archway. It was part of Mondavi's wider vision to make his winery, as he described it, a "joyous space where we [can] celebrate the joys of wine and food, of music and heart." In other words, he wanted to establish a tourist attraction to help market his wine.

It was not entirely without precedent in Northern California. Other wineries, including Charles Krug, had built tasting rooms, for instance, and it was not unusual for a winery (again, including Krug) to host concerts, but Mondavi set out to attract tourists from the beginning. That was what made him different from the start. His bucolic domain would be about not only fine wine but also the lifestyle that might come with it, the sort of romantic, wine-centric European lifestyle that had seduced him in France a few years before. Visitors at the Robert Mondavi Winery, itself styled on Spanish and Italian architecture, could sit or amble in the shadow of the bell tower, their languid fingers toying with long-stemmed, bulbous glasses as the sun slinked behind the mountains and the cool night layered the warmth the wine provided, thoughts perhaps meandering from the stresses of life to those "joys of wine and food, of music and heart." This wider vision would prove to be immensely influential in the American fine wine movement and in wider American culture, much more so than what Mondavi bottled—at least that first year.

As it happened, the Robert Mondavi Winery sold 2,579 cases of wine in 1967. Its first offering was what Mondavi described as a "cheerful, drinkable" Gamay Rosé; it retailed for $1.79 a bottle, slightly pricier than most fine wine bottles then available in the United States. While the winery also initially worked with Pinot Noir, Chardonnay, Riesling, and that specialty of To Kalon, Cabernet Sauvignon, it was Mondavi's spin on Sauvignon Blanc that proved to be the true game changer. It all started in that frantic run-up to the 1967 debut when Mondavi realized his growers had supplied him with a decent yield of the white wine grape that then covered only around two thousand acres of California. Most of the Sauvignon Blanc produced by American vintners, however, was of dubious quality, dogged by cleanliness issues and a dearth of technical know-how.

Mondavi knew that in France the Sauvignon Blanc grape could ballast some fantastic white wines, including Sancerre, Blanc Fumé, and the Pouilly Fumé that had so captivated Julia Child in Rouen. He aged his yield of Sauvignon Blanc in French barrels. By 1968 he produced, in the words of one critic, a "light, dry, golden wine" that was "long, silky [and] ideal with fish." Not only was the wine a revelation stylistically and technically, it was commercially coveted and helped Mondavi's case sales quadruple in that second full year of operation. Part of those sales surely sprang from the sort of savvy marketing Mondavi had already displayed in his winery's physical makeup. Over a few samples, Robert Mondavi, his son Michael, and his partners Ivan Shoch and Fred Holmes invented a name for the Sauvignon Blanc that was a direct challenge to purveyors in France, the undisputed leader in fine wine, as much as it was a way to separate Mondavi's Sauvignon Blanc from the American pack: they called their creation Fumé Blanc.

It was a simple inversion of one of the Sauvignon Blanc style names. It was also totally made up, but there it was: a gutsy shot across the bow of French fine wine from a tiny start-up on the western edge of the American empire.

GREYHOUND BUS TO PARADISE

1968 | Desne, Croatia—Howell Mountain, California

Professor Hebrang checked to see if any Communist agents were nearby. Confident he would not be overheard, he leaned toward his pupils and whispered, "California is a paradise."

The pupils had asked Hebrang, an enology professor at the University of Zagreb in Yugoslavia, what he thought of California wines after his recent sabbatical there in 1953. His answer grabbed one of his students in particular and held him for the rest of his long life.

Born in April 1923, in Desne, a Croatian town of about one thousand souls barely five miles from the Adriatic Sea, Miljenko Grgich grew up the youngest of eleven children. He learned to farm early, as his family, along with much of Desne, grew their own food and raised their own livestock. At the age of six, Grgich was put in charge of the family sheep, surreptitiously sneaking them onto public land in the late afternoons, after school, because that was the best place for the sheep to eat. His mother made clothes from the sheep's wool, and her large brood even got their shoes from the hides of animals they slaughtered. The family's social life revolved around Desne's Catholic parish, which they attended every Sunday and on feast days, and around the Grgichs' fireplace, from which Miljenko's father would serve him cooked eggs, a particular treat the youngster seemed to enjoy as much for the taste as for the time spent with his father, who took particular care in dipping bread into the slightly runny yolk.

There was also wine. The family had a small vineyard, with half its grapes for themselves and half for sale, grapes being one of the Grgichs' few cash crops. Soon after he stopped breastfeeding, Grgich regularly partook in *bevanda*, a mixture of water and red wine his parents saw as no less innocuous for children than water itself (maybe even better, it turned out, as the wine helped sanitize the often dirty water, which was gathered from a rain-collecting cistern). Grgich's mother even boiled wine in the fireplace when her children were ill, adding sugar and delivering it piping hot to the patient; though it burned their mouths, the children inevitably felt a little better come morning. By age four, Grgich was stomping grapes at harvest time; by age eleven, he was lowering himself morning and night into the fermentation vat in the cellar to tamp down the skins and seeds collecting on the top to let out the built-up carbon dioxide.

A precocious youngster, Grgich was able to attend school for eight years—an unusually long time then—before his family finally yanked him at age fourteen so he could manage the general store his cousin owned in Desne. While he might have wanted to continue his education, Grgich's life was rather idyllic, its rhythms still dictated by family, church, and wine, its nucleus still the big hearth in his parents' house, where he continued to live.

Then, in 1939, World War II shattered the idyll. Armies began marching and flying across Europe, the Grgichs' little corner of Croatia in Yugoslavia just another point on the map, one that changed hands over the next several years. In April 1941 the Axis powers led by Germany invaded Yugoslavia, which was itself already two years into a fresh round of ethnic and political infighting that seemed to define the Balkans. By 1943 Communist partisans gained control of Desne and looted voraciously, including the store Grgich ran for his cousin. The twenty-year-old fled to a neighboring town only to see it and much of the rest of the region overrun by the Germans again. They destroyed nearly every house in Desne. When the war finally ended in the summer of 1945, the Communists held a firm grip on Yugoslavia, and Grgich faced a bleak future. Just past the cusp of adulthood, the best he could do was to study to be a bookkeeper at a university in Split, Croatia's second-biggest city; he worked reluctantly at keeping the books at a state-owned co-op.

His mind, though, drifted often to wine. He had yanked up the vineyards at his parents' house as the war started, his father believing the land could be better used to grow crops like wheat and corn that would surely be in short supply amid the coming conquests and counter-conquests; he realized too late it would have been better to grow grapes during the war, as wine became a sort of currency. Grgich knew he had enough knowledge, however, to work with grapes again, to make wine—besides, he was unhappy as a bookkeeping cog in a jittery totalitarian machine. So one day in 1949, he walked seven miles in the predawn hours from where he was then staying to the University of Zagreb to sign up for a viticulture and enology program. In that inimitable communistic way, out of the hundreds of prospective students in line by dawn, only the first twelve were admitted. Grgich was one of them.

He worked odd jobs, he studied hard, he got back into wine, and, crucially, he found himself talking to Professor Hebrang, back from sabbatical in the apparent paradise that was California.

"What about the farming equipment?" a fellow student asked.

"Almost all the farmers have a tractor," the professor replied. "But every five years they get a new one because the new model is so much better than the old one and more efficient."

Everyone had a tractor! The students, Grgich among them, couldn't believe it. He made up his mind to get to California, whatever the odds. He applied for a United Nations fellowship to study wine in West Germany, leaving Yugoslavia in August 1954, with a passport good for only four months and a false bottom on one of his shoes to hide the thirty-two American dollars he'd gotten on the black market. Grgich was not going back to Yugoslavia.

He passed nearly two bucolic years doing research and working on a farm between Stuttgart and Frankfurt, all the while trying unsuccessfully to gain entry into the States. He finally went to the Canadian consulate in Munich at the end of 1955, and got a visa the same day. A consulate official asked him where he'd like to emigrate, and Grgich quickly pointed to Vancouver, the biggest Canadian city closest to California as well as right across the border from Washington State, where he had relatives. With $200 sent by his brother-in-law in Washington, Grgich departed via Hamburg on the ship *Italia*, bound for Halifax in Nova Scotia. After a days-long train crawl across Canada, he settled into the Vancouver area, working basically any job that would have him, including as a dishwasher and a waiter at a high school run by the Christian Brothers, a Roman Catholic order, and—more germane to his training back in Zagreb—as a quality-control inspector at a paper factory.

Just as wine had lasted through the war and through Communism, it lasted as Grgich's dream through the dreary workaday life of Greater Vancouver. Grgich wanted to get across into Washington and down to California, and he did so by posting an advertisement in the newsletter of the San Francisco–based Wine Institute. He presented his credentials in the ad, including his education in Zagreb and his wine training in West Germany. None other than Lee Stewart at Souverain, who would go on to serve as the acerbic mentor to Warren Winiarski, responded to the ad, giving Grgich, then in his mid-thirties, the job he needed for an American work visa.

Four years after he'd left Croatia with thirty-two dollars in his fake heel, Grgich boarded a Greyhound for St. Helena, California, in mid-August 1958, arriving at the corner of Railroad Ave. and Adams St. just past 10:00 PM, the only soul to disembark in what looked to Grgich like every other small town

the bus had just rolled interminably through. He carried two cardboard suitcases and wore a black beret atop his wiry five-foot-six frame. Not finding
his prospective employer awaiting him, Grgich rang Stewart at the winery.

"Hello," Stewart gruffly answered after a couple of rings.

"This is Mike Grgich," Grgich answered, using the Anglicized nickname
he'd adopted in Canada. "I'm supposed to start working at the Souverain
Cellars. Are you Mr. Stewart?"

"Yes, I've been expecting you. But it's too late now for me to drive down
to St. Helena and get you. Why don't you just go to a hotel, and I'll come and
pick you up in the morning. You can find a hotel right near where you are."

Stewart hung up, leaving the newcomer to once again find his way in a
strange land. This land in particular appeared deserted, with the few small
shops near the bus drop-off already closed. California—or at least this slice
of it in Napa Valley—didn't look like the paradise Professor Hebrang had
described; it looked hardscrabble, like its best days either lay well behind it
or far ahead.

Grgich tried the first hotel he saw. It was closed; he could see no one
through the windows, and no one answered his knocks on the door. He lugged
his two suitcases to Main Street and spied the sign for the Hotel St. Helena.
There was a lone light shining from what turned out to be a downstairs bar.
Grgich approached the bartender. "Do you have any rooms?"

"We have twenty-four rooms."

"Any empty?"

"We have twenty-four empty rooms," the bartender said.

"Can I get one of the rooms?"

"Two bucks. Go upstairs and take any room you want."

Grgich took the first room at the top of the stairs. The next morning,
Stewart picked him up, and he started a rocky tenure at Souverain that lasted
a mere four months of sixteen-hour days. He and the often-domineering
Stewart didn't get along, and besides, Souverain at the time seemed a decidedly
unambitious, if not precarious, place. Stewart produced about four thousand
cases annually, a relatively small amount, and he once paid a particularly
industrious worker a Christmas bonus of exactly one dollar; Stewart, his
wife, and their tenant Grgich often dined on bread and beans. Such thrift at
a well-regarded winery—it had won thirty-four prizes at the California State
Fair in the ten years before Grgich joined—spoke volumes for the shakiness
of the American fine wine movement in general. For starters, no one up to
that time had built a major winery in Napa Valley since Prohibition, and the
number of wineries in California had stayed relatively the same since Repeal

in 1933. If Grgich was going to gain a more stable foothold in this supposed paradise, he would have to move on.

He did. He studied wine part-time at UC Davis and briefly worked at the Napa Valley winery of his old Vancouver patrons, the Christian Brothers. Then Grgich won a spot at Beaulieu Vineyards in Rutherford, under Andre Tchelistcheff, a fellow Slavic émigré who had made it rather big in American wine. After a two-month tryout, Tchelistcheff hired Grgich as a wine chemist for what Grgich considered a princely sum of $3.25 an hour; Tchelistcheff soon added quality control to the newcomer's responsibilities. Grgich worked at Beaulieu for nine knowledge-absorbing years. In 1968 he looked around for a fresh challenge. A man named Warren Winiarski—who was itching to strike out on his own after realizing he could only rise so high in someone else's family business—had just left the Robert Mondavi Winery in nearby St. Helena, the same forgettable burg the Greyhound had dropped Grgich off in a decade earlier. He went there.

GOING FOR BROKE
1968–1969 | Oakville, California

"**M**ike," Robert Mondavi said, "if you join my company, I'll make out of you a little Andre Tchelistcheff!"

It was 1968, only a few weeks after Warren Winiarski had moved on after two crushes with the Robert Mondavi Winery. Mike Grgich and Mondavi were sitting on a bench near the winery's arched entryway Cliff May had designed a few short years before. It was a sunny day, and Mondavi's enthusiasm was intoxicating. Grgich, in demand after nearly a decade under Tchelistcheff at Beaulieu, found himself unable to say no. He came on as the director of quality control for Mondavi—though, in effect, he would oversee wine-making.

The first significant new winery in Napa Valley since Prohibition was slowly gaining a commercial foothold, though it would be years more before it was clear whether Mondavi and his partners' move was a moneymaker. Its case sales nearly quadrupled in 1968, behind such offerings as Fumé Blanc, and would triple from there to more than thirty thousand in 1969. While this paled against the generic producers such as E. & J. Gallo, which sold many times more than that—the Modesto-based company could store nearly thirty-six million cases of wine in its various facilities at one time—such sales further opened the market for American fine wine.

If one were to survey a liquor store's wine selection in a major American city such as San Francisco in the year Mondavi pitched Grgich on joining his team, it would be apparent that more than 75 percent of the brands offered came from the likes of Gallo: cheaper, stronger, sweeter screwtops made from lower-end, utilitarian grapes like Carignan, even green Thompson seedless grapes, a particular favorite of Gallo's. The smaller, fine wine–producing likes of John Daniel's Inglenook, the Latours' Beaulieu, or Mondavi's seedling might comprise no more than 10 percent of the selection; maybe another 15 percent or so of the wine bottles on the liquor store's shelves would come from European wineries, though anything of particular note, like a First Growth from Bordeaux, would have been rare. Finally, these European bottles would likely be set apart from the American ones of whatever quality, perhaps even placed horizontally to preserve the moisture of the cork and thus its seal. And this was a wine selection in a major American city; in smaller cities and towns, it was often generic wine or nothing. Robert Mondavi Fumé Blanc would have been like something from Mars.

A big part of the dearth of domestically produced fine wine throughout much of the nation was due largely to the indifference, or understandable ignorance, of the drinking public. Another part sprang from the ease of producing cheaper, sweeter wines versus pricier, drier wines. Yet another part was attributable to distribution, a domain that bigger players dominated. Gallo, again, was the dominant of the dominant: beginning in the late 1930s, it developed a strategy of buying distributorships to get around the so-called "three-tier system" under which most states operated when it came to alcohol.

Spooked by the speakeasies and rumrunners of Prohibition who knew no barrier between maker and taker, most states required alcohol sales to go from a producer to a distributor (or wholesaler) to a retailer, thus preventing a winery, brewery, or distillery from selling directly to the consumer. Some states even inserted themselves into the three-tier system by becoming the wholesaler for certain types of alcohol. A small winery had to rely on either self-distribution (if authorities allowed it) or the good graces of distributors not controlled by—or dependent upon—the bigger players. What distributor was going to carry something called Fumé Blanc that might not sell that much when they could carry a brand such as Gallo's Pink Chablis that sold regularly? The three-tier system seemed to virtually ensure that Mondavi's wines would never make it much beyond California.

Still, the winery soldiered on, the infectious enthusiasm of its leader, who had drawn Mike Grgich into his orbit, powering innovations that would come to have lasting influence on American fine wine. Mondavi threw himself into every aspect of the winery, from production to sales to marketing to human resources. The staff stayed skeletal for years—basically Mondavi, Grgich, and Mondavi's eldest son, Michael, who had returned from National Guard service and was working as vice president of wine-making. Seasonal help was brought in for crushes, but otherwise the winery hummed along from a little after dawn—when Grgich and Mondavi would arrive—to the early evenings with as few people as necessary.

While Mondavi might have skimped on labor, he did not skimp on equipment. One of his major innovations was to purchase new French oak barrels for aging, a novelty in Napa Valley; Mondavi picked up the concept during his overseas travels at the start of the decade. The technology had worked well, too, outside of the Valley, at the Hanzell Vineyards just beyond the border of the town of Sonoma to the south. It was there, beginning in the late 1940s, that James Zellerbach—a paper magnate, Marshall Plan administrator, and US ambassador to Italy—erected a winery dedicated to Chardonnay and Pinot Noir. Smitten with the wines of Burgundy, France, Zellerbach patterned his winery after an old monastic one, Clos de Vougeot, near Dijon, and his techniques after the winemakers of Burgundy. Those techniques included aging wines in oak barrels—French oak barrels from Limousin. The first Hanzell white, a 1956 Chardonnay, achieved exactly the result Zellerbach had aimed for: critics at the time agreed it "did indeed share some subtle nuances usually associated with better white Burgundies."

A lot of those nuances came from the oak, and from Hanzell onward, oak became integral to the American fine wine movement. Zellerbach's Chardonnays of the 1950s were a turning point, according to British critic Hugh Johnson. The liberal use of the wood added a complexity and lushness that would one day find expression in the oft-used enological adjective *oaky*. Aging in oak barrels, especially for red wines, might also weed out astringencies that could make the wine taste bitter, leaving it softer and infinitely more drinkable. Like Zellerbach in Sonoma, Mondavi in Napa looked past the perfectly decent American oak available and went straight to what was then the top wine-making culture on earth. Though pricier, his barrels were bought from a French cooperage that also supplied barrels to the best châteaus of Bordeaux. He also eschewed the wooden fermenting vats smaller wineries favored (largely for economic reasons) for brand-new stainless steel ones. Mondavi also spent freely as he experimented with different kinds of grape presses; the same went for bottling techniques, including the method the winery devised to expel wine-spoiling air from bottle necks right before corking.

It was once the wine was in the bottles that Mondavi really shined, though. He befriended Robert Lawrence Balzer, and his wine-making exploits became regular fodder for Balzer's *Los Angeles Times* column, still the biggest regular newspaper coverage of fine wine in the United States. After visiting "Senor Mondavi" in early November 1969—around the time his winery bottled a Cabernet Sauvignon that would win a blind tasting the columnist organized three years later—Balzar wrote:

> Robert Mondavi of the Napa Valley has a theory about the difference in taste between French and California Clarets. Both wines are basically from the same grape, Cabernet Sauvignon, and if given relatively similar soil and weather conditions, and comparable winemaking techniques, should have a kissing-cousin resemblance.

Alas, the French seemed to have an advantage: newer oak barrels. It was one of the innovations that winemaker and consultant Émile Peynaud had pushed in the last two decades in France: he had convinced his clients to discard older oak barrels—often rife with bacteria, reeking of overuse, and unable after a few years to impart flavors to the wine inside—in favor of rotating in newer ones regularly. It was a practice American winemakers were generally slow to adopt, though when Mondavi, Zellerbach, and others did finally pick up the concept of barrel rotation, they never looked back. "Robert Mondavi believes 'age in wood,' if it's new oak, spells the difference between California and French Claret," Balzer wrote of the reds on the market then, "and has put his money where his opinion falls." Oak-barrel aging, and the rotation of barrels after a few years, became de rigueur in American fine wine–making.

Also in 1969, the winery launched its summer concert series and opened its tasting rooms, wood-drenched affairs done with the same Spanish-infused flair as the exterior. Mondavi talked to anyone and everyone who might be of influence in the small universe of American fine wine, and he wasn't shy about dispatching blood to help. In the winery's earliest days, Michael Mondavi, the striking image of his father, was known to drive deliberately slowly down Highway 29, traffic building behind him, until he turned delicately into the winery's drive, right next to its sign, invariably taking a car or two of curious motorists with him. He'd then stop, spring from the car near the arched entryway, and greet the curious drivers with, "Hi, I'm Michael Mondavi. Would you like a tour?"

More and more people would take him up on his offer, and more and more would want the wine as well. While not yet in the same critical league as a winery like Beaulieu or Inglenook, Mondavi was gaining its acolytes; as it gained, it ramped up production. In 1969, in the first harvest Grgich was involved with, the winery crushed five hundred tons of grapes, several times the twenty tons it had crushed in its start-up year of 1966. The increased pace took its toll. Grgich worried aloud that he could not control the quality of every wine, insisting Mondavi hire another winemaker to handle everything but the brand-making Chardonnays and Cabernets; Mondavi nixed the idea. At the same time, Mondavi's business partners, Ivan Shoch and Fred Holmes, fretted they would never recoup their investments, given Mondavi's free-spending habits. The winery was running out of capital less than a few years in and wasn't profitable. Despite Mondavi's innovations in wine production and the increase in visitors and demand, it looked like Robert's Folly was just that.

Then beer stepped in. Shoch and Holmes in early 1968 sold their stakes in the Mondavi winery to the Rainier Brewing Company, one of the few regional breweries left in the United States, then dominated beer-wise by the likes of Anheuser-Busch and Miller. The brewery was looking to invest in a growth industry not dominated by such behemoths, and fine wine looked promising.

With bitter memories of his banishment from Charles Krug, Mondavi retained management control of the winery in a fifty-fifty deal with Rainier. That deal infused the winery with capital to grow, which it did in part through buying up hundreds more acres of To Kalon, thereby basically saving the entire operation—and with it the promise of the American fine wine movement. Still, the growth remained frantic, the Rainier monies only seeming to embolden Mondavi further in his expensive experiments and marketing. The Rainier Brewing Company wanted the winery to eventually sell two hundred thousand cases annually, a staggeringly high total; Charles Krug, for instance, was selling more than five hundred thousand cases a year by the late 1960s, but that was after decades in the business. How could Mondavi scale heights like those while still making wine meant to compete critically with the likes of Beaulieu and Inglenook? Moreover, how could it sell that amount using distribution that didn't extend beyond California?

Grgich, for his part, did not believe the growth was good, whatever the boundless optimism of his boss. Things moved too fast, too loosely for the winemaker who had learned his meticulousness at the elbow of Andre Tchelistcheff. Besides, fast growth for a winery with aspirations to take on

First and Second Growth French châteaus seemed ridiculous, given the numbers: by 1969 most of the wine consumed in the United States was still of the sweeter, cheaper generic variety. It seemed it would take a lot more than summer concerts and tasting rooms and a brewery's checkbook to turn Americans on to drier, more expensive fine wine, especially enough to justify so much production.

Grgich knew he would be happier elsewhere. He left the Robert Mondavi Winery in 1972, having lasted two more crushes than Warren Winiarski.

$50,000 DOWN PAYMENT
1968–1970 | Silverado Trail, California

This is fabulous, just fabulous! Warren Winiarski thought. The Cabernet he was sampling this particular spring afternoon in 1969 smelled of black cherries and spices he couldn't quite place; and its taste was complex, with a fine-grained texture and a long, lingering aftertaste.

The Cabernet came from a batch made at the home of Nathan Fay, a vineyard owner about seven miles down Highway 29 from the Robert Mondavi Winery, which Winiarski had left less than a year before. Fay, like many vineyard owners, made small batches of wine with the grapes he grew. In Fay's case, they were the rather revolutionary Cabernet Sauvignon. A farm equipment salesman who turned to farming, Fay bought 205 acres in 1953 along Napa's Silverado Trail in an area where most farmers, if they grew grapes at all, grew lower-quality, higher-yield workhorses like Carignan and Alicante Bouschet. Fay had a different idea: working with an adviser from the University of California, Davis, he began cultivating Cabernet Sauvignon grapes in 1961. According to Maynard Amerine and Albert Winkler's groundbreaking classifications, the southern slice of Napa Valley where Fay tilled wasn't given to Cabernet cultivation. Still, he persisted, adding acreage each year to the fifteen he started with in 1961, when he ripped up plum orchards. Soon, Fay had clients like Charles Krug and Heitz buying his Cabernet Sauvignon grapes for their fine wines.

One of the ways Fay was able to grow such grapes was through irrigation, the very topic Winiarski was there that day to talk with him about. The last few years had proven a rough go for the Chicago émigré's own grape-growing efforts. In August 1965, while still working at Lee Stewart's Souverain, Winiarski had paid $15,000 for fifteen acres high up Howell Mountain off an unpaved road; it was rocky, untilled land, nineteen hundred feet above sea level—exactly the sort of soil and climate inhospitable to higher-end grapes. Still, Winiarski and his wife, Barbara, plunged ahead, hiring help to prepare the soil through tilling and irrigation and, in the fall of 1966, to graft Cabernet Sauvignon buds onto rootstock they'd planted.

Most of the buds, however, did not take, and Winiarski found himself back at square one after spending thousands of dollars and devoting more than two years of work to the endeavor. He tried again, in 1968, this time with better irrigation, and achieved better results. But it was clear that the high-altitude vineyard would never support a winery. In the fall of 1968, about three years after buying it, Winiarski sold the Howell Mountain land to the owner of a San Francisco furniture store; the buyer hired Winiarski back to manage the vineyard, which, with the help of a well installed by the new owner, did eventually start yielding small crops of Cabernet Sauvignon.

Despite Winiarski's failure on Howell Mountain—due to the vagaries of climate and geography and not to Winiarski's skill, which had grown by leaps and bounds since his arrival in the valley—he was determined to try again. That's what brought him to Nathan Fay's vineyard in the spring of 1969, and to the revelatory sample of Cabernet Sauvignon. This was the kind of wine Winiarski wanted to make, and it turned out he might have a better than decent shot this time: a fifty-acre property next to Fay's, called Heid Ranch, was on sale for $120,000. The then-current owners were harvesting apples, plums, cherries, and low-end grapes there, but Winiarski saw potential in the soil for growing the sorts of high-end grapes that undergirded Fay's fantastic homemade wine. Winiarski negotiated the price down to $110,000 and then cobbled together enough from his mother and from savings off the Howell Mountain sale for the $50,000 down payment.

On February 22, 1970, not even two years after he'd left the Robert Mondavi Winery and fewer than five years after his first, ill-fated stab at vineyard ownership, Winiarski closed on the sale of Heid Ranch. He called it Stag's Leap Wine Cellars, named after the rocky terrain just beyond his second act.

NATIONWIDE

1968–1971 | Napa County, California—Sonoma County, California— Roseburg, Oregon—Cutchogue, New York—Fauquier County, Virginia

In 1967 Al Brounstein, a Saskatchewan native who went to college in Minnesota before building a wholesale beauty supply company in Los Angeles, bought land on Diamond Mountain in the northern slice of Napa Valley near Calistoga; the following year he opened California's first new winery dedicated exclusively to Cabernet Sauvignon and called it Diamond Creek Vineyards, with production capped at about three thousand cases annually. Also in 1968, Barney Fetzer and wife Kathleen released the first twenty-five hundred cases of Cabernet Sauvignon and Zinfandel harvested for their eponymous winery from their 720-acre farm in Mendocino County. Barney, a merchant marine from Southern California, and Kathleen, who grew up in Minnesota before moving in with a sister in Oakland, had been growing grapes on the farm since the late 1950s.

Brounstein and the Fetzers were among other pioneers of the late 1960s joining the likes of Robert Mondavi, Andre Tchelistcheff, Warren Winiarski, Mike Grgich, and Joe Heitz. They arrived at the industry from myriad backgrounds, rarely from wine directly, and from myriad geographies, all ending up in a decidedly uncertain niche market. Yet, for their different starting points and pathways, these newcomers shared a few characteristics. They were indeed new, for one thing; most either pioneered fine wine production in a particular location or with a particular grape type. They were also generally affluent to begin with, though that was not as much of a prerequisite as it would later become in American fine wine. And they all dealt with the same frustratingly indifferent marketplace, which had little firsthand experience with American fine wine and which saw their finished fares as inferior to French brands besides. These newcomers' enological fortunes would sink or swim based on consumer reception; that is, no one appears to have arrived to the party in the late 1960s as a hobbyist. They meant business.

This group of fine wine hopefuls also included Gene Trefethen, a top executive with industrial behemoth Kaiser, who had worked on such projects as the Hoover Dam and the San Francisco–Oakland Bay Bridge. In 1968, intent on forging a second career, Trefethen paid $3,000 per acre for a six-hundred-acre former winery and vineyard called Eschol just north of Napa off Highway 29. Trefethen and his wife, Katie, set about replanting most of the acres with higher-end grapes and just generally fixing up the place, which had fallen into disrepair shortly after Repeal (in the early 1970s, their son and daughter would start turning out noted wines, Chardonnays in particular, from the vineyard). In 1969 another family, the Corleys, also planted roots just north of Napa in what became known as the Oak Knoll District. Jay Corley, who was fluent in Spanish and Italian, had been a translator for the National Security Agency while living in northern Virginia. A midwesterner by birth, he eventually made his way to Southern California to work in finance and then to eighty Napa acres of mostly prune trees, which he set about supplanting with Chardonnay and Pinot Noir for what became the Monticello Vineyards & Winery.

In 1970 a San Franciscan with no experience in the wine trade named Martin Lee Sr., along with two sons, a son-in-law, and a friend of equally virginal track records, bought an old winery in Sonoma County called Pagani Brothers Winery. It dated from 1906, though Lee and his partners redubbed it Kenwood Vineyards after the town where it was located. Martin's twenty-six-year-old son, Mike, who had a business degree from the University of San Francisco, took over day-to-day operations, learning the wine trade hands-on as well as through courses at UC Davis. Kenwood became particularly noted for its Sauvignon Blanc.

Then in 1971 Jim Barrett, a successful real estate attorney in the Los Angeles area, partnered with one of his clients, developer Ernest Hahn, to buy the controlling interest in another decrepit Napa winery called Chateau Montelena. Dating from the 1880s, the 150-acre property had fallen largely into disrepair and by the 1970s was mostly producing lower-end grapes for clients like Gallo. Barrett and Hahn knew they would have to tear up most of the vines and replant.

Perhaps most portentously for Northern California, two scions of noted Bordeaux families ended their worldwide search for a suitable place to re-create higher-end French wines in Napa Valley in 1971, a little south of Warren Winiarski's Stag's Leap. John Goelet, whose ancestor cofounded the oldest Bordeaux wine trading firm in 1802, had hired Bernard Portet, whose father was the technical director at First Growth winery Château Lafite Rothschild, to scour the earth for the best spots to make French wine outside of France. Portet looked in Australia and Europe, and finally settled on Napa Valley, where he and Goelet opened Clos Du Val Winery off the Silverado Trail in 1971. It would specialize in Cabernets and Zinfandels.

There were enological machinations beyond Northern California around that time, too, though the region, particularly Napa Valley, was already America's premier area to grow wine grapes and to make wine. Between 1965 and 1975 the number of small wineries in the United States doubled, with pockets of start-ups or reanimated old operations in Southern California, the Pacific Northwest, even pre-Prohibition stalwarts like Virginia, Ohio, and New York. The majority of these newly opened wineries were looking in some mad way to craft wines from higher-end grapes.

People thought Richard Sommer, for instance, was wasting his time when, in 1961, he planted Cabernet Sauvignon, Pinot Noir, and Sauvignon Blanc vines on an old turkey farm in Roseburg, Oregon, that he dubbed HillCrest Vineyard. In 1963, however, the vineyard near the South Umpqua River yielded enough for Sommer to start production, with two hundred gallons of wine rolling out of HillCrest that year. In 1967 the ten-acre vineyard ultimately yielded six thousand gallons of juice, including enough to produce Oregon's first Pinot Noir. Sommer quit his day job as an appraiser the same year.

Other Oregonians followed him into wine-making in the late 1960s, with similar success right off the bat, including David and Diana Lett (Eyrie Vineyards), Richard and Nancy Ponzi (Ponzi Vineyards), and Dick Erath (Erath Winery). Several vineyards formed the state's first wine-promoting trade group in 1969, and the inaugural Oregon Wine Festival was held the following year, at around the time that Oregon State University started mimicking UC Davis in conducting serious wine research. It didn't hurt, either, that James Beard, the nation's leading food writer, was an Oregon native known to talk up the state's wine-making potential.

On the other side of the country, in 1973, two twenty-something Harvard graduates, Alex and Louisa Hargrave, planted seventeen acres of Cabernet Sauvignon, Pinot Noir, and Sauvignon Blanc on an old potato farm in the town of Cutchogue to create Long Island's first vineyard since Prohibition. Further upstate, in the Finger Lakes region between Rochester and Syracuse, older wineries, including those that had survived Prohibition, mingled with newcomers such as Bully Hill, founded by Walter Taylor in 1970, shortly after he unwittingly imitated Robert Mondavi in getting banished from his family's winery for insisting a little too forcefully on using higher-end grapes rather than the utilitarian ones long favored by New York vintners.

Jim Barrett and partners took control of Chateau Montelena in the early 1970s. It, like other Napa Valley wineries, had fallen either into disrepair or dire financial straits.
COURTESY OF CHATEAU MONTELENA

Meanwhile, the Finger Lakes' fine wine revival was led by Konstantin Frank, a Ukrainian immigrant trained in wine-making back home. Upon arriving in New York City in 1951, he was consigned to working as a dishwasher, largely because of the language barrier. Undaunted, Frank—whose doctoral thesis at Odessa Polytechnic Institute had been on growing higher-end grapes in cold climates—saved up enough money for a bus ticket to Ithaca, where he hoped to persuade researchers at Cornell University that his thesis could be put into practice in the United States, as it had been in the Soviet Union. He found himself working as a janitor at the university instead. He remained so animatedly adamant, however, about the possibilities of higher-end grapes succeeding in Upstate New York's colder climes that those around him at Cornell considered having him committed to a mental hospital. Finally, at a wine conference in 1953, he met Charles Fournier, a Frenchman working in sparkling wines in the Finger Lakes. The two fell to talking in French, one of the nine languages Frank knew, and Fournier hired the fervent viticulturist on the spot. Within ten years, Frank had his own eponymous winery a few miles from Hammondsport and his own fine wine vintage: a 1962 Riesling made from grapes grown in Upstate New York.

Frank was taking the work of a man named Philip Wagner that much further. Wagner, a journalist who succeeded the legendary wit H. L. Mencken as editorial page editor of the *Baltimore Sun* in 1938 and eventually wrote about wine for the newspaper, wanted to grow "wines that taste like wine." The Maryland climate was not hospitable to higher-end grapes, at least with the technology available in the 1930s and 1940s. So Wagner, who grew up drinking wine at his parents' table in Ann Arbor, Michigan, developed hybrid grapes, combinations of higher-end French grapes and more utilitarian American ones. He opened Boordy Vineyards northeast of the Baltimore area in 1945, specializing in wines crafted from these hybrids; Wagner also built a brisk side business providing vines to other would-be winemakers wanting to beat the Mid-Atlantic and Northeast's unforgiving winters and brutish summers.

Charles Fournier with Konstantin Frank, the Ukrainian immigrant who Fournier rescued from janitorial work at Cornell and who decisively proved that higher-end grapes could grow in colder climates.
COURTESY OF DR. KONSTANTIN FRANK

In Ohio the government took the lead, with academia as its partner. Researchers from Ohio State University started an experimental winery in 1963 in Wooster, about sixty miles from Cleveland, in the Buckeye State's northern half; this followed the planting of an equally experimental vineyard in the Ohio River Valley near the West Virginia border, one of the nation's leading growing areas for wine grapes in the nineteenth century. Following the public university's lead privately, Wistar and Ursula Marting in 1967 opened Tarula Farms in Clarksville, northeast of Cincinnati, the first new post-Prohibition winery in what was once called America's Rhineland. The following year, farther north, in Conneaut, near Lake Erie, one of Konstantin Frank's apprentices, Arnulf Esterer, started the Markko Vineyard, a nine-acre plot that quickly became noted for producing Chardonnay, Riesling, and Cabernet Sauvignon grapes.

Down in Virginia, where wine had been made for centuries before Prohibition but where wine grapes covered perhaps only fifteen acres by 1960, a seventy-five-year-old dairy farmer from Chicago named Elizabeth Furness turned over most of her Fauquier County property to grape-growing in the early 1970s. She had lived in France as a young girl, and her childhood memories helped spur her to start Piedmont Vineyards, the Old Dominion's first fine winery since Prohibition, which was quickly followed by others, including Archie Smith's Meredyth Vineyards and Al Weed's Mountain Cove Vineyards. Academics at Virginia Tech had told Furness that the Chardonnay and Sémillon vines she imported from California would never take; Francophile Thomas Jefferson himself failed at producing fine wine in Virginia two centuries before. Furness's vines did take, however, with the help of bug spray not available to the Sage of Monticello.

CHANGING HANDS

1959–1973 | Napa—Hartford, Connecticut—Minneapolis

Despite all these seedlings on both coasts and in the Ohio Valley in the late 1960s and early 1970s, the American fine wine movement continued to orbit a relatively small patch of Northern California: Napa Valley. Accidents of geography and climate, as well as the groundbreaking research at the University of California, Davis, a short drive up Interstate 80, and the influx decades before of European immigrants such as Cesare Mondavi and Andre Tchelistcheff, ensured that however Napa went, so would likely go the rest of America when it came to fine wine. And there were promising signs that, despite the financial struggles and relatively paltry sales of the newer wineries, things were going well.

For one thing, the local government swung crucially behind agriculture, including grape-growing, as Napa's future. In early 1968 both the Napa

County Planning Commission and the Napa County Board of Supervisors unanimously voted to create the Napa Valley Agricultural Preserve, the first such land classification of its kind in the nation. Although often overlooked as a turning point in the history of American fine wine, had the authorities ruled the other way, it is entirely within reason to think the whole American fine wine movement would have croaked in its infancy; the nation's top region for higher-end grapes would likely have become a vast suburban savanna rather than an enological gold mine, its landscape sprinkled with vineyards and wineries rather than dominated by them. The authorities plainly spelled out the new preserve's purpose for contemporaries and for posterity:

> This district classification is intended to be applied in the fertile valley and foothill areas of Napa County in which agriculture is and should continue to be the pre-dominant land use, where uses incompatible to agriculture should be precluded and where development of urban type uses would be detrimental to the continuance of agriculture and the maintenance of open spaces which are economic and aesthetic attributes and assets of the County of Napa.

The preserve covered roughly 4.5 percent of the county, twenty-three thousand acres, and was not without controversy. The idea of turning a huge swath between San Francisco and Sacramento over exclusively to farming rather than, say, shopping malls or condominiums struck many as absurd. So many opponents packed the first public hearing on the subject that it had to be held in a junior high auditorium.

California was growing by leaps and bounds economically and demographically, its many metro regions only recently better connected by the Interstate Highway System. The state's population truly boomed during the Great Depression as downtrodden Americans, like those depicted in John Steinbeck's *The Grapes of Wrath*, split westward in search of work, California as much an idea of opportunity, of new beginnings, as a reality. Between 1940 and 1960 California added more than nine million residents; in 1963, it displaced New York as America's most populous state. With the new arrivals came a stereotype of an entire California lifestyle: breezier and more carefree than stuffier state counterparts to the east, a place of big backyards reachable by steaming, gleaming oceans of asphalt highways, where industries of the future, such as computers and aviation, were taking off. Wine-making, especially fine wine–making, seemed decidedly retro and economically irrelevant.

Yet here came people like Warren Winiarski, one of the newer arrivals himself, saying that tens of thousands of acres of prime land between Northern California's largest metro area and the state capital should be eternally set aside for growing food. It seemed so foolish in light of agricultural trends, which showed a dwindling amount of Napa land actually being used for commercial farming: there were fewer than sixty-five wineries, for instance, in 1968. "Prunes and walnuts were going to hell," the chairman of the county board of supervisors put it. "And people were saying grapes would do the same."

The naysayers were wrong, of course, and that was the second thing that fine wine in Napa—and, by extension, America—had going for it: always at least a notable presence in Napa, wine grapes—in particular, higher-end varieties such as Cabernet Sauvignon, Merlot, and Chardonnay—began creeping over ever more acreage. By the early 1970s, the inky purple writing was on the wall. In 1959 wine grapes covered 9,623 acres of the county; by 1969, 12,151 acres; by 1973, after the first wave of new wineries opened following Robert Mondavi's lead, wine grapes covered 13,142 acres. The Napa County Agricultural Department's annual report for 1973 described the gains in grapes thusly:

> Wine grapes continue to be the leading agricultural crop with a gross value of $33,916,000, a $14,449 increase over 1972. This all-time record was due to a number of factors, favorable weather, 600 additional acreages coming into production and increased price per ton. An additional 2,400 new acreages were planted to wine grapes in 1973.

The report also declared agriculture the number one industry in Napa County, further vindicating the preserve that winemakers in part pushed a few years earlier.

Robert Mondavi, however, saw a different trend in Napa. In 1964 John Daniel, smarting from the same financial pressures that dogged other wineries specializing in fine wines—including limited distribution and consumer indifference—sold Inglenook Vineyard, the respected concern started by his granduncle in the 1870s, to conglomerate United Vintners for $1.2 million. A few years later, United's parent, the Allied Grape Growers cooperative, turned around and sold the winery to food-and-drink giant Heublein in a $100 million deal that included other Allied properties such as generic wine kingpin Italian Swiss Colony, Gallo's main competitor. The moves—first Daniel's, then Allied's—shocked Mondavi and the growers of Napa Valley.

The same fate befell Heublein's other big 1969 purchase: Beaulieu. The winery founded by Bordeaux immigrants Georges and Fernande de Latour was then controlled by their daughter and granddaughter, the latter having married an American businessman who assessed the struggling winery's prospects and didn't like what he saw. The vaunted expertise of Andre Tchelistcheff was not enough to make Beaulieu consistently profitable; instead, it made it marquee enough to be a feather in a large firm's cap. Heublein's holdings ranged from breweries to liquor brands such as Smirnoff vodka to fast-food joints (the firm would buy Kentucky Fried Chicken in 1971). From its headquarters in Hartford, Connecticut, the company's executives—led by a CEO from the advertising industry—saw fine Napa Valley wineries less as potential cash cows and more as window dressing for Heublein's other ventures.

After much negotiation, including the offer, and rejection, of a stock swap, the Latours' heirs accepted a cash offer of approximately $8.5 million. Beaulieu and Inglenook were then under the same corporate umbrella. Despite pledges to keep production small and quality inviolate, Heublein almost immediately set about ramping up production at both wineries, from a few thousand cases annually per winery to a few million.

Mondavi viewed the Heublein takeovers—as well as Switzerland-based Nestlé's 1971 acquisition of Beringer Vineyards, a St. Helena winery dating from the 1870s—as terrible losses for a fine wine industry just then coming into its own. The emphasis of the new corporate masters, as he saw it, was on production instead of quality. While some of Mondavi's concerns were justified—Heublein did crank up production of an Inglenook jug wine line that became one of the biggest in the United States—in other ways he was hyperbolic. For one thing, Tchelistcheff remained Beaulieu's winemaker; for another, Mondavi's own winery romped merrily along with brewery Rainier as a stakeholder pushing for greater production.

Finally, other American wine-making pockets such as Sonoma County and New York's Finger Lakes did not share Napa's shock at the corporate takeovers. The American fine wine movement remained a small universe, with a relative handful of people caring what John Daniel did with Inglenook or whether Andre Tchelistcheff stuck around Beaulieu, never mind that business with Robert Mondavi in St. Helena. The biggest Napa Valley fine wine producers, including Charles Krug and Christian Brothers, relied on cheaper, blander brands for most of their revenue; even then, their sales, perhaps as much as ten million cases each annually by the late 1960s, paled in comparison to generic behemoths such as Gallo, which might sell three times as much. For all the growth of the last few years, the American fine wine movement in the early 1970s did not seem like an actual growth industry.

Nothing illustrated this better than the last great Napa takeover of those years. In 1970, Lee Stewart, ornery as ever, sold Chateau Souverain to a group of investors, who, in turn, sold it to Pillsbury, the Minneapolis-based company best known for its giggling doughboy mascot and its recently acquired Burger King fast-food chain. Pillsbury opened another Souverain winery in Sonoma County and set about trying to capitalize on fine wine, only to find itself within a few years losing $6 million annually and desperate to sell.

STILL ONLY FOR COOKING

1964–1974 | Paris—Gainesville, Florida—New York City

In 1964 Maynard Amerine, the pioneering wine researcher at the University of California, Davis, visited Beaulieu Vineyards in Rutherford to talk to its winemaker, Andre Tchelistcheff. Amerine was scheduled to travel to Bordeaux, the world's premier wine-making region, to speak at a symposium. He was nervous.

"What can I tell the French about wine-making?" Amerine asked Tchelistcheff.

"Don't be so humble," Tchelistcheff replied. "We are doing many things in California that they don't know about. Tell them about controlled malolactic fermentation and tell them about micro-filtering wine to stabilize it biologically. Those are two things we are doing here that even the French do not fully appreciate."

In 1967 Joseph Alioto, a lawyer and Mondavi family confidant who would become San Francisco's mayor the following year, took his son and new daughter-in-law to the famed Parisian restaurant Maxim's near the Place de la Concorde. He ordered a bottle of Charles Krug Cabernet Sauvignon.

The French waiter looked at him quizzically. It was a fine California wine, Alioto explained.

The waiter drew himself up haughtily. "Monsieur, we only use California wines for cooking."

Opinions of American wine, as well as of Americans' appreciation for the drink, seemed frozen in aspic for all time on one side of the Atlantic as the calendar flipped over from the 1960s; on the other side, there were baby steps of change everywhere among consumers and critics.

In 1969 Craig Goldwyn, a journalism student at the University of Florida, bought a bottle of white wine made by Château Carbonnieux, one of the oldest wineries in Bordeaux, at the ABC liquor store on West Newbury Road in Gainesville. He paid $3.99, a sizable sum for a bottle of wine then, and took it to a party hosted by a fraternity brother and his wife.

All anyone could talk about was the complexity and the wonderfulness of the wine.

In 1971, the British wine merchant and critic Harry Waugh declared Napa Valley "the most fascinating, the most exhilarating grape-growing district in the world."

Waugh had been visiting Northern California since 1965, having discovered its wines during a tasting in New York City the year before; he would ship back to England cases of Souverain Cabernet Sauvignon and Heitz Chardonnay. Waugh's praise of America made him a lone voice in the European wine press, and he knew it: "I am sticking my neck out rather dangerously," he wrote around that time. Why? He had dared go as far as suggesting parity between California and France in some types of wine.

In 1973 Robert Lawrence Balzer, the irrepressible wine writer for the *Los Angeles Times*, organized a blind taste test in New York City of twenty-three Chardonnays from California, New York State, and France before 250 members of the New York Food and Wine Society. The Californians swept the first four spots, chosen by a fourteen-judge panel that included Alexis Lichine, the Bordeaux vintner who had famously declared in 1951 that "the greatest wines on earth come from France." A French Chardonnay did not make an appearance until fifth place.

Shortly after, California wines, in particular a Robert Mondavi Chardonnay and a Robert Mondavi Pinot Noir, swept a similar tasting hosted by *Home* magazine. "Solid French titles, with centuries of tradition and fame," Balzer explained to millions of *Los Angeles Times* readers, "trailed among the also-ran contenders in the judgment of fifteen internationally recognized experts."

Although it would be years before people were able to take full stock of the shift under way, the American fine wine movement was definitely turning a corner in the early 1970s from a statistical standpoint. While overall consumption totals still favored sweeter generics such as Gallo's Pink Chablis, sales of drier fine wines had surpassed the generics years before (in 1967 roughly 87,600,500 gallons of fine wine sold versus around 79,000,000 gallons of generics). In 1972 the difference would be nearly 100 million as the sale of fine wines almost doubled. Moreover, the 1967 sales figure represented more than a twenty-million-gallon leap from just five years before. Old habits dying hard explain the generics' consumption lead (though that was waning, too).

Why the shift, and why starting in the mid-1960s? No one was quite sure, though pet theories abounded. One held that simple labeling changes advocated since the 1930s by Frank Schoonmaker, coupled with the publicity and marketing pushes of Robert Mondavi and a handful of others—including the San Francisco–based Wine Institute—had swayed consumers. Another proffered that the sorts of technological changes—such as malolactic and cold fermentation as well as aging in French barrels and a renewed emphasis on cleanliness, championed by Andre Tchelistcheff, Mike Grgich, and the Mondavis—had ensured that those consumers drawn by the marketing stayed for the product, finding it of uniformly better quality than ever before. A corollary to this theory, of course, held that Maynard Amerine and Albert Winkler's research at UC Davis was integral to steering winemakers to the right higher-end grapes in the first place.

Still others drew a straight line from the likes of Julia Child, Ruth Ellen Church, and Robert Lawrence Balzer to the renewed national interest in fine wine, which fostered, if not created, the marketplace the wineries and their advocates could tap into. Some said the 1960s counterculture had opted for wine in rebellion against their parents' preference for hard liquor. There was yet another theory, this one grimmer: the sorts of southern European immigrants who had always made their own wine at home, right through Prohibition, were dying without leaving their expertise to their children and grandchildren, who, in turn, looked to the marketplace for the sorts of drier wines they were used to.

Curiously, this sales shift came as the number of American wineries shrank. In 1945, two years after the Mondavis acquired Charles Krug, Napa Valley's oldest winery, there were 903 wineries in the United States, 414 of them in California. In 1965, the year Robert Mondavi struck out on his own, there were 424 wineries nationwide, 232 in California (and approximately 30 percent of those in Napa County). Those numbers remained roughly the same into the new decade, and it would be many years before they again reached the levels seen in the couple of decades after Repeal.

Most of the new wineries were smaller ones specializing in wines made from higher-end, European-style grapes. They faced tough financial situations from day one that were often exacerbated by stifling distribution networks and an indifferent marketplace, success in a previous professional life no guarantee of success in the new one. If there was a single-most-prominent financial trend in American fine wine by the early 1970s, it wasn't success—it was consolidation within a larger, sometimes global company; in this, fine wine was following a trend seen in myriad American industries after World War II, from accounting to media to soda pop. While the technology was in place, while the critical backing was there, while the numbers were trending in the right direction, the American fine wine movement, nearly a decade after Robert Mondavi swaggered onto the scene, was a precarious one. It looked like the perception would have to shift before the economics could. Joseph Alioto's Parisian waiter spoke for most: "We only use California wines for cooking."

Robert Lawrence Balzer spoke for far fewer people, nearly all of them fellow Americans. He ended that December 1974 column extolling Mondavi's wins in the *Home* magazine blind tasting with an observation that could also be read as a prediction:

> Meanwhile, American wine consumers, who've already found their way to the more reasonable delights of California wines, over the extravagance of inflated French titles, are continuing to enjoy our native heritage. Consumption figures of California table wines continue to climb. Our "service ceiling" is the wild blue yonder where, with a firm grasp on the controls and open minds, the Mondavis and other leading winemakers are accepting the challenge.

The French, the undisputed world champions of wine, would soon accept the challenge, too.

PART II

AN ENGLISHMAN ABROAD
1970–1971 | London—Paris

O ne late autumn day in 1970, Steven Spurrier, an Englishman from a well-to-do family, was walking with a lawyer friend of his along one of those impossibly quaint passages in Paris, near the Place de la Madeleine in the posh Eighth Arrondissement. They passed an aged wine shop, and Spurrier remarked that it was exactly the kind of place he would like to own.

It turned out the shop was for sale. The elderly Frenchwoman selling it, however, was not interested in Spurrier's offer. How could an Englishman possibly run the wine business her late husband had built up? What did he know? Spurrier made the woman a deal: he would work for her gratis for six months, a sort of apprenticeship to prove his worthiness to take over. She agreed. Spurrier could be very charming, especially when wine was involved.

He had come to wine through his parents, though it was his grandfather who first piqued his interest by giving him a glass of port one Christmas in the 1950s.

"What's this, Grandpa?"

"Cockburn's '08, my boy," came the reply, noting both the maker and the year made.

Spurrier realized then that wine was something tied intimately to time and place—and to people. It was similar to stamps, which he collected at the time, and it jelled nicely with the geography and history he was studying at school. He began to collect information on wine regions years before he could legally drink wine in Great Britain; his parents let him and his older brother sample wines, however, during teenage trips to Spain, Italy, and France. It was his mother, a onetime employee of legendary restaurateur and wine merchant Tommy Layton, who suggested he apply for a job at Christopher and Co., then the oldest wine merchant in London. In February 1964 Spurrier joined the company as a trainee, the lowest rung on the British wine-trading ladder.

It was enough, however, for the twenty-two-year-old fresh out of the London School of Economics and Political Science. He inhaled the wine writings of Layton, Harry Waugh, Michael Broadbent, and especially Alexis Lichine; he read *Wine* magazine, an English publication, and kept up with French wine publications as well.

In 1965, shortly after the New Year and armed with introductory letters to Christopher's principal suppliers, Spurrier embarked on a nine-month educational tour of France, Germany, Spain, and Portugal, working in the cellars and vineyards of some of the world's most prominent wineries. (He skipped Italy, as the only Italian wines then well-known in the United Kingdom were Chianti in straw-caked flasks and Marsala, the sweet Sicilian wine, for cooking.) Along the way, Spurrier met and, in some cases, befriended prominent winemakers and château owners. He took a six-week break from the tour in July and August but returned in time for that year's crush. Spurrier returned to London newly emboldened in his career path—only to find no full-time employment offer from Christopher.

Undeterred, Spurrier took a job with a smaller merchant and continued his enological education, fixated—as the entire wine world had been for decades—on France. In early 1968 he made the leap across the Channel, settling with his new wife, Bella, on land in Provence, in the south of France, where the couple set about fixing up a dilapidated farmhouse. By 1970, however, Spurrier wanted back into the wine trade, and that meant a return to Paris. He knew the situation he would find there: the capital of wine had little in the form of a wine trade. Paris, in fact, ran behind London in the formality of its wine-selling industry, with merchants there exhibiting nowhere near the level of sophistication and attention to detail as the merchants at places like Christopher and Co. Instead, the Parisian wine trade consisted of wholesalers, chain stores, and the odd shop, or cave, where *cavistes* sold what the French called "*vin ordinaire*," which was exactly what it sounded like: cheap, ordinary, everyday wine usually sold in bulk, not unlike post-Prohibition brands in California.

It was a shop like this that Spurrier passed that autumn day in 1970. The old woman who ran it relied upon customers who bought their undistinguished wine in bulk, often lugging bottles and jugs from home to fill; otherwise, the shop's stock consisted of liquors, liqueurs, and the odd Champagne. In a land where wine wasn't exotic, ordinary fare sufficed. The woman's new apprentice had different ideas.

Spurrier did his six-month apprenticeship, and on April 1, 1971, for three hundred thousand francs, he became controlling owner of Les Caves de la Madeleine. He set about rejiggering the shop from vin ordinaire to vin extraordinaire, so to speak, molding its selection more in his own bolder image. Spurrier wore his brown hair long in a Beatles cut, curated a flouncy mustache, wore pin-striped suits with creamy linen shirts, and lived on a 130-foot barge in the Seine with Bella. He was not your grandfather's caviste. The move away from bulk sales to pricier trades of bottles with distinct geographies and chronologies was a risky one; not only would it alienate the shop's traditional clientele, but the French in the early 1970s were actually starting to drink less wine, a trend that would not become evident for decades but that had the potential to hit the bottom line of an ambitious young merchant.

Spurrier had a couple of aces up his sleeve. One was his knowledge of fine wine, of what was out there beyond the ordinary. The other was that he was English, in two senses of the word: Spurrier came from a London wine trade that valued salesmanship, and he also spoke the native tongue of potential expat consumers. The day after he bought control of Les Caves de la Madeleine, he took out an advertisement in the *International Herald Tribune*, the European newspaper then run by the *New York Times* and the *Washington Post*. Its headine? YOUR WINE MERCHANT SPEAKS ENGLISH.

CHEZ AMERICAN
1971–1972 | Calistoga, California—Berkeley, California—San Diego

To Mike Grgich, it was an offer he couldn't refuse. Jim Barrett, the principal owner of Chateau Montelena in Calistoga, not only offered Grgich the position of winemaker but also dangled the possibility of eventually owning up to 10 percent of the winery. The Croatian immigrant who had fourteen years before rolled into Napa Valley on a Greyhound with two suitcases and not much else to his young, unknown name suddenly had the American Dream–like chance to co-own a winery in the nation's most prominent grape-growing region.

And why not? Grgich's work at Souverain under Lee Stewart, Beaulieu under Andre Tchelistcheff, and, since 1968, at Robert Mondavi under that buzzy winery's namesake had made him one of the most sought-after winemakers in Northern California. Grgich talked the offer over with Mondavi, who frankly told him that his future at that winery was limited: Mondavi planned to pass it on to his children. After two weeks trying out the reins at Chateau Montelena, Grgich left Mondavi for good and, on May 8, 1972, started full-time at Barrett's operation.

That operation wasn't much, even six months after Barrett and Ernest Hahn had saved the ghost of the original nineteenth-century winery from oblivion. A pile of rocks, albeit beautiful ones, passed for the winery; its equipment was outmoded; and the vines that remained still bore largely lower-end, utilitarian grapes. Grgich recognized the challenge before him right away—and the cost.

"What's going on here?" Barrett asked him when Grgich presented his plans for remaking Chateau Montelena. It included a budget that presupposed no income for five years.

"That's the minimum of how long it's going to take to get any income from Cabernet," Grgich replied. "We first have to rip out the old vines and plant Cabernet grapes. Then for the first couple of years, you won't get much of a crop, and after that the wine will have to age in oak barrels for about two years."

"Mike," Barrett said, "we're going to be broke before that happens. We haven't got that kind of money. We've got to figure out some other way of doing it."

Grgich had an idea that would prove revolutionary not only for Chateau Montelena but for American fine wine: "We could make white wines first." They would buy the grapes from other growers, like Robert Mondavi often did, and make the wine at Chateau Montelena, thereby eliminating the growing time needed for the winery's vineyards. "We could crush Riesling grapes in October and sell it in March. Chardonnay takes a little longer. It has to age in barrels for about eight months, but you'll be selling it about two years after we crush the grapes."

"OK," Barrett said, "let's try it." His one caveat: they had to buy the best available grapes.

Barrett, a wine-making novice and a newcomer to Napa Valley to boot, wanted Chateau Montelena's wines to stand among California's—and therefore America's—best. He was an experienced pilot, and he flew to the vineyard from the Torrance Airport near Los Angeles in his twin-engine Aztec as often as possible, landing at the small airport at Santa Rosa about sixty miles north of San Francisco. From there it was a half-hour drive to Calistoga, where Barrett threw himself wholesale into his winery, sleeping in a room on the grounds equipped with a twin bed and a hot plate. At first Barrett, a trim ex–Navy officer with salt-and-pepper hair and prominently bushy eyebrows, spent a lot of his time visiting potential grape growers as well as figuring out which equipment to buy. After he and Grgich got the mechanics of Chateau Montelena up and running, Barrett turned his attention to marketing.

It was here that his efforts dovetailed nicely with a wider trend in American cuisine. Around the time he, Hahn, and their partners acquired Chateau Montelena, a restaurant opened in Berkeley, California, specializing not only in French food but in using ingredients from local sources. It was a novel concept in an America of TV dinners and fast-food joints. The restaurant would spawn myriad imitators, which, along with media forces such as Julia Child and Robert Lawrence Balzer, as well as the winemakers themselves, would form one of the three legs of a stool supporting the entire fine wine movement.

Alice Waters got the idea for her restaurant while she was overseas. A native of East Orange, New Jersey, she studied abroad in France while attending the University of California at Berkeley. There she absorbed the country's food—genuine crepes, Belon oysters, the hard ciders of Normandy, the wines of Bordeaux—and the culture surrounding it. The French anchored that culture not only in preparing meals but in enjoying them, too; it was the antithesis of the faster, utilitarian approach to eating and drinking then taking firm hold in the United States. The French whom Waters encountered also used local ingredients whenever they could and prepared simple yet robust meals that were often distinct region to region, even town to town; food in the United States, on the other hand, was becoming increasingly homogenized. More than one-third of the domestically produced wine sold in the country, for instance, came from E. & J. Gallo.

Waters took those lessons in leisurely cooking and dining, as well as in using locally sourced ingredients, back to California, and in 1971 she opened Chez Panisse in an old house on Berkeley's Shattuck Avenue. The restaurant was a game changer. It quickly gained a reputation for slowly prepared, simple French meals culled as much as possible from local ingredients—and often accompanied by a wine from Chez Panisse's growing list of French imports. Celebrities such as Francis Ford Coppola, Danny Kaye, and Mikhail Baryshnikov became regulars; and the media ladled praise upon the place and its owner. The *New York Times* declared Waters "a chef of international repute" whose "cunningly designed, somewhat raffish establishment" was unique in the western United States. Even the French recognized what Waters was going for. The noted Parisian restaurant critic Christian Millau praised Waters's use of "good and beautiful products of her native land."

Jim Barrett in Chateau Montelena's vineyards.
COURTESY OF CHATEAU MONTELENA

Jim Barrett wanted to get some of his own good and beautiful products into more eateries, including Chez Panisse. He had come to wine through retail, not restaurants, his ability to sample different bottles off the shelf tied directly to the fortunes of his law firm, which, thankfully for his palate and the future of American fine wine, had grown. Barrett, however, believed that a Chateau Montelena on the menu was good for business: diners might buy that particular bottle as well as tell others about it. Besides, he also believed food and wine went well together. To that end, Barrett hired a sales rep to work San Francisco–area restaurants, and he launched a Chateau Montelena news-letter. "The wines of Chateau Montelena will be instantly recognizable by the distinctive style of the wines when you taste them," declared one early edition.

Would they, though? Grgich crushed 12,147 gallons worth of Cabernet from Sonoma and Napa grapes, but a long stretch of rain had spawned mold on the all-important skins. A taste of the aging wine told him and Barrett that the wine they produced would never do as Chateau Montelena's first commercial red wine offering. The white wines, on the other hand, came along quite nicely. The winery's first offering triumphed in a tasting of ten California Rieslings that Robert Lawrence Balzer organized for the *Los Angeles Times*. Chateau Montelena's crisp, clear, citrus-laden Chardonnay from the same vintage, 1972, was a critical hit as well, though on a more modest scale than the contest the state's largest newspaper sanctioned: A tasting club in San Diego in 1974 held a blind tasting of two Chardonnays, one the Chateau Montelena retailing for $6.50 a bottle and the other a 1972 Bâtard-Montrachet, from a leading winery in Burgundy, France, that sold for around $17.50 a pop. Chateau Montelena beat the French wine.

BACK TO SCHOOL

1972 | Paris

Evening visitors from American companies in the Eighth Arrondissement— including banks and law firms, as well as the French headquarters of IBM— started showing up fairly quickly to Steven Spurrier's Caves de la Madeleine. They sampled the increasing number of bottled wines Spurrier had brought in since taking over the shop in April 1971, and listened gratefully as someone, in their own language, explained the intricacies of French fine wine.

The leap from these informal classes to more formalized, and paying, ones was not that chasmic, especially after Spurrier connected with Jon Winroth, a native Chicagoan who came to Paris on a Fulbright scholarship in 1956 and never left. Winroth wrote about wine for the *International Herald Tribune*, the same widely read English-language organ in which Spurrier had advertised. Spurrier had cultivated a relationship with Winroth, going so far as to show up cold at the newspaper's offices to introduce himself to the young wine writer. The pair later spent hours after that first encounter drinking and talking wine. Spurrier knew that the imprimatur of a noted wine writer, even one who wasn't French, could be good for business. Winroth, for his part, was already teaching small groups of American college students about wine in the musty backs of cafés. In late 1972 an opportunity to partner presented itself in the form of real estate: the locksmith next door to Les Caves de la Madeleine went out of business, and Spurrier acquired that space to host what became, improbably, the first private wine school in the world's leading wine country. Spurrier and Winroth called it L'Académie du Vin. After six months of renovations, including the installation of a horseshoe-shaped bar, it hosted its first class in the spring of 1973.

Spurrier and Winroth had to cobble together their first class; pretty soon, however, they were turning away not only Brits, Americans, and Canadians but also the French themselves. As many as a dozen students at a time packed into the old locksmith shop for a curriculum based on Michael Broadbent's 1967 book *Wine Tasting*, itself a groundbreaking idea, being the first book written in English on the topic. Students at L'Académie du Vin learned about terroir; about what to expect from different varietals; how to appreciate the various aspects of wine, from its color to its smell to its taste; the different wine regions of France—all in six weekly lessons costing five hundred francs, or about one hundred dollars, total.

Spurrier and Winroth soon hired some American help for their growing school. Patricia Gallagher was in her early twenties and stringing for the *Wilmington Morning News*, the daily newspaper for the largest city in her home state of Delaware. As did many English-language journalists in Paris then looking for ready feature fodder, she interviewed Spurrier about his novel little shop. Later, when she was looking for a way to stay in the French capital, she approached Spurrier about teaching at L'Académie du Vin. She didn't know much about wine; Spurrier, however, filled her in fast, and soon Gallagher was an integral part of an expanding curriculum. Decades later, one student would be able to recall a lesson Gallagher taught on tannins: Gallagher talked about the furry sensation the astringent red wine substances can leave in the mouth—until every student agreed that, yes, he or she was, indeed, tasting the tannins.

Within a couple years, the ambitions of L'Académie du Vin had expanded dramatically. The six-lesson introductory curriculum continued, and Spurrier and company added advanced courses on the reds of Bordeaux and the whites of Burgundy as well as an in-depth look at wine analysis based on methods devised at the University of Bordeaux, some taught by guest instructors with impressive CVs to their names. Winroth drifted away from L'Académie du Vin to focus again on writing about wine, but Spurrier and Gallagher continued to hammer away at the school's scope as well as their own enological educations, often traveling around France to visit this château or that.

Spurrier's star rose with both the wine shop and the school. He found himself the main retail point person in Paris not only for certain French wineries but for ones overseas, too, including from his native England. Responding to the added attention and ever aware that his image might translate into further success for Les Caves de la Madeleine and L'Académie du Vin, Spurrier shaved his mustache, trimmed his hair, and started donning tony Savile Row suits; he also moved himself, Bella, and their children from the Seine barge to an apartment near the site of the Bastille, the prison famously liberated at the start of the French Revolution.

For all the attention to sartorial detail, the traveling, and the marketing, Spurrier's trade by the mid-1970s continued to spring primarily from English-speaking customers—and from French fine wine. Eventually, though, some California vintners started bringing in samples of their Chardonnays and Cabernet Sauvignons. Spurrier was no fan. He didn't like the American wine he had tasted to that point, fine or otherwise. American wines were virtually unavailable commercially in France, too, and, besides, everyone who worked in the business knew French wine was the best in the world, with Italian perhaps a distant second and American beyond forgettable. Still, these customers were passionate. They told Spurrier of the changes afoot over the past decade, especially in California, of the new, smaller wineries and their emphasis on wines from higher-end grapes, and Spurrier had to admit the bottles they brought him weren't terrible. In fact, the bottles of American wine gave him an idea.

THE YEAR OF THE WINE WRITER
1972 | San Francisco—New York—Paris

For Robert Finigan, it all started at Harvard. One of his classmates came from a vineyard-owning family in France, and the young, handsome Virginian with bushy eyebrows and an impish grin soon developed a taste not only for wine but for good food as well. He took that enthusiasm for food and drink with him when he traveled westward and settled into a management consultancy in San Francisco in the 1960s. It was there, amid the burgeoning American fine wine movement gestating just northeast of the City by the Bay, that Finigan made his name as an unlikely wine critic.

Finigan traveled often to the wine regions of France, as well as just up Highway 101 to Sonoma and Napa Counties, a fact known to the purveyors at Esquin's, his local wine store in San Francisco. They asked him to taste the 1969 vintages in Bordeaux on his next trip over; Finigan obliged in 1970, returning to tell Esquin's not to buy the bottles. He had tasted the châteaus' wares from the barrel and had found them wanting. Esquin's took his advice and ended up avoiding one of the most forgettable vintages in the history of the storied wine region.

Two years later, Finigan came out with *Robert Finigan's Private Guide to Wines*, a self-published newsletter for the Bay Area. Unlike the writings of Robert Lawrence Balzer or Frank Schoonmaker—or, for that matter, French critics such as Alexis Lichine or British ones such as Harry Waugh—Finigan's production did not come from the hand of someone connected with the wine industry's inner workings; instead he was an independent appreciator, not likely to organize a blind tasting on behalf of wineries and not involved in selling or marketing bottles. His guide, too, was more direct than anything that had come before, penned in a brusque manner that was in its way refreshingly American. Finigan bracketed each wine he tasted into one of four groups—Outstanding, Above Average, Average, or Below Average—and moved on. No signs of British diffidence in Finigan's declaring some later Bordeauxs "barely drinkable swill." No French finesse in declaring certain Burgundies "trash." Budding aficionados weaned on the cheery floridity of Balzer or the servicey simplicity of the *Chicago Tribune*'s Ruth Ellen Church would have certainly been surprised at the frankness in Finigan's takedown of a beloved Bordeaux brand:

> As usual, Mouton-Cadet isn't even vaguely worth its seemingly attractive price (note that it doesn't even qualify as "Bordeaux Superieur"); the house wines of most French country bistros are not nearly so harsh and flavor-shy.

By the time he started proselytizing to Steven Spurrier about California fine wines in the early 1970s, Robert Finigan was the most powerful wine critic in the most important wine region in the United States: Northern California. His *Private Guide to Wines*, still a self-published affair, found its way into major shops like Esquin's, its subscriber count swelling toward ten thousand, enough to help pay his way to France for tastings, which is what led Finigan to Spurrier's Caves de la Madeleine, the leading Parisian shop for English-speaking oenophiles.

Finigan was not the only American wine writer to drop by. Les Caves de la Madeleine and the adjoining Académie du Vin served as a fertile hub of fine wine discourse, arguably the single most influential spot on earth in the early 1970s when it came to American fine wine.

Alexis Bespaloff was born in the Romanian capital of Bucharest in 1934, though his family soon moved in quick succession to Belgium, Brazil, and then the United States. He attended the tony Horace Mann School in New York City before going on to Amherst College—where he organized wine tastings for friends—and, for a brief period, to Harvard Business School. After a stint as a publicist at Simon & Schuster, he moved into the wine business, working in Bordeaux for a wine importer and, later, for the noted merchant Sherry-Lehmann in New York.

Soon, though, Bespaloff followed Frank Schoonmaker's path in reverse and moved from selling wine to writing about it. His 1971 work, *The Signet Book of Wine*, belied Bespaloff's own views on the subject. Where the book was a nontechnical guide that would prove very popular commercially—the original and subsequent editions sold more than one million copies—Bespaloff, an urbane ballet lover who studied English literature in college, saw wine, in the words of one admirer, "not so much as a commercial product but as an integral part of Western culture." A trenchant wit—his answering machine once went, "I cannot take your call right now, but if it's an emergency, white with fish and red with meat"—Bespaloff nevertheless kept his wine writing simple for his readers.

And he had quite a few new readers beginning in 1972. That year, Bespaloff started writing the first regular wine column in a major publication in New York City since G. Selmer Fougner's "Along the Wine Trail" column in the now-defunct *New York Sun* ended with the restaurant critic's death in 1941. Bespaloff's groundbreaker came not through the nation's newspaper of record, the *New York Times*, nor through that arbiter of the highbrow, the *New Yorker*, but through the four-year-old *New York* magazine, a weekly still in its New Journalism heyday. There, amid articles on the Vietnam War, the Rolling Stones, and the women's movement by the likes of Tom Wolfe and David Halberstam, Bespaloff delivered to perhaps the nation's most influential consumer audience his verdicts on French and, increasingly, American fine wines. Again, despite his literary leanings, Bespaloff eschewed jargon and flowery language, delivering direct descriptors like "well-made," "balanced and mature," and "more forceful than charming."

Frank J. Prial favored the same sort of straightforward writing in his initial furtive steps as the *New York Times'* first-ever regular wine writer, also beginning in 1972. Born in 1930 in Newark, New Jersey, Prial graduated from Georgetown University in 1951 and served in the coast guard during the Korean War. He then went into the shoe-leather scramble of beat reporting, working for newspapers in Newark and New York before joining the *Wall Street Journal* as a feature writer. In 1970, Prial moved to the *Times*, where he roamed a wide habitat, from covering the United Nations to profiling the

English tour guide of the grand cathedral in Chartres, France, to detailing crime on the streets of a spiraling Gotham. The wine column in 1972 started as a tentative, part-time thing, based more on his editor's enthusiasm for the food writing Prial would sometimes file during his trips to France with his wife.

Reflecting the dearth, even by the early 1970s, of American interest in fine wine, even among the sorts of more cosmopolitan Americans who inhabited the *Times'* readership, Prial himself worried that he wouldn't have enough to write about when he did start writing about the subject regularly. Was there enough going on to sustain a weekly column? he wondered. Would there be any reader interest? As it was, by 1973, he had enough material to go on, and the *Times'* "Wine Talk" was on its way to becoming one of the most influential corners of the entire enological universe. Prial, like Bespaloff and Robert Finigan, pivoted away from the Robert Lawrence Balzer school of wine writing, preferring unadorned, direct critiques rather than flowery language and references to antiquity. In a July 21, 1973, column on why there weren't more wine tastings aimed at the average drinker, Prial wrote:

> It was an instructive and well-planned event. One gripe, however. There was some good Brie cheese on the table, but it really doesn't go with the white wines. Fruit is better and some people say the best accompaniment for these wines is a plate of walnuts.

Prial, we can imagine, was just as directly matter-of-fact with Steven Spurrier on his visits to Les Caves de la Madeleine. Bespaloff, for his part, buttonholed the wine merchant at a dinner party to sing the praises of California fine wine by the early 1970s. Spurrier dismissed them, however, as "rather cooked," meaning they were higher in alcohol than he thought they should be and tasted burnt. Still, Prial, Bespaloff, and other writers—including Gerald Asher, a British expat in the United States who traveled regularly to France—kept talking.

Asher, born in the early 1930s like Prial and Bespaloff, got into wine through a part-time job selling it while in college in London. By the mid-1950s, after studying wine in Spain, West Germany, and France, he started a mail-order business for the stuff, gaining notoriety as an importer of some of the rarer French vintages to find their ways into Britain. By the 1970s he was working as a vice president at the New York City importer Austin Nichols, and in 1974 he relocated to San Francisco for a similar role at another firm. It was in New York, however, that the editor of *Gourmet* magazine asked him out of the blue to write a regular wine column. Like Prial, Asher fretted over what to write about—and whether he'd have enough to write about. Working off his experience in the wine trade, he came up with plenty of material. Asher's *Gourmet* column first appeared in 1972 and continued to appear for decades.

IMPACT

1972–1973 | San Diego—Los Angeles—San Francisco—New York

O ther wine writers plied their trade around the same time as Robert Finigan, Frank Prial, Alexis Bespaloff, and Gerald Asher. If 1972 was the year of the wine writer, the early 1970s in general was the era of such a scribe, the American fine wine movement of the previous decade seeding the grounds for such content, and content creators, to grow. The world was perhaps still ignoring American fine wine, but Americans were paying more attention than at any time since Repeal in the 1930s.

American consumers were also paying greater attention to what they were eating and drinking overall, perhaps more so than at any time in the nation's nearly two-hundred-year history. In November 1965 a thirty-two-year-old lawyer named Ralph Nader published *Unsafe at Any Speed: The Designed-In Dangers of the American Automobile,* a book detailing the resistance of major automakers to implementing safety features such as seat belts into cars. The bestseller not only transformed its author and his legion of idealistic Nader's Raiders lawyers into oft-quoted media darlings but also helped spawn a nationwide pivot in consumer expectations for everything from cars to food to detergent.

The idea of an educated consumer, active in his or her buying decisions, emerged, as did new regulations about truth in advertising (the very phrase "educated consumer" seems to have emerged at this time). The establishment of Earth Day and new federal bodies such as the Environmental Protection Agency in 1970, as well as the creation of the Consumer Product Safety Commission two years later, further hammered into the nation's psyche the notion of the educated, or informed, consumer. So, too, did the Watergate scandal in 1973 and 1974—if you couldn't trust the president to properly police things, who could you trust? American consumers felt more emboldened than ever to opt out of a product they found wanting and go their own way when it came to what they spent their money on. As Nader pointed out in an October 1975 interview, consumers' skepticism of a national food supply that factory farming increasingly dominated was "tied to the fact that twelve million home gardens have been started in this country in the past two years."

It would be a mistake to overstate the effects of this informational pivot in regard to American fine wine. People were not en masse reverting to home wine-making as in the days of Prohibition, nor were they besieging their local merchants for bottles of Chardonnays and Cabernet Sauvignons tenderly crafted by the likes of Mike Grgich and Andre Tchelistcheff. There was, though, a palpable shift reflected in wine sales and consumption figures, and ordinary consumers—who might have come to fine wine only recently and who may have barely known of names such as Montelena and Mondavi—felt emboldened to give their opinions. Nothing illustrates this sea change in public perception of wine more than the flowering of wine writing during the early 1970s, especially among those like Robert Finigan who simply started entrepreneurially putting pen to paper and finger to keyboard to walk fellow consumers through their next purchases by stating a wine's pros and cons.

Charles Olken, for one, thought Robert Lawrence Balzer and other long-established critics spent too much time writing about European wines and not enough time writing about those from California. He and Earl Singer—who found themselves with time on their hands after the Nixon administration squeezed the federal poverty program they worked on—started the *Connoisseurs' Guide to California Wine* in late 1974, creating what would become the oldest wine magazine in the state. The same year, an engineer in San Diego named Nick Ponomareff started a newsletter called the *California Grapevine*. Like Olken and Singer's *Connoisseurs' Guide to California Wine*, it focused on straightforward reviews of American as well as European wines. Both publications grew organically—the *Connoisseurs' Guide* gained its first subscribers through an ad in the more-established *Vintage* magazine—though it would be many years before either numbered their subscribers in the thousands; still, out of the newsletters and magazines that emerged in this era, theirs, along with Robert Finigan's, proved the most durable.

Less organic and more traditional were the successors of Ruth Ellen Church and Balzer (who started his own *Private Guide to Food & Wine* in 1970). Nathan Chroman, a personal injury lawyer in Beverly Hills who taught wine appreciation classes through the extension program at the University of California, Los Angeles, started writing a wine column in the *Los Angeles Times* in 1971. Hank Rubin, a pioneer in Berkeley in what would come to be called the locavore movement, wrote a similar column in the *San Francisco Chronicle* through the late 1960s and 1970s. By 1974, then, in an epoch when people still got most of their news from newspapers, several of the nation's leading newspapers (the *New York Times*, the *Los Angeles Times*, the *Chicago Tribune*, and the *San Francisco Chronicle*) had regular wine reporting—quite a leap from the decade before, even though the coverage continued to skew toward European (read: mostly French) vintages.

There were other media rumblings—not as loud as a column in a newspaper reaching millions but similarly portentous for American fine wine. In 1973 Marvin Shanken, an investment banker on Wall Street who specialized in real estate, paid $5,000 for a newsletter covering the wine and liquor industries called *Impact*, and started publishing it out of his New York apartment. Shanken's work had taken him to Northern California, where he discovered the newer wineries. A forceful personality with a passion for cigars as well as drink, the portly and bearded Shanken wanted to dominate what he recognized as the burgeoning niche market for information on American fine wine—and he would take on all comers. He was fond of quoting an adage of onetime Coca-Cola CEO Roberto Goizueta: "If you don't have an enemy, create one."

In the same year Shanken bought *Impact*, a restless young man from the Baltimore area with a similarly type A personality finished law school at the University of Maryland, where he had organized wine tastings with friends. Robert Parker Jr. didn't really want to be a lawyer, but it would do for the moment.

THE BATTLE OF VERSAILLES

1973 | Versailles, France

"**O**ther than the army of long black cars and the floodlit palace," the *New York Times* noted, "the evening would have been familiar to Marie Antoinette."

The idea for the November evening was simple enough: raise more than a quarter of a million dollars to restore Versailles, the sumptuous palace in the Parisian suburb of the same name that once housed France's monarchs, including the doomed Antoinette. The execution of the fundraiser, however, was far from simple. It was lavish, drenched in boldface names such as Princess Grace of Monaco, Christina Onassis, Andy Warhol, the Begum Aga Khan, the Duchess of Windsor, and Liza Minnelli, who kicked off the evening with a romping version of "Bonjour Paris" in Versailles's baroque Royal Opera theater. An hour-long fashion show featuring both French and American designers followed the performance, the brainchild of organizers led by the Baroness de Rothschild.

Models, including eleven African Americans (a rare sight in an often arctic-white industry), strutted the wares of French giants Dior, Ungaro, Pierre Cardin, Yves Saint Laurent, and Givenchy as well as those of lesser-known Americans Bill Blass, Anne Klein, Stephen Burrows, Halston, and Oscar de la Renta. It was rumored in the run-up to the evening that the French stylists considered their American counterparts mere sportswear designers rather than creators of the sort of haute couture that had made Paris the world's fashion capital for decades. Perhaps the Americans were only invited, some whispered, because of the potential donations they might draw for the palace restoration—and never mind their clothes.

The Americans stole the show.

"The French were good, but the Americans were sensational," said the Duchess de la Rochefoucauld, one of myriad European tastemakers stunned by the fashion sense of the Americans, whose casual-cool styles—and casual-cool models—looked so much fresher against the stuffier approaches of the established French. "C'était formidable!"

The Begum Aga Khan declared the Americans, "Extraordinary, extraordinary."

"I was so pleased, and proud," the Philadelphia-born Princess Grace told a reporter afterward.

The media blasted such reactions worldwide within two days. Within a decade, New York supplanted Paris as the world's fashion capital and the United States edged out France as the home of the industry's leading arbiters. The November 28, 1973, evening came to be called the Battle of Versailles—and the Americans had won.

SÍ, SE PUEDE

1973–1975 | Modesto—Sacramento—Napa Valley

More than ten thousand marchers stretching a mile through Modesto, California, waved red flags with a black eagle in a white circle and chanted in uproarious union, "Chavez sí, Teamsters no! Gallo wine has got to go!" It was Saturday, March 1, 1975, the end of a weeklong, 110-mile march from San Francisco to the headquarters of the biggest winery in the United States, a company that then accounted for more than one-third of the bottles bought domestically and, as such, a major force in California's grape-growing industry.

The United Farm Workers of America (UFW)—a labor union dating from the early 1960s—and its charismatic leader, Cesar Chavez, had organized the march to call attention to the unfair treatment of the often immigrant workforce that picked the grapes that undergirded American wine-making. Farmworkers usually made less than one dollar an hour toiling the entire day in often brutally hot weather, risking injury from sometimes-shoddy farming equipment and living in squalor, indoor plumbing a luxury few enjoyed. Often in the United States illegally and always outgunned, the farmworkers had little to no recourse to change things because their rights were not covered under federal labor laws.

Chavez, himself a former farmworker and a World War II navy veteran, was just shy of his thirty-eighth birthday at the time of the march. Fueled by his deep Catholic faith and angered by what he saw as a dangerous mix of discrimination and exploitation when it came to who picked the nation's produce, including grapes, Chavez had risen over the past twenty years to become a titanic force in organized labor. Despite his anger, the slight, soft-spoken Arizona native adhered to the nonviolent resistance espoused by Mohandas Gandhi and Martin Luther King Jr., which helped him draw publicity and support for his, and his union's, cause. Throughout the previous decade, Chavez enlisted the likes of King, Robert Kennedy, and Pope Paul VI in his crusade to improve the plight of farmworkers through organized labor.

The boycott proved his most effective weapon. In May 1969 Chavez called for a worldwide boycott of California grapes, including those used in winemaking; his call to action expanded on a grape boycott that had already commenced two years before and drew support as far afield as Canada and Europe. By early 1970, the state's grape growers and buyers were ready to play ball. Several struck three-year deals to allow the UFW to organize unions of their farmworkers. While things seemed settled and an uneasy truce between management and labor endured, the expiration of the contracts in 1973 brought renewed troubles. A number of wineries and vineyardists, including E. & J. Gallo, followed the lead of lettuce growers in the state and signed with the International Brotherhood of Teamsters rather than with Chavez's outfit. As Chavez and his allies saw it, the Teamsters were on the side of the grape growers, who were offering fewer workplace protections, particularly from the pesticides used to shield the vines, and less representation in negotiations with management. That management—the wineries and the vineyardists— pronounced themselves publicly flummoxed by Chavez's allegations. They saw the UFW as too disorganized to be negotiating partners, and some even grumbled that Chavez and his ilk were a Communist front at a time of ceaseless Cold War tension. Besides, the wineries reasoned, were the Teamsters not one of the nation's most powerful unions? What was the problem?

The Teamsters contract sparked two years of strikes, violence, arrests, and recriminations between the UFW, its allies, and the winemakers. Chavez's stature only seemed to grow the messier things got, while the California winemaking industry suffered both economically and in the public eye. Chavez's rallying cry of "Sí, se puede" ("Yes, we can" in Spanish) joined the national lexicon, a shorthand for labor rights generally. His actions as a labor organizer drew further support from politicians as well as from other unions just as California's—and the nation's—political climate was shifting leftward. Organizers of the Modesto march on Gallo's headquarters read aloud messages of support from several members of Congress, including Minnesota senator Walter Mondale, who would be elected vice president in 1976, and senator Alan Cranston, the California Democrat. In what turned out to be one of its most important efforts, the UFW supported California secretary of state Jerry Brown Jr. in the 1974 governor's race; when the Democrat succeeded rising Republican star Ronald Reagan the following year, Chavez found himself with a powerful ally.

In August 1975 Brown signed the California Agricultural Labor Relations Act (CALRA), the first law in the continental United States recognizing the collective bargaining rights of farmworkers. Throughout the rest of the decade, the UFW virtually ran the tables on union elections when it came to grape growers; the Teamsters largely gave up challenging the UFW for votes in the agricultural sector. As expected, though, the act did not settle every issue between the growers and the pickers. Tensions remained, sporadic strikes continued, and Chavez called for more boycotts; the UFW's footprint, moreover, never grew beyond 20 percent of the farm labor in California. Nor did the UFW succeed in really harming Gallo, its prime target that dusty March afternoon in Modesto. While hundreds of liquor stores in the state did boycott Gallo wines, the generic hegemon continued to enjoy brisk sales.

What Chavez, the United Farm Workers, and CALRA *did* do was help maintain an uneasy peace between the wine-making industry and the labor in the vineyards. The act, especially, provided a framework for the two sides to work within, not least through the regulatory board Brown created in its wake. While Chavez never targeted fine wine producers on the scale of assault he leveled at Gallo, this framework and the truce it brought steadied a volatile part of the American fine wine movement, one often ignored by the industry itself and its consumers. As it would turn out, this steadiness arrived just in time.

SKY'S THE LIMIT

1970–1976 | New York City

The views were supposed to really sell it: one acre of restaurant space more than thirteen hundred feet above America's biggest city. Joseph Baum, the restaurateur charged with making Windows on the World in the North Tower of Manhattan's World Trade Center happen by early 1976, had built his legend on such successes as Tavern on the Green in Central Park and the Four Seasons farther uptown. His new task was enviable, though by no means assured of success. The views would sell it, yes; but would New Yorkers and the legions of tourists who visited Gotham every day buy the rest of it?

Especially, would they buy the restaurant's concept in a city clearly on the decline? New York by the mid-1970s had plummeted to its late twentieth-century rock bottom. Crime was increasing, and hundreds of thousands of residents were fleeing. Things were so hopeless financially that after President Gerald Ford, in the words of the *Daily News*, told New York to "drop dead" in October 1975, the administration of mayor Abraham Beame secretly drafted a statement announcing the city's bankruptcy. For all the grandeur of its skyline and the moxie of its residents, New York City had fast become a textbook example of urban decay with no resurrection in sight.

Joseph Baum pressed ahead through that dark 1975. He enlisted French chef Jacques Pépin and food writer James Beard to help devise a menu for Windows on the World; a Hilton subsidiary would handle the restaurant's management. Milton Glaser, who would become most famous a couple years later for devising the I [Love] New York logo, designed the menus, dishware patterns, and emblem (a big, yellow moon with rays of light shooting from it and stars twinkling below, clouds shunted to the corners). Baum brought in modernist architect Warren Platner to craft an open space of clean lines and curves, all of which led eyes to those spectacular New York skyline views.

All the attention to detail was a good thing, too, as the original menu of Windows on the World did not necessarily bowl discerning diners over. It put too much emphasis on the last word of the restaurant's name: there were dishes from Holland, South Africa, China, all sorts of other global locales, with little to link them thematically. Shortly after its April 1976 opening, one *New York Times* reviewer noted that meals at Windows on the World "revealed many flaws that still have to be ironed out." Baum took the critique to heart and retooled, bringing on a new chef who took inspiration from Alice Waters's Chez Panisse in Berkeley, California, and soon the menu of the highest restaurant in the United States was revolving around simple, American meals made from the freshest ingredients possible.

Windows on the World's eighteen private suites and five restaurant spaces began attracting the politically powerful, New York governor Hugh Carey and secretary of state Henry Kissinger among them; European royalty, including the recently minted king and queen of Spain as well as the prince of Monaco; journalists such as Walter Cronkite and John Chancellor; and celebrities such as actors Robert Redford and Kim Novak. *New York* magazine soon declared the buzzy aerie "the most spectacular restaurant in the world," one that seemed to scrub clean the messy world just beyond it:

> Even New Jersey looks good from here. Down below are all of Manhattan and helicopters and clouds. Everything to hate and fear is invisible. Pollution is but a cloud. A fire raging below Washington

Square is a dream, silent, almost unreal, though you can see the arc of water licking flame. Default is a silly nightmare. There is no doggy doo. Garbage is an illusion.

Baum's effort was a hit. He and his partners then hatched a plan to add an accoutrement that suddenly seemed a must-have in 1976, even in a restaurant doing so haughtily well: a wine bar called Cellar in the Sky. And so, from that nearly quarter-mile-high perch, by the mid-1970s patrons with the right set of eyes might survey an American fine wine movement of profound potential.

The United States was by then the world's third-largest producer of wine, with nearly 90 percent of commercially available wine coming from inside the country and more of it than ever coming from higher-end grapes. California wineries had for several years been producing more than five million gallons annually of varietally labeled wine, the sort a lonely Frank Schoonmaker championed after Prohibition, telling consumers the type of higher-end grape primarily used to make the wine and the winery from which the bottle sprung; even generic kingpin E. & J. Gallo had introduced some varietally labeled wine in 1974.

Sales were up too, and not just in coastal enclaves such as the San Francisco Bay Area or metropolitan New York. From 1970 to 1971, for instance, wine sales rose 59 percent in Wisconsin, 65 percent in Vermont, and 98 percent in Rhode Island—driven in no small measure by the quality of the newer fine wines as well as their evangelists in the media and the industry. Crucially, while the average American was knocking back more wine, fine or otherwise, than at any other time since Prohibition (roughly two and a half gallons per year by the early 1970s), he had nothing on the average Italian or Frenchmen (who might put away thirty or so). That suggested room for growth in America, a margin for new entrepreneurs to play in.

This margin for growth encouraged experimentation, including with styles rather out of fashion in terms of cultivation and usage. Take Zinfandel. Beginning in 1972, Bob Trinchero, winemaker and co-owner of the Sutter Home Winery in St. Helena, had been making an intensely dark, unusually dry Zinfandel by draining a lot of the juice from batches and leaving the skins to deepen the color (red-wine juice is generally white; the skins give it its deeper hue). He called it White Zinfandel, after a style that may have gone back as far as the 1860s but that had long fallen out of vogue. In 1975, a sluggish fermentation and Trinchero's addition of natural sugar resulted in a pinkish version of the wine, which quickly became a smash hit. By the mid-1980s Sutter Home would be selling more than one and a half million cases of White Zinfandel annually. The style, with its uncomplicated softness and hints of freshly picked berries, served as a kind of gateway fine wine for consumers, a lower-priced first toe-dip into an expanding marketplace, winning "over Americans who thought they didn't like wine." Although many moved on to more complex, and more expensive, styles, Sutter Home's White Zinfandel sales, and those of later imitators, never lagged; it remained the biggest-selling fine wine varietal in the United States well into the 1990s. Ironically— but understandably—Trinchero's father, Mario, had encouraged his son, just out of the air force in 1958, to seek another line of work rather than the family winery, saying there was little future in American wine.

On the other side of the country, around the same time as Trinchero's accidental innovation, the flowering of wine coverage continued unabated with the formations of the Wine Critics Circle and the Wine Media Guild, both in New York City, for wine scribes nationwide who wanted to add a bit of associational oomph to their reputations.

These twin events illustrate, however, the main drawback of the American fine wine movement a decade after Robert Mondavi's ballyhooed opening: it was an archipelago of potential. A lot was happening on the coasts and some points in between; yet because of the vagaries of climate and the accidents of geography, as well as a larger public indifference to American-made fine wine, frustratingly little was happening in vast swathes of the nation.

Things were still busiest in California. In Napa Valley in 1973, Moët Hennessy—the centuries-old French concern most famous for Moët & Chandon Champagne—bought two thousand acres and became the first French winery to grow its grapes outside of France. The following year, in Lake County, almost sixty miles north of Napa, Jess Jackson and Jane Kendall bought an eighty-acre pear and walnut farm and tore it up to start anew with grapes. California beachheads like theirs showed the state's enological promise beyond the two primary wine counties, Sonoma and Napa, from as far south as San Diego and up to the Oregon border. That state, too, was a hive of enological activity a good eight years after Richard Sommer's first Pinot Noir. The same went farther north, in Washington State. There the number of fine wineries was nearing double digits, with ten friends, including six faculty members at the University of Washington, having started the first one in 1962 in the lush Yakima Valley. Columbia Winery's initial test batches, in fact, were made in the Seattle garage of its first winemaker, Lloyd Woodburne, a psychology professor who figured the cost of helping start a winery then was comparable to the cost of joining a decent country club.

Founder Richard Sommer at Hillcrest, Oregon's oldest fine winery and one of the few started beyond Northern California before the early 1970s.
COURTESY OF HILLCREST

There were also pockets throughout Ohio, in Virginia, and especially up the Hudson River and to its west in New York State, which then accounted for around one-tenth of all wine sold in the United States. At the start of 1976, the nation had 579 wineries, more than at any time since the post-Repeal generic peak in the mid-1950s; more than 56 percent were in California. Despite wineries having plunged to a numerical nadir right before Robert Mondavi, it was suddenly not so inconceivable to speak of more than a thousand American wineries and more than five hundred in California alone in the next decade, most predicated on wines from higher-end grapes. Conservative estimates already pegged investment in the entire US wine industry at $1 billion from 1967 to 1974, with three-quarters of that money going into vineyards and the remaining $250 million into the wineries themselves. Smart money, from inside and outside the industry, talked of people drinking hundreds of millions, even a billion, gallons of American wine annually by the close of the century. Things had changed dramatically, yet the most momentous changes were still to come.

TALES IN TWO CITIES
1975 | New York City—Chicago

Adam Strum's job could have been tougher. Twenty-three years old in 1975, he had grown up around wine as the son of a wine salesman, something he himself segued into after college. His sales territory included Greenwich Village, the Manhattan neighborhood that was then commencing a long transition from a grittier hangout for beatniks and hippies into one for affluent families and upwardly mobile young professionals. Going were hootenannies in Washington Square Park; coming were haute cuisine restaurants. The neighborhood's liquor stores, however, had not started to transition when it came to wine, something that worked to Strum's advantage; he was a sales rep for E. & J. Gallo.

Strum, a born salesman acutely aware of the larger changes in American wine, found it relatively easy to regularly unload dozens of cases of Gallo's sweeter generics at each of his accounts. The retailers knew the brand, and their customers knew the contents. Gallo meant domestic wine for most Americans, even ten years after the founding of the Robert Mondavi Winery in St. Helena, California. So Strum busied himself not so much with the sales as with the promotion. It was still a struggle, even in a cosmopolitan place such as New York City's Greenwich Village, to garner shelf space for wine, particularly American wine. The stock of a typical Village liquor store was around 70 percent distilled spirits, with beer, wine, and liqueur, both import and domestic, left to duke it out for the remaining space, never mind the prime, eyeball-grabbing locations such as the front of a shop or the midlevel shelves.

Being Gallo's man on the ground, then, made Strum's working life that much easier. The Modesto, California, concern started by brothers Ernest and Julio forty years earlier still accounted for around one-third of all wine sold in the United States. A November 1972 cover story in *Time* magazine, by far the nation's largest newsweekly, featured a photo of the siblings on the label of a wine bottle beside a headline declaring, AMERICAN WINE: THERE'S

Gold in Them Thar Grapes, likening the boom in California wine to the state's nineteenth-century gold rush. And what a rush for Gallo, according to the article: "The Gallo Winery sold 100 million gallons last year—almost half of all California wine and nearly twice as much as its nearest competitor, United Vintners."

While the five-page article expended most of its coverage on the brothers' concern, it did include references to the fine wine movement that had arisen in opposition to that jug-wine juggernaut: "A Brief Guide to California Wine" explained the different higher-end grape types, such as Chardonnay and Cabernet Sauvignon. The explanations, predictably enough, took refuge in comparisons to French regions and styles (thus Chardonnay: "a dry white that resembles the whites of Burgundy"). That *Time*'s Manhattan-based editorial staff felt compelled to include the explanations itself speaks to the lack of wider fine wine familiarity in the nation; one could not imagine a French magazine of similar stature feeling the need to explain Chardonnay to its public.

Strum was aware of *Time*'s coverage of his boss Gallo and of the fine wine movement it touched upon. That was how he recognized Marcia Mondavi, who in 1975 was schlepping to many of the same Greenwich Village accounts as Strum on behalf of her father, Robert. The elder Mondavi, as handsomely gregarious as ever in his early sixties, had spent much of the previous decade promoting not only his own wine but those of Napa Valley in general, traveling often to New York City to host tastings and regularly courting the swelling ranks of wine writers. He would never elicit the kind of coverage that Gallo got, nor its sales, but he remained the single biggest industry force in American fine wine, his winery a moneymaker at last, his vintages increasingly prized by critics.

One would not have guessed at Mondavi's success, however, when watching his only daughter try to sell Robert Mondavi wines in the nation's number one consumer marketplace. Strum noticed that where he might unload thirty, forty, even fifty cases of Gallo at a time to Greenwich Village retailers, his competitor was lucky to unload a single case of Mondavi at any one liquor store at any one time—and that case usually had to be mixed, with a few bottles of Fumé Blanc, a few bottles of Cabernet Sauvignon, etc., rather than an entire case of a single variety. There remained in 1975 that much hesitancy, even in worldly Gotham.

Shortly after his graduation from the University of Florida in 1971, Craig Goldwyn hitched a camper to the back of his pickup truck and headed north out of Gainesville. He ran into some hitchhikers trying to get back to Detroit. They were working the automobile assembly lines there for $3.50 an hour, they told him. Holy shit, Goldwyn thought, I'm going to Detroit.

He really had no plans beyond getting out of Florida, though Detroit did not quite turn out to be the financial Valhalla he expected. He rolled into the Motor City in August, when the automakers were retooling their lines, and the people on them, to handle the more recent car models. There was not as much work as he thought, certainly little at $3.50 an hour. While plotting his next move, Goldwyn visited Chicago to check out a photography exhibit of an old professor; he fell in thrall to the Windy City and moved there as quickly as his truck would take him. He settled into a role familiar to him from part-time work in Gainesville: clerking at a liquor store chain.

This time his employer was Foremost Liquors, where Goldwyn worked his way up to being the wine buyer and seller for the Skokie, Illinois, location. He had a little bar for tastings, and every year he drove to California wine country, where he ordered cases of the latest vintages from the myriad start-up wineries for the store back in Illinois. He arranged deliveries through Freemark Abbey, the St. Helena winery dating from the 1880s and rejuvenated with a change of ownership in 1967. Goldwyn's trips westward ensured his Foremost Liquors had a sizable California contingent, unlike his liquor store in Gainesville. There, as if a microcosm of a typical American wine selection in the early 1970s, only a few California bottles, including Robert Mondavi and Charles Krug, might be shelved upright alongside the many rows of jugs from the likes of Gallo; only the European wines warranted proper storage on racks at forty-five-degree angles to prevent the corks from drying out and letting ruinous oxygen in.

Chicago was different; enthusiasts such as Goldwyn in America's third-largest city could sense a perfect storm coming in American fine wine. It was as if just one more condition needed to materialize for the clouds to burst. As it happened—and as was increasingly common at the time—Goldwyn produced a wine newsletter, working off a typesetting machine in his home. One day in 1975, he scribbled this rationale in the marginalia of his newsletter, next to an entry describing the 1973 Chateau Montelena Chardonnay crafted by Mike Grgich at Jim Barrett's winery in Calistoga, California: "I know $7.39 sounds like a lot of money for an American Chardonnay, but it's just as good as any Meursault that you can find, which is similarly priced." Meursault was one of the most vaunted grape-growing areas in France.

Goldwyn put the newsletter aside and didn't think much of it until later.

"AH, BACK TO FRANCE!"
1976 | Paris

On page fifty-eight of the *Time* magazine dated Monday, June 7, 1976, the following lead introduced a 362-word article under the headline JUDGMENT OF PARIS:

> Americans abroad have been boasting for years about California wines, only to be greeted in most cases by polite disbelief—or worse. Among the few fervent and respected admirers of le vin de Californie in France is a transplanted Englishman, Steven Spurrier, 34, who owns the Cave de la Madeleine wine shop, one of the best in Paris, and the Academic du Vin, a wine school whose six-week courses are attended by the French Restaurant Association's chefs and sommeliers. Last week in Paris, at a formal wine tasting organized by Spurrier, the unthinkable happened: California defeated all Gaul.

The article went on to explain the wine tasting's parameters. There were nine French judges culled from the upper echelons of that nation's wine and hospitality industries (industries that were sometimes indistinguishable), including Raymond Oliver, owner of Paris's Le Grand Véfour restaurant and "doyen of French culinary writers," and Pierre Tari, secretary-general of the augustly named trade group the Association des Grands Cru Classes. The judges were charged with assessing four whites from Bourgogne versus six California Chardonnays, and four reds from Bordeaux versus six California Cabernet Sauvignons. Then the article moved to the judges' judgments:

> As they swirled, sniffed, sipped and spat, some judges were instantly able to separate an imported upstart from an aristocrat. More often, the panel was confused. "Ah, back to France!" exclaimed Oliver after sipping a 1972 Chardonnay from the Napa Valley. "That is definitely California. It has no nose," said another judge—after downing

a Batard Montrachet '73. Other comments included such Gallic gems as "this is nervous and agreeable," "a good nose but not too much in the mouth," and "this soars out of the ordinary."

When the ballots were cast, the top-soaring red was Stag's Leap Wine Cellars' '72 from the Napa Valley, followed by Mouton Rothschild '70, Haut-Brion '70, and Montrose '70. The four winning whites were, in order, Chateau Mont-helena '73 from Napa, French Meursault-Charmes '73, and two other Californians: Chalone '74 from Monterey County and Napa's Spring Mountain '73. The US winners were little known to wine lovers, since they were in short supply even in California and rather expensive (upward of six dollars). Jim Barrett, Montelena's general manager and part owner, said, "Not bad for kids from the sticks."

The article ran in the "Modern Living" section toward the front of the magazine, sharing a page with a longer article about a new theme park in Atlanta. As was *Time*'s custom then, the article did not carry a byline, or a photo for that matter. The magazine itself, however, carried tremendous import. *Time* was far and away America's largest newsweekly, if not the largest English-language news magazine in the world, at a pre-Web time when most people—including television news producers, who often spun the daily print headlines into the nightly newscast—got their news from the printed page. Roughly four million people read *Time* every week, its cover images an arbiter of what passed for important, its articles a barometer of what mattered in the world.

For those in wine paying attention, then, this short piece was no less than earth shattering. Nothing would be the same again.

EIGHT-YEAR-OLDS DRINKING WINE
1960–1976 | Washington, DC—Bonn—Paris

The reporter behind *Time*'s "Judgment of Paris" article ended up at Steven Spurrier's tasting accidentally. That is, George Taber had taken a circuitous route to an interest in fine wine that had placed him within the expat orbit of Spurrier's Caves de la Madeleine and adjoining Académie du Vin, an orbit that in turn put the Los Angeles–area native on a collision course with American history.

Taber had gone east in 1960 for college at Georgetown University in Washington, DC. He spent his junior year studying abroad in Tours, France, about 150 miles southwest of Paris. It was there, on his first night with his host family—a husband and wife and their two sons, ages eight and twenty— that his mind was thoroughly blown regarding wine. Taber commenced the evening using his approximately fifteen words of French to make small talk while the man of the house, a cab driver who gave tours of the area's aged châteaus, served the adults an aperitif. They then shifted to the table for dinner, where the mother poured some red wine for her sons—including the eight-year-old. Taber watched in wonderment as the mother matter-of-factly filled the child's glass halfway with wine and then topped it off with water. His own earlier experiences with wine back in the States had enwreathed it in exoticness; the first glass he could ever remember drinking was during a Thanksgiving meal in 1960, with an Italian family who'd invited him over. In the United States, it took a major holiday feast to warrant wine; in France, it was commonplace, part of the culture, something even children drank!

The college student was, of course, but the latest in a long line of Americans who had discovered such European attitudes toward wine, particularly in France. This relationship with wine—uncomplicated, commonplace—was one of the reasons Taber quickly fell in love with Europe. He began laying plans for living and working there after he was done with college.

At a time when the continent was coming together into what would become the European Union, Taber earned his master's degree studying European integration at a graduate school in Bruges, Belgium. Then he spent a summer in Charlestown, West Virginia, reporting for United Press International. Taber's two worlds, current affairs and journalism, came together beginning in December 1965, when he started stringing for *Time* out of Brussels for twenty-five dollars an article. The magazine offered him a full-time spot a year and a half in, though it meant a return to the United States—specifically to Washington, DC, where he mostly covered business. The pull of Europe remained, however, and the tall, shuffling Taber, with crystal blue eyes and fashionable brown sideburns, was back—this time in Bonn, the West German capital—by the close of the 1960s.

Curiously enough, his return was just in time for his first dabble in wine writing. Taber was invited to a wine tasting in Bonn, where he was shocked to see a bottle of German wine retailing for the equivalent of one hundred dollars. The priciest French ones went for maybe fifty, the best California ones for no more than ten. One hundred dollars? It seemed to Taber unbelievable, and he took to the pages of *Time* in December 1969 to pen an article on the wine named Trockenbeerenauslese, "probably the world's most expensive wine." (It's worth noting that for his American readers Taber immediately compared the German concoction to French wine rather than anything back in the States.)

In 1973, after a stint as the American spokesman for the precursor to the European Union, he went to work in *Time*'s Paris bureau, working again mostly on business stories. It was there that Taber, like so many other native English speakers, became a regular customer at Steven Spurrier's Caves de la Madeleine. And it was from that, that Taber, on the day before his thirty-fourth birthday, found himself the only journalist present at what would become known for all time by his article's headline: the Judgment of Paris. Luckily, by then he spoke French pretty well.

HAPPY BIRTHDAY, AMERICA—LOVE, FRANCE
1976 | Yorktown, Virginia

On Monday, May 17, 1976, the Concorde carrying French president Valéry Giscard d'Estaing landed at Andrews Air Force Base near Washington, DC, so quietly that the dignitaries awaiting it never heard its powerful engines. Giscard's choice of the supersonic jet for his transatlantic crossing was no accident: a French invention, the Concorde was meant to emphasize the Fifth Republic's technological prowess. Social unrest driven by double-digit inflation and more than one million unemployed might be wracking France, but it could still be a world leader in other things, supersonic travel being one.

Fine wine, of course, was another. It did not go unremarked that during his five-day swing, the French president seemed to savor the California fine wines served to him at functions, including a state dinner at the White House. Nor did the timing of Giscard's visit escape comment. The United States would mark its two hundredth birthday in July, and what more appropriate visitor in the run-up than the president of France, America's top ally in its war for independence against Great Britain?

President Valéry Giscard d'Estaing (left) and US president Gerald Ford on the White House lawn during a mid–May 1976 summit that wrapped just before France's epic loss in the Judgment of Paris. The summit, ironically, was meant to showcase French prowess.
COURTESY OF THE GERALD R. FORD PRESIDENTIAL LIBRARY AND MUSEUM

Symbolism infused Giscard's trip. He showed off his excellent English. He visited Philadelphia, where the Declaration of Independence was signed on July 4, 1776. He toured the battle site at Yorktown, Virginia, where French forces helped the Continental Army finish off the British in 1781. He then visited Mount Vernon, George Washington's Potomac-side estate, where he presented President Gerald Ford with a bicentennial gift: a $1.2 million spectacle depicting Washington's life in sound and light. Then he headed west, first to Houston, where he talked up business opportunities in France with Texas tycoons, and then to New Orleans, the onetime headquarters of France's New World empire in lower North America.

In the end, the visit was a success for Giscard. America's bicentennial provided numerous angles for the media to hang stories on, and the French president seemed to revel in the opportunity to put a more prosperous, confident face on France, whatever the troubles back home. More than that, Giscard was able to accentuate at every turn a closer relationship between France and the United States, like when he referenced the nations' eighteenth-century alliance against Britain during a May 20 speech at Yorktown: "By virtue of the fact that it was the first your country ever made, it has earned us—and I can say this with pride—the name of oldest and foremost friend of the United States."

THE WORLD TURNED UPSIDE DOWN
1976 | Paris

Some 195 years before Valéry Giscard d'Estaing spoke at Yorktown, the British were said to have had their band strike up a seventeenth-century marching ballad upon their surrender to the Americans and the French at the same Virginia location. The song's title? "The World Turned Upside Down."

That was exactly what it felt like in the wine world after the Judgment of Paris on May 24, 1976. It was the single most significant event in wine in the latter half of the twentieth century as well as far and away the most important in the American fine wine movement. Those five syllables in French—"Ah, retour en France!"—that George Taber overheard Raymond Oliver declaring (and that he translated for *Time* readers) were essentially the most important anyone had uttered about American fine wine up to that point, even if they did reflect a mistake by their speaker.

Moreover, and more important, the industry and those that covered it understood the statement's significance immediately. The impact of the Robert Mondavi Winery's earliest bottles, the writings of Robert Lawrence Balzer and Frank Schoonmaker, the innovations of Andre Tchelistcheff and Maynard Amerine—they were all undeniably important, but it would take years of hindsight to vet their significance to the movement, not to mention their effects on the industry's bottom line. Schoonmaker banged on for decades about varietal labeling, but the custom did not become commonplace in the United States until the early 1970s. Georges de Latour brought Andre Tchelistcheff to California before World War II, but the practices the winemaker championed weren't widely adopted until two decades after that conflict's end. Not so the Judgment of Paris: as fast as other journalists nationwide could crib from Taber's *Time* article, the impact was felt.

THREE CHEERS FOR THE RED, WHITE AND CRU, cried a June 13 headline in the *Los Angeles Times*, spinning off the French wine term for growth. The same newspaper later carried a cartoon of an American cowboy dueling with a Frenchman and besting him with a popping cork instead of a pistol. CALIFORNIA WINES BEAT FRENCH WINES!, declared the *Times-Picayune* of New Orleans on June 16, exclamation point and all. The *Weekly Calistogan* back in Napa Valley, home of both of the winning vineyards—Warren Winiarski's Stag's Leap and Jim Barrett's Chateau Montelena—played off Barrett's quote to Taber in its banner headline: "KIDS FROM THE STICKS" PLACE FIRST. Perhaps the most anticipated media reaction came from the *New York Times'* Frank J. Prial, who played up the results in the nation's most prominent publication in two consecutive columns, the sort of coverage that might attend a political result or a sporting event. He devoted the first, on June 9, to the white wines, and the second, on June 16, to the reds. While both missives cast a bit of a skeptical eye on the results—Prial wrote, "One would be foolish to take Mr. Spurrier's tasting as definitive"—they nonetheless lavished praise on the California vintners Prial himself had been talking up to Steven Spurrier for years. Two of three factions championing American fine wine, the winemakers and the critics, had come so spectacularly together in Paris, with more consumers sure to follow.

Why so spectacularly, though? After all, as Prial noted in the white wine column, there had been "several other similar comparisons in which the American chardonnays bested their French rivals," one as recently as six months before in New York City. Indeed, Robert Lawrence Balzer had been hosting his own blind tastings in California for more than a decade, and there were myriad newsletters in the mid-1970s ballasted by critics sharing their often blind tasting notes on California and French wines. What made Spurrier's Judgment of Paris so impactful?

First, these were French judges. The panel Spurrier and Patricia Gallagher assembled included luminaries such as Pierre Brejoux, who oversaw the Appellation d'Origine Contrôlée, the now-oft-imitated labeling system for French wines, and Odette Kahn, the esteemed director of La Revue du Vin de France, as well as restaurateurs and critics. They were the arbiters not only of their nation's revered wine industry but, by default, of the industry throughout the world. Second, as in real estate, location counted. The judges' decisions emanated from the InterContinental Hotel in Paris's fashionable First Arrondissement. More important, of course, they emanated from Paris, the capital of what was long understood as the world's top wine nation. Anywhere in France would have done for suitable international force, but a posh hotel in a nice neighborhood of the capital only added a certain zest.

Third, as Taber would note in his own excellent history of the tasting published thirty years later, when the Judgment of Paris's impact was still very much tangible, the news of the California victory broke in a *Time* magazine that "talked directly to the American middle class, the exact group that was becoming more interested in wine." Taber wrote:

> It was those people who read the story, told their friends about it, and suddenly had a new respect for California wines. Had the news been reported only in one of the new American wine newsletters or magazines, it might have attracted attention among wine connoisseurs, but would have been little noted by the general public.

Spurrier had desperately pitched the tasting to French journalists, though none showed. And Taber only showed because he knew Spurrier and really had nothing else pressing that day. Spurrier thought French publications snubbed it because they, like him until fairly recently, had little to no interest in California wines.

The Judgment of Paris underway in May 1976. Standing with notebook in hand is George Taber, the only journalist present. Leaning farthest forward along the table is Steven Spurrier, the co-organizer.
COURTESY OF BELLA SPURRIER

Finally, the Judgment of Paris had such world-rattling impact because it broke against a bicentennial year in the United States. The nation's news was awash on any given day with tie-ins to the two hundredth anniversary of the signing of the Declaration of Independence. Even the French president and his handlers wove the celebration repeatedly into Giscard's May 1976 visit. The United States had spent the last decade in a profound existential funk clouded by political assassinations, urban riots, a messy end to the Vietnam War, a chastening oil embargo, and, finally, Watergate. Americans and their media appreciated clear wins in 1976, whatever the sport.

FLYING OFF THE SHELVES

1976 | Margaux, France—Chicago—Calistoga, California

Jim Barrett was sipping a glass of Champagne as an aperitif before lunch at the Château Lascombes in the Margaux area of Bordeaux when Joanne Dickenson told him he had a phone call from home. Fearing the worst, Dickenson, the head of the tour company that had brought Barrett and other winemakers to France, walked with him and a member of the château's staff to an office so small the principal owner of Chateau Montelena had to kneel down to talk on the phone. Barrett worried it was bad news, too.

Instead, it was George Taber calling from *Time* magazine's Paris bureau. "Have you heard that your wine came in first in the tasting that was held on Monday in Paris?" Taber asked him. He had tracked Barrett down with the help of Patricia Gallagher at L'Académie du Vin. Dickenson had escorted Gallagher around California wine country the year before when she and Spurrier were mulling the blind tasting that became the Judgment of Paris.

"No," Barrett answered, after flashing an *OK* sign to Dickenson in the tiny office. "I haven't. That's great."

"Well," Taber went on, "you won in the white wine part of it. And a California red wine also won. So it was a California sweep. What's your reaction to beating the French at their own game, and in Paris?"

Barrett hesitated, mulling just the right response in his lawyerly head. He, like everyone else in the industry who would hear or read the news via Taber, understood its significance instantly. "Not bad for kids from the sticks," he finally answered.

It was a quintessentially American response, the sort of phrase Frenchman Alexis de Tocqueville might have reveled in hearing during his tour of a young United States a century and a half before—the perfect mix of humility and braggadocio. That seemed to be the reaction of the Americans, starting with Barrett on the phone with Taber the day after the tasting. The media trumpeted the results, though not necessarily the industry, which only added to their echo. The Americans, in short, played it cool. "We've known for a long time that we could put our white Burgundy against anybody's in the world and not take a backseat," Barrett told Taber, shortly before returning to the lunch at Château Lascombes.

There, he and the other Americans, including the venerable Andre Tchelistcheff, endured a lecture from Alexis Lichine, an owner of Château Lascombes and the critic who a quarter-century before had authoritatively written, "The greatest wines on earth come from France." It was good, Lichine told his audience, that the Americans had decided to visit châteaus like his. Pay attention, he told them, and learn—and perhaps someday you Americans might craft wine of similar quality.

All the while, news of the Paris win rippled mutedly across the lunch, passing from one American to another, but never beyond. It was cinematic. Barrett, Tchelistcheff, Dickenson, and the others maintained the secrecy through gracious good-byes to their hosts and, indeed, stayed quiet until their van was safely out of sight of the château's main building. Then they cheered. Barrett and Tchelistcheff hugged.

At their next hotel, Barrett zipped off a telegram to Chateau Montelena:

STUNNING SUCCESS IN PARIS TASTING ON MAY TWENTY-FOUR STOP
TOOK FIRST PLACE OVER NINE OTHERS WITH LE PREMIER CRU WINE STOP
TOP NAMES IN FRANCE WERE THE BLIND TASTERS STOP

Shortly after Barrett detonated the telegram bomb, *Time* magazine called Mike Grgich, the winemaker behind the 1973 Chateau Montelena Chardonnay, to ask if a photographer could snap his picture (a photo of him, glass of Chardonnay in hand, ran with Frank Prial's June 9 *New York Times* column as well). Grgich started dancing around the winery, shouting in his native Croatian, "I'm born again, I'm born again!" Bo Barrett, not yet aware of the win, thought his father's winemaker had lost his mind.

Mike Grgich in the 1970s, around the time of Chateau Montelena's triumph in the Judgment of Paris.
COURTESY OF GRGICH HILLS

On a quieter note the next evening, Warren Winiarski, the owner and wine-maker at Stag's Leap, talked by phone with his wife, Barbara, from his native Chicago, where he was settling his parents' estate. She explained that Dorothy Tchelistcheff, Andre's wife, had just called after their return from three weeks in France. The winery's 1973 Cabernet Sauvignon had won "that wine tasting in Paris." Winiarski wasn't sure what his wife was talking about. "That's nice," he said.

It was indeed nice commercially, never mind critically. All eighteen hundred cases of the 1973 Chateau Montelena Chardonnay were soon gone, some bottles retailing at the unusually high price (for American wine, at least) of nearly seven dollars. Mike Grgich solemnly promised Frank Prial and his millions of *New York Times* readers that another eighteen hundred cases of the 1974 Chardonnay would be released in August and that, besides, the 1975 was "the one to watch. I think it will be the Chardonnay of the century." The winery, though it likely could have jacked the price considerably, suggested the same $6.50 retail price for the 1974 as the 1973. The 1973 Cabernet Sauvignon from Stag's Leap also sold out quickly—too quickly, in fact, for Winiarski to raise the bottle price, as his partners insisted he do. They did, however, bounce the suggested retail price of the 1974 from six dollars to $7.50.

Other American wineries that placed in the Judgment of Paris, including Heitz Wine Cellars, Clos Du Val, and Freemark Abbey, enjoyed brisker sales too. These sales came despite the wines being available in relatively few places nationwide compared with their generic and imported counterparts. Prial, for instance, spent a part of his June 9 *Times* column simply listing off the handful of New York City area shops that carried the Stag's Leap Cabernet Sauvignon. American fine wine even started showing up on the racks and shelves of Paris in noticeable numbers for the first time ever. Stories soon arose of frantic oenophiles in cities across the United States rushing into their local liquor stores and begging staff for any bottles of the winners. Some of these stories were surely apocryphal, suggesting that the Judgment of Paris made the transition from fact to legend rather fast.

Stag's Leap and Chateau Montelena's wins also reverberated through the fortunes of American wineries that Steven Spurrier and Patricia Gallagher had not chosen to include. One of those wineries was Robert Mondavi's eponymous concern, which Spurrier considered too big by then to be represented. Still, Mondavi knew a rising tide for his boat when he saw one. It didn't hurt his cheerleading that the makers of both winning wines, Mike Grgich and Warren Winiarski, had passed through his winery's storied archway off Highway 29. Mondavi later noted in his memoir:

> I was tickled to death by the outcome. I was happy and proud of Warren and Mike, our alumni, and, in a larger sense, I was even happier. I knew this tasting was going to electrify the wine world, and I was hoping that it would let the general public know, at last, how far we had come. Ten years before, I had made a bold claim and I had staked my future on it: that we in California could make wines that would stand proudly along side the best in the world. Now here we were, proving just that. On French soil, no less.

J'ACCUSE!

1976 | Paris

Steven Spurrier knew things had gotten especially problematic when he was physically tossed from the cellars of Domaine Ramonet, the august winery near France's wine-trading hub of Beaune. By that point, he was already, as he put it, "persona peu grata" (a person seldom welcomed) because of the Judgment of Paris that he had organized in May 1976. The more rebarbative nature of the French suddenly manifested itself in their reactions to once again losing to the Americans in one of their most hallowed national genres.

The reaction toward this loss, though, was so much more biting than the reaction to the Battle of Versailles in November 1973, when American designers and their models stole the show.

For one thing, wine was a bigger part of the national social and economic life than fashion. France produced around one-fifth of the world's commercial wine by the late 1970s, second only to Italy and around four times larger than America's share; the average French tippler drank a world-leading thirty-one or so gallons of wine a year, the equivalent of two kegs of beer. Yes, most of it was of the vin ordinaire that Spurrier had made a point of ditching when he took over Les Caves da la Madeleine in 1971. That was part of the point: wine was woven into the fabric of French life in a way, as we've seen, still unimaginable to most Americans.

Moreover, France's top wines—the First and Second Growths, the ones from storied regions such as Bordeaux and Burgundy—had long commanded an international reverence that had ballasted for decades an entire ecosystem in France: the châteaus and the winemakers themselves; fine restaurants and the oft-imitated French cuisine; insurers and auctioneers; government functionaries in service of the Appellation d'Origine Contrôlée and other wine-friendly programs; an inexhaustible phalanx of critics, guides, travel agents, consultants, and wine stewards; and sundry enthusiasts who might spend a delightful lifetime discovering the best wines of the best wine country in the world. Take away the reverence, though, and the whole ecosystem starts to wobble, risking collapse, like a dying star. The Judgment of Paris wasn't a deathblow for French wine, of course, but it was certainly a scare.

The fear generated a swift counterreaction in the nation's fine wine establishment. The nine French judges from the Judgment of Paris faced years of professional threats and public insults for, in the words of one observer, having "spat on the face of France." Pierre Brejoux resigned as the director of the institute behind the vaunted Appellation d'Origine Contrôlée. Odette Kahn, another judge, took to publicly accusing Spurrier of rigging the results, an allegation Spurrier denied (and that was not true besides); she also alluded in her *Revue du Vin de France* to a conspiracy to boost the California wine results by serving the good ones after bad, thus ensuring better scores. This, too, was rubbish.

Others in the French industry simply took refuge in xenophobia. Spurrier's Englishness went from being an eccentricity to a liability virtually overnight. This was another reason why the reaction to the Judgment of Paris was much bitterer than the reaction to the Battle of Versailles. That fashion event had been organized by the French for the benefit of the French—a fundraiser for the old royal palace—with the Americans bystanders in the planning. The Judgment of Paris, however, was organized by a flamboyant Englishman and his American associate, the news of its results blasted to the world by an American journalist, no less. "You've spat in our soup," one Bordeaux winemaker told Spurrier. "We allowed you into our country, and you've done this to us—perfidious Albion!" Another wine industry insider compared the tasting not to the hyperbolically named Battle of Versailles but to the actual Battle of Waterloo, the 1815 defeat of Napoleon by British-led forces.

While the French wine industry's judgment of the Judgment was swift, the nation's major media ignored it for months, in marked contrast to the bleating coverage it drew in the States almost immediately afterward. When *Le Figaro*, one of France's biggest newspapers, finally mentioned the May tasting on August 18, it assured its readers "[the results] cannot be taken seriously." *Le Monde*, France's equivalent of the *New York Times* in terms of influence, got around to the results in November, nearly six months after the event. Its analysis? That Spurrier did not realize the difficulty of staging a blind tasting and that, besides, the French wines had not had enough time to mature in the bottle. Allegations of shoddy organization dogged the tasting for years afterward, but each proved as groundless as Odette Kahn's accusation of outright manipulation by Spurrier. For instance, the French wines were as young as the California ones, a fact *Le Monde* failed to point out.

It did not matter to the French, either, that the Englishman and the American who organized the Judgment of Paris never intended for its results to be so seismic; in fact, Spurrier had never intended a blind tasting at all. He had simply wanted to connect top French palates with these hard-to-find California wines he was hearing so much about.

The ball really started rolling when Patricia Gallagher's boyfriend, later husband, returned from a Napa Valley sojourn with a wine-making book from the University of California, Davis, a wine guide to the area, and a bottle from the Robert Mondavi Winery. That whetted Gallagher's curiosity; she did her own reconnaissance in the summer of 1975, visiting wineries suggested by Robert Finigan, a tireless booster of California fine wines on his visits to Les Caves de la Madeleine and well on his way to being America's most prominent wine critic. Finally, Spurrier visited, staying with his wife, Bella, in the Alta Mira Hotel in Sausalito in March 1976, retracing many of the same steps as Gallagher eight months before. He selected the six Chardonnays and six Cabernet Sauvignons from what were considered the smaller, boutique wineries in the area and got them back to Paris for the tasting via the luggage of a group of American tourists flying out of Boston.

The idea was simply to openly showcase the twelve wines to prove the merits of American wine. A week before the tasting, however, Spurrier realized that only one judge had palatal experience with such wines: Aubert de Villaine of the famous Burgundy estate Domaine de la Romanée-Conti, who had married a woman from San Francisco. Spurrier figured the rest of the judges would be unimpressed from the get-go with American wines, rendering moot the idea of an open tasting to boost their critical profiles. So on the day of the tasting, he asked the judges if they'd be willing to taste the American wines blind against twelve French ones he had selected. Everyone agreed.

In the end, the French wine industry's rending of garments over the subsequent results faded into a wider white noise about the epochal 1976 event. As Taber pointed out decades later, "The results of the Paris Tasting have been the subject of more discussion and debate than any wine event since the Bordeaux classification of 1855." For our story of the American fine wine movement, all that matters is that this discussion and debate must always end with US winemakers winning a game-changing victory.

PART III

OODLES OF FRUIT

1976–1978 | College Park, Maryland—Parkton, Maryland

A ny American who had gone to high school would recognize the point scale that was to become all but synonymous with fine wine in the United States. To Robert Parker Jr. and Victor Morgenroth, developing the point scale was less about familiarity and more about having greater flexibility to rate wines.

The scale worked like this: each wine they tasted got fifty points just for being drinkable; it scored more points for other attributes, such as smell and taste, all the way up to one hundred. A wine that scored in the nineties—an A, or pretty close for any high schooler—was therefore a very good wine; one in the eighties was pretty good; one that scored in the sixties or seventies was bad. The simple scale would profoundly influence wine, food, and drink in general, the world over. In 1976, though, it was merely the wide-ranging plaything of a couple of buddies in suburban Maryland, a lawyer and a toxicologist, who liked to talk and taste wine.

The two met through a bimonthly wine-tasting group Parker had arranged while a law student at the University of Maryland in College Park in the late 1960s. The pair truly bonded, however, over a Château Lafite Rothschild from the late 1950s that retailed in the DC-Baltimore area for the astronomical price of $12.50 a bottle and that came from a winery, as they discovered from their research, that like many Bordeaux operations enjoyed unvarnished critical acclaim.

Then they sipped it.

"Do you all think what I'm thinking?" Parker asked Morgenroth and the rest of the tasting group.

"Yeah!" Morgenroth responded. "This tastes like cat piss."

The disappointment in such a critically vaunted wine echoed into the next decade. Parker and Morgenroth settled into their professions and continued tasting wine together; then wine started taking over their lives. Parker married his high school sweetheart, Pat, a French teacher who had introduced him to fine wine and the palatal delights of France after a visit to the Alsace region in the summer of 1969. They soon began visiting regularly, at least once a year, including Paris for their honeymoon and Bordeaux for the wines straight from their châteaus.

Parker insisted their first place together, a basement apartment just outside of College Park, be kept at 55 degrees for the benefit of the dozens of bottles of wine he stored in the living room on a makeshift wine rack of bricks and wooden planks. They ate cheaply, too—hot dogs, mac and cheese—with Pat grateful for the free coffee she could get at the local public high school where she taught (her $6,900 salary was their only income as Parker studied law). The sacrifices were in service of drinking fine wine nightly, most of it French and a lot of it with friends, whom Parker had begun to pick based largely on whether they liked wine.

Still, after a few years, the financial toll became a sore point between Robert and Pat: Parker was spending up to $4,000 annually on wine. Even with the salary from his new post–law school job working bankruptcy and commercial proceedings at the government-backed Farm Credit Bank of Baltimore, the sums were a stretch. Morgenroth faced a similar financial conundrum. The solution? Join the ranks of those self-publishing wine newsletters. At least then, the two reasoned, they could write off their wine purchases. Not really interested in American wines, Parker and Morgenroth picked bottles of 1973 Bordeaux as the subject of their first newsletter, tentatively scheduled for 1977; they then began mapping how their review would look, which led to the one-hundred-point scale.

If wine critics in the late 1970s used points to rate wine, they more than likely used a twenty-point system that pioneering researcher Maynard Amerine and his staff at the University of California, Davis, devised in 1959. A score of 17 or above indicated an outstanding wine with no defects; a score of 13 to 16 meant a wine was merely normal—not outstanding, but not terrible, either; anything below 13 denoted a wine that really had nothing to recommend it. In the second edition of their 1951 book on wine production, Amerine and food researcher Alexander Joslyn dismissed the idea of a one-hundred-point scale for judging wine: "Although scoring systems of 0 to 100 are frequently proposed, it is difficult for inexperienced judges to distinguish a range of more than 10 to 15 grades, while 20 to 25 is about the usable range possible for experienced judges."

It's not clear whether Parker and Morgenroth knew about Amerine's critiques of the one-hundred-point scale—and it's not clear whether they would have cared. They saw their newsletter as a reaction against the enological establishment that had shepherded them to that awful, and awfully expensive, bottle of Château Lafite Rothschild. The two had devoured the works of Alexis Lichine, Frank Schoonmaker, and other noted wine writers; they were familiar with contemporary critics such as Robert Finigan, who did not use a numbered scale in his reviews . . . and they had found it all so wanting. Parker and Morgenroth hoped to make their newsletter a consumer guide akin to Charles Olken's *Connoisseurs' Guide to California Wine* or Nick Ponomareff's *Grapevine*—though, again, it's not clear whether these Marylanders were familiar with the larger West Coast publications.

The isolation in which even latter-day wine critics operated until about the mid-1990s, and the effects this isolation had on their ideas, has often been overlooked. These were days before widespread use of e-mail, before the World Wide Web, before cell phones; the US Mail might be the fastest communication tool, the nearest public library branch or bookstore the quickest search engine. Budding critics such as Parker and Morgenroth could devise, plan, and execute ways of writing about wine without necessarily being well versed in what was already out there, however deep their general knowledge. This isolation provided the benefit of unsullied confidence. By not fully comprehending the competition, a from-scratch newsletter skewering some of the most venerable brand names in fine wine, complete with a one-hundred-point scale, did not seem so crazy.

Nor did the newsletter's central premise: a fanatical impartiality. Parker and Morgenroth would buy all the wine they rated, taking no freebies from the industry, as they believed too many critics did. (Again, it's likely Parker and Morgenroth simply didn't know the full story, or maybe confused it: some critics, such as Alexis Lichine, wrote from within the industry, but most outside of it do not appear to have been awash in free bottles, with critiques generally stemming from tastings that wineries or trade groups arranged.) They would write in plain English, their tasting notes sure to connect with America's swelling ranks of wine enthusiasts; they would be consumer advocates for wine in the mold of Ralph Nader, who Parker, a fellow lawyer, especially admired for his dogged pursuit of manufacturers when it came to the validity of their products. Their newsletter would pioneer a quietly seismic shift in approaching fine wine as if it were just another consumer product, such as an automobile or baby food, rather than some sort of vaunted gift from the grape gods as so many critics had approached it for so long. It is impossible to draw a straight line from Robert Lawrence Balzer's "Fine wines, like beautiful women . . . " article in the *Los Angeles Times* in 1964 or Hugh Johnson's "mistress of the vine" observation in the

World Atlas of Wine in 1971 to the publication that Parker and Morgenroth had in mind years later.

As it turned out, Morgenroth's employer, the Food and Drug Administration, was not keen on him moonlighting as a wine critic, so he dropped out of the venture right before the launch of the first newsletter in 1978. Parker, whose years as a high school soccer standout still left him with a square jaw and compact frame despite his passionate bibulousness, pressed on, borrowing $2,000 from his mother and charming his way to acquiring mailing lists from area liquor stores and other wine-tasting groups. He paid his legal secretary to type out the first issue from handwritten notes, and he printed some sixty-five hundred copies on an old mimeograph machine. He and Pat, along with his parents, spent a sultry August evening in the couple's living room in Parkton, Maryland—a tiny community of a few thousand souls about thirty miles north of Baltimore—stapling copies of what Parker called the *Baltimore-Washington Wine Advocate.* If the title didn't hammer home his point, both the subtitle—*An Independent Consumer's Bimonthly Guide to Fine Wine*—and Parker's introductory exhortation of "Subscribe now because you may spend $10 for the wrong bottle of wine" did.

True to the newsletter's original conceit, in that first year of the *Wine Advocate* Parker tore into wines he felt didn't live up to their hype, such as the 1973 Bordeaux. The '73 from Château Margaux, one of France's First Growths, was "a terrible wine . . . very thin and acidic with a dull, dumb bouquet and taste. A poorly made wine that should be avoided." Another noted Bordeaux was deemed "atrocious" and "devoid of any redeeming social value." Parker did laud certain vintages that first year. He praised the 1973 Zinfandel from Clos Du Val, the Napa winery Bordeaux transplants John Goelet and Bernard Portet started in 1971, for its "oodles of fruit." Fruitiness would be the one attribute that really seemed to light up Parker's palate based on the number of times he applauded its presence, particularly in the French wines that were finding their ways to the Baltimore-Washington area.

This palatal preference would loom large in his critical career—and large over the American fine wine movement. Much of it stemmed from Parker's self-education; he came to fine wine in a France whose wine-making industry had been transformed by the winemaker and consultant Émile Peynaud in the 1950s and 1960s. Whereas French wines might have been inconsistent in quality and drier in taste, by the time Parker had a whack at them in the late 1960s and early 1970s during those early trips over with his wife, Pat, they were generally lusher and of uniformly better quality. The fine wine Parker fell in love with was fruitier; it was no surprise that he loved fruitier wines later on. And given his status as an American consumer in the late twentieth century, the odds were also in favor of him liking heavier, stronger fare.

Praise for Clos Du Val and for a handful of other fruit-full operations—including the French First Growth Haut-Brion—notwithstanding, Parker mostly reveled in tasting notes that he felt, as he wrote in that inaugural issue, exposed "mediocre and poor wines as well as overpriced wines." Adjectives such as *terrible* were not outside his comfort zone. Though the *Wine Advocate* at first only drew about one hundred subscribers at ten dollars a pop, Parker was convinced he had an audience for such fervently straightforward tasting notes. The thing was, though, all anyone could talk about after a while was that one-hundred-point scale.

GOING MAINSTREAM

1976–1980 | New York City—Egg Harbor City, New Jersey—Slaton, Texas—Snake River Valley, Idaho

A sumptuous photograph of a basket full of baguettes, cured meats, and vegetables, with a bottle of fine wine to its left, filled the screen along with the white blocky words, *The French Chef*. The audience's applause died down, and the culinary tableau gave way to a homey kitchen with a lone soul.

"Welcome, I'm Julia Child," said the comedian in drag. "And tonight we're going to make a holiday feast—or, la fête d'holiday."

It was the December 9, 1978, episode of *Saturday Night Live*, NBC's phenomenally successful three-year-old sketch-comedy show, and everything about Dan Aykroyd's impersonation of America's favorite French chef as she deboned a whole chicken was over the top: the intoxicating effects of the clearly half-drunk glass of red wine, the high-pitched voice, the conversational digressions, the tangential advice ("Save the liver!"), the sharp movements of the chef's tall frame. Aykroyd's skit ended with Child accidentally slicing her hand while cutting the chicken, blood spurting everywhere, the chef's advice for her audience growing more and more disjointed—"Now, every kitchen should have the emergency number written on it somewhere"—before, finally, she collapsed over the counter, but not before chirping her trademark "Bon appétit!"

The real *French Chef* had gone off the air in 1973 after a remarkable ten-year run that turned millions of Americans on to, if not cooking French food, then certainly eating it, accompanied by fine wine. Child remained a talk show staple and routinely published recipes and guides. Her breakthrough cookbook, 1961's *Mastering the Art of French Cooking*, had gone through more than two dozen printings by 1978; she even had a fresh television show in the works, *Julia Child & Company*. So when Aykroyd, a thirty-six-year-old Canadian native who was actually an inch shorter than his target, turned toward the cameras that Saturday night, the audience, in the Rockefeller Center studio and in millions of living rooms, was in on the joke.

The Judgment of Paris in 1976 had not happened in a vacuum. As Jim Barrett's Chateau Montelena and Warren Winiarski's Stag's Leap were providing the American fine wine movement with its single-biggest jolt before or since, myriad events and initiatives were strengthening that movement more and more. The episodic, coastal growth of the movement at the start of the 1970s was snowballing into a more widespread one by the decade's end. Fine wine at all its price points and in all its stylistic iterations was going ever more mainstream.

The numbers by themselves could tell the story. In 1970 Americans consumed 1.31 gallons of wine annually per person; in 1978, that number had risen to 1.96 gallons. In 1970, total US wine consumption stood at 267 million gallons, an impressive enough figure compared with the 163 million consumed in 1960 but paling against the 435 million swallowed in 1978. As for fine wine, Americans drank 133 million gallons in 1970—again, formidable against the 53 million consumed a decade earlier but much less than the 305 million gallons of fine wine Americans quaffed in 1978.

Moreover, fine wine's share of overall wine consumption grew in the 1970s—from about 49 percent in 1970 to more than 70 percent in 1978—strongly suggesting a permanent palatal shift in what Americans preferred when it came to wine. And while it's difficult to pinpoint aggregate production figures for this period, we can gauge that the fine wine output of America's wineries bounced considerably during the 1970s. For one thing, there were a lot more of them: 920 nationwide in 1980, compared with 441 ten years before; and, in California, 508 versus 240. Around this time, nearly two-thirds of the California grapes crushed annually were of the fine wine varieties—the Merlots, Cabernet Sauvignons, Chardonnays, Pinot Noirs, and others that would have been seen as curiosities, if not bad for business, to vineyards less than a generation before.

Within these numbers lay myriad stories that again showed galloping growth. As of the mid-1970s, around twenty states, led by California and New York, had serious commercial wine-making operations; nearly all of the newer ones, and not a few of the ones old enough to have survived Prohibition, staked their futures on higher-end grapes. These operations could be found not only in vastly different parts of the country but in areas never before associated with fine wine.

Southern California, long in the shadow of Northern California, was producing large amounts of fine wine; in particular, the region's central coast, beginning about one hundred miles northwest of Los Angeles, was starting to spawn new wineries as technology trumped what had been considered harsher climatic conditions for higher-end grapes. New Jersey had twelve wineries by 1976—including Renault in Egg Harbor City, the nation's oldest continuously operating winery, which had just started making wines from higher-end grapes, as had a couple of newer arrivals. Around the same time, Carl Banholzer, a founder of the Tabor Hill Winery in Michigan, harvested northern Indiana's first Cabernet Sauvignon grapes for sale through his and wife Janet's eponymous winery in Hesston. "They laughed when I said I was going to grow European wine grapes," Banholzer told a reporter of his Hoosier neighbors. In 1976, Texas's first winery since Prohibition, Llano Estacado, launched in Slaton, seventeen miles southeast of Lubbock; cofounders Robert Reed and Doc McPherson grew their commercial venture out of an experimental winery they helped start at Texas Tech four years before. Llano Estacado was only the second winery in what was then the nation's third-most-populous state; the first Texas winery was the century-old Val Verde, which specialized in generic wines.

Even farther afield that year of the Judgment of Paris, Dick Symms, a fruit farmer and brother of congressman—later senator—Steven Symms, launched a winery he called Ste. Chapelle in Idaho's Snake River Valley. It was the first post-Prohibition winery in Idaho and one of a handful in the entire western United States beyond California, Washington, and Oregon. Symms named his winery for the famed thirteenth-century chapel in Paris and designed it in a way Robert Mondavi would have readily appreciated: vaulted ceilings, lots of wood, cathedral-grade windows for sunlight to pour through—the sort of winery as perfect for production as for tourism.

A SURER THING

1976–1980 | Hudson Valley and Finger Lakes, New York—Sonoma County— Long Island

N ever before in the nation's history had so many people traveled such wide distances to visit wineries and sample their wares the way they were doing by the late 1970s. Robert Mondavi's pioneering emphasis on hospitality as well as production had birthed an outpouring of imitators. Woody tasting rooms accentuated with oak barrels (rare things in American wineries as recently as fifteen years ago), bulbous glasses readily refilled, soaring windows offering expansive vistas, earnest tutorials from knowledgeable staff—these were the physical realities of the newer wineries especially, though the older ones also jumped in with renovations and expansions.

The changes were designed to capitalize on what, in some cases, were extraordinary bounces in tourism. The venerable Christian Brothers, for instance, reported a 20 percent jump in tourism from 1975 to 1976, and Beringer a 12 percent increase, with both Napa operations guesstimating that East Coast tourists were driving the jumps. Two of New York State's prime grape-growing regions, the Finger Lakes and the younger Hudson Valley north of New York City, proved so popular for visitors by the mid-1970s that the *New York Times* cautioned its readers: "[V]intners are independent people. They are liable to shut everything down in the off season to go fishing. So, except for the biggest wineries, it is good to call in advance to make sure they are open and receiving and to check on harvest dates."

The California numbers would eventually swell so much that some smaller Napa and Sonoma wineries simply ceased giving tours—or if they did host them, there were no free samples at the end.

This spike in interest, and the increase in the consumption of fine wine that went with it, spurred a rise in the price of grape-growing land on both coasts. Just as more consumers were piling into the market, so too were investors, often novices as new to the likes of Chardonnay and Merlot as their potential customers. Vineyard land in California was going for $10,000 an acre in the mid-1970s; on the East End of Long Island, it was going for about half that. Both sums represented profound jumps from a few years before, when the fine wine movement's nascent growth seemed a passing fad. Add the Judgment of Paris and the consumer shifts, and owning a vineyard—or part of one—seemed not only a sound business move but a way to enrobe oneself in enviable social cachet: "You're nowhere in San Francisco society if you can't talk about your vineyard," wine historian Leon Adams only half-jokingly put it to the *New York Times'* Frank Prial.

This elitist attitude and the skyrocketing land prices gave birth to one of the biggest misconceptions of the American fine wine movement: that moneyed interests, particularly that subspecies known as yuppies, got involved only later on, in the 1980s and 1990s, after American fine wine was a proven commodity. As we've seen, however, the movement was always the provenance of people with money—or, at least, of people with the means to get it. Robert Mondavi lined up affluent investors as well as financing from Bank of America for his 1965 start-up; Jim Barrett, a successful real estate attorney, gathered moneyed backers, including his client, developer Ernest Hahn, to buy control of Chateau Montelena in 1971; even Warren Winiarski, the ex-academic from the Midwest, built Stag's Leap with generous financial aid from his mother. Winemakers needed a great deal of money to accommodate the hefty start-up costs of new wineries, which could quickly run into the hundreds of thousands of dollars. Plus they often needed to wait several years before vines would produce the appropriate grapes, and too often what these grapes produced, according to an October 1977 *Newsweek* article on fine wine's arrivistes, were vintages of "Chateau Debacle."

A new winery owner, then, needed his or her own capital to blow through, or fresh capital to come to the rescue (or in rare cases, a certain fatalistic comfort level with going slowly but happily broke). Consider Mondavi's life-saving partnership with Rainier Brewing, or the troubles that even a corporation like Pillsbury had making money from its acquisition and expansion of Lee Stewart's Souverain. The high barriers to entry had not changed after the Judgment of Paris—the chances of a payoff had. None other than Coca-Cola, with $420 million in net income, jumped into fine wine in the summer of 1977, Pillsbury's experience be damned. The soft-drink giant, spooked a bit by flattening soda sales, bought control of Sterling Vineyards in Calistoga, California, which had gained notoriety for the pioneering work winemaker Ric Forman had done on Merlot. Foreign concerns were jumping in around the same time: at least ten California wineries were bought in part or whole by investors as far afield as Thailand, Japan, and West Germany.

Nothing illustrated the predominance of moneyed individuals in American fine wine, even before the Judgment of Paris, better than the entry of celebrities. Tommy and Dick Smothers, whose controversial CBS variety show *The Smothers Brothers Comedy Hour* had been the nation's number one prime-time television program in the late 1960s, bought up vineyards in Sonoma County as well as near San Jose; Tom established Remick Ridge Vineyards in 1977 in Sonoma, with its fifty acres for Cabernet Sauvignon, and Dick built Vine Hill Wines on sixteen acres in the Santa Cruz Mountains, initially producing Riesling and Chardonnay. In 1975 the director and screenwriter Francis Ford Coppola—whose Oscar-laden *Godfather* films earlier in the decade represented perhaps the finest hours ever of American cinema, and who was a regular at Alice Waters's Chez Panisse in Berkeley—bought seventeen hundred acres of the Rutherford, California, estate of Gustave Ferdinand Niebaum, the nineteenth-century Finnish immigrant who started the respected Inglenook winery, which his grandnephew, John Daniel, sold in 1964. Coppola, like many Italian Americans of the previous couple of generations, had grown up around wine; it was always at the table in his parents' Long Island home, served to children with water or—preferably, as far as Coppola was concerned—with ginger ale. What he and wife Eleanor called the Niebaum-Coppola Estate reaped its first harvest in 1978.

And lest one assume such celebrity wineries were the playthings of jaded arrivistes, Dick Smothers told a reporter frankly that his winery was not "a hobby" but was in fact designed to make money, as he had already "made a lot of investments that didn't work out." To symbolize his own dedication, Coppola named the wine made from that first harvest—a blend of Cabernet Sauvignon, Cabernet Franc, and Merlot—Rubicon, as in the Northern Italian river Julius Caesar crossed on his way to conquering Rome, knowing there was no turning back. The *New York Times* deemed Rubicon "a wine of extremely high quality that will compete with the best cabernets of California."

For the first time since Prohibition, American fine wine in the late 1970s was a uniformly alluring business for individuals and companies with the means to get in. Yuppies would join their ranks in the coming decade, along with all manner of corporate and individual risk-takers, but they had ancestors in these earlier years attracted not only by the romance of the vine but by the financial prospects. Coppola, for one, put up his winery as collateral for a loan to make the movie *Apocalypse Now*, which came out in 1979.

Newcomers to the industry also enjoyed a level of unprecedented government support, particularly from state capitals. Most levels of government had long held wine at the same legal arm's length as hard liquor, throwing up arduously time-consuming roadblocks, if not to wine's actual production, then to its distribution and sales. Nearly one-fifth of America's counties forbade wine sales outright as late as the early 1970s, such opposition a vestige of Prohibition and the crimes that the manufactured black market spawned. Things started to change dramatically in the late 1970s. More distributors began noticing the rise of American fine wine through the new crop of wine writers that had arisen during the decade's early years; their reviews and news often placed an up-and-coming winery's name and wares before the eyeballs of a distributorship's management.

Moreover, in 1978 the federal Bureau of Alcohol, Tobacco, Firearms and Explosives introduced regulations that codified the concept of varietals (wines made mostly from one type of grape); it was a regulatory watershed that was spurred by the movement's growth. The new rules required wines to have at least 75 percent of a higher-end grape variety before calling itself by that grape. For states such as Texas, which could not yet grow enough higher-end grapes to label their bottles Chardonnay, Merlot, and so on, the rules proved cumbersome. Wineries had to instead improvise generic monikers such as Cibola Roja; these etymological throwbacks to Gallo's Pink Chablis could hurt not only the winemaker's pride but also sales. For states with more established fine wine repertoires, however, the new federal rules proved a marketing boon. Frank Schoonmaker decades before had proselytized that consumers should know what was in their wines, and all the better if their wines contained the best European-style grapes available. The industry, drunk on huge sales of generics, by and large had ignored him; suddenly that industry rushed, where it could, to emblazon its labels with grape types in big, bold letters. Some wineries even upped the federal ante. Oregon, for one, enacted in 1978 a 90 percent grape minimum for wines that wanted to call themselves Pinot Noir or Chardonnay.

As the market for American fine wine grew dramatically in the 1970s, states and local governments swung behind it. Many, knowingly or not, mimicked the Napa County Board of Supervisors' pioneering 1968 creation of the Napa Valley Agricultural Preserve. The legislature of Suffolk County, which covers the eastern end of Long Island, voted in October 1976 to buy up $21 million in development rights throughout the county, leaving the land titles with the farmers already there, many of whom had started growing at least some grapes as New York's fine wine industry picked up steam. In the same year, the state enacted a farm winery bill that allowed small wineries to sell their bottles on-site and also lowered annual licensing fees.

New York's move, which was widely backed politically as well as industrially, was enacted less in response to boosting wine sales—though that was a motive in the nation's second-biggest wine-producing state—than in response to a thirty-thousand-ton grape surplus that left farmers in a financial lurch. Like dozens of other states that would pass bills throughout the 1970s and early 1980s lowering winery licensing fees and allowing on-site sales, New York's farm winery act could be seen as a Trojan horse of sorts: it publicly promoted agriculture, but like Napa County's 1968 preserve, it was really about the fine wine.

BARRELING TOWARD THE BULL

1975–1979 | Sonoma, California—New York City—San Diego

The simply engraved invitation described the May 7, 1977, event as "the Consecration of the New Albion Brewery." It would start at three in the afternoon on Wednesday at the brewery's nearly year-old location in half of a converted grape-processing warehouse in Sonoma, California, and there would be an after-party nearby.

The gathering was reminiscent of the consecration almost eleven years earlier of the Robert Mondavi Winery about twenty miles northeast. There were other parallels as well between the first start-up craft brewery in the United States since Prohibition and the first start-up winery in Napa Valley. Both benefited heavily from research conducted by the University of California, Davis. Jack McAuliffe, New Albion's principal founder, had taught himself how to brew at home while he was a navy mechanic stationed in Scotland, augmenting his knowledge through UC Davis, which had been just as pioneering in beer research as it had been in wine. Both New Albion and Robert Mondavi shared geography, obviously, though the winery was much more at the mercy of climatic variations than the brewery, which could have operated pretty much anywhere McAuliffe found cheap enough space. The two also struggled to turn a profit in their earliest years, relying on the personal salesmanship of their founders and often confronting the blank indifference of a market that didn't know what to make of their products. Theirs were markets dominated by major players all making much the same thing—whether sweet, fortified wines or watery, yellowy lagers—using short-cuts such as additives and pouring money into marketing. Both New Albion and Robert Mondavi also shared a technological prowess born of necessity. In Mondavi's case, it meant pioneering techniques such as stainless-steel fermentation and oak-barrel aging; in New Albion's, it meant things such as rigging an entire brewing system powered by gravity from spare cola and dairy equipment.

Finally, McAuliffe and Mondavi themselves were keenly aware that they stood on the cusp of something. Both knew of Alice Waters's groundbreaking Chez Panisse in Berkeley and admired its emphasis on local foodstuffs; they had spent time in Europe and seen how their respective libations were not only a respected part of the culture but were crafted more deliberately and slowly than in the United States. Mondavi had for decades been immersed in a similar wine-centric subculture in and around San Francisco; McAuliffe had visited that city's Anchor Brewing, America's first modern craft brewery. Home appliance heir Fritz Maytag had rescued Anchor from closure in August 1965 and unwittingly kicked off the American craft beer movement a full year before Mondavi kicked off the American fine wine movement with his sacral groundbreaking in September 1966. The nation's fledgling interest in traditionally made beers from smaller, independent operations was one of many social and economic tangents complementing American fine wine at its point of greatest growth so far. These went beyond the more direct jolts of the Judgment of Paris and the government legislation.

On the other side of the continent, around the same time McAuliffe was cobbling together his brewery in 1976, the posh Four Seasons restaurant was starting what would quickly become the premier East Coast wine-tasting event, if not the most talked-about one in the nation. When the Four Seasons opened in 1959 on East 52nd Street, *New York Times* food critic Craig Claiborne declared it "perhaps the most exciting restaurant to open in New York within the last two decades." The cuisine, he assured the *Times*' millions of readers, was "not exquisite in the sense that la grande cuisine francaise at its superlative best is exquisite." But it was serviceable, ballasted by one of the city's—and therefore the nation's—most extensive French wine lists. Besides, the Four Seasons' decor was what made it stand out in a prosperous Gotham teeming with trendy clubs and restaurants. Its massive plants changed with the seasons; thousands of brass rods hung from the ceiling in the bar area, producing a sculptured chandelier effect; Picassos and Pollocks dotted the walls; a two-foot-deep square pool of white marble, constantly bubbling and watched over by ceiling-high ficus trees at each corner, stood in the middle of the main dining room. It was all so, in Claiborne's words, "spectacular, modern, and audacious." Plus, it was exclusive, in no small part because of its prices; dinner for two, with a bottle of French wine, might run up to forty dollars.

The Four Seasons lost a little of its luster over the next decade as the city surrounding it changed for the worse. By the mid-1970s, however, its new owners intended to restore the restaurant's prelapsarian exclusivity, in part through showcasing American fine wines at what they hoped to again make a fine American restaurant. Paul Kovi and Tom Margittai worked with Gerald Asher, *Gourmet*'s wine columnist and a British expat in San Francisco, to craft "the wine trade's most glittering social event," the California Barrel Tasting.

At least that was the vague plan for the first tasting in March 1976. Who knew if a celebration of American fine wine would take? The menu at the Four Seasons had long been dominated by French wines that sold for roughly twice the price of what that same menu called "domestic" wines—not "American" or "Californian" but "domestic," a dismissive semantic catchall that would gradually disappear from the national wine lexicon after the Judgment of Paris.

Representatives from eighteen California wineries were invited to the first barrel tasting. They were grateful and excited. Warren Winiarski thought his invitation was the first time his Stag's Leap had been taken seriously outside of California. Robert Mondavi's eponymous operation had been trying for years to make serious inroads on the East Coast, particularly in New York; he was happy, as he told the crowd at the second California Barrel Tasting in March 1977, to come "to the center of public relations of the world to tell our story."

As it was, the first California Barrel Tasting was a buzzed-about success. It lasted from around 7:00 PM until well after 2:00 AM, with the winemakers allowed plenty of time to sing their wares' praises as well as declaim on the terroir of California before a crowd of alcohol industry representatives, hospitality managers, journalists, and publicists. The American triumph in Paris two months later only cast a heartening afterglow on the event, and soon Kovi and Margittai were turning away hundreds of would-be attendees willing to pay the price of a good meal for a ticket, since their restaurant was able to hold only two hundred for the tastings.

The owners and Asher dropped the number of California wineries to fourteen after the inaugural event and curtailed the talk time for their representatives; the festivities still routinely went past midnight. More important, every year the Four Seasons' California Barrel Tasting drew a cadre of perhaps a dozen wine writers who, like Asher, were arbiters of taste for the millions of Americans turned on to fine wine in the late 1970s. These writers went forth from the restaurant on East 52nd Street into the pages of their magazines, newsletters, and newspapers to evangelize about the American wines they had just tasted and the people behind them.

The audience for this wine writing was increasingly composed of members of one of the most affluent and educated generations in history: the American baby boomers. It is almost impossible to overstate the economic impact, never mind the social impact, of the approximately forty-three million Americans born from the end of World War II through the beginning of the Kennedy administration in the early 1960s. Their parents spent huge sums on baby products as well as housing, cars, and school construction in the 1940s and 1950s, transforming the national landscape with wholly new suburban communities, complete with those newfangled supermarkets as well as the Interstate Highway System; by 1960, one in four Americans lived in a suburb, a proportion that would only grow. Then, in the 1960s, baby boomers' spending as teenagers started injecting $20 billion annually into the US economy; everything from clothing to television to music catered to their consumer tastes. Four-year college enrollment hit an all-time high in the United States in 1969. Many of these college students emerged in the early 1970s as young, comfortably compensated professionals, further ballast for an economy that, even with the oil embargo of those years and the costs of winding down America's disastrous war in Vietnam, was the financial envy of the world. US households in 1973 collectively earned more than $1 trillion—a record amount for the nation, perhaps for *any* nation.

The baby boomers were the latest members of the newest wine-tasting clubs nationwide. There were, for instance, more than two hundred chapters of Les Amis du Vin by 1977, a tasting club started out of Washington, DC, in the early 1960s. The baby boomers were the passengers on the increasing number of international flights that followed the federal government's deregulation of the airline industry in 1978, which also dramatically drove down ticket prices. These consumers were the ones Adam Strum, the former E. & J. Gallo salesman in New York City, had in mind when he and his wife, Sybil, a television producer, started a mail-order catalog in 1979 out of their attic in Mount Kisco, New York, for wine accoutrements such as corkscrews and glasses. They received one hundred orders for products that first year, though their sales numbers steadily swelled as what they called the Wine Enthusiast Companies quickly connected with more and more Americans who were just that: wine enthusiasts. "We have a bumper crop of wine drinkers and wine cultists now," a restaurateur in San Antonio, Texas, told a reporter from Los Angeles in 1980.

The baby boomers were also the advertising demographic for *Saturday Night Live*, with its Dan Aykroyd spoof of Julia Child. Boomers were the subscription base for new publications such as the monthly *International Review of Food and Wine* (later simply *Food & Wine*) launched out of Manhattan in 1978 by Michael and Ariane Batterby and quickly gaining a quarter-million subscribers; *Wine Advocate*, launched the same year by Robert Parker; and *Wine Spectator*, the magazine that investment banker Marvin Shanken acquired for $40,000 in 1979. Shanken had owned the wine and liquor industry newsletter *Impact* since 1973, but he saw something in the tabloid newspaper *Wine Spectator* published twice monthy by founder Bob Morrisey. Morrisey, a marine major who turned to public relations and marketing as well as wine writing after leaving the service, had started *Wine Spectator* in 1976 out of San Diego, printing three thousand copies of the inaugural twelve-page edition. It broke ground as a consumer source for wine-industry information, though remained, as Shanken put it, "very unprofitable" for years despite a circulation of ten thousand and a bare-bones staff.

Neither Morrisey (born in 1927), who remained *Wine Spectator*'s associate publisher after the deal, nor Shanken (born in 1943), who soon left Wall Street to throw himself full-time into wine, were baby boomers like Parker (born in 1947). Nor was Robert Finigan a boomer; he was thirty-five in 1977, the year his *Private Guide to Wines* went national. Finigan, still based out of San Francisco, made the move after he realized more than 20 percent of his subscribers lived outside of California.

Such generational lines, even those drawn with the thickness of only a few years, are particularly important to the story of the American fine wine movement. For one thing, the fine wine of the 1960s and 1970s differed taste-wise from the fine wine produced in the decades before; this was particularly unmistakable in France, where Émile Peynaud's revolutionary efforts had transformed that nation's wine-making industry, particularly in Bordeaux. Given the high, holy predominance of France, then, its lusher, rounder, fruitier wines could not help but set the trends, including in the United States; Americans growing up and into fine wine in the 1960s and 1970s were weaned on this round and fruity taste.

Moreover, there was time's simple march. People such as Morrisey, Shanken, and Finigan had no real memory of Prohibition, either having not been alive when it was the law of the land before 1933 or being too young to appreciate its ill effects on the wine industry, never mind the nation's wider wine culture. They were old enough, however, to appreciate the changes American fine wine had already wrought, the seismic shifts in preferences and consumption, in production and sales, in attention, both from overseas and domestically.

Baby boomers such as Parker—who was eighteen when Robert Mondavi broke ground on his winery and twenty when fine wine overtook generic wine in sales—were not old enough to have paralleled the movement's transformation. For them, an American fine wine culture, if not a robust industry itself, had always seemed to be there, personified by the likes of Julia Child, heralded by the regular coverage of Ruth Ellen Church, Robert Lawrence Balzer, and myriad others since at least the early 1960s, a staple of popular culture as well as the local liquor store's shelves. Simply put, unlike their elders, the majority of the baby boomers could not really remember fine wine, American or otherwise, as that exotic. This familiarity was about to collide with bull markets in both money and wine.

BE THE JUDGE OF IT

1980 | Chicago

The twenty-five expert tasters sat in crisp white jackets at five V-shaped folding tables in the airy wine warehouse in downtown Chicago. Around them buzzed similarly attired pourers, volunteers from local culinary schools, refilling the phalanxes of tulip-shaped glasses spread before each taster with splashes of Chardonnays from all over the world, including the United States, France, and more unusual locales such as Australia and Bulgaria. Event organizers, representatives from local liquor stores, and Craig Goldwyn, the *Chicago Tribune*'s wine critic, watched it all in whispered quietude. To Goldwyn, what would come to be called the Great Chardonnay Showdown looked like a painting by metaphysical master Giorgio de Chirico—mysterious, yet recognizable. Given the attire and the hushed earnestness, the single-biggest blind tasting ever of the wine style could also have been mistaken for a convention of doctors or busboys.

The idea for the two-part tasting, held during the spring of 1980, came from the Society of Wine Educators, a group Goldwyn cofounded in 1977 to lay down some standards and certifications for industry professionals and judges. The society held regular conclaves, one of which grew into the Chardonnay showdown. Goldwyn, who had picked up where Ruth Ellen Church had left off at the *Tribune*, suggested a Chardonnay tasting because he saw it as "the finest dry white wine in the world," an opinion reinforced by Chateau Montelena's top-place finish at the still-reverberating Judgment of Paris in 1976.

All 221 showdown Chardonnays were culled from Chicago-area stores, itself a notable feat given the fine wine desert that the nation's third-largest city was only a decade before. The twenty-five tasters, who came from across the United States and worked off a twenty-point scale, knew the wines were Chardonnay and in what price range they retailed in the Windy City; otherwise, they knew nothing. The pourers served six wines at a time in numbered glasses every twenty minutes for four hours, with ten-minute breaks; that translated into about forty-four wines for each five-judge panel. The wines were pared to a final nineteen, which a ten-judge panel then whittled down to a final winner a couple of weeks later. The winner was a Chardonnay by Mike Grgich—the same Mike Grgich who made the triumphant Chardonnay at the Judgment of Paris.

Grgich had left Jim Barrett's Chateau Montelena shortly after the world-rattling victory and struck out on his own, fulfilling the American dream he had rolled into Napa Valley with on that Greyhound bus barely two decades before. He partnered with Austin Hills of the San Francisco–based Hills Bros. Coffee company to open Grgich Hills Cellar off Highway 29 in Rutherford, breaking ground on July 4, 1977—Independence Day. The winery's first vintage was the Chardonnay from that year, made from Sonoma County grapes; its victory in the Great Chardonnay Showdown in 1980 put Grgich's new operation on America's ever-expanding enological map. A decade and a half would pass after the win before Grgich Hill's production satisfied consumer demand for its Chardonnay.

The importance of critical acclaim, or disdain, in American fine wine had ballooned by the 1980s. The previous decade had seen in the Judgment of Paris the single most influential event in American fine wine. Take away the French judges' accolades for Chateau Montelena, Stag's Leap, and a handful of other high-ranking California wines, and you take away much of the growth in stature, if not sales and production, of American fine wine. It would have grown through the 1970s, make no mistake, but Steven Spurrier's contest had raised the stakes, made careers, and dramatically realigned consumer expectations. As Bo Barrett, Jim's son and Chateau Montelena's new wine-maker, put it, the Paris triumph pushed the American fine wine movement ahead twenty years in a day. Expert tastings were important when it came to a drink that might vary from harvest to harvest or be altered by variables as diffuse as the weather and the artificial lighting on a liquor store shelf; the labels might stay the same—the winemakers and the vineyards, too—but the wine could change vintage to vintage, season to season.

As could the price. The prices of wine in the United States, both imported and domestically produced, appear to have outpaced inflation during the 1970s, the decade of American fine wine's most pronounced growth in terms of visibility. One analysis compared wine prices in Washington, DC, in 1973 with wine prices in the capital in 1979 and concluded that "wine inflation was about one hundred and fifty percent, almost the same as ground beef, while increases on all consumer goods averaged about one hundred percent over the same period." A bottle of American fine wine that might have cost $3.99 in 1973 cost $5.99 in 1979; the increase in cost for French First Growths was even steeper. This was at a time when, as Frank Prial noted in the *New York Times* in June 1975, "most American consumers [thought] a $4 bottle of wine [was] a rather expensive proposition."

Some wineries, of course, saw more pronounced price growth than others; as we've noted, Chateau Montelena and Stag's Leap were both able to raise the prices on their Chardonnay and Cabernet Sauvignon following their wins in the Judgment of Paris. Wines from the grand châteaus of Bordeaux, despite dramatic drops in wholesale prices in the mid-1970s, still commanded formidable markups in the States, particularly in restaurants. Oddly enough, the prices these higher-end French wines fetched at US auctions sometimes outpaced what they went for on liquor store shelves in cities such as New York, suggesting that simply publicly bidding on wine could accrete to it an artificial premium. In general, whatever the source and wherever it was sold, prices for fine wine in the United States appear to have risen—and risen sharply in many instances—leading up to the 1980s. To consumers, it was all so maddeningly arbitrary.

Add to this madness an unprecedented boom in five-figure bottle sales, often through highly publicized auctions that might move thousands of bottles in a single day. In 1978 a restaurateur from Memphis named John Grisanti paid $18,000 for an 1864 Château Lafite. The following year, Syracuse, New York, wine merchant Charlie Mara paid $28,000 for a bottle of 1806 Château Lafite at an auction in Chicago—or $1,120 an ounce, roughly four times the price of gold then. The year after that, in 1980, Grisanti again set a single-bottle record, paying $31,000 for yet another bottle of Lafite, this one from 1822. Interspersed in those years were more modest purchases of around $14,000 to $16,000.

The auctions were like gambling, according to an employee of Heublein Inc. The company had started hosting an annual auction in 1969, the same year the food-and-drink giant bought the Beaulieu winery in Rutherford, California, with the august British wine critic and merchant Michael Broadbent as auctioneer. Some bottles at the auctions didn't always get what their sellers wanted, further muddying the pricing waters for consumers on the lower ends of the pricing scale who might read about the results in major newspapers and magazines. They might read, too, about scandals in the wine world, including the doctoring of millions of bottles of Bordeaux and Burgundy through no-nos such as the blending in of lower-quality wines from less-regarded regions.

All this market distortion, coupled with the reality that prices at the wholesale and retail levels were indeed going up, put tasters at events such as the Great Chardonnay Showdown in positions of unusual power. They became arbiters not only of taste when it came to wine—which vintages, wineries, regions, and even nations were better than others—but also of the economics of the industry, in a way that critics in most other fields could only dream of. The government was little help, preferring to leave price-setting to the free market and sticking instead to fresh regulations regarding styles. The Bureau of Alcohol, Tobacco, Firearms and Explosives did develop what it called American Viticultural Areas (AVA); they were in the mold of France's oft-copied Appellation d'Origine Contrôlée, a sort of seal of approval letting consumers know wines originated in certain areas with certain reputations to maintain. Curiously enough, in another sign of the American fine wine movement's growth, in June 1980 the feds designated acreage centered on the town of Augusta, Missouri, about forty-five miles west of St. Louis, as the first AVA; Napa Valley would follow in 1981.

The tasters themselves were scant help when it came to pricing. There were not really any uniform tasting standards or benchmarks, or even ways of conducting blind tastings. Some tastings, for instance, might use all the same bottles covered in brown paper bags or toweling; others might pour from the bottles the wine came in, the bottle type and size sometimes a dead giveaway for the wine's national or regional origins. Some tastings might involve tasters sampling dozens, perhaps hundreds, of wines in a single day, certainly a reality for individual critics churning out newsletters, magazines, and guidebooks. Other tastings, and other critics, might limit themselves to a handful of wines daily. Some spit out the wine, others swallowed. Some took care to avoid certain foods before a tasting that might affect their palates, others simply sidled up and got on with it. Some rated by stars, others by points, still others by letters (and the points, as we've seen, could run to twenty, fifty, one hundred).

The lack of uniformity was not for want of trying. In a 1979 speech, no less eminent a personage than the by-then-retired Maynard Amerine, whose research at the University of California, Davis, had done so much to move higher-end grape cultivation forward in the United States, urged wine writers to adopt a stricter methodology when it came to judging wine. In 1981 Craig Goldwyn founded the Beverage Testing Institute, aimed at "producing fair and impartial wine reviews for consumers." As Goldwyn and others saw it, the measure of accuracy was repeatability. Too much variation in wine-tasting results, and what good were they to consumers, retailers, wholesalers, and the wineries themselves?

Calls for such measurement and methodology fell on deaf ears. By the 1980s, subjectivity was in, objectivity was largely out. Or, to be more precise, objectivity was subjective. Individual critics and tastings set their own methodologies and standards; and their judgments oftentimes set prices throughout the spectrum of American fine wine as well as for imports. This led not only to a notorious flowering of adjectival redolence as the swelling ranks of wine critics struggled to put into words their verdicts on bottle after bottle of often the same style, but to more power for critics—for one critic in particular. The vast sea changes that the American fine wine movement had experienced in the 1970s would pale against what was coming next: an era when the underdog found itself top dog.

TUSCANY, CALIFORNIA
1981 | Napa Valley

Rushing trumpets blare as a panorama of San Francisco Bay shrinks to a Rolls-Royce Silver Cloud II as it races northward on the Golden Gate Bridge. The scene bleeds seamlessly into a shot of the same car cutting across a two-lane highway through fields that do not become entirely clear until the camera peels away to reveal them as lush, green vineyards, which give way to an opulently apportioned white mansion. Then suddenly appears a crest straight out of medieval heraldry superimposed on the image of a falcon, its wings splayed and talons clenched—finally, as if to dispel any confusion, the words *Falcon Crest* splash across the screen. "*Dallas* with grapes" had hit prime time.

The hour-long soap opera *Falcon Crest* premiered on CBS at 10:00 PM on Friday, December 4, 1981. It centered around the seamy adventures—the opening scenes involved a murder and the cover-up after—of a wine-making dynasty presided over by the elegantly ruthless dowager Angela Channing, played by Jane Wyman (she was the one in the Rolls-Royce in the opening credits). Set in a fictitious California grape-growing region called Tuscany Valley, *Falcon Crest* unapologetically piggybacked on America's relatively newfound interest in fine wine. Not only were there innumerable geographical clues—the shots of Tuscany Valley were taken in Napa Valley, the road that Channing/Wyman's Rolls sped down was Oak Knoll Avenue near Highway 29, and so on—but the show's creator, Earl Hamner Jr., conceived of the drama after a trip to France piqued his interest in fine wine. Hamner, who shot to TV's A-list after creating *The Waltons* and who originally titled his new creation *The Vintage Years*, even owned vineyards around Sacramento.

While critics derided *Falcon Crest* early on as little more than a knockoff of its fellow CBS franchise *Dallas*, where the money came from oil instead of grapes, it soon became a breakaway hit, the first successful new prime-time drama of the new decade, one of the ten most-watched shows in all of American television. Within a couple of seasons, more than twenty million households weekly were watching Angela Channing and her vine-powered brood scheme.

Falcon Crest, of course, exaggerated the wealth of most American wine-makers, as well as their familial drama (the Mondavi brothers perhaps excepted). It did, however, reflect how far wine had come in American pop-ular culture. Not even a generation before the assumed accoutrement of an often-imagined elite or the exotic beverage of foreigners and first-generation immigrants, fine wine had become fodder for a prime-time smash created by a television writer who had bought vineyards because he saw them as "a good investment."

Such a hearty sentiment in itself reflected the ever-widening American fine wine movement. In 1981 the number of American wineries crested one thousand for the first time since before World War II. More than half were in California, though they continued to pop up in states as varied as Texas, Indiana, New Jersey, Idaho, and Hawaii. In 1980 Emil Tedeschi, son of a Napa Valley vineyard owner, and wife Joanne bottled Hawaii's first commercial wines from a grape called Carnelian cultivated on the island of Maui; developed at the University of California, Davis, the grape was a hybrid of Cabernet Sauvignon, Grenache, and that juicy Prohibition-era workhorse, Carignan, meant to yield a slightly fruitier version of Cabernet that Tedeschi Vineyards hoped to start selling in 1984.

There would undoubtedly be a market for it. Analysts who once might have talked of a dwindling number of American wineries, and fine wine consumers, suddenly spoke boldly of ever-growing sales. There were commercial wineries in at least thirty-six states; in New York, still the runner-up to California, the number of small wineries had doubled from 1979 through 1981 to around fifty, following the state's farm winery bill. At the start of the 1980s, Americans were drinking more wine than at any time since Prohibition—roughly half a billion gallons a year—and most of that was fine wine.

Such an appetite came amid a national economy providing many reasons to drink—all of them the wrong ones. The United States had been in a recession since at least July 1981, though the economy had been in a funk for years. The Dow Jones Industrial Average, the best measure of the health of publicly traded companies in the United States, was on its way to a recession low of 776.92 in August 1982. Double-digit inflation "seemed a permanent curse," as did high interest rates; home buyers might pay more than 10 percent on a mortgage loan. Major industries such as appliance manufacturers and automakers reported dismal production statistics and lackluster consumer demand. Perhaps most depressing, the new Reagan administration warned Americans to expect a high unemployment rate for several more years.

Then things began to turn around. The nation would soon be able to look back at the early 1980s as an economic nadir, a holding pen for a bull market that tore through the remaining years of the decade, which were a rapacious time personified by shows such as *Dallas* and *Falcon Crest*, with their amoral characters' lust for money. It was an era of generational change as the baby boomers asserted their claims to the reins steering finance, commerce, the arts, politics, media, universities, you name it. It was a time of excess and hubris, and fine wine was not exempt. It, too, would ride that bull.

WINE FUTURES

1980–1981 | Washington, DC—Manhattan

Phyllis Richman needed a wine critic. The newly minted food editor of the *Washington Post* was busy running the newspaper's dining and cooking coverage as well as writing its restaurant reviews, which meant at least a couple of nights out a week incognito, parsing the District's commercial cuisine. (Richman was so good at maintaining her anonymity that some in the restaurant trade were convinced her feminine name was nothing but a pseudonym to mask the man behind the reviews.) Her predecessor as food editor, William Rice, had written the *Post*'s wine column, but he had gone to New York to edit the two-year-old *Food & Wine* magazine.

Rice, an Upstate New York native who had studied at the famed Le Cordon Bleu cooking school in Paris as well as worked in a restaurant in Burgundy and on a vineyard in Bordeaux before returning stateside, had hired Richman as restaurant critic in that revolutionary year of 1976. The *Washington Post* was still a paper basking in its Watergate afterglow, the third-biggest daily in circulation behind the *New York Times* and the *Los Angeles Times*, read not only by the denizens of Capitol Hill and the West Wing but by the increasingly affluent residents of suburban Maryland and northern Virginia, areas that had seen explosive growth in population and real estate prices in recent years.

Richman had always been into food and drink and writing, making her an anomaly as a teenager in postwar Greenbelt, Maryland. She put her writing aside at Brandeis University, however, intimidated by her better-prepped peers, and instead pursued a master's in sociology. Along the way, she did time in the Philadelphia City Planning Commission while taking urban planning classes at the University of Pennsylvania; and she also lived in West Lafayette, Indiana, where "there wasn't much to do," but where her husband had landed a teaching job at Purdue University.

When she and her family returned to the DC area, she rekindled her love for writing, freelancing as a restaurant critic for newspapers and magazines in Baltimore and Washington—earning sometimes no more than a hundred dollars per column, which was also expected to pay for the food reviewed—and for national publications, which paid considerably better. She made perhaps her biggest splash nationally after *Esquire* bought her tongue-in-cheek idea for "The Watergate Gourmet," reviews of restaurants identified in the Watergate hearings from the angle of privacy. When the *Post* came calling, Richman, whose master's thesis in sociology had mercifully fallen apart, took a pay cut to work at the newspaper edited by Ben Bradlee Jr., the old Kennedy associate, and published by Katharine Graham, whose position as publisher of the *Washington Post* made her one of the most famous women in the world.

It was a sign of the ubiquity of wine criticism that it was understood that Rice would be replaced when he left in the fall of 1980. A newspaper of the *Post*'s prominence simply had to have a wine critic by that point. Maybe not on staff, like at the *New York Times*—where Frank Prial then shared wine-writing duties with financial reporter Terry Robards—but there had to be *somebody*. Richman was inundated with offers to be the *Post*'s new wine critic. All the comers seemed perspicaciously versed in both American and European vintages as well as aware of the sea changes that had washed over the wine world during the previous several years. It was an enviable position no editor would have found herself or himself in a decade before: so much fine wine knowledge and such a willingness to write about it.

To separate the wheat from the chaff, Richman decided to hold a blind tasting over two nights. She selected several California Pinot Noirs and Cabernets, sheathed them in brown paper bags, and invited about a dozen people—both the aspiring wine critics and random guests—to Katharine Graham's private dining room at the *Post* headquarters just north of the National Mall. Absurdity ensued. Nobody guessed which wines were which, and almost nobody could tell that on both nights two of the wines were duplicates of others already in the tasting. Worse, the random guests overall did about as well in identifying wines and wine styles as the applicants. These applicants, Richman realized, were fine writers who knew the nuts and bolts of the expanding American wine world, but none would make a decent critic for a place like the *Post*.

Still, the tasting gave her an idea. Several people mentioned the name Robert Parker Jr.; a few of the applicants even pitched a feature on the man, though Rice himself had already written about the suburban Baltimore lawyer and his self-published, subscriber-driven newsletter for the *Post*. Richman, who hired Parker at $150 per bimonthly column, was impressed with what she saw as Parker's "pitch-perfect taste" and could tell that he had a lot he wanted to say.

Another editor of Parker's around this time echoed Richman's observation. Two of William Rice's first hires at *Food & Wine* were Elin McCoy and John Frederick Walker, a married couple, whom he brought on as wine editors. Parker by that point was using any excuse to visit New York City, and at Rice's suggestion he dropped by the magazine's Midtown headquarters to meet with the couple in their office during one of his trips in 1981. His big, tall frame seemed to fill the office, making it feel immediately cramped. That and he was carting a couple of cardboard wine boxes as well as an envelope stuffed with recent copies of what was by then simply called the *Wine Advocate*. He started talking, according to McCoy, in "an excited, nonstop style, the words rushing out and spilling rapidly over one another." The boxes, he excitedly explained, held half-sized bottles of a vintage from the First Growth Château d'Yquem that he'd just found—just found!—at a wine shop around the corner. "What a coup!" he exclaimed.

That was Parker: a bubbling cauldron of enology, always up for wine talk, sniffing out finds for himself and his growing number of subscribers. That number would climb to seven thousand by the end of 1982, devilishly close to enough to allow the thirty-five-year-old Parker to quit his day job. The *Wine Advocate* already dominated the lives of him and his wife, Pat, including their finances. They traveled to Bordeaux at least twice a year, beginning in 1978, and Parker made other excursions in pursuit of vintages perhaps unfamiliar to his readership; he also continued to buy the wines he tasted, eschewing free samples from wineries. He wrote in a tiny spare bedroom in their Parkton, Maryland, house and usually tasted alone in the kitchen, sometimes with Pat, their weekends and nights given over to wine, Parker increasingly only grudgingly clocking in at the Farm Credit Bank of Baltimore. While he did surround himself with a group of supportive friends who also helped out in blind tastings, his wine work remained mostly a solo pursuit, a mixture of doggedness and self-assuredness, Parker still taking his intellectual cue from Ralph Nader. He literally saw himself as what his newsletter was called: an advocate on behalf of the consumer in a rapidly expanding American wine marketplace.

Parker was different—or, more to the point, presented himself differently—than just about any wine critic with a serious following. About a month before his visit to *Food & Wine*'s offices, the magazine had hosted Hugh Johnson, the Cambridge University–educated British critic who had penned the canonical *World Atlas of Wine*, published in 1971. To McCoy, the contrast could not have been starker: Johnson was "very much the great man holding court" for an hour in the magazine's dining room, recounting bibulous excursions to famed châteaus and other enviable real estate, all in a clipped and practiced accent that seemed to drip exclusivity; Parker, on the other hand, had a warm and inviting smile, "almost Midwestern," and seemed uncomfortable in his suit and tie. Even compared with Robert Finigan, the leading American wine critic who could be just as blunt in his judgments, Parker came off differently. Perhaps it was that Finigan was educated at Harvard in the early 1960s and Parker at the University of Maryland in the late 1960s; or that some of Finigan's critiques read as whiny, while Parker's were shorn of all emotionality save for that reserved for the wine; or maybe it was just that Parker wrote about more wines that more people could afford. He wasn't exclusive, he was Everyman.

As such, Parker continued to think of his tasting notes—direct, acerbic when they had to be, unadorned always—as what drew readers in and guided their purchases. Meanwhile, his wine scores from the one-hundred-point scale he and Victor Morgenroth devised were starting to pop up next to bottles on store shelves, an instantly recognizable metric for any American who'd gone through high school. Parker might describe one particular Cabernet as having "the finesse of a horny hippopotamus," but it was likely the low score that stuck with consumers when they hit the liquor store. He had readers in places as varied as Detroit and Richmond, Virginia, never mind the great cities of the East, such as Washington, Baltimore, Philadelphia, and New York. Many of them came to the *Wine Advocate* through their local wine merchant, who was often the first subscriber in a particular geographic area.

Parker's geographic reach spread without the newsletter as well, first with the *Post* column and then, following that 1981 visit to the Manhattan offices of *Food & Wine*, his first magazine piece. It was published in March 1982, and based on a rather wry assignment from McCoy and Walker: taste and find the most drinkable jug wines on the market. As for his first newspaper column, published on the front page of the *Washington Post* food section on Sunday, May 31, 1981 (and blasted to other outlets on the *Post*'s formidable newswire), Parker picked an auspicious topic, given what his writing would spawn in just the next couple of years: wine futures, the buying of vintages while they're still in the barrel, and less expensive, with the anticipation that the commercial price for the wines will later increase, perhaps dramatically. Phyllis Richman had introduced the columnist to *Post* readers a few weeks before, explaining Parker's growing influence not just regionally but nationally: "In the meantime, our notes on Robert Parker read: young and fresh, clean, a touch of sweetness with a nice balance. Enough backbone so you can expect him to develop well over the years . . ."

THE BIRTH OF THE WINE BAR

1974–1979 | San Francisco—New York—Chicago—Washington, DC

The Sunday before Robert Parker's first column, the *Washington Post* ran another article on wine. It began with a simple enough question: "What is a wine bar?" The answer turned out to be complicated, especially in the United States.

Fine wine in post-Prohibition America had never been a drink for bars or pubs; it showed up in restaurants, of course, and at bars, for that matter, though those bars undoubtedly served liquor, beer, and food as well. But Americans had never made it a habit to stroll to their local pub for a glass of wine the same way they might drop in for a shot and a beer. That began to change through the introduction of the wine bar in the late 1970s, which speaks again to the larger sea change that American fine wine underwent in that decade.

The first American wine bar was the incongruously named London Wine Bar, which opened in 1974 in San Francisco's Financial District. From there, the concept, like the American fine wine movement itself, trickled eastward, though it would be several years—decades even—before wine bars started popping up in major cities, never mind smaller ones. The first post-Prohibition wine bar in New York opened in 1979, for instance, the first one in Chicago in 1994. Still, the American wine bar was enough of a reality at the start of the 1980s for Frank Prial to try to explain to his *New York Times* readers exactly what it was:

> A modern wine bar is, more or less, an attractive tavern where glasses of wine are served by people reputed to know what they are doing. Bottles are available, of course, but the true function of a wine bar is to serve wine by the glass. And not just any wine.
>
> A Frenchman elbows his way to the counter at his neighborhood snug, drops a coin on the zinc and says "Beaujolais." The bartender replies: "You got it."

A New Yorker hoisting himself—or herself—onto a bar stool at, say, the Wine Bar in Soho, will say, "Do you have the '81 Georges Duboeuf Beaujolais Villages?" To which the barman might answer: "No, we prefer the Paul [Beaudet] or the Jadot. We had a staff tasting, and the Duboeuf came off just a smidge too tannic."

Prial's imagined exchange at the Wine Bar in Soho, that first Gotham wine bar, said a lot about who frequented these and who staffed them, as well as a lot about how wide and varied many Americans' fine wine knowledge had quickly become. Unlike their counterparts in France or Great Britain, where they had caught on with particular fervor, American wine bars reveled in wide selections. San Francisco's London Wine Bar offered some 350 wines; the Wine Bar in Soho had up to 40 wines available by the glass at any one time; the Carlton Wine Bar in Washington, DC—the capital's first successful wine bar, dating from 1979—offered patrons approximately 100 wines, most of them American made. These wine bars also usually served food, though dining was not the focal point, nor were other drinks. That seemed the salient feature of American wine bars: wine was the focus to the exclusion of just about every other beverage except water; take away wine as the angle, and a wine bar became a bar that served wine.

Make no mistake: wine bars wanted to move wine, not merely to provide ambiance for tipplers. A Frenchman might be encouraged to spend a couple of hours sipping his cheaper Beaujolais; an American was expected to order more than one glass, if not an entire bottle, of the more expensive Paul Beaudet or Louis Jadot. It was both practical and financially sound for American wine bars to push their wares in ways that were aggressive by international standards: the wine had to be sold before it spoiled. Some wine bars adopted Cruvinets, airtight cabinets full of nitrogen gas to prevent oxidation in opened bottles and therefore to help them survive longer unspoiled; but the best protection against wasting a bottle on one or two glasses was selling that many glasses more until it was empty. Enter the sommelier.

THE GONG SHOW

1977–1981 | Seattle

The Chinese gong would sound and a red-suited figure crowned by a turban would then stride into the dining room of Seattle's Olympic Hotel, the swanky Jazz Age inn on University Street. The inquiring patron would be told to order a bottle of First Growth French wine, likely the menu's priciest selection. Such was the work before the 1970s of the only sommelier in Washington State's largest city. It was a mix of theater and the hard sell: put on a show because questions about fine wine were so rare, and selling a bottle of it was such a big financial deal to the restaurant. Diners at the Olympic were otherwise apt to order the latest generic from California.

The titanic growth of the American fine wine movement in the 1970s had already boosted wine-related tourism to areas such as Northern California and Upstate New York, as well as expanded the coverage of fine wine in newsletters, magazines, and newspapers. The growth also turned wine expertise on its head, seeding fertile ground for an explosion in the ranks of sommeliers, wine stewards, and masters of wine. The American industry had difficulty defining these titles, all of which had been around for years in different semantic iterations.

The sole prerequisite for any of these titles seemed to be a deep knowledge of wine, one that went beyond appreciation or trivia. It was not enough, for example, to know the First Growth châteaus of France; a sommelier or a steward needed to know which recent vintages were worth a patron's money, and why. Training became paramount. A sommelier's education might come through the industry itself—Foremost-McKesson, perhaps the nation's biggest distributor of wine and liquor, ran the California Sommelier Academy, which in the early 1980s charged $800 for its six-day courses—or the training might come through more independent bodies, such as the elegantly titled Court of Master Sommeliers, a British trade group started in 1977. Finally, a sommelier's training might simply come through a sort of homeschooling, including visits to wine bars and the increasing number of restaurants with extensive wine lists, as well as regular consumption of the widely expanding canon of wine writing.

Larry Stone traveled all three training routes. A precocious youngster growing up in Seattle in the 1950s and 1960s, he entertained and impressed his parents by guessing styles from wine samples he was not allowed to swallow; admittedly, the dearth of fine wine in the city eventually made his guessing easy. He moved on to making wine—and whiskey—as a teenager, all the while voraciously reading Hugh Johnson, Steven Spurrier, and especially Alexis Lichine. He traveled in Europe as a Fulbright scholar, visiting major wine regions as well as gastronomically inclined relatives in the Austrian capital of Vienna, the entire time considering wine a pleasure, however intensely enjoyed, and not a career path. He had visited some of the earliest post-Prohibition Napa Valley wineries with his father in the 1960s; they seemed such bold, foolhardy affairs. One winery owner would leave bottles for Stone's father to in turn leave cash for, an honor system that worked in that pre-tourism era before the Judgment of Paris changed everything. Stone, too, knew of the gong-rattling sommelier at the Olympic Hotel in his hometown. Neither that nor the wineries seemed a way for a young man with a felicity for both language and science to make a living.

Yet during what would turn out to be a decade-plus run toward a PhD in comparative literature, a friend recommended in 1981 that Stone interview for an assistant sommelier job at the Red Cabbage restaurant on the Seattle waterfront; it was perhaps one of two or three sommelier positions in the entire city. Stone aced the interview with the restaurant's owner, who ripped queries directly from Lichine's *Encyclopedia of Wines & Spirits*, a book in excess of seven hundred pages that Stone had all but memorized. The owner gave the arriviste the Monday and Sunday shifts, not exactly the busiest days at any restaurant, but Stone was happy, as it would afford him more time for academic work. Soon, though, he was moving more wine on those two days than the head sommelier was moving on Fridays and Saturdays. So the owner replaced him and made Stone the head sommelier. Soon Stone was no longer an academic, at least not in any official sense. He went on to train in the 1980s through the Court of Master Sommeliers, becoming America's ninth master sommelier (the first, Eddie Osterland, a would-be behavioral psychologist, was crowned in 1973).

Stone's path—a mixture of self-education and industrial certification that led from enthusiast to professional—became more common as the new decade wore on. Like with wine bars, however, the rise in the number of sommeliers and wine stewards was slow and sporadic. These wine professionals primarily worked at high-end restaurants and novel wine bars in the nation's largest cities, and their presence (and training) made a significant difference in the number of bottles sold. A master sommelier, for instance, could move twice as many bottles of wine as could a wine steward. Stone was living proof that having a sound mind for wine encouraged customers to purchase more—and better—bottles. The number of customers at these restaurants and bars swelled in the 1980s, as did the prices of fine wine. Sommeliers, and experts in general, came to represent the best and the worst of the American fine wine movement as it barreled further into the new decade.

UGLY DUCKLINGS

1979–1984 | Beverly Hills—Bonny Doon, California

The Great American Pinot Noir. The idea hove into Randall Grahm's view in the late 1970s at just the right time in his life. Grahm was born in 1953 in Los Angeles and went to school in neighboring Beverly Hills. In the early 1970s, he decamped a few hundred miles up the coast to study philosophy at the University of California, Santa Cruz, and there led an easeful lifestyle famously typical of that college town; but it was quickly leading him nowhere.

Then he discovered fine wine. First, while spending a summer in Europe, he met a woman in Denmark who made elderflower wine in her bathroom, a straightforward enough process that nevertheless struck the young Grahm as some sort of alchemy. Then in 1975 he got a low-end job sweeping floors and stocking shelves at the Wine Merchant in Beverly Hills, the shop restaurateur Dennis Overstreet started in 1971 and that eventually amassed a celebrity clientele not unlike the concern that Robert Lawrence Balzer's family ran in Hollywood forty-odd years before. Overstreet allowed his staff to sample top-flight wines, including French First Growths. Grahm was hooked; he was eventually promoted to salesman at the Wine Merchant, his knowledge gaining depth though not necessarily breadth. He expanded his wine repertoire by leaving his philosophy degree unfinished at UC Santa Cruz and, after taking the requisite science courses at UCLA, enrolling in UC Davis's vaunted Viticulture and Enology Department, which Maynard Amerine and Albert Winkler had made industrially famous. In 1979, nearly a decade after starting college, Grahm—who resembled John Lennon during that ex-Beatle's New York City years, with round glasses, a thin nose, and long hair—completed a degree in plant science. He then set his sights on, as he put it, developing the Great American Pinot Noir.

It would be a steep climb and an even steeper learning curve. Pinot Noir had never been a very popular grape in California, and the wines it undergirded were never that critically great or commercially popular. As late as 1960, the single-biggest block of Pinot Noir vineyard in Napa Valley was likely the seventy acres of Louis Martini's eponymous winery off Highway 29; outside of Napa and Sonoma Counties, in the rest of California, there were few acres of the grape. Earlier attempts at its successful cultivation in the state, including at James Zellerbach's Clos de Vougeot and Jay Corley's Monticello Vineyards & Winery, were as notable for their quality as for their very existence. According to one history of the grape in North America, by the 1960s and 1970s most California Pinot Noirs "were not just disappointing or mediocre; on the contrary, they were plainly flawed and actively unpleasant." Charlie Olken's *Connoisseurs' Guide to California Wine* would frequently describe Pinot Noirs from the 1970s as "dull" and "short." In hindsight, critics would blame the grape's often heavier-handed treatment during fermentation and aging, noting that Pinot Noir grapes might be a little more delicate than other high-end red wine grapes, such as Zinfandel or Cabernet Sauvignon. Wineries only compounded the problem by adding lower-end grapes, such as that old, plump workhorse Carignan, to fill out body and color as Pinot Noir invariably lost both during the aging process.

Whatever the reasons, by the late 1970s Pinot Noir was not a promising wine style for a California vintner, especially a new vintner such as Grahm. Older, more established wineries, such as Heitz Cellars and Sterling, dropped their Pinot Noir lines during this time. Lusher-tasting Cabernet Sauvignon was the money grape when it came to red wine—the Judgment of Paris and the ensuing media attention had made sure of that. Even before the 1976 tasting, Cabernet Sauvignon's post-Prohibition creep in California had been trending exponentially upward. Surveying the scene in 1964, Albert Winkler found that Cabernet Sauvignon's California acreage increased 133 percent from the 1950s to 1963—more than fourteen thousand acres in total. It blew past twenty-five thousand acres at the time of the Judgment of Paris, becoming the second-most-planted higher-end variety of red wine grape in the Golden State behind only Zinfandel. It went on to best that, though, in the century's closing decades, with Cabernet Sauvignon emerging as the undisputed commercial king of red wine grapes in California; the failure of Pinot Noir to catch on only buoyed its fortunes. In the wine world as in other businesses, oftentimes nothing succeeds like success.

Still, Grahm pressed on with his dream of popularizing Pinot Noir. He used family money to purchase a vineyard in the Santa Cruz Mountains, about seventy-five miles south of San Francisco, in an area called Bonny Doon, which he took as the name of his winery. Grahm then set about joining the pantheon of California vintners who made so-so Pinot Noir—he later chose the word *prosaic* to describe the finished product. He also realized that the Pinot Noir grapes he was growing in California had nothing on the quality of the ones grown in Oregon. Rather than continue producing passable plonk from the mercurial grape, Grahm reached into his past. During his time at UC Davis, he had patronized the Berkeley wine shop of importer Kermit Lynch, whose stock included higher-end wines born in southern France's Rhone region. If American consumers had found Cabernet Sauvignon obscure before the Judgment of Paris, these grapes—ones such as Grenache, Syrah, and Mourvèdre—were positively anonymous. Most were barely grown anywhere in the United States, including in its top grape-growing state, California, and they were rarely used in any domestically made fine wines. After consulting Lynch and conducting research on his own, Grahm decided nonetheless to stake his reputation on these "ugly duckling grape varietals."

The move proved pioneering. Bonny Doon's first commercial release was a twelve-hundred-case run of a blend that Grahm called Le Cigare Volant, after the French slang for "flying saucer" and in reference to actual anti-UFO legislation Rhone officials enacted in the 1950s. Indeed, harvested in 1984 from vineyards beyond Grahm's original Pinot Noir spread and released in 1986, Bonny Doon's blend was out of this world for American-made fine wine. It was 72 percent Grenache, 25 percent Syrah, and 3 percent Mourvèdre. Pleased critics struggled for years to describe the taste these three rarely blended grapes produced; "earthy" popped up a lot, as did "black cherry" and "licorice." Part of this struggle stemmed from Grahm—who was ever willing to experiment once he was free of his Great American Pinot Noir pursuit—changing up in subsequent vintages the ratio of grapes, giving each release a subtly different taste, which only seemed to increase the wine's allure. Bonny Doon never produced more than 3,600 cases annually of Le Cigare Volant during the 1980s, and it remained more of a cult hit rather than a commercial smash. Still, Grahm's move into Rhone varieties, and a later move into Italian grape types, opened an intellectual pathway for other vintners, not to mention the move made him a star. *Wine Spectator* slapped him on its April 1989 cover beneath the block-lettered tagline, THE RHONE RANGER.

Grahm is decked out in Lone Ranger attire, complete with eye mask and sidearm, his left hand holding the reins of a white horse. The attention, and the nickname, only emboldened him to focus more on Grenache, Mourvèdre, and others. The grapes might not have been as financially remunerative as Cabernet Sauvignon, or Chardonnay when it came to whites, but Americans *could* still produce enviable fine wines from them.

The predominance of those two titanic stalwarts of French fruit, Cabernet Sauvignon and Chardonnay, in American fine wine production is one of the little-explored aftershocks of the Judgment of Paris. The triumphs of vintages made with those grapes marked the beginning of "the end of history" for American fine wine–making according to one analysis that charted the growth in Chardonnay and Cabernet Sauvignon acreage in California from the Judgment of Paris in 1976 into the next century. In a paper subtitled *Winning Is Winning Forty Years after the 1976 Judgment of Paris*, Susan Arrhenius and Leo McCloskey noted that there were 20,345 acres producing Cabernet Sauvignon grapes in 1976; that placed the grape second among higher-end varieties in California, behind Zinfandel, which was itself behind the old workhorse Carignan. Chardonnay wasn't even in the top five.

Randall Grahm, founder of Bonny Doon and a pioneer of American fine wines that are not Cabernet Sauvignon or Chardonnay.
COURTESY OF BONNY DOON

What a difference a generation made. By 2012, at more than ninety-five thousand acres, Chardonnay would cover more of California wine country than any other grape, higher-end or otherwise; Cabernet Sauvignon would be second with just more than eighty thousand acres. This coverage sprang directly from consumer—and therefore winery—demand for the grapes. Zinfandel ran a distant third with fewer than fifty thousand acres (Carignan, to no one's surprise, was no longer in the top five). Pinot Noir, interestingly, would be the fifth-most-planted in 2012, at around thirty-nine thousand acres, representing a generational sea change as winemakers figured out how to make the more delicate grape work for them. For the foreseeable future, though, it was all about finding ways to make Chardonnay and Cabernet Sauvignon—not Pinot Noir, and certainly not the likes of Grenache and Mourvèdre—work in a US marketplace bigger than most could have imagined a decade before.

GRAPES THAT CAN FIGHT

1983 | Glen Ellen, California—Lake County, California

One day in 1983, Mike Benziger was meeting with his winemaker, Bruce Rector, at the Glen Ellen Winery in the Sonoma County area of the same name when the phone rang. It was Benziger's father, Bruno Benziger. He was in a sales meeting with a New York distributor on behalf of the winery, sipping Scotch, as was his wont; the elder Benziger had had an idea.

He was an ex-marine who fought in World War II and pioneered the importation of Scotch while at the family firm based in White Plains, New York. In 1979, Mike, one of Benziger's seven children, moved to California to learn winemaking. By 1981 his father joined him and the two, along with several other relatives, bought a winery and began building it up on an eighty-five-acre ranch in Sonoma with a restored farmhouse dating from the nineteenth century. It did a respectable trade in both generic and fine wines, shipping fifty thousand cases annually. Still, Bruno Benziger was rooting around for more cash flow. Thus the sudden phone call from the other side of the continent.

He asked his son and Rector, "Could you guys put in 25 percent more Chardonnay to the Proprietor's Reserve White, and we'll call it Chardonnay?"

The pair was skeptical. Rector knew that his boss would not want to introduce a new product without the sales demand for it in place first. Besides, what exactly was this new product that Bruno Benziger was proposing? Glen Ellen's Proprietor's Reserve White was half Chardonnay and half French Colombard, a widely planted, lower-end grape often used in the brandies Cognac and Armagnac. That extra 25 percent would tip it to 75 percent Chardonnay and, under federal labeling regulations for varietals, allow the winery to market it as a Chardonnay rather than as a generic white. The inclusion of the cheaper French Colombard would allow for a lower price than a typical California Chardonnay in the early 1980s. Benziger's technical knockout, a fine wine at a lower price, harbingered a coming divide in the American industry and marketplace.

Still, what to call this new blend? Weeks later, during another well-lubricated sales meeting, this time with Glen Ellen's California distributor, Bruno Benziger threw out the phrase "fighting varietals" while discussing wines that wineries utilized to gain market share. The neologism stuck. Glen Ellen would release that 1983 Proprietor's Reserve Chardonnay two years later, sparking gigantic sales jumps in American fine wine. Glen Ellen's own numbers told the tale: its output ratcheted from those fifty thousand cases annually in 1983 to more than two and a half million cases five years later. As many as fifteen trucks would pull up to and depart from the winery every day, dropping off empty bottles and leaving with full ones to satiate demand. It wasn't just the low price—Glen Ellen's suggested retail price for its Chardonnay was five dollars for *two* bottles—but the wine's presentation. Like other wineries dealing in fine wine, Glen Ellen clearly listed the higher-end grape variety on the label; in fact, the biggest word on the label was the grape name, as loud a visual trumpet as one could blow to show this was not generic plonk. Should that somehow be lost on the consumer, Glen Ellen had a backup: its bottles, the same 750ml ones that had become the standard for fine wine, were corked.

Beginning January 1, 1979, the federal government required all newly bottled wines and liquors to come in one of six different metric sizes that replaced earlier nomenclature such as "miniature," "half-pint," "pint," and so forth that might have been harder for consumers to grasp. Fine wine gravitated toward the 750ml size, which replaced the old "fifth" container and equated to about twenty-five ounces in nonmetric terms. Europe soon followed the United States, and fine wines by the 1980s were uniformly arriving on American shelves in 750ml bottles.

As for corks, the wood-derived seals had been a staple of wine packaging for centuries. Despite the very real possibility of damage to wine due to a cork's occasional porosity, a certain ritualistic romance had attached itself to the cork—or, more to the point, to the uncorking of the cork. The screwtops that topped most generics, on the other hand, were considered cheaper—they were, in fact, from a winery's perspective—as utilitarian and unremarkable as the grapes that had made the wine they sealed. So Glen Ellen's packaging for its 1983 Proprietor's Reserve Chardonnay contributed mightily to creating what George Taber, the chronicler of the Judgment of Paris, described as "a classy, attractive product at a reasonable price."

These were fine wines with which Americans could play tentative ball, even more so than the White Zinfandel that Bob Trinchero's Sutter Home popularized several years before. White Zinfandel was not as familiar a style for consumers, having largely disappeared for decades; Chardonnay and the other fighting-varietal styles were. Like Trinchero's White Zinfandel, though, these freshly introduced wines were retailing for relatively low prices. If ever there were, or would be, gateway wines in the American fine wine movement, fighting varietals were them. Other wineries would rush into the breach that Glen Ellen cleaved, including more established brand names that—though they might not have adopted Bruno Benziger's moniker "fighting varietals"—saw a market for less expensive fine wines produced in small part with lower-end grapes.

Glen Ellen's biggest initial competitor proved to be one of those more established names. Kendall-Jackson, the Lake County, California, concern Jess Jackson and Jane Kendall started in the mid-1970s, released its Vintner's Reserve Chardonnay in 1983 in corked bottles with an elegantly simple label playing up the grape type, the winery, and the vintage year. It was critically praised as well as served at the Reagan White House, and it helped power the winery to sales of one million cases within ten years. None other than generic giant E. & J. Gallo released what it called a vintage Chardonnay in 1983, priced at five dollars a bottle, as inescapable a nod as any to the potential market that fighting varietals had opened for American fine wine in general.

Much of the growth of fighting varietals had to do with the changing US wine marketplace, where drier fine wines were consistently outselling sweeter generic ones. While variations on the maxim that "Americans were drinking less, but better" seemed omnipresent in industry coverage in the early 1980s, it was wrong: Americans were drinking more wine than at any time since Repeal—and better stuff, at that. California's Wine Institute estimated that the average American put away 2.25 gallons of wine in 1983, the year the fighting varietals started storming the marketplace, up from around two gallons in both 1979 and 1980, and way up from the approximately 1.33 gallons in 1970. Americans per capita were drinking about five more 750ml bottles of wine a year at the start of the 1980s than at the start of the 1970s. (Most of these bottles were likely white wines; that shade of the grape accounted for perhaps 70 percent of the wine consumed in the United States by 1980, red's market share having steadily dropped since the early 1960s.)

There was another reason for fighting varietals' success, for their very existence, in fact: lots of good grapes. Years of planting ever more higher-end grape varieties had left the wine-making industry with a major surplus. Napa County's crop reports illustrated the trend markedly: In 1973 Chardonnay vines covered 1,702 acres. In 1983 the grape covered 5,662 acres. At the same time, the acreage of that post-Prohibition workhorse, Alicante Bouschet, dropped to twenty, from an already paltry fifty-eight in 1973. Demand for the fruits of higher-end grapes had risen sharply, though not enough to consume all that were being harvested each year. That meant that wineries could buy the grapes more cheaply and pass the savings on to consumers, providing, as Bruno Benziger put it to a reporter, "plenty of good wine at ridiculous prices." Take away the wine-grape surplus—some even called it a glut—and it's unlikely varietal smashes such as Glen Ellen's or Kendall-Jackson's Chardonnays would have been possible, at least not at the prices they were offered. Frank Prial broke it down in the *New York Times* the week before Christmas 1983: "Even if every year is a good year for fans, 1984 bids fair to be even better than usual. Put as simply as possible, there is a lot of excellent wine around at very attractive prices." With Gallo's vintage offering, Prial predicted that "1984 may see more Americans drinking fine wine than ever before."

A good thing for France. Like California in the United States, its main wine-making region needed to move some bottles, too.

WHEN ROBERT MET ROBERT

1982–1983 | Bordeaux—Manhattan

The news traveled fast around the eighth annual California Barrel Tasting at the Four Seasons in New York City: Robert Parker was back from Bordeaux. The tasting had become, in the words of one regular attendee, "the single most important event on the New York wine calendar," a kind of gastronomic Olympics that could decide the critical and commercial fates of California's newest vintages. At the tasting, the restaurant served seven courses, not including dessert, each accompanied by six wines, including barrel samples from the 1982 vintage; the final course, for instance, was filet of venison served with a half-dozen Pinot Noir samples. The tasters knew where the wines came from, and they were expected to taste them fully. Four Seasons owners Paul Kovi and Tom Margittai insisted guests swallow, not spit, invariably turning the five-hour dinner into a boozy, if not decadent, affair as the sampling thoroughly lubricated the latest industry gossip. Topic No. 1 on this particular Monday, March 21, 1983? The Bordeaux wines from the previous year, which would soon be available for sale.

Parker had gone to the Four Seasons in Manhattan directly from John F. Kennedy International Airport in Queens, having jetted in from Paris that day. He had spent seven straight twelve-hour days tasting his way through Bordeaux, sampling the 1982 vintages from château barrels and interviewing many of the winemakers. He had arrived in France's premier wine-making region apprehensive about what he would taste. Parker was a fan of Bordeaux, his fine wine epiphany—like those of so many other Americans—having come in France, through French wines. The terroir of Bordeaux yielded an immense grape harvest in September 1982, swelling with dark-skinned, juicy grapes grown during what turned out to be freakishly ideal weather: warm, dry, some rain, but not too much. Parker worried whether such huge volume could translate into the sort of concentrated, fruity wine he and others had come to associate with Bordeaux. Or would the grapes translate into another vintage of watery, thin wine?

After the extraordinary run following World War II due in no small part to the exertions of consultant Émile Peynaud, Bordeaux had had a string of unremarkable years. Critics found several vintages in the 1960s, particularly the 1965, subpar. Then, after a couple of good years to kick off the decade, the vintages of the 1970s fared similarly poorly, with the 1973 a particular bugbear of critics. Parker himself found the wines of that rain-drenched harvest "lightish" and used it as the metric against which he measured the potential of the 1982. Bordeaux had been solid from the tail end of the 1970s through 1981, though it produced nothing particularly stunning—there had not been a stunning Bordeaux vintage since 1961, critics agreed, and perhaps only five in the entire twentieth century so far.

The uneven performance only exacerbated the financial woes of Bordeaux winemakers. A major labeling scandal as well as an anemic French economy and a drop-off in exports drove down prices for Bordeaux wines 50 percent in the early 1970s. At the same time, several Bordeaux winemakers, including First Growth giant Château Margaux, struggled with debt to the point of having to sell, and an abnormally abundant 1979 grape harvest left châteaus with more wine than they could sell at the higher prices they wanted, further depressing revenue. Couple all of these dire indicators with the twin existential shocks of losing to the Americans at the 1976 Judgment of Paris and so many middling vintages, and it was clear: like an aging pop star hoping to stage a comeback, Bordeaux needed a hit.

This explained the buzz about Parker at the California Barrel Tasting. It wasn't necessarily that this was the first one that he had attended; Parker, careful to cultivate his outsider image for the *Wine Advocate*, was based in suburban Maryland, well outside of Gotham's media orbit. Nor was it necessarily that he was a wine critic for the *Washington Post* and the publisher-editor of a newsletter that by then counted more than seven thousand subscribers. It was instead, simply, that he had been to Bordeaux and tasted the latest vintage.

The châteaus had already engineered a fair amount of publicity surrounding the quality of the '82 Bordeaux. Frank Prial wrote in the *New York Times* at the beginning of March that "early signs indicate that the 1982 vintage in Bordeaux is going to be one of the greats," the region having benefited from "a California summer" of warm, sunny days. Terry Robards had written in the same pages a few weeks before that it was "too early to know how the wines will evolve, but the early prognosis is that the vintage will turn out to be the best since 1961, although it may lack the longevity of that great year." French critic Michel Bettane went even further, calling '82 the best Bordeaux since 1929. Peynaud, who consulted for dozens of wineries, said the '82 could turn out better than the '81, which he had given a seventeen and a half out of twenty. Peynaud was one of the few commenting on the vintage who had actually tasted it. Parker was one of those few, too. His fellow critics at the barrel tasting wanted to know one thing, then: what did he think of the '82 Bordeaux? Elin McCoy, his editor at *Food & Wine*, popped the question.

"Phenomenal," Parker replied, though he found it strange to be talking France at a California tasting. "They're great!"

As emphatic as his answer was, it wasn't entirely clear what Parker meant. He was undoubtedly excited about the vintage. Normally a serene flier—he jetted to France at least twice a year—he had been nervous on that day's flight, fearful the plane would crash before he could tell the world of the quality of the '82. He had jammed his black notebook during his tasting tour with adjectives such as *blockbuster, stunning, heavyweight,* and *incredible*. He had torn through Bordeaux at breakneck speeds in his rental car, fitting in as many châteaus in a day as he could. Parker had done all of this before, though. He was known in the industry and to his readers as an unabashed Bordeaux partisan, a not-unusual position—the region had produced some of the world's best wine for centuries.

Parker had spent years peppering the *Wine Advocate* with high scores and rhapsodic praise for Bordeaux wines. He had bestowed a ninety-four on the 1975s from the region's Pomerol area, one of his highest vintage scores to date; the Barsac/Sauternes from the same year rated a ninety. It would not have been unusual, then, for Parker to praise the latest wines from Bordeaux or even to praise them highly, especially given that other critics such as Bettane, Prial, and Robards, as well as the highly respected Peynaud, a force in the shaping of modern French wines, had already nodded to the quality of the '82s. (Nor, we should note, would it have been extraordinary for Parker to hammer the region's wines, as he had done in the past, doling out seventies and low eighties, or ignoring years altogether.) Parker's Bordeaux praise, or condemnation, would surely have receded into the general din of buzz already building about the latest offerings from France's top, though troubled, wine-making region.

Later during the barrel tasting, as the West Coast winemakers continued to extoll their offerings and the Four Seasons' waitstaff diligently refilled oft-emptied glasses, McCoy and her husband, John Frederick Walker, introduced Parker to Robert Finigan, the nation's top wine critic. The two had never met. It's not entirely clear if they had ever communicated by phone or mail, either. Finigan later claimed that Parker had reached out to him when he launched the *Wine Advocate* in 1978; Parker said he had never heard of Finigan before then.

Parker's unfamiliarity might have been understandable at the time, though in the ensuing five years Finigan's star rose well beyond its San Francisco horizons. His *Private Guide to Wines* had gone national, with more than ten thousand subscribers; he was a frequent guest of Alexis Lichine at his Bordeaux château and Fifth Avenue apartment; he seemed to know everybody in wine, from restaurateurs such as Alice Waters to importers such as Kermit Lynch to scores of vintners and merchants, including Steven Spurrier before the Judgment of Paris. A rating of *Outstanding* from Finigan could send bottles flying off shelves, if not move the sales needle on an entire vintage nationwide; Parker himself would come to think of Finigan as "the dean of wine writers." Erudite, lean, forceful, the Harvard-educated Finigan cut a fearsome figure. Parker was no slouch himself: he opined in the *Washington Post* and *Food & Wine*, had thousands of subscribers of his own, and had access to wineries on both sides of the Atlantic. But he was still the arriviste, a thirty-five-year-old suburbanite commuting most weekdays fifteen minutes or so to an office park just outside of Baltimore for a day job specializing in uniform commercial code and bankruptcy law at the Farm Credit Bank. Finigan did wine full-time. And at forty years old in 1983, his dominance of wine criticism seemed unassailable, a kind of lexical fortress no other American writer could breach.

After McCoy and Walker introduced the two Roberts, they fell into polite conversation about the topic of the evening: the '82 Bordeaux, which Finigan had also recently sampled in its natural habitat.

The older critic was aloof, cool to the younger man's enthusiasm for the vintage. Finigan had been disappointed by it, underwhelmed even.

Parker was shocked. If he really writes that, he thought, he's gotta be a fool.

The two parted ways. Finigan would not remember meeting Parker at the barrel tasting; Parker would never forget meeting Finigan.

"A MONUMENTAL VINTAGE"

1983 | Parkton, Maryland

Robert Parker introduced the twenty-sixth edition of his newsletter with an urgent message:

This volume contains my annual preview report of the new Bordeaux vintage, in this case the 1982s. The format of *The Wine Advocate* has been changed for this issue only, because of my extensive notes on this marvelous vintage, which is destined to be one of the very great years of this century. I have also reassessed the 1981 Bordeaux vintage and provided an updated report on this very good, but somewhat irregular vintage. If this issue seems too Bordeaux oriented, I apologize, but I believe the consumer is **now** in the best position in the last twenty years to take advantage of the buying power of America's strong dollar to stock up on some sensational Bordeaux wines. What has happened in the last five years in Bordeaux is unparalleled in the history of the region. Never have there been four out of five vintages of such quality, and even the off-vintage of 1980 is not nearly as miserable as so many irresponsible journalists have indicated.

The edition was a love letter to Bordeaux, complete with a history of Parker's recent visit to the region as well as a summation of the conditions that had "produced very great wines, the quality of which I predict will go down in the annals of Bordeaux wine history with such legendary vintages as 1929, 1945, 1947, 1959 and 1961." To remove any ambiguity possibly left by this effusive language and the very abnormality of the edition's layout, those remarkable years were splayed in big, blocky font across the upper middle of the first page with ". . . 1982!" following "1961."

Parker closed the issue on April 11, 1983, three weeks after the California Barrel Tasting and his first encounter with Robert Finigan, whose lukewarm assessments of the '82s so flabbergasted him. Finigan had already committed those assessments to print, though not yet to his subscribers, by the time of the run-in with Parker at the tasting. The March 30 edition of Finigan's *Private Guide to Wines* dismissed the '82s as—yes—"disappointing," even "oafish," with too much alcohol and too little subtlety, the traditional hallmarks of wine from such a high grape yield. As to all the buzz about the vintage, Finigan warned: "No—the proverbial thousand times no—it was not the 'vintage of the century.'" It's clear from all accounts that when Parker stepped onto Manhattan's East 52nd Street outside the Four Seasons at the end of that raucous, revelatory spring evening, on his way back to Maryland and his day job as a commodities and real estate attorney, he knew his assessment of the '82s would stand in stark contrast to that of the most powerful wine critic in America.

He would not be alone in his views. Though the legend would build that Parker was some sort of enological John the Baptist, solitarily telling a disbelieving English-speaking world of the coming of the '82 Bordeaux, he was one of several critics then touting its merits—and he was not the first. Frank Prial assessed the '82s for an immensely larger audience than the *Private Guide to Wines* and the *Wine Advocate* combined in his March 9 missive for the *New York Times* about his own tasting trip through Bordeaux. "Everything in the wine," Prial wrote of one château visit, "supported the now widely prevalent prediction that 1982 could be one of the major vintages of the last few decades. . . . Across the board, the '82s easily outclass the '81s, and it must be remembered that '81 was a very good year." Where Prial put forth the conditional *could*, however, Parker went for broke.

Take Finigan's critique that the '82s were too high in alcohol, too in your face, a view other critics shared, including Craig Goldwyn, the organizer of 1980's Great Chardonnay Showdown who would eventually take over Parker's role at the *Washington Post*. Bordeaux wines were traditionally balanced and complex, with the alcohol resting amid that complexity and not predominant. To Parker, the alcohol's unexpected predominance, spurred in part by the unusually warm weather right before the harvest, was one of the three reasons the '82s were so exceptional, the other two being their dense color and their "unbelievable lushness, richness and fat, fleshy character." Parker appeared to adore the heaviness of the wines, the zestful fruitiness, the very lack of subtlety that Finigan had expected—had hoped—to find in a Bordeaux vintage. The "astounding" alcohol content—in the case of the Cabernet Sauvignons, several châteaus reported their highest natural levels since 1947—contributed mightily to this character, in Parker's singular opinion. Similarly alcoholic Merlot grapes used in Bordeaux's Pomerol section, in particular, produced "astonishingly rich, fat, full-bodied, intensely flavored wines." Where Finigan and others saw problems, Parker saw only glory.

Ironically, the sole chastisement in this love letter to Bordeaux concerned alcohol content. "As spectacular as the red wines are," Parker wrote, "the dry white wines of Graves are good, but seem too alcoholic and lack the finesse of the very finely made 1981s." In the next sentence, he dismissed the sweeter dessert wines of the Sauternes and Barsac areas of Bordeaux as "very mediocre" this go-round. Otherwise, the *Wine Advocate*'s twenty-sixth edition heralded an unabashed triumph for Bordeaux wines. In another break with tradition, Parker dispensed with scores in this edition, instead going into detail about different areas and châteaus of Bordeaux and the wines they had produced; he also speculated in-depth about the price of Bordeaux thanks to the "tremendous consumer interest in the 1982 vintage." A region that had teetered financially of late, within a nation still teetering, might, Parker wrote, see "price increases of 8% to 20% for the 1982 Bordeaux over and above the 1981 vintage." He was perhaps the only critic to be so precise that year in his pricing estimates for Bordeaux as well as in advising his readers on whether they should buy futures of the '82s (his effusive praise told them yes without actually saying so). He would declare in a newsletter in early August that he was "absolutely certain that the wines in most demand will be significantly more expensive (perhaps as much as 70 percent more) in two years." Eventually, Parker advised his readers to "buy as much great 1982 as you can afford because there may not be another vintage this great for 50 years."

It was in a later issue that Parker unveiled his regional scores for the '82s. The Bordeaux from St. Emilion rated a ninety-four; those "fat, full-bodied, intensely flavored wines" from Pomerol got a ninety-six; and the Bordeaux from St. Julien, Pauillac, and St. Estophe—Parker gave each of those a ninety-eight, a de facto perfect score in that he had yet to award a ninety-nine or a one hundred to any vintage from after the 1960s (and there had been only three other ninety-eights).

These wine scores, as well as the tasting notes that accompanied them, could soon be found in liquor stores nationwide, square declarations taped to shelves beneath, beside, or above the prized '82s. More frequently, subscribers clutched the newsletter itself as they searched, often in vain, for bottles from the vintage. Parker's scores from earlier newsletters for earlier vintages, from both the United States and Europe, got a second look and invariably received their own spots on the shelf, a rating system too eye-grippingly good for retailers to pass up. The *Wine Advocate*'s subscription base swelled toward twenty thousand, and Parker quit his day job as an attorney before the end of 1983. He was able to do wine full-time then, including writing books on Bordeaux for Simon & Schuster. Parker's became an enviable life of marathon tastings—often more than one hundred wines a day in his revamped kitchen in Parkton—interspersed with travels to the world's finest wine regions, his scores the most powerful currency in fine wine since perhaps the French growth appellations devised in 1855.

Later critics of the vintage swung snugly behind Parker's take, too. Marvin Shanken's *Wine Spectator*, for one, came out in August 1983 with two articles by James Suckling lauding the '82s. As for those such as Frank Prial who had offered more conditional praise, their assessments tumbled down a historical rabbit hole, never to be institutionally heard from again by the industry or the public. A happy Bordeaux also swung behind Parker's reviews—helped not in the least by the publicity efforts of an Alexis Lichine miffed at Robert Finigan's dismissal—welcoming him into a widening circle of wineries and merchant offices; Parker was sought after not only for the sales-spurring scores he might bestow but for hints he might drop regarding how to achieve those high marks. As for Finigan, the most powerful American wine critic never recovered from insufficiently praising the 1982 Bordeaux. His *Private Guide to Wines*, as he and his approximately ten thousand subscribers knew it, would cease publication within two years, and subsequent iterations would fail as well, his "Outstandings" and "Averages" ground underfoot by "98s" and "90s."

Robert Parker's assessment of the '82 Bordeaux was the third and final great event in the history of the American fine wine movement. Like the opening of the Robert Mondavi Winery in 1966 (but unlike the Judgment of Paris ten years later), it would take a while before the movement felt the impact of Parker's critique. When it was felt, the '82s undoubtedly became, in the words of Eric Asimov (who would eventually segue into Frank Prial and Terry Robards's role at the *New York Times*), "possibly the most significant wine vintage ever. Well, maybe that's an exaggeration, but certainly the most significant of the last fifty years, and arguably of the twentieth century." He noted that Parker "made his own reputation" with his praise for the vintage, in the process opening up "a wonderful world for a new generation of wine lovers." To Asimov, the '82 Bordeaux was unavoidable when considering fine wine in America:

> The soaring trajectory of interest in wine owes much to revolutions in technology, transportation, communications and food in general, but it all traces back to 1982.
>
> It's a clear dividing line between the end of the old way of making and thinking about wine, and a new way that, for better or worse, defines our current age.

From 1983 onward, the story of American fine wine becomes an exploration of the aftereffects of the clear dividing line between Parker's gushing praise of the '82 Bordeaux and Finigan's lamentation of the same. This divisive nature itself explains why any history of American fine wine has to include the critical assessment of a vintage from a French region down on its luck. The '82 Bordeaux arrived at a convergence of trends: the peaking of the spending power of the baby boomers; the unpenning of an international economic bull market; Americans' ballooning interest in all things enological, manifested by new publications and tastemakers, wine tourism, and voyeurism (think: the auctions); greatly increased sales through the fighting varietals and White Zinfandel; even one of the biggest television shows in prime time. On the earlier side of the dividing line, before 1983, things were simpler, with fewer characters and a clearer-cut trajectory toward critical respectability and commercial success for American fine wine. On the other side of the line drawn by the '82 Bordeaux is a more complicated movement, with many more players—and a lot more at stake.

PART IV

24 BRIX

1983–1984 | Syracuse, New York—San Francisco

"Wait until the world hears about this bottle and then buy two seats on a flight back to Syracuse—one for you, one for the bottle," beer critic Craig Goldwyn told Charlie Mara, owner of the Green Hills Liquor Supermarket in that city in Upstate New York. "And call your store manager, and have him send an armored car and an armed guard to the airport."

Mara took Goldwyn's advice regarding the 1806 Château Lafite bottle he'd won at a Heublein-run auction in Chicago in 1980. The sheer ostentatiousness of Mara's precautions, not to mention the victorious $28,000 bid, garnered quite a bit of publicity for him and his shop; reporters even awaited him on the tarmac in Syracuse. Three years later, and thanks to another mammoth bid, Mara enjoyed a similar burst of publicity: he became the new owner of the sole twelve-bottle case of Opus One, a Cabernet Sauvignon born of a collaboration between the Robert Mondavi Winery in Napa Valley and the Château Mouton Rothschild in Bordeaux.

Opus One had been anticipated for years by 1983. The two wineries connected in the late 1970s and started production on the wine in 1979. In 1981, while it was still in barrels, its creators entered it in the first-ever Napa Valley Wine Auction, held on a torturously hot June day beneath a big white tent on the grounds of the Meadowood Country Club. Bidders and vintners alike buzzed about the case of what Mondavi and Rothschild had decided to call Napamedoc for lack of a better placeholder. The blend of Cabernet Sauvignon, Cabernet Franc, and Merlot—harvested from the To Kalon vineyard and made entirely at Mondavi's winery in Oakville—was expected to fetch around $3,000, maybe $10,000 on the outside, though it would not be ready for years and would not be ideal for drinking for years more. The bidding for Opus One was a bet on the future—and the bettors went big.

The price for Opus One quickly soared past $10,000; six bidders remained, Mara among them. The auctioneer, noted critic and merchant Michael Broadbent, began calling out ever-escalating amounts: $12,000, $15,000, $20,000. Finally, Broadbent called $24,000. His hand trembling, Mara raised his bidding paddle.

There was a pin-drop quiet pause. No one topped Mara, and Broadbent rapped his gavel. Mara's $24,000 was the most anyone had ever paid for a case of American wine. In late 1983, Robert Mondavi, no publicity virgin himself, came to Syracuse to present Mara with it. A gold plaque affixed to the case included both men's names.

Wine critic Craig Goldwyn serving the 1806 Chateau Lafite that Upstate New York wine merchant Charlie Mara bought at auction for $28,000 in 1979. (To Goldwyn's right is wine critic Terry Robards.) Such highly publicized auctions only increased the aura of exclusivity surrounding fine wine in America.
COURTESY OF CRAIG GOLDWYN

As for the wine in the case's bottles, it received mixed reactions. Robert Parker found it "not a great wine. And certainly not a good Cabernet Sauvignon value." Still, "it was an interesting, well-made, distinctive and balanced wine." Terry Robards, who had begun writing for the *New York Post*, described it as "basically a very good California wine that will please most knowledgeable consumers." What really grabbed critics and consumers alike, however, was Opus One's marketing—including its price. Frank Prial warned *New York Times* readers the week before Christmas that the new bottles would "sell in the neighborhood of $50 a bottle. That's $600 a case, but maybe some stores will give a 5 percent case discount." This was at a time when top-shelf Champagne bottles in the United States sold for about $20 each. And, of course, there was Mara's winning bid (for a case of wine he had yet to taste) as well as Mondavi's personal delivery of the embossed case.

Taken together, the facets of the wine's aristocratic pedigree—the higher price tag, the record auction amount, its Napa creator's personal, publicized touch—signaled to many that Opus One was the start of something not altogether good for American fine wine. Shortly after Mondavi and Rothschild unveiled their Napamedoc at the Four Seasons' annual California Barrel Tasting in March 1984, Parker (by then the nation's most powerful critic on the subject, having belted Robert Finigan from his pedestal with his raves for the 1982 Bordeaux) put it this way in the *Washington Post*: "The hoopla surrounding the Opus One joint venture will, I suspect, always overshadow the wine itself." Parker also deemed Opus One's advance press "hysteria."

There had always been a touch of hoopla and even hysteria in American fine wine. Robert Mondavi, the godfather of the movement, had proved a master in moving bottles from almost the beginning of his independent winery in 1966; he opened sales avenues for other Northern California vintners that would have been inconceivable beforehand. The movement, moreover, had grown up with a phalanx of writers happy to both criticize and evangelize new wineries and new styles as well as trends. What was different about the likes of Opus One and much of what took hold wine-wise in the mid-1980s was the scope. Bigger, stronger, pricier—that seemed the mantra, the precipitation from the perfect storm of baby boomer spending power, technological advances, critical triumphs, and a general go-go ethos that infused the nation's way of doing things after, as President Jimmy Carter famously put it in the 1970s, a "crisis of confidence."

Examples abounded. The fourth annual Napa Valley Wine Auction in June 1984 featured a Nebuchadnezzar, a "vulgarly large" vessel, as one observer put it, sufficient to hold the equivalent of twenty 750ml bottles. The entire auction yielded $402,650 in winning bids, including $3,000 for a bottle of 1974 Cabernet Sauvignon from Chateau Montelena, Jim Barrett's Calistoga winery that only a decade before was struggling to find its footing; the auction total far surpassed the $250,000 mark organizers thought it would reap.

Wine Spectator's third California Wine Experience in November 1984 at San Francisco's Fairmont Hotel drew seven hundred people willing to pay $450 a pop to taste ten thousand bottles of wine from forty thousand glasses, all at a cost to the organizers of $250,000. The experience featured not only a reception with Robert Foxworth, a star of *Falcon Crest*, that television smash about a California wine dynasty, but seminars led by critical luminaries such as Michael Broadbent and Hugh Johnson. These lectures moved with a sometimes brusque efficiency, one attendee drily noting that "the organizers of the seminars behaved more like Caligula than Dom Perignon."

By the mid-1980s the United States boasted more collectors of expensive wines than any other nation, a state of affairs that manifested itself in lavish marathon tastings of famous vintages. A Miami lawyer threw a tasting of bottles from each of the sixty-one classified châteaus of Bordeaux from the 1978 vintage; an aerospace consultant in New Orleans hosted a three-day tasting for 115 bottles of Château Lafite Rothschild, some dating to the 1830s—never mind that wine rarely improves after a decade in the bottle. These tastings weren't about quality, or even quantity, but rather about status. "Acquisitiveness," Frank Prial wrote, "or, if you will, greed, is their principal motivation."

For enthusiasts without hundreds to spend on seminars or thousands to spend on single bottles, there was another way into this brave new American fine wine world. Accessories such as corkscrews, differently shaped glasses, even home cellars began selling widely. Out were the makeshift contraptions of bricks and wood for racking wine, the sort jiggered more than a decade before by Robert Parker for his first marital apartment in Maryland; in were stylish racks of shiny metal, varnished wood, even stone. Corkscrews—before the 1980s a rarity even in wine-drinking households, thanks to the previous ubiquity of screwtop bottles—started turning up in kitchen drawers nationwide. Not only that, but this relatively simple instrument for removing a squishy wooden stopper from a glass bottle ran the gamut in prices, all of them tantalizingly affordable: a consumer could buy a simple model for five dollars or a more complicated contraption that might run to more than one hundred dollars. The cost ranges and sizes of racks and, especially, cellars also became a way of sorting the casual fine wine fan from the aficionado. A small refrigerator built to hold forty-four bottles of wine at no more than fifty-seven degrees, for instance, might cost $649; substitute a French oak door in place of the thermopane one, and the price ballooned toward a cool $1,000.

If such accessories were not baroque enough, there were other options. Frank Prial cautioned his readers during one holiday shopping season about the price ($200) of "a Rube Goldberg" setup complete with "a strategically placed candle" that allowed "the pourer to watch the wine run through the neck of the bottle." The critic seemed to suggest there might be other, cheaper ways to decant wine to separate sediment from liquid. During another Christmas in the mid-1980s, shoppers perusing the *Wine Enthusiast* catalog could have themselves a "George Washington 18th-century silver-plated wine coaster, reproduced by the Smithsonian for wine lovers," for $39.50 plus another $1.75 for shipping. Or perhaps one might pick up the Home Computer Cellar Log Software retailing in the same catalog for around $50, plus $2.50 shipping: "With one simple command it becomes an amazing group tasting tool with built-in report writer and spreadsheet programs which can print tasting notes and arrive at group consensus." There was also a Pocket Wine Computer that was more utilitarian and ten dollars cheaper. Such myriad choices, none of them truly astronomical in cost when weighed against a $24,000 case of wine, allowed the *Wine Enthusiast* catalog—started by Adam and Sybil Strum in their Westchester County, New York, attic in 1979—to balloon toward twenty million annual shoppers.

A lexicon arose along with the availability of these accessories. Like the hoopla surrounding fine wine, as well as the ways of separating corks from bottles, the words and the phrases had been around for a very long time. It was only in the 1980s, however, that they took true verbal flight. Some words the marketplace made necessary. Distributors and merchants had rarely used *premium* in the US wine marketplace before the 1980s. By the middle of the decade it was in vogue to describe those fine wines still affordable—though not necessarily as affordable as, say, a fighting varietal—as "premium"; soon "premium" wines would be joined by "superpremium" or "ultra-premium" ones, or, even more literally, "top-shelf" wines to distinguish both higher price tags and the fact that retailers almost invariably plunked their priciest selections on upper shelves closer to eye level. The plump harvests on both sides of the Atlantic in the 1970s and early 1980s helped spur these adjectival additions; simply put, there was more fine wine available to Americans than ever before—and more of it being consumed: more than 400 million gallons by 1983.

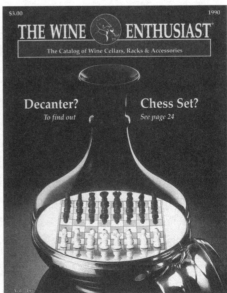

(Left) Adam Strum, a former Gallo salesman, cofounded the *Wine Enthusiast*, a company that targeted America's growing phalanx of fine wine consumers. As late as the 1970s, corkscrews were still novel in US kitchens, never mind wine glasses. (Right) A *Wine Enthusiast* catalog from 1990.
COURTESY OF *WINE ENTHUSIAST*

As with the accessories, the lexicon could border on the absurd. "It appeared that, having expressed our amazement that the dog could talk, it was time to determine what it might have to say." These were words pecked out by Frank Prial after a sojourn in Europe, when the great proponent of American fine wines had had a chance to view them in a fresh, foreign light. He saw in the wines, and in their new fans back in the States, the seeds of an exclusivity he hoped would not flower further. Prial knew he was already too late, though; the "cultists" were winning. He wrote:

> In America wine has its own newsletters, its own stars, its own clubs, even its own vocabulary. Where else in the world would someone sip a little wine and then, with a straight face, remark, "I understand they brought these grapes in at 24 Brix."
> What is or are "Brix"? Sorry, you are not a member.

How supremely ironic that at the post-Prohibition zenith of its commercial and critical prominence, American fine wine was in danger of once again becoming seen as a drink to be enjoyed only on special occasions, by well-heeled drinkers with highly specialized knowledge. "It still isn't clear why Americans insist on becoming wine experts before they can enjoy it," Prial sighed in another column later in the decade. "No one seems to have trouble working through the considerable selection of beers available. But we continue to be intimidated by wine." James Conaway, who would become a merciless chronicler of modern Napa Valley, saw the future through the present in the California Wine Experience that *Wine Spectator* organized in November 1983:

> The ongoing trend of expensive promotion of wine, as well as the mistaken notion that wine appreciation is somehow going to lift you above the masses, were better served than was the product. Learned enophiles are, after all, just people who drink more wine than other people and pronounce upon it; you would have thought, judging by the California Wine Experience, that some of them consecrated it.

THE SCOREKEEPER

1984–1988 | Parkton, Maryland—New York City

S teven Spurrier, the architect of the Judgment of Paris in 1976, knew which wines Robert Parker had recently rated highly, even without being a regular reader of the *Wine Advocate*. How did he know? The sales of certain wines at his Les Caves de la Madeleine jumped. Merchants for Château Mouton saw that venerable Bordeaux house's 1982 vintage quadruple in price after Parker awarded it a score of 100. Spurrier was not the only retailer, nor Château Mouton the only vintner, to start noticing such Parker bounces in the mid-1980s. Even vineyard owners were apt to hold back or raise the prices for certain grape varieties based on the scores of the onetime real estate attorney still working from home in Parkton, Maryland. Such was the power of what Frank Prial called "the Parker phenomenon . . . the hottest thing in wine buying."

By 1986 the *Wine Advocate* was grossing about $500,000 annually through 17,800 subscribers in thirty-seven countries paying twenty-eight dollars a year—many more subscribers than Robert Finigan had at his peak. Moreover, Parker was in demand as a speaker and as an author. His 542-page tome for Simon & Schuster, *Bordeaux: The Definitive Guide for the Wines Produced Since 1961*, not only garnered two reviews in the *New York Times* shortly after its November 1985 release but also quickly became an oft-translated bestseller; the line for a book signing on Manhattan's Upper West Side wended around the block.

As much as he put himself out there, Parker also played it cool, turning down lucrative radio and television deals as well as interview requests. His Maryland home and office were a part of his outsider allure to consumers who increasingly saw his scores, and only his scores, as their unbiased road map through an ever-crowded American fine wine marketplace. That one-hundred-point scale, the most visible example of the new American wine lexicon, proved irresistible to competitors as well: Marvin Shanken's *Wine Spectator* adopted it in 1985, and Adam Strum's *Wine Enthusiast* followed.

Shanken even offered to buy the *Wine Advocate* as its influence ballooned; Parker turned him down cold.

As if to officially signal his ascension as America's most powerful wine critic, the Four Seasons ceased its annual California Barrel Tasting, the storied critical conclaves that started in 1976 and that provided a high-profile showcase for California vintners such as Robert Mondavi and Stag's Leap. Organizers said the tasting needed more space—the Four Seasons was only ever able to seat two hundred, with as many as two thousand people turned away some years—and roomier digs in San Francisco and elsewhere seemed a better fit; but it was never the same, not least because none of the critics who gathered at the tastings, either individually or collectively, could match the power of Parker. No one said so at the time, but there seemed to be little need anymore to collect so many tastemakers when one man's score could move more of the featured wines than anybody else's.

Parker came to this power partly through luck. The critical and commercial success of American fine wine jelled in the late 1970s and early 1980s with the baby boomers' economic prowess, as well as with myriad events and trends, including the deregulation of the airline industry, the rise of craft beer, and a rise in wine tourism. Parker's easily digestible scores came along at just the right time. Indeed, paid lectures at corporate events proved one of his steadiest side gigs, as executives and middle managers wanted to know how to talk about fine wine in a business world where it was increasingly the drink of choice for lunches and dinners.

Luck took Parker only so far, however. He worked hard and logged long hours, both tasting at home and researching abroad, writing up notes on about four hundred wines per bimonthly edition of the *Wine Advocate*. He also benefited from what even his competitors recognized as a formidable palate. He was on his way by the mid-1980s to tasting about ten thousand wines a year, usually heavier reds in the mornings and lighter whites toward the end of the day. He could, he would say, remember every wine he had ever tasted as well as the score (within a few points) that he had given it. Parker would struggle to explain, however, how he could distinctly discern and remember details of dozens, perhaps hundreds, of wines tasted in quick succession to the point of assigning exacting scores that might move thousands of cases worldwide. In a profile published in the *Atlantic Monthly* titled "The Million Dollar Nose"—a nod to Parker's real-life insurance policy for his olfactory and gustatory senses—he said:

A wine goes in my mouth, and I just see it. I see it in three dimensions. The textures. The flavors. The smells. They just jump out at me. I can taste with a hundred screaming kids in a room. When I put my nose in a glass, it's like tunnel vision. I move into another world, where everything around me is just gone, and every bit of mental energy is focused on that wine.

Such apparently preternatural abilities only added to his appeal. Here was a self-made expert expounding in plain language on a subject that seemed opaque and complex. More than that, he was some kind of superman, and yet he didn't make a big fuss about it, preferring gentle suburban obscurity—a neighbor was surprised to learn of Parker's star status in the wine world—over froufrou-laden ostentatiousness, his relentless work ethic ballasting the entire endeavor. Finally, the vast majority of fine wines he raved about were relatively affordable, especially since the US economy was bullishly out of its recessionary pen. Even bottles of the vaunted 1982 Bordeaux could be had for less than fifty dollars in major metropolitan areas; the best Cabernet Sauvignons from California also peaked at fifty bucks. Without Parker's imprimatur, they might have retailed for less, but they were not astronomically expensive or that difficult to find, not anything like those wines selling at auction. They were an affordable accessory, as one writer put it, with Parker's praise serving as "a green light to the Me Generation."

What was not to like? Some of his fellow critics, particularly at Shanken's *Wine Spectator*, resented Parker's swift rise after the '82 Bordeaux raves, as did, surely, Finigan; British giants such as Hugh Johnson would also come to frown upon Parker, particularly upon his one-hundred-point scale. But, by the mid-1980s, he was unstoppable, already labeled the most powerful critic of any field ever. "When Parker spits, the world listens"—that was the message embroidered on a pillow Parker's literary agent gave him. It was true.

WARNING

1986–1988 | San Francisco—Washington, DC

For two days during the first full week of October 1988, the Robert Mondavi Winery brought together about two hundred people, including medical experts, for a symposium in San Francisco to talk openly about the health benefits of wine. The discussion was radical in that openness.

For much of the middle part of the decade, the wine industry had faced a bugbear familiar to anyone old enough to remember the industry right after Prohibition: it was frequently lumped in with hard liquor. There was a fresh twist this time, though. Not only was it lumped in with hard liquor, but, improbably enough, government officials also connected fine wine to illegal drugs; laughable as it is today, influential people, publicly at least, often tied Cabernet to cocaine. Proponents of such near-hysteria honed their messages to the point of achieving huge legal shifts throughout the United States. Activist organizations such as Mothers Against Drunk Driving (MADD), formed in 1980, and the Center for Science in the Public Interest (CSPI), started by Ralph Nader disciples in 1971, were pressing for stricter controls on alcohol—and they were winning. In 1984, with the support of President Ronald Reagan, Congress passed legislation withholding a crucial percentage of highway funds from states that did not raise their drinking age to twenty-one; the states fell into line one by one, until all had upped the age by 1988.

The legislative move came amid shifting views on alcohol, a burst of neo-Prohibitionism that caught the American fine wine movement off guard, just as it should have been basking in the hard-won financial and critical triumphs of the previous ten years. Americans were drinking less alcohol overall, fine wine included. After peaking in 1986 at 487 million gallons, or roughly 82 percent of all the wine consumed in the United States, the amount of fine wine Americans drank every year dropped steadily through the rest of the decade on its way to dipping below 400 million gallons in 1991. It was that lumping in with hard liquor, however, that rankled older pioneers such as Robert Mondavi. Throughout 1988, the same year as his San Francisco meeting, the federal government debated requiring a forty-two-word label on all alcoholic beverage containers warning consumers of the supposed health risks of drinking the contents inside, be they bottom-shelf vodka or Mondavi's legendary Fumé Blanc.

"What nonsense!" Mondavi thought. "Wine was liquid food! Wine was healthy! We had plenty of medical evidence showing that drinking wine in moderation was good for the heart, the circulatory system, the central nervous system and more. *That* should be on the wine label!" Worried about the industry's sluggish response to what he saw as a serious threat, Mondavi commissioned research on wine's health benefits as well as research into the influence of wine on culture and history, in the United States and worldwide. The San Francisco meeting was just the start; more symposia were planned in different locations nationwide.

It was not simply the antialcohol activism that nettled Mondavi and others; it was the activism's context that might prove far more financially damaging in the long run. America was in the midst of a decade-long fitness craze. Hundreds of exercise videos, designed for the proliferation of the VCR, were selling millions of copies, some so popular they spawned sequels. C. Everett Koop, President Reagan's surgeon general, intoned on television and radio, like the voice of an angry god, against everything from smoking to sloth. Gym chains such as Bally Total Fitness, Crunch, Planet Fitness, and Equinox opened hundreds of locations nationwide throughout the 1980s. A "perpetual stream" of diet books flowed onto the bestseller lists.

Robert Parker, America's most powerful wine critic and a man who had taken to gleefully referring to himself as a "hedonist," was especially annoyed by the Center for Science in the Public Interest; the nonprofit was cut from the same Naderite cloth as his *Wine Advocate*, but it seemed to find fault with nearly every legal pleasure known to an American. "Fettuccine alfredo is dangerous for your health," Parker put it to a reporter, ticking off some of CSPI's conclusions. "Kung pao chicken will destroy your life. Holy shit, the first week it's one of the classics of Italian cooking, the next week it's one of the staples of Chinese cooking! These are the people who do studies that your carry-out Chinese meals are saturated in fat . . . " The context for these conclusions was clear: the nation's socioeconomic arc seemed to be bending toward healthy living, and fine wine—unfairly or not—was increasingly seen as unhealthy.

The Reagan administration led the charge. It was simple, really: First Lady Nancy Reagan equated legal alcohol with illegal drugs, a muddying her husband, the former governor of California, did nothing to clear. On September 14, 1986, a Sunday, Mrs. Reagan joined the president for a nationally broadcast speech from the West Hall of the White House. President Reagan, in a deadly serious monotone devoid of the folksiness with which he often addressed the nation, invoked everything from the liberation of France during World War II to Abraham Lincoln's long nights of the soul in the nearby Lincoln bedroom. The cause for which the president conjured these memories? "Today," Reagan told the nation, "there's a drug and alcohol abuse epidemic in this country, and no one is safe from it—not you, not me, and certainly not our children, because this epidemic has their names written on it." His wife closed the address with a question to the cameras, a question infused with undertones of religious fervor and asked on the Christian Sabbath no less: "So won't you join us in this great new national crusade?"

Soon the federal government was amassing muscle behind its chief executive's words, which the First Lady summed up with the slogan "Just Say No." Each state was already on its way to raising the drinking age to twenty-one, amid federal threats of cutting off highway funds. Suddenly legislators who were allied with the Reagan administration proposed dire warning labels for alcoholic beverages, including wine. Federal grants and money for student loans hinged on colleges and universities implementing and enforcing "no-use" drug and alcohol policies. Even elementary and high school curricula worked in the Just Say No messaging; the Drug Abuse Resistance Education Program (D.A.R.E.) clearly stated to students that "alcohol is a gateway drug that can lead to other, stronger chemical dependencies." Obviously, D.A.R.E. organizers made no exception for fine wine in their literature, which soon included seemingly ubiquitous posters in schools nationwide.

Combined with the health craze, which itself seemed at times to emanate from the corridors of Washington power, this government enforcement toward alcohol went well beyond laudable goals such as reducing traffic fatalities and curbing abuse to simply scaring the bejesus out of parents and fostering the sort of near-hysteria that was bad for business. During the 1980s, according to legal scholar Richard Mendelsohn, "Americans came closest to re-creating the moral panic that had accompanied the march to Prohibition." Another national ban on alcohol seemed unlikely, of course, and federal agents were not pouring through wineries' doors, cracking oak barrels with axes and smashing bottles. Consumption was declining, though, amid animated worries over health risks.

The medical experts Mondavi marshalled for the San Francisco symposium sought to assuage the public and right the industry's sales ship. "We have evidence that the moderate consumption of wine is not harmful," Keith

Marton, a top physician at the Pacific Presbyterian Medical Center in San Francisco, told attendees. He defined moderate consumption as about two glasses a day, a shorthand for moderation that would gain popularity in the coming decades. Others went further. Paul Saltman, a biology professor at the University of California, San Diego, echoed Mondavi's sentiment that wine is a food, further stating that it "can be an integral part of the diet without toxic effects." As to the neo-Prohibitionists, who would never go this far when it came to any health benefits of any alcohol, the august British critic Hugh Johnson laid down a paternalistic, though memorable line: "Uncle Sam is becoming Auntie Sam in its critical view of wine's role in America." Mondavi pronounced himself pleased with the meeting and looked forward to more in both the United States and Europe. "Anthropologists, priests, ministers, rabbis, scholars and physicians will all be invited to participate," he told a reporter. He would also dispatch his formidable marketing force, the same one that had willed much of the American fine wine movement into being a generation before, to talk up not only the health benefits of wine but the contributions moderate drinking could make to conviviality, to food, to what Mondavi called "our American way of life." It was perhaps his finest hour.

And yet none of it worked. The month after the symposium, the federal government implemented the Alcoholic Beverage Labeling Act of 1988, the single-biggest consequence for fine wine of the "moral panic" of the 1980s, besides a renewed emphasis on the drink as something exotic. The forty-two-word warning began popping up in conspicuous places on alcohol packaging nationwide, fine wine bottles no exception. Not only that, but the health admonition joined another one germane to wine. In January 1987 regulators ordered winemakers to slap a sulfites warning on bottles, giving them a year to do it; by the start of 1988, consumers were confronted regularly with the blocky words "Contains Sulfites" cautioning them about the sulfur compounds occasionally used as a preservative that sometimes triggered allergic reactions in high concentrations. The sulfites warning, far from reassuring those who might suffer from the allergy, sowed confusion instead. Some wines contained no added sulfites, or did not contain enough to fall under government guidelines, and therefore didn't use the warning; most wines did, and therefore the warning seemed ubiquitous, painting all wines with the same cautionary brush. Add to this the fact that a relatively few people were actually allergic to sulfites, which had no taste besides, and it was yet another potential turn-off for new consumers. No one wanted to buy something that might trigger an allergic reaction, much less something unhealthy.

Such consumer confusion drove Mondavi and others mad. They knew they could cut through the confusion with clarity, but would they ever have the platform to do it? And would they be able to do it in time? The American fine wine industry was already in the midst of a years-long drought in some of its choicest wine-growing regions, never mind grappling with a decline in consumption, which hurt sales. Worse, phylloxera, the vine-destroying bug that had terrorized the wine world in the nineteenth century, was attacking the West Coast, munching through thousands of acres of grapes. Banks weren't returning wineries' calls for loans; some venerable names teetered on the brink of financial ruin. The industry needed a thundering voice.

Mondavi's October 1988 symposium in San Francisco grew in part out of a concern that the Wine Institute, the venerable trade arm of the California wine industry started in 1934, was not doing enough to counteract the antialcohol crowd amid the drought, the drop in wine drinking, and the phylloxera. Nor was help forthcoming from the industry's dominant player, E. & J. Gallo, which saw little threat from the attacks in particular—and presumably little benefit from helping smaller higher-end wineries since it, too, had started varietally labeling wines. The company, too, was one of the biggest producers of wine coolers, those ultra-sweet, lower-alcohol alternatives to actual wine that became popular in the 1980s; Gallo's Bartle & Jaymes, introduced in 1985, accounted for 40 percent of wine-cooler sales. In April 1988 fifty-five smaller wineries signed a petition lobbying for a louder voice in how the Wine Institute coordinated its campaigns. First up, the wineries wanted "wine with food programs to offset prohibitionist threats," the sort designed to promote the idea that "wine is the answer, not the problem." The institute appeared to drag its feet on that request, as well as on a plea to address the warning-label debate head-on, worried as it was about liability lawsuits from too aggressively promoting alcohol. So Mondavi, in his fifth decade of wine-making and his seventh decade of life, took the lead. He not only organized the research and the symposia but also raised tens of thousands of dollars to fund education efforts, including monies from Italian and French vintners worried about the neo-Prohibitionism in the important American marketplace.

It was not clear, though, whether Mondavi's efforts would have any impact at all. The industry lost on the health and sulfite warnings. There was also talk of requiring winemakers to list calories and ingredients on bottles, even toll-free numbers for alcoholism treatment centers. The national health craze banged on unabated, by then personified by George H. W. Bush, the new US president inaugurated in January 1989. The abstemious New Englander made it a habit to be seen jogging, buff Secret Service agents in tow, and he reinvigorated the President's Council on Physical Fitness and Sports, condemning millions of schoolchildren to compete through pull-ups and sprints for certificates from the White House. At the same time, the "increasingly vocal anti-alcohol advocates" continued, as one observer put it, to deliberately "not differentiate between eighteen-dollar chardonnay and two-dollar white port in their crusades" (never mind the earlier talk of alcohol as a gateway drug on the way to crack). The same liability fears that spooked the Wine Institute eventually hamstrung Mondavi. Talking of fine wine's health benefits, however tangible they might be, was decidedly out of style.

It was another supreme irony of this complicated decade for American fine wine that while it continued to broaden its commercial reach and critical appeal, it faced a serious challenge akin to what had nearly wiped it out sixty years before: Prohibitionism. Just as the cultist lexicon in the early 1980s threatened to turn consumers off from fine wine, so too did the antialcohol dogma of the decade's latter half. Ironically, another debate over fine wine's health benefits would heal just about everything.

THE FRENCH PARADOX

1991–1992 | Lyon, France

At 7:00 PM Eastern time on Sunday, November 17, 1991, twenty million households tuned in, as they had been doing for years, to the CBS newsmagazine *60 Minutes*. One of its segments that evening was titled "The French Paradox," hosted by Morley Safer, a gravelly voiced Canadian-born veteran of the network's Saigon and London bureaus who had joined the show in 1970 and who bore a resemblance to Hollywood legend William Holden. Safer set up the segment by rattling off some rather grim statistics—from an American point of view at least:

> There are several things that contribute to heart attacks. Diet, of course, is one of them. So why is it that the French, who eat 30 percent more fat than we do, suffer fewer heart attacks, even though they smoke more and exercise less? All you have to do is look at the numbers.
> If you're a middle-aged American man, your chances of dying of a heart attack are three times greater than a Frenchman of the same age.

So it's obvious that the French are doing something right, something Americans are not doing.

What might that lifestyle difference be? Safer and his crew then transported their viewers to Lyon, a city in southeastern France. Shots of a restaurant in what looked like the middle of the day, busy with diners and waitstaff, filled the screen. Safer's voiceover kept going, explaining Lyon, "the gastronomic capital of France," to Americans in a way that would surely have excited Julia Child and been recognizable to scores of people involved in the American fine wine movement:

> Chefs have the stature of quarterbacks. But their preparations would send the American Heart Association into cardiac arrest. Butter, goose fat, lard, double cream are the staples of a decent day's cooking. Lyon, a city of just over 400,000, has 2,600 restaurants, 2,300 meat shops, 115 wine stores. Shopping is not a bore; people do it with gusto and care.

It was the French approach to food and drink writ on a grand canvas. CBS's *60 Minutes* was far and away the most popular program on American television, news or otherwise; even its reruns might be the top show for a particular Sunday evening. In the era just before one-thousand-channel cable packages, watching *60 Minutes* was a ritual for more than one-fifth of the nation's households. This particular Sunday, they were being fed quite a feast.

The restaurant scene zoomed in on Safer at a window-side table with Curtis Ellison, a cardiologist and professor at the Boston University School of Medicine, who, as Safer explained, was in Lyon as part of a recently started study comparing the diets of different nations (including the United States) with the diets of the French. To illumine that particular diet, Safer began reading the restaurant's multipage menu aloud to Ellison: "A Lyonnaise salad bowl, which is pig's head pate with parsley; black pudding, which, you know, is very fatty; and potatoes in oil; double-fat sliced tripe sautéed with onions; and hot sausage with lentils and potatoes and oil." Closing the menu, Safer, who lived part-time in France, added, "This is routine stuff." Ellison quickly answered the obvious unspoken question: "The farmers have been eating this for years. They've been eating a very high-fat diet, it seems, and yet they don't get heart disease. If we took the same diet and put it into an American, you know, we would all be suffering from coronaries at an early age." Then the camera peeled away, and smack-dab between journalist and physician an unmistakable object stood at the center of the table: a half-empty bottle of red wine. "There's something about the French that seems to be protecting them, and we're not sure what it is," Ellison said. "We're looking for it."

Viewers, if they missed the clue, would have to look no further than a couple of minutes later, when Safer, with Ellison, introduced a researcher with the French government named Serge Renaud, who believed he had found causal links between drinking moderate amounts of red wine regularly and healthiness. A nutritionist in Paris also talked up the benefits of the average French citizen's annual cheese intake, a staggering forty pounds, as well as the general French approach to cooking and eating—namely, slowly and with pleasure, often from the freshest ingredients available. But wine was clearly the star of the evening. Renaud implied that regular drinking could even offset the ill effects of a diet rich in butter and cream. Cue a French wine store: square wood shelves piled high with dark wine bottles laid flat, an anonymous clerk replenishing inventory. Then fade to an earnest Safer, alone at another table, another half-empty bottle of wine before him, a very much full glass beside it. He was looking directly into the camera, at more than forty million Americans:

> The wine apparently affects the platelets, the smallest of the blood cells. It is platelets that cause blood to clot. They prevent bleeding. But they also cling to rough fatty deposits on the artery walls, clogging and finally blocking the artery and causing a heart attack. The wine has a flushing effect; it removes platelets from the artery wall.

Safer picked up the glass and smiled. "So the answer to the riddle, the explanation of the paradox, may lie in this inviting glass."

The segment ended, and the land rush began. A follow-up piece in July 1992, in which Safer concluded, "The evidence of the benefits of alcohol in moderation keeps growing," only emboldened consumers more. Sales of red wine in the United States spiked, providing a boon to an American fine wine industry that needed it. Retailers reported shoppers asking for "the same wine the French drink," and even ancillary vendors, such as those for corkscrews and glassware, saw sales jump. Newspapers and magazines, as well as diet gurus, picked up on the 60 Minutes reports and ran with them in articles and books. The original segment's very title, "The French Paradox," entered America's vocabulary, taking on an etymological life of its own; it came to be shorthand for living well and staying healthy at the same time.

It also undoubtedly contributed to a major shift in the marketplace. Drinking totals that had been on the decline for much of the late 1980s and early

1990s began to reverse themselves. Per-capita wine consumption in the United States had dropped below two gallons in 1991 for the first time since 1979; by 1999 it would be back above that benchmark. The total amount of fine wine consumed had tumbled to 394 million gallons in 1991 from nearly 490 million five years before; the total would ascend back toward that number by the end of the decade. Demand increased in particular for wineries specializing in premium fine wine, those costing at least about four dollars a bottle; shipments for those rose 16 percent annually in 1992 to $1.6 billion. The American wine industry's revenue for the fiscal year ending June 30, 1992, bounced an astounding 23 percent over the previous year's total, and fine wine shipments overall were up 10 percent annually. A lot of the financial nervousness of the previous few years evaporated—this despite a quintuple increase in the federal excise tax for wine in 1991 to $1.07 a gallon. Robert Mondavi happily drew a straight line from his efforts at pushing the health benefits of wine to the *60 Minutes* report, though Safer later said the wine-making pioneer's work had nothing to do with it. Whatever the genesis of the segment and its follow-up, their unambiguous message—a little wine now and then is good for you—was an unmitigated boost for the industry.

Never mind that a lot of this new information was bunk. For one thing, the eating and drinking habits that Safer described, and that Americans such as Child and Mondavi had fallen in love with decades before, had been in decline in France for years. Fast-food joints were the ascendant restaurant model in the Fifth Republic, not the type of urbane urban bistro where Safer and Ellison dined. Also, fewer and fewer French were drinking wine regularly, if at all. A survey taken in 1990, the year before the first *60 Minutes* segment, showed that more than half of French adults never drank wine; of those that did, fewer than one-third drank it every day. Such statistics, as Frank Prial pointed out in the *New York Times*, meant that those who did drink wine regularly drank an unhealthy lot of it. How else to account for France's aggregate consumption? Finally, and perhaps because of this decidedly immoderate consumption, France's rate of alcoholism and its proportion of deaths from liver diseases such as cirrhosis were double those of the United States. For that matter, while France did have far fewer instances of heart disease than its much more populous ally across the ocean, the disease was still the nation's number one killer. All that red wine had done little to dethrone it.

Such critiques were ultimately swallowed up by the avalanche of coverage of the French Paradox, but not before they unintentionally laid bare a profound global shift in wine. The French *were* drinking less wine; the Italians, too; most Europeans in general. The shift and its effects would become more pronounced in the decades to come—and for the time being, the average American, with two and a half gallons consumed annually, paled against the average Frenchman with his nineteen—but by the 1990s the trend was already clear: Americans were starting to drink more fine wine than the Europeans who had all but invented it.

SCENES FROM A RECOVERY

1988–1993 | Paris—Los Angeles—Manhattan—Napa— Washington, DC—Los Altos, California

During the final leg of a two-part competition in Paris in May 1988, Larry Stone, a sommelier from Seattle, listened as the other finalists for the title Best Sommelier of the World botched the identification of a white from Bordeaux. When it came his turn to answer in front of more than five hundred spectators, Stone nailed it, thereby securing his lead in the annual competition that the French government had backed since 1969 and putting him on course to become the first American to win. President Reagan sent Stone a congratulatory telegram, and the crowd in Paris cheered so loudly the organizers had to play "The Star-Spangled Banner" three times for the American national anthem to be heard.

In the Westwood neighborhood of Los Angeles, a customer bought a case of California-born Chardonnay at Wally's Wine & Spirits, the liquor store that Beverly Hills nightclub manager Steve Wallace opened in 1968 after taking tasting classes under Robert Lawrence Balzer. It was one of the first stores in Southern California to sell fine European imports and the few fine wines made upstate. The customer eventually returned eleven of the case's dozen bottles because he did not like what he tasted. Wallace refunded him. The same customer returned two weeks later and bought another case of the same wine. Wallace asked him why. The customer shrugged. "Parker just gave it a 95," he replied.

During this same period, in April 1989, Robert Parker himself conducted a Monday morning wine tasting at the Park Lane Hotel on Manhattan's Central Park South. It was part of the press conference to announce the New York City launch of the Prodigy interactive personal service, a suite of computer software created through a partnership of IBM and Sears, and launched the year before in cities such as Los Angeles and Atlanta. Subscribers could pay $9.95 monthly to get online information such as weather reports, news digests, stock quotes—and wine notes via the founder of the *Wine Advocate*. It was groundbreaking stuff technologically—there would even be a color map of the United States for those weather reports—and Prodigy was compatible with Apple IIs and IBM PCs.

Larry Stone, who in May 1988 became the first American to win France's Grand Prix de Sopexa competition— best sommelier in the world specializing in French wine and spirits.
COURTESY OF LARRY STONE

Then, on September 16, 1989, a Saturday, the Napa Valley Wine Train pulled out of McKinstry Street Station in the city of Napa for its inaugural run through the valley to St. Helena and, of course, past some of the nation's most storied wineries. Backed by Vincent DeDomenico, a San Franciscan best known for inventing Rice-A-Roni, the train had proved extraordinarily controversial, with those such as Robert Mondavi convinced of its potential for boosting tourism and alleviating automobile congestion counterbalanced by those who thought the valley had enough tourists already and preferred they come by car anyway. Both sides, along with the state and local governments, reached a grand compromise: the train could run, but riders could not get off to visit wineries along the way. They would have their curiosity whetted but would have to find another means of transport to satiate it.

Shortly before Christmas 1990, Robert Mondavi announced that he was turning over day-to-day management and decision-making at his pioneering eponymous winery to his sons Tim and Michael. He would remain as chairman—and as the best-known promoter of American fine wine, "an enological Billy Graham, preaching the gospel." Encomiums burst forth following the announcement. Mondavi was the first American winemaker, as Frank Prial put it, to make "a single fine wine label recognizable coast to coast." His tireless marketing prowess aside, there had been technical triumphs as well; for one, numerous winemakers, including Warren Winiarski and Mike Grgich, had passed through the mission-style archway off Highway 29.

The following March, MacArthur Beverages, a liquor store in Washington, DC's Palisades neighborhood started in 1957 by Addy and Ruth Bassin (the same couple that had provided Robert Parker with a chunk of his initial *Wine Advocate* mailing list), divided its annual California Futures Barrel Tasting into two slots for the first time to satisfy demand. The event, initially held in 1986, drew dozens of California wineries for perhaps the biggest East Coast airing of barrel samples since the California Barrel Tasting at the Four Seasons in Manhattan ceased in 1985. MacArthur's tasting, with food pairings, was also held at a Four Seasons, this one in Washington. Tickets to each 1991 session were seventy-five dollars.

Several months later, during the last weekend in October 1991, Marvin Shanken's *Wine Spectator* hosted its tenth annual Wine Experience at the Marriott Marquis in Manhattan's Times Square. Each of the three time slots included all 165 wines and cost $150 per session. Various multiday passes, ranging from $625 to $750, sold out by the start of the month. Attendees were promised luminaries such as Robert Mondavi, Alexis Bespaloff from *New York* magazine, and at least two Rothschilds.

In August 1993 Bob Trinchero's Sutter Home, the St. Helena progenitor of the wildly successful White Zinfandel style, became the largest winery in the nation to seal its larger varietally labeled bottles with a screwtop rather than a cork. The winery had already pioneered the sale of smaller, so-called airplane bottles, also with screwtops, but the 1993 move heralded real change, with more than one million cases shipped with the new seal. Still, most wineries clung to cork, for image more than anything; that did not stop critics from predicting the beginning of the end for corked wine.

Andre Tchelistcheff died in Napa on April 7, 1994, of esophageal cancer at age ninety-two. Though mostly associated with Beaulieu Vineyards and its signature Georges de Latour Private Reserve Cabernet Sauvignon, he influenced numerous wineries and winemakers as a consultant, including perhaps most auspiciously Robert Mondavi. Other pioneers of the American fine wine movement had passed and would pass in the 1990s, including two figures essential to cultivation of fine-wine grapes in the United States: Dr. Konstantin Frank, who made them grow in colder climates such as Upstate New York, and Maynard Amerine, whose research convinced vineyardists they were worth the trouble in California.

In late summer 1995, the one-year-old Los Altos, California–based company Virtual Vineyards became the first online retailer to accept encrypted credit card payments through any World Wide Web browser. New technology allowed wine buyers to enter their credit card and billing address information into a system that Virtual Vineyards could then use to process the order. The company promised that buying wine would be "as easy as a few keystrokes."

The ten vignettes in this chapter, from the late 1980s and early 1990s, illuminate the breadth and activity of an American fine wine movement once again in growth mode, one a half-generation from the Judgment of Paris and a decade from the 1982 Bordeaux. In 1995 there were 1,820 wineries in the United States, the most since before World War II, with the majority focused on fine wine. Every state had at least one, except for the Dakotas, Wyoming, and Alaska (and South Dakota's first, Valiant Vineyards in Vermillion, near the Iowa border, would open in 1996, shortly after passage of that state's Farm Winery Act). California still claimed the vast majority, 944, with most located in the San Francisco Bay Area. New York and Washington were a distant second and third, respectively.

None of this happened in isolation. Take the World Wide Web. Created by English programmer Tim Berners-Lee and launched in 1992, it busted open the Internet, for decades largely the domain of academics and government workers. With the emergence of browsers such as Marc Andreessen's Mosaic starting in 1993, it became easier than ever to upload graphics and photos; the number of websites, the very parlance of the Web, exploded throughout the decade, with wine and wineries a part of that explosion. Web-based stocks, too, contributed to the overall economic boom of the 1990s. The nation had pivoted out of another recession in 1992, the recovery a precursor to another bull run in the financial markets. Such a bull run undergirded bounces in tourism, including wine tourism, and international travel, including to some of the world's top wine regions outside of the United States. And it seemed, as it did in the early 1980s, unstoppable.

MADE IN AMERICA

1993 | Washington, DC—High Point, North Carolina

The nation's "center of attention," as a front-page story in the *New York Times* on November 9, 1993, put it, was shifting to the Washington, DC, studios of CNN. It would be there, on that Tuesday evening edition of *Larry King Live*, that Vice President Al Gore would debate Texas businessman Ross Perot, the third-place finisher in the presidential election of the previous fall. Their topic had officialdom in Washington—as well as the business hubs in Chicago and on both coasts—humming already: whether Congress should pass the North American Free Trade Agreement (NAFTA) that President Bill Clinton supported. The agreement would open up trade with Mexico and Canada to an unprecedented degree, ostensibly lowering prices on consumer goods and boosting companies' bottom lines so they could create more jobs, particularly in manufacturing. Or at least that was the theory supporters proffered.

Most unions adamantly opposed NAFTA, seeing the Clinton administration's push not only as a betrayal of a core Democratic constituency but as an open invitation for companies to shed jobs in the United States and resurrect them at a fraction of the cost in Mexico. Much of Congress was opposed too, with Clinton pressing legislators for support at White House get-togethers and employing the help of deputies such as Treasury Secretary Lloyd Bentsen to get to the 218-vote threshold he needed to pass NAFTA during a House tally scheduled for late November. Then there was Perot, who had placed himself at the vanguard of the opposition during the 1992 presidential race, colorfully summing up the job-loss fears from NAFTA as "a giant sucking sound." His November 9 debate with Gore took on the portentous aura of a major sporting event; neither opponent disappointed, one speaking slowly in a Tennessee drawl, the other in a rat-a-tat-tat Texas twang. Here was an early exchange between the two as King, the host, sat mutely:

Perot: Do you guys ever do anything but propaganda?
Gore: Isn't that your business also?
Perot: Would you even know the truth if you saw it?
Gore: Oh, yes, I—
Perot: I don't believe you would. You've been up here too long.

Zings and barbs aside, a very real concern about American manufacturing undergirded the NAFTA debate. Between 1979 and 1992, the United States lost more than three million manufacturing jobs as companies chased cheaper labor overseas and greater automation rendered some positions obsolete. Textiles, furniture, automobiles, even the hardware of the personal computer industry—these iconic industries' manufacturing jobs were disappearing and were by and large not coming back. Such sharp contractions in employment decimated the industries and the employees themselves in many cases; they also wreaked havoc on their host communities.

Take furniture. Since at least the late nineteenth century, furniture production had animated a huge swath of central North Carolina, from just north of Charlotte to the Virginia border. By the early 1980s, the small city of High Point, near Greensboro, had, in fact, earned the nickname the Furniture Capital of the World, in no small part because it hosted the world's biggest annual home-furnishings trade show. The furniture that factories in High Point and nearby areas produced was a source of local pride and an economic engine for the region. By the 1990s, the engine was sputtering; it was clear that employment in North Carolina's furniture industry had peaked and would never really rise again. Overseas competition—particularly from China, where furniture could be made much more cheaply with less expensive materials—was chipping away at local sales, and soon at factory orders as well. While local politicians and industry executives talked up greater automation as a way out, others took a colder, soberer view, especially when it came to employment. A Duke University study of the furniture industry's decline put it this way: "The chance of finding a new job in the furniture industry is probably very low for most displaced workers." Furniture as an economic driver in North Carolina was done.

The scenario would repeat itself in regions and cities nationwide; the old factories of places such as Pittsburgh, Chicago, and New York would soon find new lives as luxury condominiums and apartments, their vaunted manufacturing pasts nothing more than marketing-material fodder for real estate agents. Growth in service sector jobs, as well as retail, soon ran way ahead of any having to do with manufacturing; growth in health-care jobs looked like it would outpace every category, a function—in part—of the aging baby boomers. It would still be a few years before America's manufacturing sector walked off a statistical cliff hand in hand with a good deal of the national psyche. But that cliff clearly loomed.

Congress in the end did pass NAFTA, and President Clinton signed it, Ross Perot's protestations notwithstanding. The globalization it furthered, the "giant sucking sound" it loosed, did contribute mightily to the economic contractions that swept the nation in the 1990s and beyond.

Then there was fine wine. Wine and wine-making were bright spots in America's economic landscape and in its manufacturing sector in particular. As the job losses mounted in the sector overall, the reverse held true in wine. By the middle of the following decade, the California wine industry alone would employ more than 200,000 people, with that number growing to 330,000 by 2013, twenty years after the Gore-Perot debate (the nationwide figure would then stand at 820,000). A sizable reason for this growth was also an obvious one: domestic wine-making could not be outsourced. On the contrary, the world would beat a path to the United States for its enological know-how as the nation's number of wineries and their output crested toward all-time highs during the 1990s. The industry, moreover, created its own job-making ecosystem, from financing to production to packaging to distribution to sales to writing about it to serving it at restaurants and elsewhere. Yes, globalization would come to American fine wine—it would go wherever it pleased after a while—though not in the ways it visited itself upon other, unluckier industries.

CULTS, CHRIST, AND FRANKENSTEIN

1989–2000 | San Francisco—Sonoma—Manhattan

One morning in December 1989, Richard (Dick) Graff gathered the winemakers from his Chalone Wine Group in the company's San Francisco headquarters on Spear Street. They were there to taste four Pinot Noirs from each winery that Chalone controlled, including Acacia, Edna Valley, and Carmenet. The bottles also included four selected from Chalone Vineyard itself, which a Frenchman planted just before Prohibition in 1920 and which Graff took over in 1965 with financial help from his mother.

A 1958 Harvard graduate with a degree in music who served three years as a navy officer after college, Graff came from a family that had already dipped a toe in fine wine: they owned a stake in northern Sonoma County's Windsor Vineyards. It was there that Graff learned a lot of the trade from Windsor owner Rodney Strong, who had acquired it in 1962 after getting a taste for fine wine as a ballet dancer in Paris in the 1950s. ("I could not be an old dancer," Strong would tell people, "but I could be an old winemaker.")

Strong focused on Chardonnay, Cabernet Sauvignon, and Merlot at Windsor, which was one of the first wineries to really push those varietals in that area of Sonoma. Graff took an appreciation for all three to Chalone; his 1974 Chardonnay placed third among the whites at the Judgment of Paris. He branched out as well, including into Pinot Noir, that mercurial grape so many found so difficult to master in the 1960s and 1970s. Production improvements, including tailoring fermentation to the grape rather than using a one-size-fits-all-red-wines approach, had California wineries—including the wineries under Chalone's expanding corporate umbrella—turning out solid Pinot Noirs during the 1980s, even if it was yet to be much of a commercial boon.

Shortly before the blind tasting's scheduled 9:00 AM start, a sandy-haired, blue-eyed ex-winemaker-turned-consultant named Leo McCloskey placed an envelope in the center of the table around which the winemakers had gathered. He did so with a deliberate rhetorical flourish designed to grab the tasters by their collars: "I have placed in this envelope the rank order you will come up with tasting these Pinot Noirs." McCloskey then walked away, and the tasting commenced. The tasting was expected to last an hour; it soon stretched past 10:00 AM, then past 11:00. Finally, around noon, the winemakers voted. The results vindicated McCloskey: he had picked the top three finishers in order, as well as the last three and much of the middle.

How did he do that? McCloskey had developed a mathematical algorithm that could, he was convinced, predict the future taste of wine. The algorithm married the French-developed concept of terroir with the chemistry inherent in grapes and wine-making. The two were symbiotic, after all, if not essentially the same: time and place often dictated the quality of the grape and therefore the quality of the wine. The Chalone tasting was the algorithm's first big test, and it had passed. From there, McCloskey spent the next six months enticing other wineries to sign with him as clients. He figured he needed a dozen to launch his consultancy successfully; he got those, primarily in California but also in the Pacific Northwest, and then got some more.

McCloskey got his start in American fine wine in the early 1970s, near where he went to high school in Cupertino, just down the street from a new software firm called Apple. In 1959 a Stanford researcher named David Bennion, who made wine in his spare time, partnered with fellow scientists—including Carl Djerassi, credited with inventing the birth control pill—to launch Ridge Vineyards in the Santa Cruz Mountains to the west of Cupertino and its larger neighbor San Jose. Ten years later, Ridge hired Paul Draper as winemaker. Draper, who knew about Ridge from his time as a philosophy student at Stanford, had spent time exploring fine wine and fine wine culture in Europe, first in Italy with the US Army and then afterward on his own in France. After a stint at Lee Stewart's Souverain in Napa Valley, Draper decamped to Chile with a friend from Stanford named Fritz Maytag, who in 1965, using money from his family's home-appliance fortune, rescued San Francisco's Anchor Brewing Co. from financial ruin and thus unwittingly sparked the American craft beer movement. The two worked together on a nonprofit vineyard project on the Chilean coast, with Draper returning to the States by 1969 to take up his post at Ridge.

Two years later, the winery hired McCloskey, a recently minted Oregon State University general sciences graduate, to clean barrels. Ridge's owners recognized his acumen early on; within a year, McCloskey was in charge of Ridge's fledgling laboratory. The position, as he would later realize, gave him a bird's-eye view to "observe the separation of the life history of Chardonnay and Cabernet winemakers from all those who would make other new California varietal wines." McCloskey was soon doing research, delivering lectures, and writing academic papers on how to improve both Cabernet Sauvignon and Chardonnay as well as other wine styles made in the United States. No less an eminence than Maynard Amerine of the University of California, Davis, encouraged McCloskey to formally further his studies in enology (Amerine wanted the twenty-something to join the UC Davis viticulture faculty). McCloskey did complete a master's in enology at San Jose University in 1973. When it came to a doctorate, however, he took the advice of Carl Djerassi, who pushed him to study "things like chemistry and mathematics, which actually have principles," lumping enology in with the social, rather than the hard, sciences. McCloskey chose chemistry—chemical ecology, to be precise—enrolling in a doctoral program at the University of California, Santa Cruz, while remaining a paid consultant at Ridge and other wineries, including those of the comedian Smothers brothers in the San Francisco Bay Area.

In 1976, while pursuing his doctorate, McCloskey cofounded and then ran the start-up Felton Empire Winery in Santa Cruz County; it became particularly noted for its Rieslings. (That turned out to be the same year that

Ridge's 1971 Monte Bello Cabernet Sauvignon placed fifth among the reds in the Judgment of Paris.)

By the mid-1980s, Felton Empire had been sold and McCloskey was done with his doctorate. It was an auspicious time to be thirty-something and a veteran of the American fine wine movement. The power of critics was ballooning, particularly that of Robert Parker and his one-hundred-point scale; so, too, was the power of baby boomers in the fine wine marketplace. McCloskey watched the twin developments and realized that, whatever the industry might think of the critics and their effects on consumers, "the critics were going to win because Americans wanted to reduce their risk of purchase and winemakers weren't filling the information void." If anything, during the 1980s, the industry was getting rolled by the neo-Prohibitionists, its sales and reputation suffering amid a general fever-pitch panic about alcohol consumption. Wineries, McCloskey concluded, would want help safeguarding their gains in this brave new post–1982 Bordeaux world.

Along came his algorithm, which sought to take the guesswork out of wine-making by predicting quality based upon the grapes themselves rather than on any one wine-making technique. After the algorithm came McCloskey's consultancy, which he based in Sonoma and called Enologix. He developed computer software to run the algorithm through, having identified what he considered the most important chemical components of wine: the ones that bequeathed sensations such as taste and smell.

Enologix's client roster swelled through the 1990s from the original dozen that began with Dick Graff's Chalone. While it would become the most prominent, it was not the only firm to pop up during the decade promising innovations that would make wines just so, never mind the winemakers. An equally futuristic-sounding firm called Vinovation pioneered the techniques of reverse osmosis and micro-oxygenation. In reverse osmosis, high pressure separated the alcohol and the acid from wine that would otherwise have been ruined. Micro-oxygenation, which pumped oxygen bubbles into barrels holding wine, did away with the need for the centuries-old practice of racking to separate wine from fermentation residue such as spent yeast. There were also new firms specializing in "emergency rescues" of iffy batches, through these techniques and others. Such firms were controversial, with some winemakers declaring their necessity only when a batch did indeed need rescuing and others happily signing up for the uniformity that micro-oxygenation promoted; in a single year in the late 1990s, Vinovation sold one thousand micro-oxygenation systems for $2,000 each. None of these firms, though, was as blunt and unapologetic as McCloskey's Enologix: *Give us your wine, or simply the makings of your wine, and we'll deliver the finished product you and your critics want.*

The work of McCloskey and his firm would represent the triumph of uniformity in wine-making, for good and ill, sapping much of the romance and the uncertainty that had defined it for so long but adding a profound layer of reassurance for both vintners and their customers. This went leaps beyond Émile Peynaud's innovations in the 1940s and 1950s, which helped to drastically increase the uniformity of wine techniques and therefore quality. Here was a way to drastically increase the uniformity of wine *outcomes*, to make a particular wine taste the same—starting before the grapes were even harvested. One observer compared McCloskey to Jesus Christ, collecting disciples in the industry as he performed similar miracles. Others called him Dr. Frankenstein. He was robbing wine of its surprises, of its sense of place, of its allure grounded in that aged French concept of terroir. How dare he!

What was the revolutionary French classification Appellation d'Origine Contrôlée save a nod to place in wine-making? The Four Seasons' now-legendary California Barrel Tastings were just that, were they not? Tastings of new wines from a specific state in the union. The hit 1980s television drama *Falcon Crest* could not have been set anywhere but in California for the public to have understood its connection to wine. The pivotal debate over the quality of the 1982 Bordeaux could never have happened but for the fact that the grapes came from a certain part of France in a certain year. Cultivation of fine wine grapes in New York State's Finger Lakes region presented a certain set of challenges not presented to vineyardists in southern Ohio or northern Virginia, and left the grapes with an almost apple-like taste. On and on went place's influence upon the gustatory realities of fine wine. Negate it through algorithms and computer software, through making wines taste a certain way regardless of terroir, and suddenly it did not matter all that much where a wine came from so long as it tasted the way consumers, or critics, wanted it to taste time and again. Such an approach made wine-making more akin to brewing, where repetition was prized and the origin of ingredients was not all that important. It was also, McCloskey's critics said, analogous to fast food and any number of processed, mass-produced foodstuffs.

Not quite. Much of the fine wine produced in the United States by the start of the twenty-first century was adulterated in some major way. Some in the industry pegged the percentage of significantly doctored wine at more than half. Usually, the adulteration came through the addition of compounds such as Mega Purple and Ultra Red, which were exactly what their brand names sound like: ways to make red wines darker in color and richer in texture.

These were adulterations well beyond the norm, and the public might be none the wiser about them; the government did not require ingredients on packaging such as labels (in fact, it often forbade wineries from listing them), and wineries who did significantly doctor their products were, of course, none too keen on sharing that with an increasingly informed buying public. "Who among them," Eric Asimov asked rhetorically in the *New York Times* in August 2012, "wants to 'fess up to adding Mega Purple or Ultra Red, grape concentrates used to darken color and plump up the texture in red wines? Who wants it known that they added tannins, removed alcohol or relied on Velcorin, a common wine and soft-drink additive that combats spoilage and then chemically dissipates?" It was one thing to add sulfur dioxide as a preservative, something winemakers had been doing since the ancient Roman era, or nutrients for the yeast to feast on or even to use micro-oxygenation to save a potentially spoiled barrel of saleable wine; it was another thing entirely to almost completely change the appearance, the taste, and the texture of a wine, often after fermentation and aging.

The surest proof of the prevalence of such adulteration came from the wineries that did *not* do it. Randall Grahm started listing all the ingredients on his bottles of Bonny Doon in 2008. It was a simple, straightforward affair; these were the ingredients for a Bonny Doon Syrah:

> Syrah grapes, tartaric acid, and sulfur dioxide. In the winemaking process, the following were utilized: indigenous yeast, yeast nutrients, and French oak barrels. At time of bottling, this product contained 65 ppm total SO2 and 25 ppm free SO2.

Few wineries followed Grahm's lead. One, interestingly enough, was Ridge Vineyards, where Leo McCloskey got his start in wine in the early 1970s; Ridge had tried listing ingredients as far back as the 1980s, but the federal government stepped in to stop them. The fact that Bonny Doon, Ridge, and a handful of others even attempted the labeling showed that significant adulteration was going on regularly and that it was widespread enough to have spawned a countertrend. It could be argued—and some winemakers did make this argument—that such adulterations divorced wine so much from grapes that the fruits mattered little in the finished product. What McCloskey was doing, however, was hanging almost everything on the grapes, on finding and divining which ones should be used and when they should be harvested to produce the wines that his clients wanted. His algorithmic approach to winemaking, his critics notwithstanding, was a celebration of terroir. Enologix's schemata reached back to the harvesting advice of pioneering French consultant Émile Peynaud in the 1940s and 1950s, industry-altering advice that hinged on when and what to pick.

Such a grape-centric approach de-emphasized fermentation and aging. It also marginalized what had come to be called, not always derisively, the "cult of the winemaker" or "cult winemaker." The term appeared to have emerged in the 2000s to describe either particularly celebrated winemakers or the craft of wine-making itself. Cult winemakers were rock stars, the men and occasionally women who brought the party to people's mouths and who often featured prominently on winery tours and in the trade press. As with so many of the prominent trends in the American fine wine movement around the turn of the century, the term was fresh but the trend itself was not. "The cult of the winemaker as hero has recently been described as a new phenomenon," wrote Charles Olken in his *Connoisseurs' Guide to California Wine*. "I think we all know better." To Olken, it could have started with the monk Dom Pérignon, whose wine-making skills in the late 1600s and early 1700s were so celebrated that his name came to be literally synonymous with a top-shelf Champagne. "But I am not sure," Olken concluded, "because I am guessing that the wealthy classes who raised wine into a product to be worshipped probably had their heroes back as long as there were people who believed that they had to have the best wine."

People in more recent times did highly regard the likes of Andre Tchelistcheff, Konstantin Frank, Mike Grgich, and Warren Winiarski; no one, however, talked or wrote widely about winemakers as "superstars" until the twenty-first century. With that greater notoriety, one that the greater amount of fine wine on American shelves and menus only heightened, came a sense of the winemaker as some sort of mad-genius magician. Here was how a profile of one Long Island winemaker started:

> From the outside, a winery in winter looks as dormant as its grapevines. The chaos in the vine fields subsides. The stream of tasting room tourists slows to a trickle. But deep inside the bowels of the cave, the grape juice is maturing and the winemaker is buzzing— sampling, blending, brewing, and passing judgment. He engages in a sort of alchemy.

We also found that said winemaker "keeps no spreadsheets. The information rests in his head." Then there was this general description from a British newspaper at the start of the century's second decade: "There are even characters who work in obscure corners of Europe and harvest only under certain phases of the moon, so fuelling the cult of the winemaker." In the sometimes quiet awe in which consumers—and, more often than not, the media—held them, cult winemakers were similar to the small-scale, independent winemakers called *garagistes* who arose around the same time.

To be sure, the American fine wine movement in the 2000s included fantastically precise and well-trained winemakers; the industry as a whole by then employed more than one million full-time workers in varied roles. However, the certainty that Leo McCloskey and others sold, beginning in the early 1990s, threatened the reputation of winemakers as magicians. If the quality of a fine wine could be predicted at, or even before, harvest, and if certain sketchy batches could be saved in the barrel, how much was the winemaker's expertise really worth? It was a debate that remained ongoing, one likely impossible to resolve as the calendar flew further past 2000, given the reticence on all sides to fully disclose clients, adjuncts, failure rates, and techniques.

"We've sold the math of the flavor of wine," McCloskey would say. This math included the calculations of critics such as Robert Parker. Graff himself had come to McCloskey in the late 1980s, concerned about the influence the assessments of Parker and other critics were exerting on fine wine. McCloskey prided himself on being able to deliver to clients the scores they wanted for their more prized offerings, and to make it easier for them to replicate that wine in larger quantities without risking consistent quality. He could often— again starting with the grape, before harvest—steer a client toward earning a 91 or a 92 in Parker's *Wine Advocate* if the client wanted that. The wine might ultimately score a 90 or a 93, but, really, who was quibbling? American baby boomers would snatch it up.

Shortly after that December 1989 blind tasting at Chalone, Dick Graff introduced McCloskey to the owners of Château Lafite Rothschild, the vaunted First Growth winery in Bordeaux. Might he assess the quality of their coming harvest? McCloskey did, successfully predicting from which lots in the vineyards the winery's best wines, or Grand Vins, would emerge. Château Lafite Rothschild became another Enologix client.

GLOBAL WINE

1995–2000 | Nationwide

Critics of Leo McCloskey and his Enologix company would pin nicknames on what they believed were the end results of his and his competitors' efforts: global wine, international wine, big wine. The nicknames implied homogenization as well as a sort of unstoppable nature. *Global* and *international* meant worldwide, *big* meant powerful, indefatigable; they also signaled an inevitable interconnectivity, with producers from regions as diffuse as Oregon's Willamette Valley, Australia's Limestone Coast, and Argentina's Mendoza colliding on the same supermarket shelves.

In retrospect, what this book will call global wine would seem, by the media coverage at the time, to have washed over the American fine wine movement like a tidal wave in the 1990s and early 2000s. It didn't. It seeped in gradually. Enologix, for one, had only sixty-five clients by the start of the 2000s out of the hundreds of wineries in California alone. Moreover, never before the late 1990s had fine wine from so many different places been available to American consumers, adding a certain irony to the harrumphing about global wine. Australia and New Zealand made their first big inroads into the American marketplace, with imports from these nations, including relatively novel varietals Sauvignon Blanc and Syrah, up 17 percent annually in 1998 to 3.2 million cases. *Wine Spectator* picked a red wine from Australia's Penfolds winery as its Wine of the Year in 1995, the first time it had ever chosen one from outside of California or France. Bottles from other nations never before commercially prominent in the United States also started popping up on shelves; Brazilian imports jumped 45 percent in 1996, Chilean imports 60 percent. There was even talk of Peru making a go of it in the United States, and Spain was reasserting itself among leading European exporters.

Meanwhile, the traditional European hegemons, France and Italy, grappled with both changing drinking habits and overproduction at home, which translated into more exports to the United States. "There's a snobbism among the producers," an analyst in Milan explained of Italian winemakers in the late

1990s. "They spend to bring people to their castles in Tuscany, and prefer to invest in journalists who write for wine magazines, rather than buyers for the half-dozen supermarket chains that sell the volume." As a consequence, Italian imports were up annually around 70 percent in 1998, four times the combined total of Australia and New Zealand. In France, wine drinking was steadily declining as an every-day or even every-other-day habit, whatever Americans' newfound quasi-religious belief in the French Paradox. That decline meant more exports to the United States, though not nearly at the annual growth rates of newer entrants such as Australia.

Add to this exports boom the growth in the number of American wineries as well as an industry beyond the weeds of neo-Prohibitionism, poor harvests, and phylloxera, and you have an unusually diverse US wine market, perhaps more diverse brand- and style-wise than any nation's at any time ever. True, the United States may not yet have developed the sort of wine culture hoped for by the likes of Robert Mondavi and Julia Child—one of glasses with lovingly prepared dinners (and lunches), certainly not one to rival that of France, even with its struggles, or of Italy—but what wine culture did exist was impressively varied. By mid-decade, the average Italian drank sixteen gallons annually, the average French person around the same; the average American put away about two gallons. Granted, too, most of the fine wine that American wineries produced stemmed from either Cabernet Sauvignon, Chardonnay, or blends relying on both, grinding under commercial foot other varietals such as the Syrah and Riesling that Randall Grahm at Bonny Doon and Konstantin Frank at his eponymous New York winery had tried to place before a wider audience.

Still, whatever this grapey dominance and this temperate drinking, or in spite of both, the entire American enological ecosystem, from vineyardists to winemakers to distributors to retailers, enjoyed a bracingly strong market as the curtain dropped on the twentieth century. This was the best of times commercially in American fine wine, after some of the worst. The full brunt of the maturing baby boomer generation was finally being felt. Sales of California-made fine wine were up 11 percent in 1997 over 1996, an impressive enough feat coming off the decade's rocky start; all the more impressive, however, when we take the long view. In 1985 California winemakers shipped twenty million cases of fine wine; in 1996, that figure was more than seventy-seven million. And 1997 was a stronger year than 1996. Moreover, while a generation before fine wine ran neck and neck with generic for predominance, fine wine had started accounting for an astounding 88 percent of all wine consumed in the United States, with the cheaper generics claiming a nearly single-digit percentage of the marketplace. The long view again rendered the trend even more starkly: in 1985, California winemakers shipped almost 86 million cases of generics, mostly the screwtop jug wines ballasting the likes of E. & J. Gallo; in 1996 they shipped 52.5 million.

Production was up in California and elsewhere, due in part to the growth in the number of wineries. Also, wine bars and restaurants with extensive wine lists, once anomalous even in the nation's largest cities, began popping up in places such as Cleveland and Detroit; the number of sommeliers and wine stewards ballooned, too, as did the number of American Viticultural Areas the federal government designated—more than half of the fifty states had at least one. Sales of wine gadgetry—the cellars, racks, decanters, aerators, and cork removers that suddenly seemed essential to the enjoyment of what twenty years before would have been an exotic presence in most households—jumped as well. The *Wine Enthusiast*'s catalogue reached a peak of around twenty-two million users in the 1990s.

All of this growth got passed on to the consumer not only in terms of kaleidoscopic variety, but cost, too. Greater demand from the drinking public appeared to outpace even the beefier supply, especially for premium bottles. Also, the widely publicized auctions, the critical acclaim (and the acclaim for certain critics), and the immortal perception among many that wine was something so very special only served as further boons for producers, distributors, and retailers when it came to pricing. Whereas once even top imports such as the 1982 Bordeaux might have been within the financial reach of the average accountant or attorney in the late 1980s, that was no longer the case—at least not within regular, reasonable reach. Bottles of Robert Mondavi Reserve Cabernet Sauvignon and Warren Winiarski's Stag's Leap Wine Cellars Case 23 were retailing for $75; the Lake Vineyard Cabernet from Al Brounstein's Diamond Creek in northern Napa might go for $250 a pop. As for fine French wines on American shelves, First Growth bottles acquired "years ago at reasonable prices" were fetching $350 at auctions, leaving their American owners in the conundrum of either drinking something gaining so rapidly in value or selling it. Wine futures for American wines, never a financially comfortable option for most, were being routinely traded for more than $200 a case, if not twice that.

Prices were bouncing for non-premium fine wines as well. Those bottles costing eight dollars a few years back now cost twelve; those costing twelve now cost twenty. "For all but a small group of consumers," Frank Prial wrote in the *New York Times* in September 1997, "twenty dollars is too much for a bottle of wine for dinner at home." The markups at restaurants and wine bars did not help matters. Nor were things mitigated by retailers' markdowns, perhaps as much as 10 percent in some cities, or the planting of thousands of acres of additional vineyards to make up for those that phylloxera blighted. Prices did not appear to be going down . . . ever. Fine wine in the United States, whether from top-shelf foreign producers, the California game changers, or from all the newcomers, was destined always to be that much pricier than, say, most six-packs of beer or a jug of sweeter plonk, both of which could be had for well under ten dollars in the late 1990s.

Such pricing left the consumer seeking two things more than ever: reassurance and bargains. "In most wine stores, you go in and you either have to know what you want or find a good salesperson," Joshua Wesson told a reporter in 2000. "If you can't do either, then you're wandering in the desert." Four years before, Wesson, a sommelier, cofounded Best Cellars, a retail chain specializing both in fine wine costing no more than ten dollars a bottle and in shearing the subject of verbosity (Wesson grouped the wines under only eight categories, for instance, including *juicy*, *luscious*, and *sweet*). The "anti-wine store" quickly proved a hit, especially at its flagship on Manhattan's Upper East Side, spawning imitators bent on attracting drive-by shoppers who couldn't be bothered to read the *Wine Advocate* or *Wine Spectator.*

For the "small group" shopping the middle and higher ends (the bottles starting at twenty dollars) the critics still played a marketplace-shaping role, one that those buying from the lower shelves might watch as well. As the twentieth century closed, consumers in general continued to ascribe to Robert Parker's warning in the early editions of the *Wine Advocate*—"Subscribe now because you may spend $10 for the wrong bottle of wine"—only the dollar amount had changed.

That change, though, meant that tipplers, wherever on the fine wine spectrum they fell, were paying more than ever before for wines or wine styles. Based on their own experiences and the best advice, they understandably expected them to taste a certain way. A juicy wine had better taste like fruit; a drier wine had to taste just so; one that Parker scored as a 92 had better taste like liquid sunshine. And they had better taste like that every time.

SCREWED

1997–2002 | Manhattan—Oakville, California

Shortly after noon on October 2, 2002, a Wednesday, a steel-gray 1937 Buick hearse pulled alongside the curb outside the Vanderbilt Avenue entrance of Manhattan's Grand Central Terminal. Four pallbearers emerged, three in black and one in impossibly loud purple. They removed an equally steel-gray casket from the hearse and marched it solemnly into one of the nation's busiest train stations, led by a trumpeter blowing "Taps." Amid the curious stares and glances of hurried onlookers, the pallbearers foisted the casket to the Campbell Apartment restaurant and bar at the station's southeast corner. There, amid the beaux-arts capaciousness of Grand Central, they placed the casket on a catafalque before the Campbell's stone fireplace, between a lectern and a wreath ringing a portrait of a cork tree. Finally, the pallbearers solemnly opened the casket. There before them and the assembled mourners lay the *corkpse* of M. Thierry Bouchon (1585–2002).

The pallbearer in purple stepped to the lectern. "I would like to thank you for attending this very heartfelt wake for the old stinker," Randall Grahm said.

The "old stinker" in question was the wine cork ("Thierry Bouchon" being a play on *tire-bouchon*, the French word for *corkscrew*). Grahm's Bonny Doon Vineyard south of San Francisco would hold five such events on both coasts to mark its transition from corks to exclusively screwtops. At this particular one in Manhattan, media capital of the planet, the esteemed British wine critic Jancis Robinson delivered the eulogy: "How we shall miss thy cylindrical barky majesty," she began. "Thy uniquely obstructive presence in the bottlenecks of our favorite drink. Thy utter darned ridiculousness as a twenty-first century stopper." It wasn't all madcap humor. Grahm wanted to drive home a point, and Robinson seemed to oblige. The critic finished her eulogy with an unmistakable critique of the centuries-old enclosure:

But we will not mourn the social posturing you have—perhaps unwittingly—given rise to over the past centuries. The sniffing of the cork. How ridiculous is that when the most hideously tainted wines can be topped by perfectly sweet-smelling corks, and the most divine wines emerge from under a stink-bomb of a cork?

Message: Corks, wooden or synthetic plastic, could be unreliable. Screwtops were better. (Bonny Doon had flirted with synthetics for a couple of years before taking the screwtop plunge exclusively.) The trade press had gotten the message a while before, in fact, sometimes complaining about the damage cork rot could inflict on wines and musing aloud about alternatives. It was this critical kvetching that inspired Grahm to stage the wakes. *If I can mobilize the press*, he thought, *I can really turn this to my advantage.* It would prove a tough sell to American consumers, however, one that began well before the macabre festivities in Grand Central. Bob Trinchero's Sutter Home in St. Helena, California, had been moving millions of cases of its screwtop White Zinfandel since the early 1990s; fine wineries in New Zealand and Australia had used screwtops as far back as the 1950s. The real game changer, however—or at least what *looked* like the real game changer—came in June 2000, when the PlumpJack Winery in Napa Valley announced it would seal half of its Reserve Cabernet Sauvignon from grapes harvested that year with screwtops.

Beyond the technicalities of sealing with a screwtop rather than a cork, PlumpJack was breaking profound ground. It was one of those ultra-premium wineries that had sprung forth from the fine wine movement's flush wave beginning in the early 1990s, with the neo-Prohibitionists vanquished—or at least kept at bay—and the baby boomers undergirding an entire enological biosphere. The founding of PlumpJack served as an excellent example of that by-then decades-old aspect of American fine wine: the convergence of money and ambition in a region held sacred worldwide for its grape-growing abilities.

Gavin Newsom had started a wine store called PlumpJack Wine & Spirits on San Francisco's trendy Fillmore Street in 1992; much of the seed money for the store sprang from the Getty family. The Newsom and Getty families went back a ways. Newsom's father, a state appellate court justice, had been friends since high school in the 1940s with Gordon Getty, a music composer and a son of J. Paul Getty, one of the world's wealthiest men. The Gettys were a dynasty that oil made rich and that subsequent investments, including the photograph-sharing service Getty Images, made richer. It was the elder Newsom and a few others who traveled to southern Italy after the abduction of J. Paul Getty III—nephew of Gordon and grandson of J. Paul—to deliver the multimillion-dollar ransom that freed the teenager. Gordon Getty would end up underwriting many of Newsom's ventures in the San Francisco Bay Area after Newsom graduated from college in 1989, including in real estate development, hospitality, and restaurants. It was inevitable that fine wine would make an appearance in the young entrepreneur's portfolio.

Armed with Getty's financial backing, Newsom went for broke, leasing forty-two acres in Oakville and launching a winery on the vineyard in 1995. Such a location, as well as the reputations of the winery's principals, fueled much of the pearl-clutching that arose in the wake of the 1997 screwtop announcement from PlumpJack, which was named after one of Getty's operas as well as a Shakespearean character. Sutter Home and White Zinfandel—lighter in flavor and less expensive in price—using screwtops was one thing. But PlumpJack's Reserve Cabernet Sauvignon, sprung from the same Oakville soil that Robert Mondavi had three decades ago sanctified in critics' eyes, if not consumers'—that was an entirely different proposition. Moreover, Gordon Getty wasn't just any financial backer, he was from California nobility; and Newsom—tall, movie-star handsome, and whip-smart in front of a microphone—seemed destined for politics (he would indeed serve two terms as San Francisco mayor, before being elected California's lieutenant governor in 2010).

Finally, PlumpJack, in keeping with their ultra-premium milieu, aimed for the topmost end of the marketplace with the 1997 Reserve Cabernet Sauvignon pricing: when the inaugural 282 cases first appeared in late 2000, they were priced at $135 a bottle, hardly in the lower-priced league of Sutter Home White Zinfandel. PlumpJack even deliberately priced its corked Reserve Cabernet Sauvignon ten dollars *cheaper* than the screwtop version to drive home the point that the screwtopped bottle was just as worthy of consumer attention (the winery also sold them in two-packs—one corked, one capped—for $260).

The industry itself generally supported the move, particularly the production side. Winemakers saw the screwtop bottles, with their firmer, longer-lasting seal, as a solution to the oxygen-fueled degradation that can seep into wine from corks that might dry out. At the time of PlumpJack's initial screwtop bottling, corks failed to adequately protect the contents within about 8 percent of the time, rendering the wines unsellable, never mind undrinkable. This was an embarrassingly high rate in particular for ultra-premium wineries that might sell their wares for north of one hundred dollars a bottle and with the expectation that they would age well. Moreover, some winemakers thought their cork producers and suppliers were not taking the problem all that seriously. Randall Grahm, for one, pronounced himself "fed up." Screwtops promised a stronger, or at least more consistent, seal. Also, contrary to a myth that would dog PlumpJack's move for years, screwtops were not all that cheap to use. It cost the winery $150,000 for the first five hundred cases worth of screwtopped bottles, and PlumpJack had to commit four vintages to the endeavor if the pricing was going to work; finally, the winery had to turn to an Italian glassmaker for the bottles, so rare were domestically made 750ml ones with the necessary openings for screwtops.

The two-pack of the 1997 PlumpJack Cabernet Sauvignon—one with screwtop, the other with cork—marked a revolution in American fine wine's approach to bottling.
COURTESY OF PLUMPJACK

While the production wing of the industry nodded quiet approval toward PlumpJack's 2000 announcement, the marketing side, so important in an industry where perception might dictate much of price, was aghast. "This is the end of your career," a colleague at another winery told John Conover, who joined PlumpJack in 1999 as general manager, just as the winery was preparing to bottle its first screwtops. "You'll be known as the screwcap winery."

That skepticism carried over to consumers for the same reason: screw-tops were seen as a sign of wine being cheap, cheap, cheap, no matter the cost it took to use them. The cheesy ghost of E. & J. Gallo's Pink Chablis—or Thunderbird, or any number of fortified wines designed to wallop rather than to impress—loomed collectively large. It also loomed particularly large for PlumpJack's clientele in general, which skewed demographically older; simply put, these sixty- and seventy-year-olds, with long memories, were less apt to roll their financial dice on a screwtop wine, however fine. "Millions have long been used for whiskey, vodka and other liquors and for inexpensive wines. Which is the problem," wrote Frank Prial in the *New York Times* on October 31, 2001. "For most wine consumers, screw caps are indelibly associated with jug wines and—worse—cheap fortified wines with a largely skid-row clientele. Time and again, consumers have rejected screw-on bottle tops."

It would take a while for the perception to even start to shift, at least when it came to American fine wine at the premium or ultra-premium ends. But PlumpJack's 1997 Reserve Cabernet Sauvignon did sell out—before it was even officially on sale. Robert Parker's rave review in a December 1998 *Wine Advocate* ensured robust preorders. "The wine boasts an opaque purple color," he wrote of early samples, "followed by a stunning bouquet of flowers, black currants, minerals, and toasty oak. Rich and powerful . . ." PlumpJack would continue to seal many of its wines, particularly whites, with screwtops; the practice helped make it one of the more profitable ultra-premium wineries in Napa Valley, with a production level by 2006 of 10,500 cases annually (again, the winery was in a different league than Sutter Home, with its hundreds of thousands of cases of screwtop White Zinfandel alone).

Few ultra-premium American wineries besides Randall Grahm's Bonny Doon followed in PlumpJack's risky wake during that new decade. The modest sales of screwtop wines in the United States sprang largely from wineries in South America, New Zealand, and Australia, as well as from domestic producers such as Sutter Home that were working the lower-price end of the market. It would be several years before screwtop fine wines made a serious dent in the United States; one estimate pegged 2013 as the first year that screwtops flirted with a double-digit percentage presence in the US marketplace. The vast majority of 750ml bottles remained sealed by natural wooden corks; the share might have been as high as 80 percent as recently as 2014.

Not that screwtops were infallible. If not properly sealed, screwtops could cause "reduction," a term covering a broad range of things that can go wrong with some wine styles if they don't get just enough air; these underoxygenated wines might end up smelling sulfurous, like rotten eggs. Reduction was rare, though, affecting perhaps fewer than 3 percent of bottles sealed with screwtops. Otherwise, there appeared to be no technical downside. Scientific studies as well as critical blind tastings would reveal almost no difference in either taste or quality when it came to screwtops versus corks. One such study, published in 2005, came from the redoubtable Viticulture & Enology Department at the University of California, Davis; it tested six bottles of 2002 Sauvignon Blanc from New Zealand, half sealed with screwtops and half with traditional corks. The bottles were filled to different levels and treated with different levels of sulfur dioxide (a.k.a. sulfites); they were also stored either upright, in the case of the screwtops, or lying down, in the case of the corked bottles, which are supposed to lie flat so as to keep the cork moistened. Researchers stored all six bottles in the same cellar at the same temperature with the same level of humidity.

And they came out tasting the same:

> When a trained panel of 12 judges was presented the wines in pairs and asked the question: "Are they the same or different?", there was no significant difference. When the same panel was asked to rate the intensity of 6 self-generated attributes (passion fruit/sweet, passion fruit/stalk, capsicum, cat urine, grassy, and lemon peel) using an unstructured scale, the intensities were similar for the three sample wines compared.

Similar studies would roll in comparing screwtopped wines with corks, both traditional and plastic, and would reach similar conclusions. Critics, too, couldn't help themselves. Whether as part of these studies or on their own, they sized up this relatively new sealant on the American fine wine market against the one everyone always associated with Merlot, Chardonnay, et al. The critic Richard Jennings described the results of a March 2011 tasting of three bottles, including the 1997 PlumpJack Reserve Cabernet Sauvignon, under both cork and screwtop:

> I was guessing that the bottle under cork would show greater maturity and development, so I assumed my favorite in the tast-

ing, bottle A, which showed the most development, would be the Plump[J]ack under cork. . . . So between the two closures of PlumpJack, I definitely preferred our bottle C, the screw cap version, which had a plush cassis and menthol nose, was also tight, but showing more fruit than the cork sealed bottle, with more integrated oak.

If anything, indeed, critics, who had been calling the end of cork's predominance since at least the mid-1990s, gave the edge to the screwtopped wines. In 2009 a writer for *Forbes* magazine tasted some such bottles with George Taber, chronicler of the Judgment of Paris and an early chronicler as well of the screwtop versus cork debate in the United States. Regarding a PlumpJack Reserve Cabernet Sauvignon retailing for ninety dollars, they had this to say: "We noticed, however, that the screw-cap version seems a bit richer and fruitier."

Consumers began to notice the difference in quality, too—or at least they stopped caring so much about the romance of the cork. It became another sign of the American fine wine movement's evolution. Critics aware of the history of screwtopped jug wines, of E. & J. Gallo's Pink Chablis and Thunderbird, might fret about the differences in sealants; and the industry might worry about those judgments. Not consumers. For them, especially those born in the late 1970s and early 1980s—and therefore just able to legally drink—screwtopped bottles were just another facet of the fine wine cornucopia that America had become by the twenty-first century; they were not the older customer base of wineries such as PlumpJack. The screwtop market share would remain small compared with cork, but the numbers were trending decisively less than a decade after PlumpJack's 2000 announcement and barely fifteen years after Sutter Home's moves. In 2006 the increase in domestic sales of screwtopped wines would outpace overall domestic sales 25 percent to 11 percent; a survey that same year showed that more than one-third of wine drinkers who had at least one glass weekly had bought a wine sealed with a screwtop, up from just over 27 percent in 2005.

In yet another improbable twist, the United States, despite the production head starts of Australia and New Zealand, was on its way to becoming the single-biggest market for screwtop wines. In fact, as the twentieth century shuffled into oblivion, America was poised to become the biggest wine market, period.

FAT BASTARDS AND SMOKING LOONS

1998—2004 | Languedoc-Roussillon, France—Alexander Valley, California— Bonny Doon, California

Bottles of Fat Bastard Chardonnay (left) and Fat Bastard Merlot. The phenomenally selling brand kicked off a new era in packaging and marketing fine wine in the United States.
COURTESY OF FAT BASTARD

Early one week in late 1994, Guy Anderson, an English winemaker who had worked in Italy and France, dropped in on Thierry Boudinaud, a winemaker who cut his teeth in California, Australia, and New Zealand before settling in the Languedoc-Roussillon region in the southern part of his native France. The pair, both barely into their thirties, had met the year before and worked together on producing and marketing different wines. They quickly fell to talking shop in Boudinaud's cold, damp cellar.

Anderson had just come from a week of tasting wines in Bourgogne, divining the right varietals and blends he might eventually bring to market in the United Kingdom. Boudinaud handed him a Chardonnay to try, a yeasty gambit he had been toying with in one of the tanks at the back of the cellar. Anderson was impressed.

"This is every bit as good as one of the Bâtard-Montrachets I was making last week," he said, referencing a Bourgogne village named after what in the past would have been called a "bastard," or son born out of wedlock. Boudinaud's wine was full-bodied, with a rich, fruity taste that lingered on the palate and a deep straw-like color that belied its 100 percent sourcing from Chardonnay grapes in Languedoc-Roussillon.

His friend's praise aside, Boudinaud was modest. "Well," he replied, "I don't know if it's Bâtard-Montrachet quality, but it is one fat bastard of a wine."

The two laughed at the description, delivered as it was in the Frenchman's heavily accented English. They wrote the name *Fat Bastard* on the tank and moved on to the next option. Later another wine merchant dropped by, and Boudinaud again poured a sample of his experimental Chardonnay. The merchant, like Anderson before, was impressed—deeply impressed.

"This is really special," the merchant said. "I'll take it all. Does it have a name?"

It did now. The name that Boudinaud and Anderson had scribbled on the tank became the name of the new Chardonnay. And the new Chardonnay, Fat Bastard, became a smash hit. The first eight hundred cases released in the United Kingdom sold out quickly. In 1998 Fat Bastard Chardonnay climbed ashore in the United States in the form of 2,049 cases; that number grew by more than 600 percent the following year and crested more than forty-five thousand cases in 2000. In 2004, by which time the Fat Bastards were retailing for around ten dollars a bottle, the case count had grown to 550,000. In six short years, Fat Bastard had very likely become the best-selling French-made Chardonnay ever in America.

Boudinaud and Anderson quickly rolled out an entire line of Fat Bastard wines, including reds such as a richly dark Fat Bastard Merlot, which tasted heavily of black cherries and plums, and other whites, including Fat Bastard Sauvignon Blanc, a veritable citrus-fruit bomb complete with a lemony hue. Fruitiness dominated all of the Fat Bastard wines, which perhaps went far toward explaining the popularity that each enjoyed in an America that seemed to have an insatiable appetite for lusher, fruitier, fuller-tasting wines.

Or was it the name?

During what Boudinaud and Anderson called their Living Large tour of the Northeast in the spring of 2004 to promote the debut of that Fat

Bastard Merlot, people from Boston to Annapolis besieged them with requests for branded merchandise. It did not hurt the winemakers' cause that the hit 1999 movie *Austin Powers: The Spy Who Shagged Me* had included a morbidly obese character called Fat Bastard, played by *Saturday Night Live* alumnus Mike Myers. Boudinaud and Anderson lustily responded to the merchandising requests, dispensing Fat Bastard T-shirts, bumper stickers, baseball caps, and boxer shorts from their RV, with its eight-foot inflatable Fat Bastard hippopotamus above it, or from the wine shops and nightclubs along the eighteen-day jaunt that saw them treated "like rock stars," in the words of one journalist who beheld the wine-soaked spectacle. There were even Fat Bastard colored condoms. At the most compulsive heights of his promotional powers, it would be impossible to imagine Robert Mondavi tossing out Robert Mondavi condoms; it would be equally herculean to imagine a name anywhere near as ribald as Fat Bastard appearing on a label of a Robert Mondavi wine, wherever it might fall on the price spectrum.

Go back to the 1960s and 1970s, even much of the 1980s, and American fine wine labels inevitably presented a somber, serious product within. The names were often surnames or locations, and the information was exactingly direct. Oftentimes, the labels offered no more than the winery, the grape type(s), the vintage year, and perhaps a graphic, such as a crest or a rendering of the winery itself. Take that groundbreaking Robert Mondavi Cabernet Sauvignon from the 1960s. Its label stated in a seven-level ascending order the vintage year, the geography ("Napa Valley"), the grape type, the alcoholic content, and a three-tiered explanation of its production: "Produced and Bottled by/Robert Mondavi Winery/Oakville, California." A yellow-and-black sketch of the Cliff May–designed winery off Highway 29 crowned the words; the only other color on the label was the vintage year done in red.

Such was the simple, stark template for the vast majority of fine wine produced, or sold, in the United States starting in the 1960s—and it was a hard-fought simplicity at that. Pioneers such as the writer and merchant Frank Schoonmaker had had to convince wineries to list grape types and geographic origin clearly, and the industry itself had had to convince the federal government to abstain from further admonitions beyond those warning of sulfites and the potential health dangers of too much drink. Fine wine labels in the United States into the twenty-first century put an aesthetic premium on directness; on the back label, often alongside those government warnings, there might be further explanations, but the front was generally shorn of euphemism or double meaning. Barring cork rot or poor storage, what buyers saw was what they got when they opened the bottle. It was, it seemed, a conscious imitation of European packaging. Elements of that packaging might be different (especially because in the United States labels placed more emphasis on the grape types used), but by the time of the American fine wine movement, labels had adopted that sonorously serious directness.

And why shouldn't labels have appeared serious and straightforward? From a marketing perspective, it was a smart business move, especially for less expensive fine wines; given the role that pricing and perception had come to play in consumers' minds—trends helped massively along by critics and the industry itself—a more genteel label might be the decisive factor for a wine shopper. Again, we can look to Mondavi as an example. Labels for its lower-priced Woodbridge line, named after the town near the grape growers' cooperative that the winery acquired in California's Central Valley in 1979, offered a harmonious pastiche of rolling vineyards soothingly capped in big, bold letters with WOODBRIDGE BY ROBERT MONDAVI. The name itself, as well as the names of competitors such as Coastal Estates, Beaulieu's lower-priced offering, could be mistaken for "suburban subdivisions" as the *New York Times* saw it.

Fat Bastard upended this more straightforward approach in the United States. More to the point, its commercial success upended things. Prior to its success, other wineries working with higher-end grapes had put forth similarly risqué names. Alexander Valley Vineyards launched in Sonoma County in 1975, on farmland the Wetzel family had owned since the early 1960s, and specialized in—what else?—Chardonnay and Cabernet Sauvignon, as well as in selling grapes to other wineries. In 1978, however, winemaker Hank Wetzel crafted a Zinfandel from grapes left over from that year's harvest; his sister, Katie Wetzel Murphy, who handled the winery's marketing, dubbed it Sin Zin, complete with a scantily clad figure in seductive repose splayed across the largely black-and-red label. Originally, it was simply an inside joke, a gift to friends and family. Encouraged by the reaction, however, the Wetzels were soon selling the spicy, plummy Sin Zin commercially. They dropped the name for a time in the mid-1980s in favor of the staid Alexander Valley Vineyards name, but customer complaints soon compelled Sin Zin's rerelease as well as their release of other irreverent Zinfandel brands, including Temptation and Redemption.

A bottle of Inglenook 1941 Cabernet Sauvignon (left) and a bottle of Chateau Montelena 1973 Chardonnay. Both are examples of the classic straightforward packaging inherited from European winemakers.
COURTESY OF INGLENOOK; CHATEAU, MONTELENA

Randall Grahm's Bonny Doon also enjoyed success from the early 1990s onward with an indecorously named Zinfandel—in his case, Cardinal Zin. A wickedly amorphous-looking Catholic cardinal dominated the label designed by British illustrator Ralph Steadman, who was most famous for his collaborations with writer Hunter S. Thompson. Grahm's copy for the back label all but taunted potential buyers with lines such as, "We anticipate its greedy acquisition by consumers lusting for a complete gluttonous, sorry, that supersonic gastronomic experience." Sonorous descriptions of Old World charm this was not. Around the same time, Grahm also launched a brand called Big House, inspired by the state prison in the California city of Soledad, where he bought land in 1992 (one such Big House production: a Syrah called the Slammer). Both Big House and Cardinal Zin proved commercial hits for Bonny Doon, helping the winery scale up to around $27 million in annual revenue by the time Grahm sold both brands in 2006.

Still, while Bonny Doon might have sold 175,000 cases annually of its Big House brands, Boudinaud and Anderson's Fat Bastard, with its half-million-plus case runs, stood in a class by itself among this newer trend in naughtier marketing. Their late 1990s creation soon spawned a run of etymological imitators bent less on reassuring consumers than on surprising them—or at least eliciting a chuckle. Make no mistake: the wine inside still had to be decent, if not terrific. An analysis of wine labels, prices, and consumer choices presented at California Polytechnic State University in March 2010 put it this way:

> In all, a wine label's value is only as good as the wine itself. . . . If there is a correlation between the aesthetics of wine labels and which bottle of wine the average consumer purchases on a Tuesday night, it is a choice that is not statistical or mathematical. Some of the wines that receive the highest Parker scores have the simplest labels and some of the most intricate labels are the least expensive. So, like a book, don't judge a wine by its label.

Consumers couldn't help it, though, as the sales numbers of Fat Bastard and later imitators suggested. It was America's tradition of free speech, including in commercial branding, that allowed for just about anything on a wine label save for disparagement of a competitor, something truly obscene, or misleading or incorrect information. Brands such as Ball Buster, BigAss Red, Bitch, Jealous Bitch, and Royal Bitch, as well as less rascally though equally incongruous ones such as Smoking Loon, Cupcake, Jam Jar, Layer Cake, and Bored Doe (get it?), would crowd American shelves and menus into the new century, coating fine wine in a sort of schoolyard insouciance that would have been scandalous—or at least laughable—to American and French winemakers a generation before. It was no coincidence that Boudinaud and Anderson were themselves not even teenagers at the time of the Judgment of Paris in 1976; it is unlikely members of an earlier generation could have divined a name like Fat Bastard or crafted a marketing approach that involved boxer shorts and an enormous fake hippo.

Labels from Bonny Doon's Cardinal Zin, a Zinfandel (left), and Le Cigare Volante, a blend (right). Both labels helped push American fine wine packaging in new directions.
COURTESY OF BONNY DOON

"We're more like a beer brand than a wine," Anderson told a reporter during the Fat Bastard Merlot tour. Now *that* was scandalous! Anderson was not referencing the growing ranks of American craft beers that independent breweries were making in small batches with traditional ingredients; he was referencing enormous brewing concerns such as Anheuser-Busch and Miller, and their tacky advertising that often featured ex-jocks, comedians such as Rodney Dangerfield, and bowling. This was not the American fine wine movement of even ten years before, much less twenty or thirty.

That was, of course, the point—one that became incandescently clear as fine wine burrowed further and further into the heart of American popular culture. During that Fat Bastard Merlot tour in 2004, Boudinaud and Anderson encountered some men in their twenties who, as Anderson described it, were "just turned on to wine, and Fat Bastard was down with them." New generations were arising, ones that did not, that *could* not, see fine wine in America as their parents and grandparents had. Yet a red by any other name smelled pretty much like ripe fruit.

SIR ROBERT AND THE FRUIT BOMBS

1999–2001 | Paris—New York City

Robert Parker was not supposed to say anything while French president Jacques Chirac pinned France's highest accolade on him, but he couldn't help himself. "Merci, le President!" a sweatily nervous Parker exclaimed. Tears in his eyes, he answered a startled Chirac's two European-style airpecks with large kisses on the president's cheeks, the men ending their encounter—before a crowd of about one hundred in the reception salon of Paris's Élysée Palace—with manly smacks on the shoulders.

On June 22, 1999, a Tuesday, Parker became the first wine critic ever to receive the Legion of Honor, the blue, green, gold, and white medal Napoleon Bonaparte established in 1802 to reward extraordinary contributions to France. Parker was the only American to receive the honor that day, though it had been bestowed already on a number of US military veterans who fought in France during the world wars, as well as on figures such as Ronald Reagan and

Neil Armstrong. But Parker enjoyed the rare honor of receiving the medal—officially the Chevalier de Légion d'Honneur—directly from the president of the Republic, who called Parker "the man who taught America about French wine [and] the most respected and influential critic of French wines in the entire world." Chirac's pronouncement was difficult to dispute: the onetime attorney at the Farm Credit Bank in suburban Baltimore, who parlayed his passion for fine wine into a self-published newsletter in 1978 and who seized his editorial moment five years later with the 1982 Bordeaux, was indeed the most powerful critic of French wines—of any wines, including American.

Myriad examples of Parker's influence abounded at the close of the 1990s, whether it was his ability to hyper-boost the sales of an unheralded California winery or destroy the fortunes of an ancient French one. In general, his coverage had only boosted the French wine industry, lifting it from its existential doldrums after the Judgment of Paris in 1976 and turning his own free-spending generation, the baby boomers, on to the joys of French appellations, particularly Bordeaux, through his best-selling guides and his bimonthly newsletter. That newsletter's numbers belied his influence. The *Wine Advocate* had forty thousand subscribers by the new century, and his disciples followed him with a fervency few critics in any field could hope to engender; their detractors even slapped an appropriately lemming-like nickname on them, which they embraced: Parker Sheep. The flock was always ready, often online, to counter any criticism of their shepherd's palate, any impugning of his hard-earned integrity (the *Wine Advocate* continued to rely on subscribers paying forty dollars annually, rather than on advertisers who might prod Parker for a certain angle); and they snatched up his highest-rated bottles en masse, which was the important thing.

Not everyone shared in President Chirac's hearty congratulations, however. Gilles Pudlowski, a prominent wine critic in France, sniffed that Parker tended to prefer fruitier, heavier wines, what those in the Bordeaux industry called "vin de putes"—or whore's wine. "In other words," Pudlowski explained to a reporter, "a wine that gives immediate pleasure without a culture of depth." It was an accusation that had dogged Parker since he broke through after the '82 Bordeaux reviews: He only liked, and therefore only highly praised, big fruit bombs laden with alcohol. As his old editor-turned-biographer Elin McCoy put it:

> The 100-point wines were more often those Parker described as "massive and powerful" than "delicate and subtle." Some of his "perfect" and "near perfect" reds resembled a "dry vintage port," as he put

it, although other palates might be more reminded of cough syrup. Many had high alcohol, even upwards of 16 percent. The sensation of ripe fruit was paramount. Parker was fond of asking, "How much enjoyment do you get eating a pear that's not ripe? If they're not ripe, they're green, they're acidic, they're just not flavorful, and they're not fun." He himself had admitted in print that when it came to Bordeaux he had "a stylistic preference for more opulently textured wines with lower acidity."

Parker seemed to personify this preference for big, strong wines. Fifty-one when Chirac knighted him, he weighed 265 pounds, the chiseled-chin look of his jocular high school days long gone, replaced by a rotund face of comfortable jowls; journalists couldn't help but describe his walk at the time as a "waddle," and he had gout. Still, he remained unapologetic, a "hedonist" in his own words, happy to taste deeply and fully of the food and drink available to the world's most powerful wine critic. Health scares didn't seem to bother him, never mind those admonishments from the neo-Prohibitionist crowd, which Parker took particular pleasure in loathing. In 1997, during a ten-course meal at a French restaurant in Manhattan, Parker turned gray and began to sweat profusely; he heard a high-pitched whine in his ears and grew weak. As he and his anxious dinner mates awaited an ambulance, George Pataki, the governor of New York, arrived for a meal of his own. Parker looked up at him "from the edge of death" and found humor in the moment: "Don't eat the scallops!" he warned Pataki. It wasn't the scallops, though, nor a feared heart attack, but a bleeding ulcer that doctors quickly fixed. Such an appetite for opulence meant two things in the American fine wine movement: One, it meant that Parker's praise elided many of the subtler, drier wine styles in favor of the heavier, wetter ones. Two, those heavier, wetter wines became that much heavier and wetter (read: fruitier)—and uniformly so.

A little while after Parker received his singular honor at the Élysée Palace, Alice Feiring, who was writing the official wine guidebook for *Food & Wine* and who would soon go on to cover the subject for *Time* magazine, started noticing something in her work: a lot of the wines available in her hometown of New York City, whatever their terroir or their vintage, tasted similar. A Cabernet Sauvignon from one part of California tasted like a Cabernet Sauvignon from another part of the Golden State; a Chardonnay from France could pass for one from the United States. Subtlety seemed to Feiring suddenly nonexistent in legendary varietals such as Barolo from northern Italy and Champagne from northern France. Some styles appeared to be vanishing altogether, dragging the wineries that made them down the memory hole as well.

Feiring—a plain-talking, spectacled Brooklyn native introduced to fine wine through friends in graduate school in Cambridge, Massachusetts—saw things as particularly dire, especially when it came to California wines. Never a jewel in that state's fine wine crown, Pinot Noirs had become particularly off-putting in their fruity uniformity. "How could anybody drink this shit?" she wondered. Then she asked *why* they drank it. A friend told her about firms such as Leo McCloskey's Enologix that were advising an increasing number of wineries on how to cater their wares to Robert Parker's palate, therefore garnering high scores and the resultant high sales. Feiring knew of Parker—it was hard not to by the early 2000s—though she did not read the *Wine Advocate*. She had not, however, fully grasped Parker's power. Feiring soon placed herself at the vanguard of a reaction against Parker and his taste for opulent wines, a reaction delineated by age (Feiring was several years younger than Parker, born at the tail end of the baby boom rather than toward the beginning) and by a generous helping of irony.

"I AM NOT DRINKING ANY FUCKING MERLOT"
2000–2009 | Cambridge, Massachusetts

"**I am very, very proud**," Julia Child told the crowd at the Hotel Méridien in Cambridge, Massachussets, barely two miles from the house where she and her husband, Paul, had lived for decades, the same house from which she had called producer Russell Morash at WGBH in Boston to request a hot plate for that first public-television appearance in early 1962.

The crowd of about two hundred had gathered on Sunday, November 19, 2000, to see the California native awarded the Legion of Honor. Renowned chef Jacques Pépin served as master of ceremonies; restaurateur Roger Fessaguet, a chevalier in the legion himself, presented the medal. Child, still whimsically spry at eighty-eight, organized for the occasion what she described as her "dream meal": foie gras, roast duck with chanterelle mushrooms and pearl onions, sole with cucumber, and profiteroles with vanilla ice cream and chocolate sauce. Wine, naturally, was on the menu, the Christian Sabbath be damned: a 1990 Château Suduiraut Sauternes, a 1998 Louis Latour Pouilly-Fuissé, and a 1997 E. Guigal Côte Rôtie. No American wines were served, but that was kind of the point. "Before Julia Child, America was still a meat-and-potatoes country," Fessaguet said. "But then Julia gave chefs instructions to make French cuisine with ingredients they could find in American super-markets. She helped to make cooking the culture it is today."

That culture included fine wine. Child had helped mightily to demystify the beverage for her fellow Americans, to reach back past Prohibition and rescue it from the exoticness that the thirteen-year ban as well as government actions (and reactions) had left it mired in. Fine wine, in Child's televised and published universe, became but an accoutrement to cooking and con-viviality, something you bought on the way home and drank with dinner or perhaps even sipped with lunch. At the advent of the twenty-first century the United States still lagged behind European cultures in terms of wine drinking, though the numbers were clearly shifting. That was due in no small part to that shift in perception from exotic to more commonplace; and we can trace a straight line from Child's lunchtime epiphany in Rouen in 1948, when the waiter nonchalantly served her that crisp, white Pouilly Fumé from France's Loire region, to that perception shift two generations later. Fine wine, from the lower-priced table brands to the superpremium bottles costing in the hundreds of dollars, was part of food in America now; more important, it was part of a foodie culture you could not escape, no matter your tastes.

This foodie culture came with many nicknames. The word *foodie* itself seems to have bubbled up from the mid-1980s into the American media ver-nacular by the end of the twentieth century; the comedian Jerry Seinfeld even dropped the word, albeit mockingly, during a bit to introduce a June 1991 episode of his hit NBC sitcom *Seinfeld*.

There was also Slow Food, the somewhat messianic movement that a handful of Italians from that nation's prime wine-making region, Piedmont, hatched after the world's largest McDonald's opened near the Spanish Steps in Rome in April 1986. The 248-word Slow Food manifesto, released in Decem-ber 1989 with the input of American members, spelled out its reactionary yet simple premise:

> We are enslaved by speed and have all succumbed to the same insidious virus: Fast Life, which disrupts our habits, pervades the pri-vacy of our homes and forces us to eat Fast Foods. . . . Our defense should begin at the table with Slow Food. Let us rediscover the

flavors and savors of regional cooking and banish the degrading effects of Fast Food.

Slow Food's membership numbers swelled in the United States throughout the 1990s and into the 2000s, with Slow Food USA, the domestic wing of the group, launching out of San Francisco in 1998. Alice Waters, who had taken essentially the same slow-going approach to the cuisine of her pioneering Berkeley restaurant in the 1970s, was among Slow Food USA's early leaders, and several area winemakers were among its cheerleaders.

Slow Food jelled nicely, too, with what had come to be called "locavorism," an equally reactionary push to cook and consume mostly local ingredients and foodstuffs, whether they be beef from cattle raised on a nearby farm or wine sourced from grapes grown in the vineyard down the road. Locavorism would within a few years end up undergirding an entire foodie ecosystem in itself, from trendy eateries in major cities such as New York and Chicago, to grocers and other vendors (including online), to books and shorter missives espousing the joys of locally produced food and drink. More wineries, too, were adding options for sampling their wares at the source. "Today, from Mattituck, N.Y., to Mendocino County, Calif.," Frank Prial wrote in May 2001, "hundreds of wineries devote almost as much time and money to their tasting rooms as to their cellars."

At the same time and not by chance, whole companies sprang up to satiate the newfound demand for what was being called "artisanal" or "artisan" food. Artisan bread was in the 1990s "the next food craze," one that flowered in the following decade with upscale bakeries and cafes peppering metropolitan areas such as Boston, San Francisco, and Austin. There were even national chains of these types of restaurants, including Au Bon Pain and the St. Louis Bread Company, which Au Bon Pain would absorb and reposition as Panera Bread. Coffee, too, saw a tremendous pivot from utilitarian morning fuel to a kind of socioeconomic bellwether with its own language and rituals. Starbucks in 1987 had fifteen locations in the Seattle area; fifteen years later, in 2002, it had 5,689 locations in twenty-eight countries. Its entry into a neighborhood, or the entry of competitors such as Caribou Coffee and Peet's Coffee, often harbingered gentrification, as did the debut of a wine bar. Longtime residents often opposed such gentrification, which by definition usually brought higher real estate prices along with the higher-paid new neighbors. The opening of a wine bar that actor Bruce Willis co-owned in Manhattan's once-gritty East Village in June 2008 drew protesters waving signs that read DIE HARD

YUPPIE SCUM, referencing Willis's canonical action movie in their rage against by-the-glass Cabernet.

The yuppies, those young professionals of the 1980s and 1990s, and their progeny, often labeled "hipsters" or "Generation X," tended to be artisanally omnivorous and omnibibulous nonetheless. "They drink wine and boutique beers (and can discuss them expertly) but only in moderation, and they hardly ever smoke cigarettes," said the *Economist* of the generation that came of age in the 1990s and 2000s. American fine wine, exotic to some of their parents and certainly to their grandparents, had become a part of the consumerist milieu, a wine shop a feather in any urban developer's ground-floor retail cap, a capacious wine aisle a feature of your average suburban grocery store. In 2002, for instance, the A&P supermarket chain, one of the nation's largest retailers, acquired Joshua Wesson's Best Cellars, the fine wine emporium that grouped bottles by taste rather than origin.

This ubiquity fed a craving among consumers for information about artisanal wares, including fine wine, and the media world responded. In April 2002 the *New York Times* expanded its "Dining In, Dining Out" New York City section nationwide, explaining that it would have "an increased focus on the food scene including a new wine-tasting feature, and more national coverage of chefs and restaurants." Its two main national competitors, the *Wall Street Journal* and *USA Today*, started wine clubs, as did the *Times* itself, the *San Francisco Chronicle*, and *Forbes* magazine. At the same time, "dozens of great wine books" were hitting the shelves, many updated editions of earlier works, such as British critic Hugh Johnson and Jancis Robinson's *World Atlas of Wine*, Robert Parker's *Parker's Wine Buyer's Guide*, and *Wine Spectator's California Wine* by James Laube, a senior editor at the magazine; other works were brand-new, including *The Pleasures of Wine* by Gerald Asher, the architect of the old California Barrel Tastings at the Four Seasons. The early and mid-2000s, in fact, represented the greatest burst of fine wine writing since the early 1970s.

A lot of this came through the World Wide Web, that decade-old development of English programmer Tim Berners-Lee. Alder Yarrow was born on a hippie commune in Sonoma County and grew up in Aspen, Colorado. He spent his summers back at the commune, where he would often tag along with adult relatives to wine tastings (his first might have been a late-harvested Sauvignon Blanc). While studying abroad at Oxford University in England in the early 1990s, the round-faced, curly-haired Stanford student began testing and tasting wines in the most straightforward way: too intimidated to ask for help from clerks, he picked the cheap bottles on the lower shelves, working his way through styles and unwittingly into an expanding body of knowledge. By the end of the decade, Yarrow, then working in software in the San Francisco Bay Area, was the go-to guy for his friends when it came to wine advice. Tired of answering the same questions repeatedly, one day in late 2003, Yarrow typed *wine blog* into Google on his IBM ThinkPad. No hits appeared. (Were he to have skimmed the major American newspapers of the day, it's unlikely he would have seen the phrase there, either.) Yarrow typed in *vinography* next. No hits again. He had his idea and the name for it.

The wine blog Vinography launched on January 15, 2004, and within eight months it stood at the vanguard of an expanding warren of US wine blogs; to his surprise, Yarrow was even drawing comments from readers. He reviewed restaurants in the Bay Area as well as wines, mostly from California, suggesting food pairings for the latter and scoring each on a ten-point scale. "Excellent light style lets the fruit and floral aspects of the wine shine through without being caked in the butter that comes from malolactic fermentation or the oakiness that I would have expected had I read the winemaker's notes before drinking," went one January 28, 2004, review of a Chardonnay from a winery in California's Santa Cruz Mountains. Yarrow's conversational tone and direct writing was not unlike that of Robert Parker or even Robert Finigan decades before in the golden age of printed wine newsletters (Parker's *Wine Advocate* launched its own website in 2002). Other wine bloggers followed Yarrow's lead, and by 2010 there were at least five hundred English-language blogs about wine, many in the United States.

The wine blogs would never enjoy the influence of the wine newsletters, however. The American fine wine movement was profoundly different in 2004, when Yarrow launched Vinography, than in 1978, when Parker launched the *Wine Advocate*, or even in 1983, when he pronounced upon the '82 Bordeaux. Winemakers and their wares were just coming into their own in the wider US marketplace following 1976's Judgment of Paris, the baby boomers had yet to start expending their capital in volume, most areas of the country lacked ready retail access to American-made fine wines, and information was simply much more diffuse. To get information about the latest Cabernet from Bordeaux or the latest Chardonnay from Napa Valley, one had to wait for a newsletter or magazine to arrive in the mailbox, or visit the wineries themselves, or hope for a missive in the local newspaper. The technology of the Internet, and the ease of the Web it spun, quickly turned such information dissemination on its head; news and views became nearly instantaneously accessible, consumers became critics seemingly overnight. All that consumers required was the technology itself, affordable for most households by the end of the 1990s and high-speed soon after, and a dedication to sussing out the *mishegoss* of a much more pervasive American fine wine industry.

The democratization brought dilution; so much information was so readily available from so many freshly published voices that wine criticism quickly lost its novelty. Only a handful of wine blogs, including Yarrow's Vinography, appeared to exert any sort of sales power in the marketplace; otherwise, consumers continued to turn to established critics and writers such as Parker and Frank Prial (and Prial's successor, Eric Asimov, who became the *New York Times'* chief wine critic in 2004). The vast sea of wine bloggers continued typing away nonetheless, their evangelism both a boon to American fine wine and, in its adjectival redolence, often ripe for lampooning. Ron Washam, a former television comedy writer and sommelier who launched the satirical HoseMaster of Wine blog in 2008 out of his Healdsburg home in northern Napa County, wrote of the blogging community, "Basically, the whole wine blog world is like the floor of the New York Stock Exchange, a whole bunch of loudmouths trying to shout over each other, only less dressy." Whatever their collective dearth of influence relative to their deadwood forebears, these bloggers helped to widen Americans' awareness of their nation's fine wine movement that much further.

Also aiding in the popularization of fine wine was its representation on the big and small screens, which reached exponentially more eyeballs than the books, Web, and newspaper coverage. The decade saw not only the dawn of reality-television food shows such as *Top Chef*, *Kitchen Nightmares*, and *The Winemakers* (a PBS vehicle that tracked twelve contestants as they vied to create their own wine brand in California) but also a flowering of cooking shows in general. Their stars, such as Mario Batali and Lidia Bastianich, made much of their love of fine wine and its role in food. These shows, particularly those in prime time, returned solid ratings, spawning spin-offs and buoying entire networks. *Top Chef*, for instance, quickly became the Bravo network's No. 1 show, as did *Cake Boss*, a reality series pivoting on baking, for The Learning Channel. The Food Network, which launched in November 1993, drew its greatest number of prime-time viewers ever in 2009. More Americans were eating and drinking better; and more were clearly lapping up the larger foodie culture as well.

Perhaps nothing in the fresh decade demonstrated this interest more than the success of *Sideways*, a feature-length film that Fox Searchlight Pictures produced and released domestically in the fall of 2004. It tells the story of Miles, a shlubby, frustrated novelist with a borderline addiction to fine wine played by actor Paul Giamatti, taking his soon-to-marry college roommate Jack, a shameless roué portrayed by Thomas Haden Church, around parts of California wine country. The pair, both on the northern side of forty, drink their way through high jinks and romantic trysts, with the vineyards, the bottles, the glasses, the vistas, and the tasting rooms main characters in and of themselves. *Sideways* slowly ascended into the upper reaches of weekly box-office tallies, suggesting not only the persuasiveness of film critics, who uniformly adored it, but word-of-mouth praise among viewers. It went on to gross more than $100 million worldwide and to win an Oscar for the adaptation of Rex Pickett's novel of the same name. It also damaged Merlot sales. "I am not drinking any fucking Merlot," Miles rages at Jack in an early scene, birthing perhaps the film's only catchphrase. Meanwhile, Miles's partisanship toward Pinot Noir boosted demand for that style.

Five years after *Sideways*, another movie dropped in the United States, this one a much more immediate hit. *Julie & Julia* traces the efforts of a young New York City blogger to cook all 524 recipes in the original *Mastering the Art of French Cooking* in a single year. Produced by Sony Pictures and starring Meryl Streep as Julia Child in the 1940s, 1950s, and 1960s, right as she met her moment, the film opened in August 2009 as the second-top-grossing movie in the United States. It spurred further sales of Child's books and sparked renewed interest in her life and career (Child had died in 2004 at age ninety-one, suggesting there was something to be said for all that butter and red wine). It was Child's improbable career, started when she was in her forties, that shaped the world of the American fine wine movement. Quaking events such as the founding of the Robert Mondavi Winery, the Judgment of Paris, and Robert Parker's pronouncements upon the 1982 Bordeaux represented other major turning points in the movement, the great leaps forward that put the nation ahead of so many others wine-wise, that grabbed France by the lapels and shook it existentially. But without the sort of foodie culture Child and a handful of others built from a mid-century America of TV dinners and white bread into a mass movement of its own, it is hard to imagine the popularity of fine wine spreading all that far and wide in the United States. Build it they did, though: wine, food, wine with food, wine as food.

And so much of this culture, which lifted not only the fortunes of the American fine wine industry but those of other nations entering the US marketplace, might be traced to Child's damascene moment over lunch in Rouen more than a half century before. "I adore France," she told the crowd in Cambridge in 2000. France, as with Robert Parker the year before, loved her back.

A CONSTELLATION OF WINES

2004–2010 | Oakville, California

On November 3, 2004, Mike Grgich, the now-legendary winemaker behind the Chateau Montelena Chardonnay that won the Judgment of Paris and longtime owner of his own eponymous Napa Valley concern, dropped by Robert Mondavi's house in Oakville for lunch. It was a Wednesday, and the big news was Senator John Kerry's concession to President George W. Bush in the national election held the day before. For Grgich, though, the news was all about Mondavi: namely, the sale of the winery where Grgich had honed his skills nearly forty years before. He figured his friend could use some cheering up.

"Let's talk about happy things," Mondavi told him.

Anything but the sale—it had been so messy, yet seemingly so necessary. In June 1993 the Robert Mondavi Winery went public, offering 3.7 million shares at $13.50 apiece through the NASDAQ exchange. It was only the third winery in the United States to go public, and the first independent one specializing in fine wine. It had perhaps as much as $65 million in debt to settle, and the downturn of the late 1980s to shake off, including costly vine replantings, given the phylloxera blight. The winery also had to cover the millions of dollars Robert had promised the University of California, Davis, for a wine-and-food institute named in his honor. It was assumed the public offering would provide the capital and cash to deal with all those things.

The wider wine industry, in fact, greeted the move with a "cheer of liberation," seeing in it a third way to finance wine-making: not through banks (Mondavi's decades-long relationship with Bank of America had soured) or through wealthy individual investors (which had driven so much of the initial American fine wine movement) but through the stock markets, which were once again on a bullish tear in the United States after a mild recession to start the decade. "This is the most exciting thing to happen here in years," one Napa Valley analyst said of the Mondavi offering.

Some voiced warnings amid the excitement. Wine stocks, even ones from so prestigious a name as Mondavi, would never have the bounce of those from meatier industries of the day, such as the Internet, that seemed to be driving so much of the economy in the 1990s. No, these naysayers cautioned, the most Mondavi and their ilk could hope for were shareholders intent on what Wall Street called "prestige buys"—stocks bought not so much for their returns but for the social capital they might bring. One of the two other wineries to go public, for instance, Chalone Wine Group—which controlled a handful of California brands and whose Chardonnay had placed third among the Judgment of Paris whites in 1976—threw grape-soaked shindigs for its shareholders and also cut them discounts on bottles and cases. Chalone's stock, and that of the jug-wine concern Canandaigua Wine Company out of Upstate New York, had never done all that well, another warning sign for Mondavi. Both Chalone and Canandaigua traded well below their highs by 1993, Chalone barely cracking six dollars a share. Mondavi's stock that first June day of trading would finish down.

The company and its newest stakeholders, however, ignored the concerns, and a newly cash-infused Mondavi rode the wider industry wave of success into the new century. Within a decade of its initial public offering, the Robert Mondavi Winery was the sixth-largest in the nation, selling 9.3 million cases annually and posting a profit of more than $25 million. Most of this monetary muscle sprang from Mondavi's Woodbridge brand, which was sourced from grapes in California's Central Valley, around Lodi rather than from the revered To Kalon vineyard in Napa, and the wine was generally priced below ten dollars a bottle. The winery also produced a slightly pricier line called Robert Mondavi Private Selection sourced from vineyards along the Central Coast, between Los Angeles and San Francisco. Together, these two non-premium brands accounted for nearly 90 percent of Mondavi's sales and almost 80 percent of its revenue. This left the sorts of wines that put Mondavi on the map nearly two generations ago—the Fumé Blanc and the Cabernet Sauvignon harvested from To Kalon, never mind the bottles out of the Mouton Rothschild partnership known as Opus One—to trade in paltry amounts, almost as novelty items, among die-hard fans and aficionados.

Other wineries had been engaging in the same demarcation for decades, offering less expensive brands to ballast production of their most heralded; it was a way not only to support smaller, higher-end production financially but to introduce more and more consumers to fine wine in general. Pique consumers' interest, the logic often went within marketing bull sessions, and they might scale up to ever-more-expensive bottles. A winery might not run for long if it relied solely on selling a few thousand cases of the finest Cabernet Sauvignon annually. Though the Stanford business graduate in Mondavi understood the business reality, it still irked the godfather of the American fine wine movement. "We've got to get our image back," Mondavi told a reporter in 2004. The company, which Robert had stepped away from running day-to-day in 1990, got too "interested in making money and they forgot to promote Robert Mondavi Napa Valley Wines." Others agreed. "What Robert built up in terms of quality may have been traded down," Don Sebastiani, head of a nearly century-old winery in Napa Valley, told a reporter in the mid-2000s. "You walk into a Safeway and see a bottle that says 'Robert Mondavi Cabernet,' and it's featured for six-ninety-nine." Even Tim Mondavi, who, along with his brother Michael, had led the winery's shift toward this demarcation, thought it had gone a little too far. "Usurping the name 'Robert Mondavi' for the benefit of the broader wines," Tim Mondavi said at the time, did more harm than good by undercutting the higher-priced products.

Two other realities, in addition to this undercutting, made the sale of the Robert Mondavi Winery, with all its moving parts, seem even more necessary. Visiting on the next generation the drama that had gripped the family in the 1960s, Tim and Michael frequently fought over details of the winery's direction, from the look of labels to whether to go public, a rivalry their father blamed on himself. The trio was even known to quibble over details of a wine during private tastings at the legendary Oakville site, leaving attendees to shake their heads as father and sons wrestled for the microphone to get the last word. A cousin spoke for many when he pronounced himself "personally tired of seeing this same soap opera replayed." Finally, at the start of the new century, Tim Mondavi abruptly left the company for a sabbatical—echoing Robert's exit from Charles Krug in 1965, after smacking his brother Peter (who still ran that winery with his family)—and in January 2004, Robert helped force Michael out as the winery's chairman. For the first time, a non–family member took the reins of Mondavi. Rumors began rushing about the valley of a sale or of a splitting of the company between its less-expensive brands and the higher-end Oakville operation. While family members were skeptical of either, it was no longer their decision to make: the iconic American winery appeared, given its production and sales levels as well as the overall health of the domestic wine market, imminently ripe for takeover, according to a Wall Street that then called the shots. Suddenly the stock offering ten years before seemed less talisman than curse. Robert, who was ninety when a sale started to look inevitable, told people, "If I had to do it over again, I would not go public. I took a gamble."

He lost. Constellation Brands—a mammoth alcohol concern based in suburban Rochester, New York, and perhaps most famous wine-wise for its fortified Wild Irish Rose, described by one wag as "for drinkers who wanted to get hammered in a hurry"—soon put in two bids for Mondavi. Ted Hall, a former director at consultancy McKinsey & Company who became in 2004 the only non–family member to chair Mondavi, rejected the first one. In response, Richard Sands, chairman and CEO of the ballooning Constellation, invited him to lunch at Manhattan's private Harmonie Club in late October 2004—and threatened Hall with a hostile takeover.

Sands, along with investment bank Merrill Lynch as advisor, was unabashedly intent on growing his family's publicly traded concern in all directions of the alcohol industry, from beer to wine to liquor. Constellation's gross sales already stood at nearly $4 billion annually, up from just more than $200 million twelve years before. The company's very name reflected Sands's ambitions: originally named Canandaigua, after one of New York's Finger Lakes, it had been changed to the expansive-sounding Constellation in 2000. Constellation under Sands wanted, as one profiler put it, "to sell to them all—to the cash-strapped, the ultra-flush, cocktail lovers and suds guzzlers. . . . For breadth and sheer number of brands, the company is unlike anything else in its industry, an alcoholic emporium that has become all things to all drinkers." It was the antithesis of Robert Mondavi's original approach to his winery: an independently owned business carefully trying to match, or usurp, the French in fine wine–making.

No matter. Sands's firm had gobbled up fourteen companies since 1991, including Franciscan Estate, a Napa Valley winery dating from 1972, as well as Almaden and Inglenook, Napa names born before Prohibition. Sands wanted Mondavi to be acquisition number fifteen, and he would get what he wanted. The day after Mike Grgich came over for lunch, November 4, the Robert Mondavi Winery announced its sale to Constellation Brands for $1.3 billion, which included the assumption of $325 million in debt. Shareholders would take all of twelve minutes to approve the deal at their annual meeting the following month.

The news shot across the American fine wine movement. Though treated as a novel event in some media quarters, such corporate takeovers went all the way back almost to the start of the movement. Witness Coca-Cola buying control of Sterling Vineyards or Pillsbury purchasing Souverain in the 1970s. This corporate takeover was different, though. This was Robert

Mondavi, the Mondavi family, a clan that hadn't missed a vintage since 1919, even throughout Prohibition. Though they reaped a tremendous windfall of around $400 million from the Constellation deal (which spoke more to the overall health of the American wine market and not so much to that of the winery itself), the family finally lost any semblance of control. The winery would never be the same. The archway and the tower Cliff May designed all those years ago had already begun to look less and less dramatic, even agedly stumpy, as Napa became more and more crowded, cars choking Highway 29 even in the middle of winter weekdays. The gigantically influential Robert Mondavi Winery in Oakville would be just another notch, however gleaming, in Constellation's brand portfolio, which also included Corona beer and Black Velvet Canadian whisky.

Shortly after the Constellation deal, Robert and Peter Mondavi, long estranged, announced they would produce a single barrel of wine, enough for about sixty magnums, with Cabernet Sauvignon grapes sourced from the family vineyards. Calling the blend Ancora Una Volta, or "Once Again" in Italian, it was a poignant nod to the old days, when such grapes were rare in California, rare in the United States, and rarely used there to make wine. The barrel sold for $401,000 at the Napa Valley Wine Auction in 2005.

BIG MONEY

2007–2008 | Rutherford, California

One day in December 2007, Francis Ford Coppola—in a beret and scarf, eyes behind dark sunglasses, his midsection straining against the buttons of a sweater, every inch the jolly gourmand—hopped into the cockpit of a backhoe with a jackhammer affixed to the front and merrily set about commencing the demolition of an old barrel-storage building on his Napa Valley property in Rutherford.

The act was fraught with symbolism. Liquor giant Heublein had erected the concrete structure in 1975, shortly after its takeover of the storied Inglenook winery. Gustave Niebaum created Inglenook in the 1800s, and his grandnephew, John Daniel, nurtured it to renown before he had to sell it amid financial strains in 1964; it was a time just before Robert Mondavi and the Judgment of Paris, when the American fine wine movement was more promise than practice, an era when any challenge to French hegemony seemed absurd. The likes of Heublein—cut very much from the same cloth used to make E. & J. Gallo and other generic giants—appeared to be the industry's future. In fact, Heublein and United Vintners, the preceding owner of Inglenook, had not only set about rapidly altering the physical landscape of the winery but had usurped the name for a line of jug wines sourced from grapes in California's Central Valley, not Napa. Over time, even as Coppola and his wife, Eleanor, bought up parts of the old winery and began producing what they called Niebaum-Coppola vintages, the name Inglenook quickly receded from the ranks of respected American wineries. Even a top Heublein executive lamented, "Inglenook was a Picasso that somebody defamed and destroyed."

Inglenook was one of the few wineries in the United States making wine from higher-end grapes by the start of the 1960s.
COURTESY OF INGLENOOK

Nothing symbolized the defamation and destruction quite like the barrel-storage building. Composed of three thousand tons of concrete, it could hold three hundred thousand cases of wine, far beyond the production limits of most fine wine producers in the United States. As if the building were not harbinger enough of what Heublein had in mind for Inglenook, it had originally been meant as the *first of seven* to hold more than one and a half million cases. It was also ugly, an incongruous "blunder" blocking the view of

Niebaum's gorgeous chateau from Highway 29. Margrit Mondavi, Robert's second wife, could not bring herself to look leftward when she drove up the road from her husband's winery lest she spy the building. And now the building was gone. A crew followed Coppola's first thrusts with a systematic demolition over several weeks and the replacement of the eyesore with an acre of Cabernet Sauvignon grapes. Within a few years, Coppola would also have control of the Inglenook name, bathing it once again in its former fine wine glory, even hiring an estate manager in 2011 from the French First Growth Château Margaux.

Coppola's Inglenook was the reverse of the Robert Mondavi Winery story. Instead of the conglomerate taking over the vaunted independent, the vaunted independent pretty much took over the conglomerate, albeit over decades. Inglenook, however, was an anomaly in American fine wine in the new century. The trend was instead toward consolidation and conglomeration, driven by the American public's insatiable thirst. In 2007 annual per capita wine consumption in the United States reached an all-time post-Prohibition high of 2.46 gallons, or more than a dozen of those standard 750ml bottles—well more than double what Americans had been downing annually twenty-five years before. Most of it, too, nearly 90 percent, was fine wine. At the same time, the number of US wineries had reached a post-Prohibition high of 5,958, a number that itself would be eclipsed in coming years. Upon unfolding a map of the United States at the end of 2007, a consumer would be able to pinpoint at least one, if not several, wineries in each state, the vast majority producing wines from higher-end grapes and the vast majority capitalizing on America's foodie culture as well. California, with more than twenty-six hundred, still easily claimed the lion's share of wineries, though New York was no longer number two; that honor belonged to Washington State, followed by Oregon, followed at last by New York.

The increase in demand and the proliferation of competition meant wine-making costs were also on the rise. Land in the nation's prime grape-growing regions had not been particularly cheap for a long time. "I get calls from people with accents I can't understand," the mayor of Napa Valley's St. Helena told the *New York Times* in May 1981, five years after the Judgment of Paris. "And they'll pay anything, anything. . . . They're driving up the prices for real estate so that local folks can't afford it anymore." Whereas the cost of undeveloped vineyard land in Napa might have run to $5,000 an acre then or to $35,000 an acre as recently as the early 1990s, it was around $150,000 by 2007. Planting the actual vines ran to as much as $40,000 an acre, and then maintaining each of those acres could cost a further $20,000 a year. Jim Barrett saved Chateau Montelena in 1972 for roughly $1 million; Warren Winiarski bought his first acres of what became Stag's Leap for $2,000 each in 1970. Such sums would not have gotten either of them into the game in the latter half of the first decade of the twenty-first century.

The costs were similarly prohibitive in other areas. In New York State's Finger Lakes region, for instance, it cost at least $18,000 per acre to *start* a winery specializing in higher-end grapes; in the Northwest, including Oregon and Washington State, the total cost might run to more than $9,000 an acre— or roughly $9 million for a one-hundred-acre winery. This number-crunching did not include the permitting process, which might also reach seven figures, or the cost of spending the time to amass the winery itself, including parts and labor. Buying an established winery provided little financial respite, too. While purchase prices in places such as Oregon ran significantly cheaper than start-up costs—sometimes hundreds of thousands of dollars less—there was still the matter of operations, labor, distribution, and miscellany such as expansion and insurance. Finally, work on any winery, start-up or acquired, meant absence from work elsewhere, which suggested either long hours as owners fit in the winery business amid other responsibilities, or the sort of money that allowed one to toil for a long time on something with no financial return. Relatively few individuals could afford to do either; big companies could.

Thus the American fine wine movement in the 2000s was more Robert Mondavi than Inglenook. There were the consolidations and takeovers, some so stealth that it was a while before even the most die-hard oenophiles noticed, if they ever noticed at all. Brands cloaked brands. Diageo, the London-based alcohol giant that ran Guinness, Johnnie Walker, and Captain Morgan, among other spirit and beer behemoths, also controlled the vaunted Beaulieu and Sterling Vineyards; and, shortly after Constellation's blockbuster billion-plus deal for Mondavi, Diageo snapped up the Chalone Group, the other fine wine operation that went public, adding thirteen wineries to its portfolio. These included Napa operations such as Acacia, Provenance, Hewitt, and Jade Mountain. Similarly, by the middle of the decade Constellation controlled not just Mondavi (and its Woodbridge and Robert Mondavi Private Selection labels as well as two other wineries, Byron and Arrowood, and half of Opus One) but also a slew of others. US Tobacco, incorporated in Delaware and based in Connecticut, controlled wineries such as Chateau Ste. Michelle and Columbia Crest through its Stimson Lane Vineyards. Brown-Forman out of Louisville, Kentucky, famed for its Jack Daniel's whiskey, owned Fetzer Vineyards in Mendocino County. E. & J. Gallo, the old generic champion, owned several fine winemakers, including Louis M. Martini in Napa and Mirassou Winery in San Jose.

None of these, though, came close to the ubiquity of the concern that had belted Gallo off its pedestal as America's biggest winemaker: Richard Sands's Constellation. Under the umbrella of the Mission Bell winery in Madera, north of Fresno, Constellation during much of the 2000s produced Almaden, Paul Masson, Taylor, and Inglenook (before the Coppolas bought the name in 2011). Under the Franciscan Estate umbrella, the company turned out wines from Estancia, Mount Veeder, Ravenswood, and Simi. Aside from these California operations, Constellation also controlled the Columbia and Covey Run Winery in Washington State and Canandaigua, the jug-wine giant in Upstate New York.

Further muddying the branding waters, Constellation was born of Canandaigua, the firm changing its name in 2000 "to better reflect . . . its broad range of brands that satisfy a wide range of consumer preferences." Indeed, row upon row of these labels and other labels might stare from supermarket and wine store shelves, the consumer none the wiser. These operations continued to source their wines from higher-end grapes, continued to slap *Merlot, Cabernet Sauvignon*, and others upon the labels when it was warranted, continued to project that air of gastronomic enjoyment, if not refinement, that had come to walk hand in hand with American fine wine. The only thing that had changed substantially was the bottom line. American fine wine was bigger business than ever. Witness the early 2008 sale of Inglenook, Paul Masson, and Almaden to the Livermore, California–based Wine Group, maker of boxed-wine leader Franzia and other popular brands such as Cupcake and FishEye; Constellation pocketed more than $134 million—in cash.

Along with the conglomerates came the individual investors and the pools of investors. While some journalists and even veteran critics who should have known better would treat this trend as a fairly new one, fine wine, particularly in California's choicer regions, had always drawn moneyed individuals and interests. They were the ones able to absorb the risks and expend the time in what until recently had been a delicious way to hemorrhage money. Jim Barrett flew his own plane to check out Chateau Montelena; Robert Mondavi was fond of noncommercial flight as well; PlumpJack's principal backer, Gordon Getty, came from one of the wealthiest families in modern history; James Zellerbach, Mondavi's fellow pioneer in oak aging, headed a family paper concern that would eventually be worth several hundred million dollars; Inglenook was born of a nineteenth-century fur baron with connections in Russia's czarist court. And on and on . . .

Names such as Beverly Hills, Paris, Harvard, and Stanford appeared often in the curriculum vitae of the American fine wine movement's pioneers. Rags-to-riches stories, such as Konstantin Frank's or Mike Grgich's at their eponymous operations, were and remained rarities. As noted in December 2004 by Frank Prial, who was ending a fantastically meaty three-decade run chronicling the nuts and bolts of the industry for the *New York Times*: "The old wine country adage was never truer, that the way to make a little money in the wine business is to start with a lot."

Those with a lot were jumping in more than ever. One in five acres of farmable Napa Valley land was controlled by corporations by 2008. Individually, "swarms of millionaires" bought extant wineries or opened new ones. Developers, including investors from the industry, built housing within vineyards in areas as disparate as Georgia, Texas, New York, and California, similar to the housing they had been building for decades on golf courses; for prices in the low seven figures, Americans could purchase the fine wine lifestyle without necessarily taking on the risk of a working winery. The arrivistes spawned an often histrionic backlash from a small cadre of critics and historians who saw them as "showing off" with their "totalitarian architecture" dictated by "fashion, not function"—acerbic assessments that the economic collapse of late 2008 only sharpened. These critiques often walked together with lamentations over global wine, each seen as a symptom of the other. Though, as with the warren of brands the consolidations and takeovers birthed, it is unlikely that the average American fine wine consumer, by then drinking more of the stuff than ever from more places than ever, really detected the changes in the boardrooms and front offices, much less those involving the barrel-storage buildings. That did not mean these critics did not have a point.

GARAGE REVOLUTIONARIES AND VIRTUAL GIANTS

2000–2010 | Napa, California

"**W**hether you're a CEO looking for a memorable retreat for your management team or a wine aficionado wanting to get Cabernet-stained fingers this harvest, you can really get to know what goes on behind the scenes in the world of Napa Valley winemaking at MicroCrush at Judd's Hill Winery in Napa Valley." Thus began the press release that Judd Finkelstein's Napa Valley winery blasted out on July 29, 2010. The fine wine bug had bitten Finkelstein's late father, Art, in the 1970s, while he was working as an architect in Los Angeles. Art's son eventually took over at the winery, an eccentric presence in a valley of eccentrics, a self-described "Hawaiian nut" who played ukulele in a local band called the Maikai Gents Featuring the Mysterious Miss Mauna Loa.

Finkelstein's MicroCrush was one of the first of its kind: a place for non-industry types to stain their hands purple while making and blending small batches of fine wine, maybe as little as one barrel—enough for twenty-four cases or nearly three hundred standard-size bottles. MicroCrush clients would toil beneath the direction of staff at Judd's Hill Winery off the Silverado Trail and would work not with whatever grapes might be available but with those sourced from some of the best vineyards in the valley and therefore the United States. More than the logistics—the all-day blending "camp" could run to nearly $700—was the vibe behind MicroCrush: it had, as the press release explained, "literally started in the family's garage—thus aligning with today's usage, 'garagiste' winemakers."

Not every *garagiste* winery started in a bona fide garage, but the point was well taken. These operations were tiny, producing perhaps a few thousand cases yearly, and their wares were often highly coveted, if not for the quality, then for their novelty in an era of both increasing corporate consolidation in the industry and fears of global wine. These operations were invariably scrappy in that finest American entrepreneurial sense: the garagiste winemakers were usually home winemakers turned recently professional, joining the flow of the decades-long movement from a variety of other career paths.

Garagistes were, indeed, a fairly new phenomenon in the United States in the first decade of the twenty-first century, though in France they were old hat. As Frank Prial told his *New York Times* readers in October 2000, "[T]here is a revolution going on here, a wine revolution that has shaken the foundations of the most important region in France. . . . Simply stated, the garagistes make exceptionally good wines in exceptionally small quantities and sell them for exceptionally high prices." The first garagiste started in the Pomerol area of Bordeaux in the early 1980s on a five-acre vineyard called Le Pin, or the Pine Tree. The trend quickly spread, and by the late 1990s more than a dozen French garagistes were producing wines that routinely traded for several hundred dollars per bottle, with fans worldwide putting in bids over the Internet. This frenzy invited an inevitable question, as Prial saw it, especially given the fact that larger producers in the same areas made the same varieties of wine from virtually the same grapes (Le Pin, for instance, was less than a mile from vaunted Pomerol producer Petrus): "[A]re these great modern wines made by people willing to break the mold, or are they over-hyped trophies for the moneyed collector?" Some, such as the critic Robert Parker, fell on the former side—Parker's fandom for the garagistes kindled their spread in Bordeaux—while others, such as Steven Spurrier, the merchant behind the Judgment of Paris, dismissed garagistes and their superexpensive, ultrasmall batches as "a fad."

There was some truth to the fad part. Even the garagistes themselves insisted that what they were doing was nothing new. "We are not garagistes," one of Le Pin's owners told Prial, "we were making wine here a dozen years before anyone thought up the name." The name, which French writer Nicholas Baby coined to describe the makers of what he called "vins de garages," stuck, however, and soon garagistes were popping up worldwide, with especial force in the United States, where they held a manifold allure. First, Americans love an iconoclast; and the idea, if not the reality, of a garagiste fit the mold: the solo artist, the little guy, crafting away in his or her cramped surround-ings, standing athwart an increasingly globalized, supposedly homogenized market, making quality wine, and damn the price. The French word even sounded like "garage band," a phrase in the American lexicon long used to describe struggling musicians striving to make it big (in fact, it translates to "mechanic"—close enough). This iconoclasm goes a long way toward explain-ing why a custom-crush concern such as MicroCrush would want to piggy-back on the concept.

Along similar lines, American garagistes tended to buddy up when it came to distribution, promotions, and purchasing supplies such as glass and cork, creating a kind of fraternity of happy wine warriors. This symbiosis spawned another movement within the movement: the wine-making co-op or village, wherein independent winemakers shared production facilities as well as distribution avenues, allowing them to sidestep huge capital costs and get off the ground, and stay there, faster. After his family winery was acquired by the nation's biggest winemaker in 2004, Michael Mondavi helped pioneer the co-op trend through his Folio Fine Wine Partners, which he started in 2007. "Own your own vineyard, maintain your personality and style, but be interdependent on everything else," Mondavi's mantra went. The economic downturn that began the same year Folio launched and that would come to be called the Great Recession only strengthened the pull of the garagiste/co-op/village model. Times were tougher, money was more expensive to borrow, and the financial risks were greater in an ever-crowded American wine market. Going it alone on a microscale or going it alone in a group on a microscale became much more appealing to aspiring winemakers than simply going it alone.

Finally, and perhaps most alluringly for Americans, the garagistes and their progeny were real in that most literal sense: they existed. The labels on their bottles connoted a going concern made up of a small group of people producing something in small quantities. This stood in direct opposition to virtual wineries, the somewhat Orwellian moniker slapped on a trend that often fed off the frenetic consolidation in the industry at the start of the century. Virtual wineries sourced their wines from higher-end grapes but produced oceans of it, with the names on the labels—Cupcake, Smoking Loon, Mark West, Rock Rabbit, Pepperwood Grove, Layer Cake—little more than logos tied neither to a particular time nor a place.

At the start of 2010, none of America's bestselling thirty wine brands grew, produced, or bottled their own wines. Instead, conglomerates such as Constellation or Diageo crafted them, though they marketed the brands as anything but the fruits of such concentrated corporate force. "Those bottles may look beautiful, implying a bucolic wine-y setting," wrote one consultant in 2009, "but the cold hard fact is that the juice within is just a trademark coupled with a savvy marketing plan." Such lamentations missed the point. Virtual wineries were the godchildren of Robert Mondavi's Woodbridge—or of any number of fine wineries that paid the bills through non-premium and non-superpremium brands. Like with garagistes, the nickname "virtual winery" was itself new, but the trend was far from it. Moreover, had not E. & J. Gallo barely a generation before produced most of the wine drunk in the United States? Critics of virtual wineries invariably started from the false supposition that Americans since time immemorial had been into Chardonnay, Merlot, etc., produced by small, independent wineries.

Not even remotely so. It was a slow slog to the growth and ubiquity of the early twenty-first century, one driven as much by the wider culture, including the doggedness of certain writers, as by entrepreneurs in the industry and their technological leaps. Virtual wineries, and garagistes and co-ops, succeeded because the table had been set for them; they could not have come along at any other point in the American fine wine movement. For the virtual wineries, there would not have been the consumer base; for the garagistes and the co-ops, there would not have been the interest, never mind the consumer base.

People forgot this, though—and people noticed. To mark their six-month anniversary in 1982, the mother of Dyson DeMara's girlfriend gave the couple a bottle of 1978 Cabernet Sauvignon from Silver Oak Cellars. Ray Duncan, an oil and gas entrepreneur from Colorado who would also branch out into building ski resorts and raising bison, started Silver Oak Cellars in 1972 in the Alexander Valley of California, just to the northwest of Napa Valley in Sonoma County. It focused solely on Cabernet Sauvignon, with Justin Meyer, a veteran of the esteemed Christian Brothers winery in Napa, serving as winemaker. Tasting Silver Oaks' 1978 vintage changed the eighteen-year-old DeMara's life. He swung from what looked like some sort of career in finance—he studied accounting in college—to a career in the fine wine business that would take him first to Pine Ridge, a vineyard that former Olympic downhill skier Gary Andrus launched in 1978 off Napa's Silverado Trail, and then to the Robert Mondavi Winery nearby. It was there that DeMara spent more than two decades working in myriad aspects of the business, including international marketing and often in close contact with the Mondavis themselves. DeMara described working with Robert Mondavi as an almost "spiritual experience," the pioneer still exuding savvy and swagger into what would turn out to be his last decades. Finally in 2003 DeMara and his family acquired HillCrest Vineyard, the oldest fine winery in Oregon, which Richard Sommer started in the 1960s in Roseburg, near the South Umpqua River, amid much skepticism about that state's potential to foster higher-end grapes.

During the decades after his first taste of that game-changing bottle of 1978 Cabernet Sauvignon, after working so intimately with Robert Mondavi and within the storied bubbles of first Napa Valley and then Oregon, DeMara noticed something about his industry: newcomers, those who came up in the 1990s and 2000s, often did not understand the leaps and bounds that American fine wine had made. DeMara figured these newcomers thought, "history begins the day you're born. People have no concept what it was like to sell fine wine from Napa Valley even in San Francisco in 1970, where people wouldn't even taste your wine." Back then it was European fine wine, French in particular, or nothing. People weren't necessarily ignorant, DeMara thought, and certainly not willfully so; instead, it was that American fine wine had come so far, so relatively fast. A lot of people did not know the story or many of the characters in it. A big reminder was coming.

A JOURNEY ENDS

2008 | Springfield, New Jersey—Yountville, California

On Friday, June 20, 2008, a thirty-two-year-old man in a winery T-shirt that read OLD SCHOOL sat at a gray table to the left of two pro wrestling dolls and a New York Jets helmet in an austere studio that looked like anyone's hastily converted basement. Gary Vaynerchuk had a square face bookended by pointy ears and capped by closely cropped brown hair that came to a widow's peak above a forehead creased with lines from his bushy eyebrows bouncing up and down. Like the pro wrestlers the dolls represented, Vaynerchuk was a bundle of bravado and energy designed to entertain. It was the 490th episode of his Web series, *Wine Library TV* (also known as *The Thunder Show*), which regularly reached tens of thousands of viewers after a little more than two years online. The more die-hard viewers already had a nickname: Vayniacs.

The son of Belarusian immigrants, Vaynerchuk had gradually taken over and greatly expanded his father's liquor emporium in Springfield, New Jersey. The store under Vaynerchuk *fils* did about $50 million in sales annually, reaping the whirlwind of a growing American fine wine movement, sales over the Internet as well as over the counter, and a proximity to New York City barely twenty miles to the east. Beyond the retail trade and the Web series, Vaynerchuk dabbled in books and television—he famously got the daytime TV giant Ellen DeGeneres to lick soil and rocks to get a sense of the tastes of wine—and spoke regularly not only to crowds of wine devotees but to those in the new-media business as well. Vaynerchuk served as the most visible link between the two worlds of wine; he was younger than the youngest baby boomer, and it showed.

"This is why I do this show," Vaynerchuk said after swirling and swilling a glass from the second of four bottles arranged to his left, opposite the dolls. "I just tasted a wine from Oklahoma—made by college students in Oklahoma, with Oklahoma grapes!—that, I'm going to tell you, beats the living snot out of 90 percent of the California red Meritage wines that I've had under twenty US bones in the last thirty-six months. That was a lot of numbers—did you follow that? Fifteen bones, under twenty, thirty-six months. That's three years, folks." He held up three fingers on each hand and counted them off. "That was six . . ." His hands now chopped the air, his body rocking back and forth. "I'm telling you, I am baffled right now. Baffled right now! Mott, I'm sorry, you have to taste this . . ." Vaynerchuk handed the glass to his cameraman. "I am shocked right now how good this wine is!"

The wine, from the Chapel Creek Winery in El Reno, Oklahoma, sold out within days of Vaynerchuk's rave. Here was a perfect-storm example of the ubiquity, the dominance even, of American fine wine by the end of the first decade of the twenty-first century. A young man in a T-shirt, self-educated when it came to wine, had delivered a specific—however histrionic—judgment upon a bottle from a small winery in the middle of the nation, thousands of miles from both California and New York, to an audience of tens of thousands over a still relatively new medium. Almost every aspect of this would have been surprising, if not impossible, when Vaynerchuk was born in 1975. Never mind the medium itself—the English newspaper *The Independent* called Vaynerchuk "the first major wine critic of the YouTube generation"—his body of knowledge, the winery in Oklahoma, the expectation of any sizable audience to receive the knowledge about the winery, none of that would have been there in 1975, and certainly not from a thirty-two-year-old broadcasting from northern New Jersey. There it was, though: inarguable proof of how far the American fine wine movement had come in the last thirty-odd years.

The movement had commenced its journey in earnest shortly after ten in the morning on September 6, 1966, with the benediction of the Robert Mondavi Winery in Oakville, California. The winery's namesake and progenitor wanted the new operation "to be a showcase for the most advanced winemaking techniques and equipment in America, if not the world." Few outside the small world of American fine wine took any heed of Robert Mondavi's lusty boast or the opening of his small winery, designed by Cliff May, with that tower and archway just off Highway 29 so conspicuous. To that small world, he was Cesare Mondavi's son, Peter Mondavi's brother, the one who had been unceremoniously booted from the Charles Krug Winery because he was so impetuous, so damned difficult to work with. He looked destined to fill out his days spending familial tokens on trips to France and meals in San Francisco. You would hear little from Robert Mondavi.

Then the winery took, soon known in Napa Valley and parts beyond for Mondavi's contrived Fumé Blanc and his very real Cabernet Sauvignon and innovations such as oak-barrel aging on a (for America) grand scale; for being a training ground for winemakers such as Mike Grgich and Warren Winiarski, who staked their own audacious, and verified, claims in the following decade; then finally, and mostly, for Mondavi himself, a tireless promoter of not only American fine wine but of what grew up as American food culture, a slender, raptorial, Romanesque knight with a crushing handshake and a wide grin who saw around corners others had not when it came to what his countrymen would eat and drink. Had he not invited his friend James Beard, the biggest food writer in America at the time, to that benediction in 1966? Robert Mondavi knew there was a future in fine wine—and, more important, he knew how to get that knowledge out. His flirtations with disaster, going all the way back to the first years of his eponymous winery and through those very trying first years of the new century, when he and his progeny lost control (though were handsomely compensated), only seemed to burnish his image: a survivor as well as a striver—never content, never sitting still. Age finally slowed him, and Robert Mondavi died in his ninety-fourth year at home in Yountville, in Napa Valley, on May 17, 2008, a Friday.

The encomiums poured in from both sides of the Atlantic. Mondavi's death did not so much jog memories, including institutional ones, but grab them by the lapels and shake from them every last drop of appreciation. Newcomers who may have known Robert Mondavi only as a name on a bottle got schooled in his immense influence on not just fine wine—they learned about how he had changed the way Americans ate. "The California wine scene would be immeasurably different today without the pivotal role played by this great visionary," the English wine critic Jancis Robinson wrote. "Robert Mondavi *was* California, if not American, wine as far [as] non-Americans were concerned. And he represented wine itself with more sophistication and generosity of spirit than most Europeans." James Laube at the *Wine Spectator*, a publication like many others that may never have existed were it not for Mondavi, had pegged him in 1999, with the benefit of a generation of hindsight, as "the single greatest influence on modern California wine"—a judgment, he told a reporter, he saw no need to revise. Frank Prial, who followed Mondavi's career and the rise of American fine wine much more closely than most, captured the wider context of Mondavi's work and its results: "With other promoters of good living like Julia Child and Alice Waters, he tried to lead the country away from shopworn Old World ways, insisting that Americans were second to none in creating elegance and enjoying it. Few did it better than he: he lived like royalty." Or, as the Mondavis' biographer, Julia Flynn Siler, put it: "He was very successful in convincing other winemakers and consumers that wine should be a part of the good life." Bo Barrett, who had taken on an increasingly wider role at his father Jim's Chateau Montelena in Calistoga, including as winemaker, once asked Mondavi, "Did you ever think it would get this good?" Mondavi replied, "Not in my lifetime."

ON PARKERIZATION, NATURALLY
2010–2012 | Parkton, Maryland

In April 2010, the 188th issue of the *Wine Advocate* dropped, with Robert Parker's much-anticipated assessment of the 2009 Bordeaux. The wine world had been abuzz since at least the fall about the potential quality of this latest vintage, and there remained no greater arbiter of fine wine, particularly that from France, than Parker. "For some Medocs and Graves," Parker wrote, citing two sections of the region, "2009 may turn out to be the finest vintage I have tasted in 32 years of covering Bordeaux." He went on to eventually bestow a score of 100 upon nineteen wines. Never before had Parker, still working out of his Parkton, Maryland, home, rated so many bottles so highly—in essence, perfectly—and not since the vaunted '82 Bordeaux, the assessment of which made his name, had he praised a vintage so mightily.

A dry, cool September had followed a warm, sunny summer in Bordeaux, ripening the grapes just so, but not too much so, leaving those in the French wine industry to talk of conditions "so sumptuous that it is difficult to find parallel" and of having "perhaps to go back to the 1940s to find a comparable year." In short, the '09s would make the '82s seem like plonk. Many critics echoed these early words, joining Parker in thoroughly praising throughout the spring of 2010 the output of France's leading wine region. "Their ecstatic reviews reverberated through Britain, which takes its claret extremely seriously," Eric Asimov wrote in the *New York Times* in May 2010. "They rang out in Hong Kong, the leading edge of what Bordeaux hopes will be a huge Asian market. In the United States, the huzzahs resonated with collectors and wine investors, and with high-end restaurants whose clients don't mind spending hundreds or even thousands of dollars on renowned bottles."

Asimov, however, noticed something else amid the profligate praise: a lot of it was ignored. Parker's assessment in particular was greeted, as Asimov put it, with "a yawn." Some of it was fatigue with Bordeaux, so long a presence in the US marketplace, a foil for American winemakers and drinkers; most of it, though, appeared to be generational. Or perhaps it was a combination of both, as Asimov wrote:

> Not so long ago, young wine-loving Americans were practically weaned on Bordeaux, just as would-be connoisseurs had been for generations. It was the gateway to all that is wonderful about wine. Now that excitement has gone elsewhere, to Burgundy and the Loire, to Italy and Spain. Bordeaux, some young wine enthusiasts say, is stodgy and unattractive. They see it as an expensive wine for wealthy collectors, investors and point-chasers, people who seek critically approved wines for the luxury and status they convey rather than for excitement in a glass.

This Bordeaux fatigue led to a diminution in Parker's influence through-out the first decade of the new century, as did the rise of new generations. His raves about the 2010, 2011, and 2012 Napa vintages would be similarly ignored. Parker was a baby boomer who had hit it big just as the baby boomers in general hit it big in the late 1970s and 1980s. Their children and grandchildren, Generation X and the Millennials, would never match them in spending power; the Great Recession that started in 2008 finished any notion of that, as companies shed jobs by the tens of thousands and financing avenues for first homes and other equity-building assets dried up. At the same time, these younger shoppers in the fine wine marketplace could behold a selection unimaginable to their immediate forebears. Events such as the Judgment of Paris, much less the Great Chardonnay Showdown or the California Barrel Tasting, and people such as Robert Mondavi and John Daniel, rang some bells but not many; their consumer consciousness was instead formed in the 1990s and 2000s, after American fine wine's slow, hard slog to prominence.

Vast supermarket sections of colorful labels of Merlot, Chardonnay, Cabernet Sauvignon, and others; Oscar-winning movies about daring chefs and debauched wine-tasting jags; a seemingly ceaseless queue of cooking shows; newspaper columns and entire magazines dedicated solely to wine and food (and wine-related gadgetry, for that matter); and an Internet brimming with information—this was normal for Generation X and the Millennials. The world of Robert Parker—who came up a generation ear-lier, when a handful of souls, maybe fifteen at most, defined tastes, and the judgment of a single newsletter, never mind a single judge, could move markets—was distant and getting more so. "[F]ocusing on Parker's influence and the growth of American wine culture got me thinking about the comparative *lack of influence* he's had on me and what that says about *the current generation's changed perspective on wine*," Talia Baiocchi, a wine critic in her late twenties, wrote of Parker in 2012 on the foodie blog Eater National. She went on:

> I've often wondered whether my experience is something of an anomaly, mostly because I've been led to believe that I might be. I've been told that it must be because I live in an urban area, or because I went to college in New York, or drank wine as a kid. All of those things are true and they've all impacted my experience with wine, but I think my experience is less unique than it is indicative of *how much the wine world has changed* since Parker started leading the blind 30 years ago. [emphasis hers]

The Bordeaux fatigue and the generational shifts only partly explained things. There was also that sheer enormity of choice that further diluted Parker's influence. In 1983, the year of his famed '82 Bordeaux reviews, there were 1,172 wineries in the United States and Americans drank 528 million gallons of wine, most of it made from higher-end grapes; in 2010, there were 7,626 wineries, more than at any time in the nation's history, and Americans put away 784 million gallons, again most of it fine wine. California alone had more wineries in 2010 than the entire United States had in 2001; the number of New York wineries had nearly tripled in that same period. The amount of imported wine grew 32 percent just between 2005 and 2010; by 2010, 30 percent of the wine Americans consumed came from overseas, mostly from Italy and France. These imports brought new wines made from less familiar grapes such as Touriga, Grüner Veltliner, and Gewürztraminer. There were more and more wine shops and wine clubs—the simply named Wine.com had sixteen thousand members in 2005. When Parker went wine shopping in the early 1980s, he had MacArthur Liquors in Washington, DC, and perhaps a couple of other options in the entire Baltimore-Washington corridor to peruse. (In 2014, the boilerplate Safeway supermarket across the street from MacArthur Liquors unfurled a sign reading, WINE SHOP NOW OPEN.) The federal government even flirted with the idea of allowing wineries to sell directly to consumers by mail across state lines, turning the nation into one big wine store.

Critic and *Wine Advocate* founder Robert Parker at a barrel tasting in France in 2003.
COURTESY OF *WINE ADVOCATE*

Finally, Parker could not get out from under the one-hundred-point scale. It was all anyone seemed to associate with him, especially those who never seemed to have read his tasting notes. The more his critics dismissed the scale, the easier it became to dismiss Parker's entire opus, which, taken together, still stands as a remarkable achievement in its breadth and realized ambition. The nineteen perfect scores for the '09 Bordeaux didn't help matters. "And we all pretend that the score is broken down into parts like Appearance (0 to 5 points) and Aroma (0 to 15 points) when all we really do is smell it, taste it, spit it out and declare, in our authoritative voices, '89!' or '97!'" wrote Ron Washam on his HoseMaster of Wine blog in a spoof of Parker's acceptance speech at the Vintners Hall of Fame (which the Culinary Institute of America started in St. Helena in 2007). Washam continued as Parker:

> Truth and sulfites, my friends, use them sparingly. And I about peed my circus tent after I rated 19 different 2009 Bordeaux 100 points! I always wanted to do that. Just throw around hundreds like Charlie Sheen at TrannyFest. That's power. Oh, the outrage that spawned! How can there possibly be 19 perfect wines from one vintage? I don't know, maybe because I said so.

Parker's critics often wrongfully credited him with inventing the one-hundred-point scale they so thoroughly loathed. He and his *Wine Advocate* had certainly popularized it, causing it to become widely adopted, including by competitors such as *Wine Spectator* and *Decanter*. The latter, an august British publication, held out until mid-2012, when it started running the one-hundred-point scale next to the more traditional twenty-pointer developed at the University of California, Davis, in the 1950s. "*Decanter* is now a global magazine with more than half its readership outside the UK," editor Guy Woodward explained in a press release, acknowledging that those external readers may be more familiar with a certain scale popularized by a certain American writer out of Maryland. Critics of other foodstuffs, especially beer, adopted the one-hundred-point scale as well.

Its ubiquity created a kind of rite of passage for newer wine critics, especially younger ones online, who made it a point to explain why they would *not* be using the scale. "It never occurred to me that I should subscribe to the *Wine Advocate*," Talia Baiocchi wrote in 2012. "And before I even knew it was a topic of debate, *I dismissed the 100-point system*, [emphasis hers] not because I found it anti-romantic or ineffective, but because I just never felt like I needed it. I had other options that were more appealing to me." Even more disinterested critics, including fans of Parker, found it difficult at times to defend rating fine wine like high school teachers might rate social studies essays. "I've never been a fan of point-ratings or fruit bombs," wrote *Los Angeles Times* food critic S. Irene Virbila. "Or humongous comparative tastings where the boldest wines can't help but obliterate the subtler ones—in his heyday Parker could taste hundreds of wines at a sitting. But I've always marveled at Parker's stamina. And at his ability to communicate what he thinks about each of those hundreds of wines."

Those communication skills were what his harshest critics almost always overlooked—namely, the tasting notes, which, beginning with those first *Wine Advocate* issues in the late 1970s, were some of the frankest and most thorough ever written in the English language; they were a real game changer when it came to writing about wine. The tasting notes—the actual descriptions of the wines and whether they lived up to their creators' reputations or their marketers' hype—were what Parker wanted, what he had expected, people to focus on; instead, the one-hundred-point scale devoured the attention. If Parker ended up communicating anything to the masses, especially to those who may not have been regular readers of his newsletter but of his critics, it was that he preferred "the boldest wines," those "fruit bombs" that stood at the supposed vanguard of global wine, that homogenized style that American vintners, eager in the 1980s and 1990s to curry Parker's favor, seemed to have exported to the world. The critic Alice Feiring wrote an entire book (*The Battle for Wine and Love: or How I Saved the World from Parkerization*), published by Houghton Mifflin Harcourt in 2008, taking Parker to task for his role in the rise of global wine. She gave voice to the particular horror some felt at discovering the manipulations wrought by firms such as Enologix, which "was actually thriving by helping wineries shape and coerce a wine into a fat, oaky, thick, dense wine that Parker would give points to . . ." She further wrote:

> With all due apologies for painting Mr. Parker as the hit man in this book, he and his tastes have become bigger than himself. The term *Parkerized* has been added to the colloquial lexicon, and there is even a *Wikipedia* entry: *Wine Parkerization, the widespread stylization of wines to please the taste of influential wine critic Robert M. Parker Jr.*

Was Parker to blame, though? Or did he simply personify a little too easily the aspects of American fine wine that critics and consumers in the twenty-first century loved to hate: the snobbery, real or perceived; the supposed need for specialized knowledge just to pick a bottle, much less drink it; the sheer costs of the best-reviewed wines; the supposed loss of terroir, that French sense of place, amid the waves of juice that virtual wineries and others produced? A lot of these accusations were unfair (as was the focus on the one-hundred-point scale). Take the snobbery bit: Parker had launched the *Wine Advocate* from his Maryland home to cut through the jabberwocky he saw infesting a lot of wine criticism. He saw himself as a sort of Ralph Nader of fine wine, championing the ordinary consumer, which he was at the time. No matter. In the twenty-first century, people who had never met nor really read Parker felt they knew him and his motives. He had assumed an almost godly presence: distant, thought to be omnipotent, an object of praise but more often cursing, a force toward which many directed their ire and approbation about fine wine in America. And then there was surely a dose of that age-old motive: envy. Parker had, after all, arrived early to the party, bumping off Robert Finigan as the top American wine critic way back in 1983, monetizing his criticism into a comfortable living at a time when the pool of criticism was small and a little shallow.

Fast-forward thirty years, and newer critics found it pretty much impossible to transition from day-jobber to millionaire wine critic, a fact that Parker never tired of gleefully reminding them. He noted in an essay that few of the newfangled bloggers "make a living from their sites, largely because many of them are 1) lazy, 2) have narrow agendas, 3) offer little in the way of content and substance, 4) appear to be constantly whining about the failure to monetize their sites, or 5) are the antitheses of consumer advocates." Parker dismissed his critics as "false prophets of doom" and had especially needling words for those, like Feiring, who advocated natural wines.

The term *natural wines*, born in France in the 1990s, was meant to define wines made with as little adulteration as possible, as close to the vineyard as possible. Some saw it merely as a marketing ploy that washed ashore in a twenty-first-century America ripe for a clear alternative to the ever-larger number of mass-produced brands; and to be sure a great many wines presenting themselves as natural were almost undrinkable in their nostril-curdling astringency, having none of the roundness or softness that might come with wine-making techniques such as malolactic fermentation or oak-barrel aging. Whatever it was, the natural wine movement, as its adherents often styled themselves, amounted by 2012 to "no more than a tiny collection of wine-makers," according to Eric Asimov, and "a motley crew of restaurants, wine bars, consumers and writers." To Parker, though, the natural wine set was a graver threat—"one of the major scams being foisted on wine consumers"—as was the pushback against the higher-alcohol, fruitier wines that he, and the lumpen public, seemed to prefer. He considered the natural wine movement "essentially a phony anti-California, anti-New World movement by Eurocentric, self-proclaimed purists."

These "purists" kept on pummeling Parker, who not only gave as good as he got but also couldn't help being influential in ways he didn't even intend. Pierre-Antoine Rovani, a *Wine Advocate* writer whom Parker discovered when Rovani was working at MacArthur's in Washington, DC, described the controversy as "a game" to the journalist William Langewiesche, one played by Robert Parker's rules. "Why is it that at a certain age men start buying little sports cars, or the cigar boat that makes so much noise—or they get the trophy wife? How many of these guys don't even drink the wine? They call you up and they say, 'I've got twenty cases of Lafite, I've twenty cases of Le Pin . . .' These are trophies that they're collecting."

Parker may have started out in the late 1970s as Ralph Nader, but he ended up as Robin Leach. He was the most famous figure in the American fine wine movement since the early 1980s. His work had popularized California wines worldwide and had brought French wines, particularly Bordeaux, to the attention of more Americans than perhaps anyone's ever. He had also accentuated the force that wine criticism played in the movement, proving time and again that the story of the rise of American fine wine was as much a story of technical innovation and entrepreneurial verve as of shifting perceptions. Parker shifted a lot of perceptions. But did he really shift the taste of wine in the United States? Answering that question explains the American fine wine movement as it enters its second half-century.

AN "INCOMPREHENSIBLE" TRIUMPH
2004–2013 | Bordeaux—San Francisco—Seattle—Napa Valley—London

O n July 18, 2004, the most influential figure in the rise of American fine wine died in France. Émile Peynaud passed at his home just outside the port of Bordeaux near the university of the same name where he had taught for so many years. He was ninety-two and could have looked back at that point on a storied career during which he became, as the *New York Times* headline above his obituary put it, the professional "who defined 'expert'" in the wine-making field. Peynaud's innovations and advice, to students and to his myriad clients in the industry, rejuvenated first the wine of Bordeaux, then France at large, then much of the world, including the United States. His teachings led to a uniformed quality in fine wine, one that relied on precisely timed harvests, clean environments for fermentation and aging, and scientific rigor; Peynaud's efforts also led to richer, fuller, fruitier, lusher wines.

And so the coming-of-age story of American fine wine comes full circle, back to the France that the United States at first slavishly imitated and then thoroughly humbled. These were the wines that captured the imagination—as well as the dollars—of Americans beginning in the 1960s, including that of a frustrated young attorney and budding oenophile in Parkton, Maryland, named Robert Parker. The 1961 Bordeaux was indisputably considered the best vintage of the twentieth century until the 1982 came along. It was his unmitigated praise for that '82 vintage that made Parker's reputation, setting him on a course to dictate the taste for American fine wine over more than the next two decades. That taste, as his critics in the new century never tired of reminding anyone who would listen or read, was for fruitier, richer wines—exactly the kinds coming out of Bordeaux years before Parker ever stapled together the first issue of the *Baltimore-Washington Wine Advocate* in his living room.

It is doubtful whether the average—or above-average, for that matter—American wine consumer in the early twenty-first century knew of Peynaud and his influence any more than he or she may have known about the technical contributions of Andre Tchelistcheff or Maynard Amerine; or about Steven Spurrier, George Taber, and the Judgment of Paris; or even Robert Mondavi the man versus Robert Mondavi the label. It is likely, however, that this hypothetical consumer would have known about the role criticism played in fine wine. Small square placards boasting of *Wine Advocate* and *Wine Spectator* scores still stared out from supermarket shelves; magazines on the subject popped up on news racks; ever more blogs spilled onto the Internet; entire sections of newspapers had the very word in their titles, the *New York Times*' Food & Wine perhaps the most prominent; and restaurant and bar menus invariably included tasting notes beside the wines they offered. There also was another dimension to wine criticism in the new century, one that the average wine consumer would have recognized as well.

From 2005 to 2013, Richard Hodgson, an owner of a small winery in Humboldt County, experimented on the judges of the California State Fair's wine-tasting competition, the oldest of its kind in North America. With the help of the organizers, Hodgson presented a few of the same wines to the judges three times, with the wines in each instance coming from the same bottle. After the last judgment in Sacramento in June 2013, Hodgson went public with the experiment's results: Only about 10 percent of the judges, "a who's who of the American wine industry," were consistent in their assessments. "The results are disturbing," Hodgson told a writer for a British newspaper. "Chance has a great deal to do with the awards that a wine wins."

Other experiments on wine criticism showed chance playing a similarly hefty role—and not just among those trained to taste wine for competitions and media but among ordinary consumers as well. A 2008 study of six thousand blind tastings revealed that price often determined how much people said they enjoyed a wine. Another study, this one in 2001 by a faculty member at the University of Bordeaux, showed that labels profoundly affected assessments, too. The same fifty-seven experts were given the same wine in different bottles, one labeled as a Grand Cru and the other as more everyday fair. The tasters described the Grand Cru–labeled wine in more positive language, noting its complexity and balance; the wine from the other bottle was dismissed as weak, light, and flat. Journalists gleefully reported such results, and the foodie commentariat, especially online, exploded with analysis about the value, or lack thereof, of wine criticism. Princeton University economist Richard Quandt produced perhaps the most memorable piece of parsing with his autumn 2007 paper "On Wine Bullshit." Using the words, particularly the adjectives, of actual wine reviews, Quandt generated plausible-sounding critiques of fake wines. "In some instances," he wrote, "there is an unhappy marriage between a subject that especially lends itself to bullshit and bullshit artists who are impelled to comment on it. I fear that wine is one of those instances where this unholy union is in effect."

The harder science suggested at least some bullshit had permeated wine criticism. New research revealed both the vastness and the limitedness of our sense of smell, for instance. Richard Axel and Linda Buck shared the 2004 Nobel Prize in medicine for solving the mystery of how people can distinguish some ten thousand different odors, both pleasant and otherwise; it turns out that hundreds of genetically ordained receptors clustered at the top of the nasal cavity dictate such an ability. And these receptors, further research showed, get tired—or at least a little punchy: expose a person to a certain odor, and he or she can usually get so used to it after a few minutes so as not to smell it anymore. As for taste, psychologist Linda Bartoshuk concluded in the early 1990s that only about one in four people can be considered what she called "supertasters," those who perceive tastes such as bitterness and sweetness much more acutely than others; everyone else simply muddles along with average palates or worse. These discoveries cast profound doubt on the routines of many wine critics, especially those who often judged several, perhaps hundreds, of wines in a sitting. If it was a physiological crapshoot as to who really had acute tasting abilities and if humans could easily acclimate themselves to even the dankest scents, how could various critics claim to assess all those wines so distinctly? Simple: they claimed it.

Or at least some critics did. Others, such as Craig Goldwyn, the organizer of the Great Chardonnay Showdown in 1980, advocated for more stream-lined tastings, ones that did not pivot on marathon sessions of several wines at once. Others, such as Alder Yarrow and the fresh crop of critic-bloggers to arise in the new century, deliberately stood athwart the approach to wine as if it were a product like any other, ripe for rating, eschewing above all the one-hundred-point scale. Still others, such as Frank Prial, who died in November 2012 at age eighty-two, mixed a dash of nonrated reviews in with copious coverage of the industry and its trends.

Then there was that last cohort, clustered in the United States at the *Wine Advocate* and *Wine Spectator*, and led by Robert Parker. Though significantly fewer in number and diminished in influence as the twenty-first century slapped on years, their hundreds of reviews each annum continued to provide winemakers, especially those of premium and superpremium brands, "a powerful tool for inflating prices at the top end of the market, drawing all other prices up with them." That science and psychology now called into question their tasting acumen mattered little. Many consumers, especially those younger than the market-moving baby boomers, may have moved on, but others had not, including the graying boomers themselves. "I can tell you this without any qualification: When a wine receives a mid- to high-90s score from Robert Parker or another *Wine Advocate* critic, that wine sells out . . . and quickly," Tom Wark, who worked on the marketing side of the wine business and who was part of the post-2000 wave of wine blogs, wrote in December 2012. "Additionally, the wine scoring 98 points will increase in price in retail establishments and restaurants and the winery obtaining the 98 point score can easily increase the price of that wine next vintage . . . all on the weight of the great *Wine Advocate* review."

The credit and infamy for global wine was thus laid at the feet of these critics, especially Parker. He had come to represent the homogenization in the taste of American fine wine—strong and fruity—and its supposedly unfortunate export to the four corners of the earth. Yet Parker, who once described himself as a "fruit fanatic," was more a symptom of any perceived problem than the cause. Émile Peynaud had cast the die long before Parker took his fateful first trip to France in 1968, though Peynaud himself was said to be horrified by just how strong and how fruity fine wine had become. Parker can also be seen as symptomatic by stepping back and regarding the nation's tastes in those two other titanically fertile beverages of post–World War II America: beer and coffee.

By late summer 1965, there was one independently owned brewery left in the United States that made beer in small batches from traditional ingredients, the hallmarks of what would come to be called a craft brewery. Before Prohibition in 1920, there had been thousands of similar establishments. Unlike commercial wine-making, commercial brewing was pretty much wiped out by Prohibition; there were no religious exemptions, and few supplies were available to the private consumer akin to those two hundred gallons of grape juice allowed to households annually. There were hardly any breweries operating, then, when Repeal came in 1933 like there were residually operating wineries. Brewing had to start largely from scratch, and capital counted—those breweries that had money going into Prohibition had the advantage coming out.

From just before the Second World War, then, through the 1960s, consolidation ripped through the American brewing industry as the biggest players, especially names such as Anheuser-Busch and Miller, which had been big before 1920, gobbled up smaller competitors or put them out of business by muscling in on their market share. In the late 1960s, five brewing companies produced nearly half of the nation's commercially available beer, a proportion that only rose through the following decade.

At the same time, that beer had become dreadfully homogenized: a yellowy, fizzy bastardization of the Czech-developed style called pilsner—one craft brewer would later liken it to "alcoholic soda pop." What had happened to beer stylistically in the first decades after Repeal was not unlike what had happened to wine with the rise of generic hegemons such as E. & J. Gallo. And, like wine, beer began shuffling off its stylistic straitjacket in the mid-1960s, in Northern California no less. Anchor Brewing in San Francisco was the last independently owned brewery left in the United States that was making beer in small batches from traditional ingredients; it would remain the nation's sole craft brewery until 1976. Under the largesse and dedication of its owner, appliance heir Fritz Maytag, Anchor turned out magnificently groundbreaking beers through the late 1960s and early 1970s, most on the milder, lighter side. Starting in the late 1970s, however, as more craft breweries opened, a curious thing happened stylistically: the growing ranks of American craft beer drinkers gravitated toward heavier, bitterer beers—the more hops (the bittering agent in beer), the better

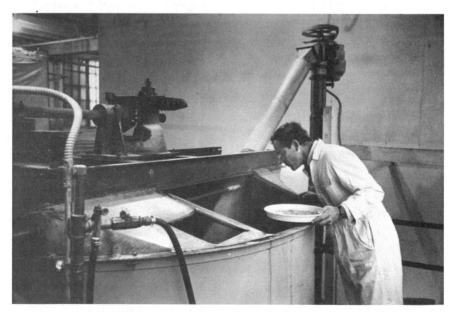

Fritz Maytag, owner of the Anchor Brewing Company in San Francisco, America's oldest craft brewery. Craft beer grew up almost in tandem with fine wine in the United States, the two industries creating ever heavier and punchier drinks for consumers' palates.
COURTESY OF ANCHOR BREWING

By 2012 the bestselling craft beer styles in the United States were season-als, such as Christmas ales and Octoberfest lagers, and India pale ales, all of which skewed toward bitter instead of mild and had high alcohol contents instead of low. No one quite knew why. Some said it was a reaction against all the sweeter colas and fruit juices baby boomers and their children grew up on; others traced it to the popularity of a 1975 release from Anchor called Liberty Ale, which was enormously bitter for its era (four times as bitter as the then-recently introduced Miller Lite, for instance). Still others ascribed the rise of bitterness to some sort of clubbiness on the part of those on the West Coast, birthplace of the bitterest styles. It should be noted, too, that the vast majority of the nation's thousands of craft breweries did not advertise, and some barely marketed. Instead, millions of consumers, from the 1960s onward, sought out these heavier, stronger beer styles on their own—and brewers happily responded, producing ever-bitterer brands, including for an international marketplace looking more and more to the United States as the world's leading beer nation.

Americans also took in droves to stronger, bitterer coffee beginning in the 1970s, with the opening of the first Starbucks coffeehouse in Seattle in April 1971. It and its handful of subsequent locations, most of them clustered in the Pacific Northwest, specialized in deeper, richer coffee blends that most Americans would have found unfamiliar, if not off-putting. Coffee consump-tion in general had been on the decline when the first Starbucks opened; Americans, if they did quaff java at all, mostly drank coffee brewed from weak, bland blends that giant brands such as Maxwell House and Folgers made. Starbucks' entrepreneurial roll of the dice paid off handsomely: by the mid-2000s, the chain was servicing more than 30 million customers weekly (about one in ten Americans) at its more than seven thousand locations in the United States alone. Also, its 1998 decision to sell its wares in grocery stores and other retail outlets reaped billions in revenue; by 2012, Starbucks' nearly 13 percent share of the market for Americans making coffee at home stood behind only much older competitors Kraft Foods, the maker of Maxwell House, and J.M. Smucker, the maker of Folgers. Starbucks' bestselling retail brand at the start of the 2010s was French Roast, its darkest roast and one with "intense and smoky flavors"—a representative for the company who worked in the wine world previously compared Starbucks' French Roast to Cabernet Sauvignon or Zinfandel. More important in the long run, Starbucks' success spurred its competitors, even fast-food chains such as McDonald's, to introduce the same sorts of complex, stronger, bitterer brews as the number of Americans who inhaled the drink daily and weekly continued to explode. What had come to be called the premium or specialty coffee market accounted in 2012 for approximately 37 percent of the coffee consumed every day in the United States—and that share was only expected to balloon.

Again, as with stronger, bitterer beers, no one could quite explain the rise of stronger, bitterer coffee in barely a generation in America. Some ascribed it to Starbucks' resuscitation of coffeehouse culture; some credited globalization for a greater availability of better beans from places such as Ethiopia, Brazil, and Southeast Asia; some saw it, again, as a reaction against the sweeter colas and fruit juices ascendant before the 1970s; still others saw it as a part of an embrace of Italian and Italian-American culture, with its espressos, lattes, and cappuccinos (the most heralded television drama of the 1990s and 2000s was, after all, HBO's *The Sopranos*). For whatever reason, millions of Americans since the 1960s had come to expect to pay a little more for coffee that would have surprised, if not befuddled, their immediate ancestors. It was a trend familiar to anyone following craft beer, and fine wine, during the same period.

Still, the debate over who or what caused global wine—and therefore whether it really existed at all—rolled on through the first decade and a half of the twenty-first century. It was the salient issue of the American fine wine movement, the one thing everyone who wrote about, traded in, or worked in wine had to have a position on. Most credited or blamed Robert Parker. "People don't want to drink wine anymore, they want to drink scores—Parker scores," sniffed one California winery manager. "If you blame anyone," retorted a prominent wine merchant who worked both sides of the Atlantic, "blame the people who follow him blindly. After all, he doesn't make the wine." Both the criticism and credit were incorrect and unwarranted. Robert Parker had merely been the latest American to fall in thrall to the lusher, richer French wines that Émile Peynaud pioneered. At the same time, he was but another American who liked his beverages strong and heavier-tasting.

A certain irony overshadowed this, the biggest wine debate of the new century. Never before had so much fine wine, from so many different producers using so many different grapes and selling at so many different prices, been available in the United States. The *New York Times*' Eric Asimov aptly termed the modern era a "golden age for wine drinkers." Even the hegemony of Chardonnay and Cabernet Sauvignon appeared much less hegemonic. An early 2014 report from the consumer-tracking service Nielsen pegged Chardonnay's sales-market share among white wines at 19 percent and Cabernet

Sauvignon's among reds at 12 percent; that meant that around four in five wines sold in the United States were made primarily from different grapes or from blends. Yet calls rang out for more diversity, the same sort of calls that had spurred the fine wine movement in the first place. "There *are* California wines as fine as the best in Europe," Robert Lawrence Balzer had written in the *Los Angeles Times* the Sunday before Thanksgiving in 1964, emphasizing the verb, as if anticipating his readers' disbelief. Preposterous! The French made the best wines in the world, everyone knew that; it had always been so and would ever be. Then, two years later, Robert Mondavi launched his tiny winery in tiny Oakville; and ten years after that George Taber reported to the world the results of the tasting Steve Spurrier and Patricia Gallagher organized in Paris; and then seven years after that Robert Parker pronounced upon the '82 Bordeaux. Such history may have gotten muddled, or forgotten altogether, but its influence remained unmistakably undiminished.

On May 24, 2006, a Wednesday, in nearly simultaneous tastings in Napa Valley and London, Spurrier and Gallagher re-created the Judgment of Paris on its thirtieth anniversary. Or at least they tried to. The French were understandably reticent to participate in another matchup of their best against America's best. "I suspect some of the wineries felt they had little to gain and much to lose in a blind tasting," one of the judges noted. To assuage Gallic passions, Spurrier and Gallagher tweaked the format of the reenactment. The older Cabernet Sauvignons, including ones involved in the original 1976 tasting, were judged against each other (the Chardonnays were not included because they were too old). The younger Cabernet Sauvignons and Chardonnays, however, were tasted separately, with the judges clearly aware of which were from California and which from France; to drive that point home, the organizers touted this particular tasting as a "celebration," not a competition. The tasting of the older Cabernet Sauvignons, each of which was at least thirty years old, remained a competition.

And California won again. The international judges awarded the top five spots to six California wines (there was one tie), including Warren Winiarski's 1973 Stag's Leap, which had won thirty years before; it placed second this go-round, behind a 1971 Cabernet Sauvignon from Ridge Vineyards, the winery west of San Jose and south of San Francisco started by David Bennion and fellow scientists, and where Enologix's Leo McCloskey began his wine career. Its win was further proof that California's climatic hospitality toward higher-end grapes extended well beyond Napa.

Some rolled their eyes at yet another reenactment—there had been similar events every five years, and there would be another, in Germany in

2011, for the thirty-fifth anniversary—but, coming as it did during a decade of tremendous growth for American fine wine that also saw the passing of giants of the movement such as Robert Mondavi, the thirtieth anniversary of the Judgment of Paris seemed particularly fraught with symbolism, as did the results. America's triumph was once again, as one French judge put it, "incomprehensible."

Epilogue

THE WORLD'S BIGGEST WINE COUNTRY

2014

The news broke on May 13, 2014, late on a Tuesday in the United States: The nation had for the first time surpassed France as the world's biggest wine market. Americans bought more than 768,740,000 gallons of wine in 2013, as recorded by the Paris-based International Organisation of Vine and Wine, while the French took home just more than 742,323,000 gallons. While the organization did not spell it out, wines from higher-end grapes were understood to comprise the bulk of these wine purchases. Also, while the figures acknowledged that the average French citizen consumed about six times what the average American did in 2013, it was also understood that more Americans than French drank wine regularly. In fact, nearly 40 percent of French men and women never drank wine. The 2014 figures represented industrial and palatal shifts that would have been unimaginable a half-century before.

Pick any statistic at random, and it would show tremendous growth in the American fine wine movement since the early 1960s, when things began to really take off. There were in 1965 barely four hundred wineries in the United States, and most made fortified or generic wines; in 2014 there were more than eight thousand, and most made wines from higher-end grapes. Those grapes continued to spread over the nation, particularly in California. Winemakers in the Golden State crushed about ninety-four thousand tons of Cabernet Sauvignon grapes in 1990, for instance; in 2012 that tonnage tickled half a million. For Chardonnay, the story was similar: about 250,000 tons crushed in the early 1990s, and more than 730,000 in 2012. In Napa County, still the premier spot in America's premier wine-producing state, fine wine grapes covered more than 43,500 acres in 2013; a generation before, at the close of the 1960s, they covered barely 12,000.

And theses grapes were immensely lucrative, with a value of more than $656 million in 2013. The estimated retail value of the more than 375 million cases of wine distributed in the United States in 2013 crested $36 billion. In

2010 the United States became the biggest wine-consuming market on Earth; in 2012, the average American wine drinker knocked back more than thirteen standard-size bottles of wine yearly, at least one a month (and that was the mere average!). Three years later, revenue from wine exports reached an all-time high of more than $1.5 billion; most of this export revenue came from Europe and Canada, but an increasing amount was pouring in from East Asia, particularly Japan and China.

That region, too, provided another piece of major news illumining just how far America had come in terms of influence. In the waning days of 2012, Robert Parker announced he was selling control of the *Wine Advocate* to three businessmen under the age of fifty from Singapore, where the company would open an office; Parker was also stepping down as editor-in-chief, with Lisa Perrotti-Brown, a former playwright from Maine whom Parker met while she was working in the Japanese wine trade, taking over. Parker would continue to write for the newsletter he started out of his Parkton living room all those years ago, including about his beloved Bordeaux, and would retain the titles of chairman and CEO; but his ceding of day-to-day duties to a group from East Asia proved irresistibly symbolic. "The move recognizes a new reality," Eric Asimov wrote in the *New York Times*, "that the center of orbit for critics like Mr. Parker is now Asia rather than North America."

As it had been Europe a generation before.

What of our other main characters in the history of American fine wine?

Maynard Amerine

The influential University of California, Davis, researcher retired in 1974 and died in 1998.

Gerald Asher

The British expat and *Gourmet* columnist who helped organize the Four Seasons' California Barrel Tastings continues to write about wine.

Robert Lawrence Balzer

The first serious wine writer in the United States after Prohibition died in 2011 at age ninety-nine.

Jim Barrett

The savior and principal owner of Chateau Montelena, crafter of the winning Chardonnay at the Judgment of Paris, died in 2013 at age eighty-six. The winery is now run by Jim's son Bo.

Mike Benziger

Benziger and his family sold Sonoma's Glen Ellen Winery, birthplace of the "fighting varietals," to Heublein in 1993. They launched the Benziger Family Winery, also in Sonoma, shortly after.

Cesar Chavez

The legendary labor leader continued to feud with California's grape-growing industry, though he never again drew the scale of attention he did in the 1970s. He died in 1993 at age sixty-six.

Paul and Julia Child

Paul Child died in May 1994 at age ninety-two, about ten years before Julia. He had served from the 1960s on as an informal adviser to his wife as her career took off.

Ruth Ellen Church

The author of the first weekly wine column in a major American newspaper, the *Chicago Tribune*, died in 1991 at age eighty-one.

Francis Ford Coppola

The legendary film director and screenwriter still owns and helps manage the Inglenook winery he and his family started piecing together in the 1970s.

John Daniel

Daniel, who lifted his granduncle Gustave Niebaum's Inglenook in Napa Valley to critical heights, died in 1971, seven years after he sold the winery.

Alice Feiring

Feiring continues to write about wine, particularly natural wines.

Robert Finigan

Finigan continued to write about wine after Robert Parker rocketed past him in the early 1980s to become America's most influential wine critic. Finigan died in 2011 at age sixty-eight.

Konstantin Frank

The man who made higher-end grapes grow in the colder climes of Upstate New York died in 1985. His family continues to run Dr. Frank Wines.

Patricia Gallagher

The co-organizer of the Judgment of Paris, who now goes by Patricia Gallagher-Gastaud, continues to write and teach about wine.

Ernest and Julio Gallo

Julio Gallo died in 1993 at age eighty-three, and Ernest Gallo in 2007 at age ninety-seven. Their company remains the world's largest family-owned winery.

Craig Goldwyn

The former *Chicago Tribune* critic who organized the Great Chardonnay Showdown in 1980 now writes widely about barbecue.

Randall Grahm

Randall Grahm sold off the Cardinal Zin and Big House brands in 2006 and has refocused Bonny Doon on smaller-scale production that emphasizes biodynamic wine-making, a sort of holistic approach that starts with terroir.

Mike Grgich

The architect of the winning Chardonnay at both the original Judgment of Paris and the Great Chardonnay Showdown in 1980 remains president of Grgich Hills Estate, which he runs with daughter Violet and nephew Ivo Jeramaz.

Alex and Louisa Hargrave

The now-divorced couple that brought fine wine to Long Island sold their eponymous concern to Castello di Borghese in 1999.

Joe Heitz

Heitz, hailed as Napa Valley's "first artisan," died in 2000 at age eighty-one. His children now run Heitz Cellars.

Leo McCloskey

McCloskey continues to work with several wineries through his Enologix firm.

Peter Mondavi

Age one hundred as of October 2014, Mondavi is still involved in the running of Charles Krug, the winery his parents bought control of in 1943.

Robert Parker

Parker still travels widely, including as a host of an international program the *Wine Advocate* launched in early 2014 called the Grand World Tour. The first event focused on Asia.

Frank Prial

The first wine critic at the *New York Times* retired from the role in 2004 and died in 2012 at age eighty-two.

Phyllis Richman

The *Washington Post* editor who hired Robert Parker retired as the newspaper's food critic in 2000 and continues to write about food and drink, including through novels.

Frank Schoonmaker

The writer-turned-merchant who advocated early on for grape labeling on American wine bottles died in 1976 at seventy years old, soon after he sold his wine-selling business to Pillsbury.

Marvin Shanken

Shanken remains the publisher of *Wine Spectator* as well as other publications, including *Cigar Aficionado*.

Richard Sommer

Sommer, who pioneered Oregon's fine wine industry, died in 2009 at age seventy-nine. Dyson DeMara acquired the HillCrest winery in 2003.

Steven Spurrier

The co-architect of the Judgment of Paris sold his hugely influential Caves de la Madeleine, as well as his stakes in other French wine concerns (including L'Académie du Vin), in 1988. He then relocated to Great Britain, where he continues to work as a consultant and writer.

Lee Stewart

The Souverain founder and cantankerous mentor to Warren Winiarski died in 1986 at age eighty-two.

Larry Stone

The first American to win Best International Sommelier in French Wines went on to work with various restaurant and winery ventures, including partnering with Francis Ford Coppola. He is now the estates manager for Napa-based Huneeus Vintners.

Adam Strum

Strum remains editor-in-chief and publisher of *Wine Enthusiast* magazine, and chairman of Wine Enthusiast Companies.

George Taber

The crucial media link to the Judgment of Paris results went on to start *NJBIZ*, a weekly newspaper covering New Jersey business, before selling it and turning to wine writing full-time in 2005.

Bob Trinchero

The man who resurrected the White Zinfandel style at Sutter Home in Napa Valley continues to help run a family company that now includes dozens of wine and spirits brands.

Gary Vaynerchuk

The frenetic former *Wine Library TV* host now manages a social-media consultancy and a $25 million seed fund for technology start-ups.

Philip Wagner

Wagner, whose cultivation of French-American hybrids in the 1930s and 1940s helped advance East Coast wine-making, died in 1997. He and his family had sold Boordy Vineyards in 1980.

Warren Winiarski

The architect of the winning Cabernet Sauvignon at the original Judgment of Paris sold his Stag's Leap in 2007 to a joint venture of Italy's Marchese Piero Antinori and Ste. Michelle Wine Estates, Washington State's biggest winery, for $185 million.

Albert Winkler

The influential University of California, Davis, researcher retired in 1963 and died in 1989 at age ninety-five.

Alder Yarrow

The pioneering blogger continues to edit and write *Vinography*.

James Zellerbach

The Sonoma pioneer of French oak usage at his Hanzell Vineyards died in 1963. His widow sold the winery shortly afterward.

ACKNOWLEDGMENTS

I **wish I had more space to** thank the many people and organizations that helped make this book possible. To start, I would like to thank those in the American fine wine industry who generously gave of their time and expertise, in particular the Robert Mondavi Winery; Bo Barrett and Chateau Montelena; Warren Winiarski; Larry Stone; Adam Strum and the *Wine Enthusiast*; the Dr. Konstantin Frank winery; Pierre Rovani; the California Wine Institute; Randall Grahm and Bonny Doon; Leo McCloskey and Enologix; John Conover and PlumpJack; Dyson DeMara and HillCrest; Harold Francis and Inglenook; and Steven Spurrier.

Also, I would like to thank the fellow writers who paid it forward in the form of interviews, archival information, or fact-checking, including George Taber, Elin McCoy, Eric Asimov, Harry Steiman, Craig Goldwyn, Alder Yarrow, Alice Feiring, and Ron Washam. I am also indebted to wine writers who are no longer with us, particularly Frank Prial, all of whom adeptly chronicled what turned out to be, in the end, one tasty yarn. I am acutely aware and very grateful that I have been able to stand on their research and analysis.

I would in particular like to credit two books: Taber's *Judgment of Paris*, which tracks not only that epochal event expertly, but much of the backstory of American fine wine up to that point; and the first volume of Thomas Pinney's magisterial *A History of Wine in America*. I have provided a fuller bibliography as well of other books I frequently consulted.

I am also grateful for research help from the Cambridge Public Library in Massachusetts; the University of California, Davis, the bibulously formidable canon of which I first encountered researching craft beer; the Beverly Hills Public Library; the special collections of the California State Polytechnic University; and the WGBH Educational Foundation. The archives of *Wines & Vines* and the *St. Helena Star*, and their respective staffs, were also helpful. The same can be said of the *Wine Advocate*.

This book, too, would not have been possible without the team at Chicago Review Press, especially my editor, Yuval Taylor, who saw the wisdom in a substantial rewrite; copyeditor Laine Morreau; and project editors Amelia Estrich and Ellen Hornor for shepherding the book to completion. Any mistakes in this volume are my own. A thank you, too, to my agent, Adam Chromy, for his frank advice and guidance.

I would also like to thank my family, especially my uncle and aunt, Roy and Anne Meyers, for help with research; my in-laws John and Suzanne Rudy for introducing me to a wider world of wine (and John's help in scrupulous proofreading); my parents, as always, especially my mother, who instilled in me a love of books and reading; and my siblings and their families. This book is dedicated to my oldest sibling, Nan Acitelli. Finally, none of this would have been possible without the love and constancy of my wife, Elizabeth, and our fearless alarm clock, Josephine.

TJA
Cambridge, Massachusetts
November 20, 2014

ENDNOTES

Prologue: The World's Biggest Wine Market

"the 'wine-ification' of beer" Clay Risen, "Craft Beer's Larger Aspirations Cause a Stir," *New York Times*, March 4, 2013, D4.

"The old American term" Jay Brooks, "Big Bottles Equals Wine," *Brookston Beer Bulletin*, March 5, 2014, accessed May 5, 2014, http://brookstonbeerbulletin.com/big-bottles -equals-wine/.

no new wineries of note Julia Flynn Siler, *The House of Mondavi: The Rise and Fall of an American Wine Dynasty* (New York: Gotham Books, 2007), 78. Nearly all the Napa Valley wineries to come out of Prohibition, fine or otherwise, were there before—and during—it.

"came in at the top" Dorothy J. Gaiter and John Brecher, "Putting Wine's Magic Into Words," *Wall Street Journal*, July 1, 2005, W6.

French Connections

Childs' conversation and lunch description Julia Child and Alex Prud'Homme, *My Life in France* (New York: A. A. Knopf, 2006), 16–7.

for the story had yet to be told Indeed, that would not happen until 2001, with the publication of Don and Petie Kladstrup's *Wine & War: The French, the Nazis & the Battle for France's Greatest Treasure* (New York: Broadway Books, 2001). Anecdotes about the Germans' love and loathing of French wine were taken from that book.

"sent shivers down" Ibid., 179–80.

"grown-up little girl" Louisa Thomas, "Julia Child's Life as a Spy," *New York Times*, April 3, 2011, BR21.

Child background Bob Spitz, *Dearie: The Remarkable Life of Julia Child* (New York: A. A. Knopf, 2012), 87–88.

The Man Who Drew a Line in French Wine

Peynaud background "Peynaud, French Wine Expert and Consultant, Dead 92," Associated Press International, July 23, 2004; Eric Asimov, "Émile Peynaud, 92, a Revolutionary Wine Expert Who Defined 'Expert'," *New York Times*, July 23, 2004, A21.

"There was really one world" Asimov, "Émile Peynaud, 92," A21.

"More than any other" Ibid.

if his white Citroën simply slowed Ibid.

was able to marry Jennifer Jordan, "Émile Peynaud: a Wine Revolutionary," Savoreachglass
.com, accessed September 21, 2014, www.savoreachglass.com/articles/emile-peynaud
-a-wine-revolutionary. Writers seemingly could not cease using *revolutionary* to
describe Peynaud and his work; and justly so.

"The greatest wines" George M. Taber, *Judgment of Paris: California vs. France and the
Historic 1976 Paris Tasting That Revolutionized Wine* (New York: Scribner, 2005), 17.

Hugh Johnson details "Hugh Johnson," Wilson Daniels, accessed October 28, 2013,
www.wilsondaniels.com/our-portfolio/royal-tokaji/biographies/.

Harry Waugh details "Harry Waugh," *Telegraph*, December 5, 2001.

cofounded the Bordeaux Club Michael Broadbent, "Obituary: Harry Waugh," Decanter.com,
December 3, 2001, accessed November 4, 2013, www.decanter.com/news
/wine-news/489013/obituary-harry-waugh.

"the undisputed mistress" Dan Halpern, ed., *Not for Bread Alone: Writers on Food, Wine,
and the Art of Eating* (New York: HarperCollins, 2009), 71. The quotation can also
be found in the original 1971 edition of *The World Atlas of Wine*.

Classification details Taber, *Judgment of Paris*, 22–23.

First Growth châteaus Baron James de Rothschild purchased Lafite in 1868. This book
will refer to it as Chateau Lafite Rothschild.

Appellation d'Origine Contrôlée details and spread Taber, *Judgment of Paris*, 19; David J.
Duman, "The DOC (or DO or AOC)," *Huffington Post*, accessed September 11, 2011,
www.huffingtonpost.com/david-j-duman/the-doc-or-do-or-aoc-nobo_b_957748.
html. The number of French wine appellations would grow to more than four hundred by the turn of the century.

not widely adopted Elin McCoy, *The Emperor of Wine: The Rise of Robert M. Parker, Jr.
and the Reign of American Taste* (New York: Ecco, 2005), 35.

"So You'd Like to Know Wines!"

Headlines from the Chicago Tribune*'s online archives.*

Ruth Ellen Church biographical details Jodi Wilgoren and Carol Haddix, "Ruth Ellen
Church, Ex-Tribune Editor," *Chicago Tribune*, August 22, 1991; "Ruth Ellen Church,
81, Food Critic and Author," *New York Times*, August 23, 1991, D17.

readership of more than three million Based on "The *Los Angeles Times*' History,"
accessed October 29, 2013, www.latimes.com/la-mediagroup-times-history
,0,2679122.htmlstory#axzz2j8VWkDYe. It says the Sunday paper's circulation regularly reached one million in 1961. The newspaper industry rule of thumb is that there
are three readers to every circulated copy.

"Many Americans are eager" Ruth Ellen Church, "So You'd Like to Know Wine!," *Chicago
Tribune*, February 16, 1962, B1.

Balzer column excerpts Robert Lawrence Balzer, "The Pride of the Vineyards," *Los Angeles
Times*, November 22, 1964.

Robert Lawrence Balzer biography Elaine Woo, "Robert Lawrence Balzer Dies at 99," *Los
Angeles Times*, December 9, 2011; Frank J. Prial, "Robert Lawrence Balzer, Wine
Writer, Dies at 99," *New York Times*, December 15, 2011, B19; "Robert L. Balzer,"
IMDB, accessed October 25, 2013, www.imdb.com/name/nm0051338/bio?ref_=nm
_ov_bio_sm; Robert Lawrence Balzer, "Buddhist Monk's Life Happy One," *Los Angeles
Times*, April 19, 1956, front page.

G. Selmer Fougner The *New York Sun* restaurant critic, who wrote that newspaper's
daily Along the Wine Trail column from 1933 until his death in 1941, appears

to have written almost exclusively about European wines (when he wrote about wines at all) amid his three-thousand-word missives on massive repasts. Per Frank J. Prial, "Affairs to Remember," *New York Times*, February 23, 1992, 52. Balzer was the first to routinely write about American wines, albeit almost exclusively California ones.

January 1939 details and excerpt Robert Lawrence Balzer, "Concerning Wines and Foods," *Beverly Hills Citizen*, January 27, 1939. The author thanks the Beverly Hills Public Library for its help in locating these early columns.

an annual barbecue Here was Mayock's first mention of the wine at the barbecue: "One part of imported Campari with seven parts of Petri's sweet Vermouth was served with the celery and giant olives as an aperitif. It was a little too sweet for me so I poured a part of it into my champagne and it came out just right." Per Robert S. Mayock, "About Wining and Dining," *Lodi News-Sentinel*, June 3, 1942.

House & Garden, for instance Thomas Pinney, *A History of Wine in America*, vol. 2, *From Prohibition to the Present* (Berkeley: University of California Press, 2005), 108.

Schoonmaker details Paul Lukacs, *American Vintage: The Rise of American Wine* (New York: Houghton Mifflin, 2000), 123–24; Frank J. Prial, "Wine Talk," *New York Times*, March 20, 1991, C9.

"No sooner had legalized wines" Prial, "Wine Talk," March 20, 1991, C9.

Pink Chablis vs. Premier Cru

"most effective commercial . . . ever" Ernest and Julio Gallo, with Bruce Henderson. *Ernest & Julio: Our Story* (New York: Random House, 1994), 213. The full quotation is: "On the verge of failure in 1965, Pink Chablis was not only saved but 'made' by what was probably the most effective commercial we have ever made."

"Gallo Pink Chablis Wine Commercial," YouTube video, 1:01, posted by AmberVon on September 5, 2008, www.youtube.com/watch?v=rxgPem4Q9lA.

when Gallo's annual sales jumped Ernest & Julio Gallo, with Bruce D. Henderson, *Our Story* (New York: Random House, 1994), 167.

"the size of oil refineries" Frank J. Prial, "A Feud and a Book Unplug the Cork on the Gallo Empire," *New York Times*, April 14, 1993, C8, *Home & Garden* section.

make their own bottles Gallos, with Henderson, *Our Story*, 167.

California wine statistics Pinney, *A History of Wine in America*, 225–26.

at the Exposition Universelle Lukacs, *American Vintage*, 90.

"unpretentious, accessible" Pinney, *A History of Wine in America*, 50.

"an article formerly contraband" Ibid., 51.

Laws and bulk-sale ban Ibid., 49–50.

Serve with Fish, Poultry, and Veal

P. Albert Duhamel details Spitz, *Dearie*, 4; Paul Doherty, "Straight Arrow," *Boston College Magazine*, accessed March 3, 2015, http://bcm.bc.edu/issues/winter_2007/linden_lane /straight-arrow.html.

Other book, show details Author's e-mail exchange with Keith Luf, archives manager at WGBH Educational Foundation, 2013–14; Calvin Tompkins, "Good Cooking," *New Yorker*, December 23, 1974; Ruth Graham, "How Julia Child Outfitted Her TV Kitchen," Boston.com, September 26, 2012, accessed September 22, 2014, www.boston.com/bostonglobe/ideas/brainiac/2012/09/three_questions.html.

Bertholle, Beck, Child details and cookbook work Spitz, *Dearie*, 219–39.

On Thursday, September 28, 1961 Ibid., 307.

"the most comprehensive" Craig Claiborne "Cookbook Review: Glorious Recipes: Art of French Cooking Does Not Concede to U.S. Tastes," *New York Times*, October 18, 1961, 47.

sold ten thousand copies Andrew F. Smith, *Eating History: 30 Turning Points in the Making of American Cuisine* (New York: Columbia University Press, 2009), 237. The book would clear one hundred thousand sales by August 1962. Per Joan Reardon, ed. *As Always, Julia: The Letters of Julia Child and Avis DeVoto* (Boston: Houghton Mifflin Harcourt, 2010), 396.

Morash-Child conversation Spitz, *Dearie*, 3–4, 87–88.

Child appearance and dialogue Spitz, *Dearie*, 12–13. Because it was filmed live, according to WGBH, no tapes of that *I've Been Reading* episode exist. The author went by Spitz's re-creation.

Child knew she was taking Dana Polan, *Julia Child's* The French Chef (Durham, NC: Duke University Press, 2011), 122.

Details about The French Chef Smith, *Eating History*, 237–38.

Beard and Lucas shows Ibid., 238.

Beard seemed to simply seize up David Kamp, *The United States of Arugula: How We Became a Gourmet Nation* (New York: Broadway Books, 2006), 94.

simple production value; use of blowtorch and bow saw Ibid., 94–95.

Verdon's first official William Grimes, "Rene Verdon, French Chef for the Kennedys, Dies at 86," *New York Times*, February 5, 2011, B8.

"Full-Bodied Dry, White Wines" Julia Child, Louisette Bertholle, and Simone Beck, *Mastering the Art of French Cooking* (New York: Alfred A. Knopf, 2010), 33.

Julia Child drank; no-endorsements policy Spitz, *Dearie*, 337; 335.

In correspondence with WGBH Polan, *Child's* French Chef, 123–24.

which outsold gas-range stovetops Southwest Museum of Engineering, Communications and Computation website, accessed March 3, 2015, www.smecc.org/microwave_oven.htm.

more than sixty million households Paul B. Johnson, "Computer Age Causes Shift in TV Industry," *High Point (NC) Enterprise*, December 12, 2011.

drop in the number of farms "Growing a Nation," National Institute of Food and Agriculture, USDA, accessed March 3, 2015, www.agclassroom.org/gan/timeline/farmers_land.htm.

Fathers and Sons and Brothers

Robert-Peter fight details Siler, *House of Mondavi*, 51; Robert Mondavi with Paul Chutkow, *Harvests of Joy: How the Good Life Became Great Business* (New York: Harcourt Brace, 1998), 16.

Cesare and Rosa Mondavi background Siler, *House of Mondavi*, 9–12; Mondavi, *Harvests*, 29–38.

Mondavi family business background Siler, *House of Mondavi*, 9–16.

"nonintoxicating" fruit juice "200 Gallons Family Limit, Dry Chief Says," *Sausalito News*, September 24, 1921.

serious critics disdained Frank Schoonmaker, *Encyclopedia of Wine* (New York: Hastings House, 1965), 358–67.

Details about Alicante Bouschet Ibid., 358; Talia Baiocchi, "Alicante Bouschet: Prohibition's Darling Grape," Eater.com, June 28, 2011, accessed November 11, 2013, http://eater.com/archives/2011/06/28/alicante-bouschet-prohibitions-darling-grape.php.

"vulgar virtues" and *"it afforded California"* Robert Lawrence Balzer, *Wines of California* (New York: Harry N. Abrams, 1978), 56.

"common" and *"baptized"* Schoonmaker, *Encyclopedia*, 358–59. The British often call Bordeaux "claret."

"sound, agreeable wine" Ibid., 358.

"no possible value" Ibid., 363.

Acreage details, including Merlot Ibid., 358–61.

wondered aloud Ibid.; Pinney, *History of Wine*, 119.

singled out for derision Ibid., 119.

A Higher Calling

five hundred thousand gallons Siler, *House of Mondavi*, 21.

Details on Mondavis' work, relationship Ibid., 19–21; James Conaway, *Napa: The Story of an American Eden* (New York: Mariner Books, 2002), 27–28.

Robert ate a particularly revelatory Mondavi, *Harvests*, 5–7.

Mondavi lifestyle, Wine Institute meetings Conaway, *Napa*, 27–28.

he was restless, worried Mondavi, *Harvests*, 4–5.

"We needed a great dream" Ibid., 10.

felt tremendously Siler, *House of Mondavi*, 54; Mondavi, *Harvests*, 16–18.

Firing and confrontation over Michael Siler, *House of Mondavi*, 54–56.

Optimism

Andre Tchelistcheff biography Frank J. Prial, "Andre Tchelistcheff, Authority on Wine," *New York Times*, April 7, 1994, B8; Conaway, *Napa*, 104–05; "The Maestro—Andrew Tchelistcheff—the Voice of Wine," The Maestro Film website, accessed November 15, 2013, www.themaestrofilm.com/thestory.htm.

Georges de Latour and Beaulieu winery details Prial, "Andre Tchelistcheff," B8; Pinney, *History of Wine*, 16.

Latour-Tchelistcheff meeting and Tchelistcheff mannerisms Prial, "Andre Tchelistcheff," B8.

became a gold standard in California reds Praise of the Georges de Latour Private Reserve Cabernet Sauvignon appears throughout wine literature. Interestingly, Latour's name was not added to the label until after his death (Pinney, *History of Wine*, 453).

rat floating in a vat of Sauvignon Blanc Taber, *Judgment*, 42.

Maynard Amerine details Dan Berger, "Maynard A. Amerine; Wine Expert," *Los Angeles Times*, March 13, 1998; Molly O'Neill, "Maynard Amerine, 87, California Wine Expert," *New York Times*, March 13, 1998, B13.

Winkler details Myrna Oliver, "Albert Winkler; Authority on Viticulture," *Los Angeles Times*, September 6, 1989.

Winkler Scale The scale has attained near-mythic proportions in American wine. The author consulted Pinney, *History of Wine*, 103–05, and Oliver's obituary as well as various other sources, including the UC Davis website.

grapes that Winkler thought Pinney, *History of Wine*, 104.

Napa Valley Technical Group Ibid., 145.

single-biggest fine wine vineyard "Oakville Vineyards & Coombsville Vineyards," Far Niente Wine Estate, accessed November 26, 2013, www.farniente.com/WinesVineyards/vineyards.html. Martin Stelling, who died in a car accident in 1950, appears to have been the biggest what-if in the early American fine wine movement.

American Society for Enology and Viticulture Pinney, *History of Wine*, 149.

Paul Garrett quotation and biographical details "The Wines of the US," *Fortune*, 1934, accessed November 21, 2013, http://features.blogs.fortune.cnn.com/2012/03/25/american-wine-fortune-1934/; "Virginia Dare Wine," North Carolina History Project, accessed November 21, 2013, www.northcarolinahistory.org/commentary/199/entry. Among other pioneering moves, Garrett very likely recorded the first radio ad for wine, American or otherwise.

Most of the sixteen thousand acres Pinney, *History of Wine*, 64.

Robert Mondavi was aware of all this Mondavi writes at length in his memoir, *Harvests of Joy*, about his thoughts around the time of starting the Robert Mondavi Winery, pages 55 to 108 in particular.

Maybe there was no market Mondavi, *Harvests*, 23.

"It's Beautiful"

Dedication details "Ceremonies Mark First Grape Crushing at New Robert Mondavi Winery," *St. Helena Star*, September 8, 1966, 1; Siler, *House of Mondavi*, 77–78.

Yet it was not to be The sort of national and international coverage that would have suggested a serious impact on American wine does not appear to have materialized until the late 1970s. Hugh Johnson's original *World Atlas of Wine*, published in 1971, for instance, did not reference it. Any significance writers have ascribed to its 1966 opening, then, has to be understood as coming solely with hindsight.

"The winery I envisioned" Mondavi, *Harvests*, 23, 55.

quickly shed the pretense Ibid., 70.

$9,000-a-year consultancy fee Siler, *House of Mondavi*, 76.

Financing sources for winery Mondavi, *Harvests*, 71.

Cliff May background Anna Almendrala, "Cliff May Classic: A Ranch House in Solvang, California," *Huffington Post*, September 14, 2010, accessed November 26, 2013, www.huffingtonpost.com/2010/09/14/cliff-may-classic-a-ranch_n_715480.html#s138142.

Site selection details and Mondavi winery vision Mondavi, *Harvests*, 58–68.

To Kalon details Ibid., 57–62; Lettie Teague, "The Most Powerful Grower in Napa," *Wall Street Journal*, March 19, 2011, D6. The closest English approximation for *Kalon* is "beautiful" (per Merriam-Webster's dictionary), though *To Kalon* could literally mean "It Good."

Mondavi liked To Kalon's proximity Mondavi, *Harvests*, 63.

Joe Heitz biographical details Frank J. Prial, "Joseph Heitz, 81, a Standout in California Winemaking," *New York Times*, December 23, 2000, B7; "Heitz Founders," Heitz Wine Cellars website, accessed November 27, 2013, www.heitzcellar.com/legacy/founders.cfm.

"distinctive expression of terroir" James Laube, "Martha's Vineyard Reaches the Heitz of California Cabernet Again," *Wine Spectator*, June 15, 2012.

"first artisan" Prial, "Joseph Heitz, 81, a Standout," B7.

On Route 66

"fantastic tomatoes" Carrie M. Golus, "Days of Wine and Prizes," *University of Chicago Magazine*, June 2002, accessed November 29, 2013, http://magazine.uchicago.edu/0602/peer/vitae.shtml; Mondavi, *Harvests*, 74.

Warren Winiarski biography details Author's interview with Warren Winiarski, March 27, 2014; Jon Bonné, "After the Leap: His Celebrated Winery Sold, Warren Winiarski

Ponders His Legacy—and His Next Move," *San Francisco Chronicle*, March 28, 2008; Golus, "Days of Wine and Prizes"; Taber, *Judgment*, 92–99.

Interestingly enough, Winiarski's Machiavelli work was translated into a chapter in the book *History of Political Philosophy*, coedited by neoconservative godfather Leo Strauss (Golus, "Days of Wine and Prizes").

Robert's Folly

"How the hell" Conaway, *Napa*, 19.

Souverain Winery details "Chateau Souverain," Atlas of Wineries, accessed December 2, 2013, www.atlasofwineries.com/wineries/chateausouverain.html. For this book, the American varietal Zinfandel is treated as a higher-end grape.

Stewart-Winiarski relationship Author's Winiarski interview; Taber, *Judgment*, 92–99; Conaway, *Napa*, 17–19.

Winiarski family living arrangements Taber, *Judgment*, 99.

Mondavi working conditions Mondavi, *Harvests*, 74.

the weather cooperated Ibid., 73; Siler, *House of Mondavi*, 77.

Charles Krug helped with the crush Mondavi, *Harvests*, 73. Curiously, in a further break with his brother (and, presumably, his mother), Robert began pronouncing his surname differently personally and professionally. He went by Mon-DAH-vee while Peter et al. went by Mon-DAY-vee, the pronunciation preferred by Cesare Mondavi (Siler, *House of Mondavi*, 79).

"Robert's Folly" Siler, *House of Mondavi*, 79.

"joyous space" Mondavi, *Harvests*, 67.

Mondavi set out Robert Mondavi makes clear in his memoir, *Harvests of Joy*, particularly in chapter 10, that he wanted to attract visitors to the winery from the start. Charles Krug's efforts, including renovating an old storage shed to serve as the tasting room, might have represented the pre–Robert Mondavi Winery apotheosis for winery hospitality in Napa Valley.

2,579 cases of wine in 1967 Siler, *House of Mondavi*, 87.

$1.79 a bottle Mondavi, *Harvests*, 75.

around two thousand acres of California Schoonmaker, *Encyclopedia of Wine*, 366–67.

"light, dry, golden wine" Balzer, *Wines of California*, 150.

Fumé Blanc creation and popularity Mondavi, *Harvests*, 75–76; Larry Olmsted, "Why You Should Drink Fume Blanc This Summer," *Forbes*, May 18, 2013; Bill Daly, "Not Your Parents' Sauvignon Blanc," *Chicago Tribune*, July 16, 2008.

Greyhound Bus to Paradise

Miljenko Grgich biographical details Taber, *Judgment*, 47–49.

Grgich working life, including with Souverain and Beaulieu Ibid., 60–72; "Miljenko 'Mike' Grgich President and Vintner's Hall of Fame inductee," Grgich Hills website, accessed December 9, 2013, www.grgich.com/mike_grgich.

Michael Mondavi had returned from National Guard service in 1967, and officially became a winemaker at Robert Mondavi. This proved frustrating for Winiarski, who had been supervising much of the day-to-day production; and he was reportedly not impressed with Michael's attention to detail. Per Siler, *House of Mondavi*, 80–81.

Going for Broke

"*Mike,*" *Robert Mondavi said* Siler, *House of Mondavi*, 82.

Mondavi's enthusiasm was intoxicating Ibid.

Wine sales figures Ibid., 87.

Survey of a typical liquor store Based on author interviews with producers and consumers back then as well as sales and production figures from the Wine Institute. Regarding Gallo's love of Thompson seedless grapes: when the winery stopped using them in 1982, the *New York Times* noted that the move "sharply depressed the market for the variety." (Per Terry Robards, "Gallo Drops a Grape Variety," *New York Times*, Sept. 8, 1982, C15.)

Gallo's distribution strategy Pinney, *History of Wine*, 198.

Grgich hiring and responsibilities Siler, *House of Mondavi*, 82.

Mondavi threw himself Siler, *House of Mondavi*, 82; Mondavi, *Harvests*, 103–08.

James Zellerbach, Hanzell details Bryan Miller, "A Matter of Taste," *New York Times Magazine*, January 5, 1986; Hanzell.com, accessed August 7, 2014, www.hanzell.com /people/ambassador-zellerbach.html; James Laube, "Former Hanzell Winemaker Bob Sessions Dies at 82," *Wine Spectator*, May 14, 2014.

"*did indeed share*" Miller, "A Matter of Taste."

a turning point Hugh Johnson, *Wine: A Life Uncorked* (Berkeley: University of California Press, 2006), 301.

stainless steel and new French oak Mondavi, *Harvests*, 101–02. Hanzell Winery in Sonoma County was using new French oak around the same time (per Mondavi, *Harvests*, 102).

Work ethic and innovations Mondavi, *Harvests*, 100–08; Siler, *House of Mondavi*, 82.

"*Robert Mondavi of the Napa Valley*" Robert Lawrence Balzer, "The Wine Connoisseur," *Los Angeles Times* magazine, November 2, 1969, 64.

Émile Peynaud had pushed Per Henrik Mansson, "Emile Peynaud, Who Influenced Wine-making Around the World, Dies at 92," *Wine Spectator*, July 21, 2004.

Michael Mondavi, the striking Siler, *House of Mondavi*, 80.

Grape tonnage Ibid., 83.

Grgich worried aloud Siler, *House of Mondavi*, 83. Mondavi did hire an assistant wine-maker for Grgich two years in named Zelma Long (per Siler, *House of Mondavi*, 83).

Details about Rainier stake and growth plans Siler, *House of Mondavi*, 87–89; Mondavi, *Harvests*, 151–55. Mondavi would come to own seven hundred acres of To Kalon (per Mondavi, *Harvests*, 152).

didn't extend beyond California According to the winery, sales beyond California likely started in the early 1970s (per e-mail exchange with winery representatives, June 2014).

Grgich, for his part, did not believe Siler, *House of Mondavi*, 83.

by 1969 most of the wine All consumption and sales figures via the Wine Institute, accessed December 12, 2013, www.wineinstitute.org/resources/statistics/article86.

still of the sweeter, cheaper generic variety In 1967, sales of fine wine finally overtook fortified ones. But according to the Wine Institute, Americans were still consuming more fortified wines than fine ones; the consumption balance would not start to tip until the early 1970s, and then only gradually. The Wine Institute's statistics can be found here: www.wineinstitute.org/resources/statistics (accessed March 4, 2015).

Grgich knew he would Siler, *House of Mondavi*, 83–84.

$50,000 Down Payment

Winiarski visit to Fay Taber, *Judgment*, 109–11.
Winiarski vineyard experience and deal Ibid., 106–11; author interview with Winiarski.

Nationwide

Diamond Creek Vineyard details Frank J. Prial, "Al Brounstein, 86, Who Made Sought-After Wines, Is Dead," *New York Times*, June 29, 2006, A4. The Wine Institute provided the author a timeline of different wineries' starts, which was checked against state incorporation records. The Wine Institute's list was deferred to when the years differed.

Fetzer Winery details Laurie Daniel, "Grapegrower Interview: Patti Fetzer," *Wines & Vines*, January 2011; Lynn Alley, "Wine Family Matriarch Kathleen Fetzer Dies at 88," *Wine Spectator*, September 20, 2010.

Gene Trefethen details "Eugene Trefethen Jr.; Industrialist, Vintner," *Los Angeles Times*, February 3, 1996. The winery eventually became known as Trefethen Family Vineyards.

Corley details "Our History," Monticello Vineyards website, accessed December 16, 2013, www.corleyfamilynapavalley.com/corley-story.php; "Monticello Vineyards—A Corley Family Affair," Bacchus & Beery Wine Blog, October 23, 2011. Corley named his winery Monticello Vineyards (per http://wine-blog.bacchusandbeery.com/wine-blog/winemaker-interview/monticello-vineyards-corley-family-affair/, accessed March 4, 2015).

Kenwood Vineyards details "In Memoriam: Mike Lee, Founder of Kenwood Vineyards," *Kenwood Press*, May 15, 2011; "Mike Lee: Pioneer, Winemaker, Gentleman," A Year in Wine blog, May 4, 2011, accessed December 16, 2013, www.ayearinwine.com/2011/05/mike-lee-pioneer-winemaker-gentleman.html.

Chateau Montelena "Honoring the Life of James L. Barrett," Chateau Montelena website, accessed December 16, 2013, www.montelena.com/jameslbarrett.aspx; "Chateau Montelena's Jim Barrett Dies, Leaves Behind Long Legacy," *Scranton Times-Tribune*, March 20, 2013. George Taber's book *Judgment of Paris* also provides myriad details about Barrett's life and the restarting of Chateau Montelena.

Portet and Goelet details John Lewis, "Worldwide Wineries," *Newcastle Herald*, April 13, 2011, 47; Mondavi, *Harvests*, 177.

was wasting his time Cara Pallone, "In Memoriam to Four Men Who Made a Difference," *Oregon Wine Press*, January 10, 2010, accessed December 20, 2013, http://oregonwinepress.com/article?articleTitle=%25232+story:+in+memoriam+to+four+men+who+made+a+difference--1262894545--237&re.

HillCrest Vineyard details Ibid.; "Oregon Wine History," Oregon Wine Board website, accessed December 20, 2013, www.oregonwine.org/wineries/history.aspx. The Ponzis were pioneers in craft beer, too, founding in 1984 the brewery that became BridgePort, Oregon's oldest surviving craft brewery.

Oregon Wine Festival and trade group Pinney, *History of Wine*, 325.

Alex and Louisa Hargrave Lettie Teague, "Louisa Hargrave, a Long Island Wine Pioneer, Looks Back and Forward," *Wall Street Journal*, July 12, 2013, A16. There were also details of Hargrave Vineyard's start on Ms. Hargrave's website, accessed March 4, 2015, www.louisahargrave.com/The_Vineyard.html.

Bully Hill and Walter Taylor Frank J. Prial, "A Farewell to the Baron of Bully Hill," *New York Times*, May 2, 2001, F1.

Konstantin Frank details, including Fournier meeting "The Legacy of Dr. Konstantin Frank," Dr. Konstantin Frank winery website, accessed December 29, 2013, www .drfrankwines.com/history; Robert J. Roberts, "A Toast to the Future: Frank Leads the Way for New York Wines," *(Hornell, NY) Evening Tribune*, May 7, 2001; "Early History of Finger Lakes Wines," Wines NY, accessed December 30, 2013, www .winesny.com/NewYorkWines/Articles/FingerLakesRiesling053108 /FingerLakesRiesling053108-History-p2.aspx.

considered having him committed Carlo DeVito, "Hybrid vs. Vinifera Part 2: Dr. Konstantin Frank," East Coast Wineries blog, accessed August 8, 2014, http://eastcoastwineries .blogspot.com/2009/09/hybrid-vs-vinifera-part-2-dr-konstatin.html.

Philip Wagner details Frank J. Prial, "Philip M. Wagner, 92, Wine Maker Who Introduced Hybrids," *New York Times*, January 3, 1997, B7. It must be noted that while Konstantin Frank may have known about Wagner's hybrid work, he remained committed to *not* making fine wine with hybrids but with the higher-end grapes alone.

"wines that taste like wine" Ibid.

Ohio wineries Pinney, *History of Wine*, 271–72; the Ohio Wine Producers Association website, accessed December 30, 2013, www.ohiowines.org/cgi-bin/winery_12.pl.

Virginia wineries John Hagarty, "In the Beginning Was Archie," June 10, 2009, accessed December 20, 2013, www.hagarty-on-wine.com/OnWineBlog/?p=1392; Kenan Heise, "Elizabeth Furness," *Chicago Tribune*, March 2, 1986; Walker Elliott Rowe, *A History of Virginia Wines: From Grapes to Glass* (Charleston, SC: History Press, 2009). Piedmont may have actually been the first commercial winery in Virginia to work with higher-end grapes irrespective of Prohibition, but given the commonwealth's long history, it's difficult to tell; it was definitely the first after Repeal.

Changing Hands

"This district classification is intended" "The Ag Preserve History," The Jack L. Davies Napa Valley Agricultural Land Preservation Fund, prepared by James A. Hickey, accessed December 23, 2013, www.jldagfund.org/history_AGpreserve.html.

California growth Tom Acitelli, *The Audacity of Hops: The History of America's Craft Beer Revolution* (Chicago: Chicago Review Press, 2013), 22. Aviation was long a huge industry in California by this time. In 1935 Boeing was the only airplane manufacturer without a California address (per "A Brief History of the California Economy," California Department of Finance, accessed March 4, 2015, www.dof.ca.gov/HTML /FS_DATA/HistoryCAEconomy/).

Grape acreage and values Crop reports from the Napa County agricultural commissioner's office. The excerpt mentioning the all-time record comes from the 1973 report. Walnuts did, indeed, go to hell: in 1959 Napa Valley farmers produced more than 4,500 tons of walnuts; in 1973, 550 tons.

Heublein takeovers of Inglenook and Beaulieu Conaway, *Napa*, 131–38; James Laube, "The Glory That Was Inglenook," *Wine Spectator*, October 17, 2001, 60.

Mondavi viewed Mondavi, *Harvests*, 154.

perhaps around ten million cases James T. Lapsley, *Bottled Poetry: Napa Winemaking from Prohibition to the Modern Era* (Berkeley: University of California Press, 1997), 143.

Pillsbury acquisition of Souverain Michael Dresser, "Revived California Winery Now Making Good Varietals," *Baltimore Sun*, March 1, 1992; Gail G. Unzelman, *Sonoma County Wineries* (Charleston, SC: Arcadia Publishing, 2006), 94; Mondavi, *Harvests*, 155.

Still Only for Cooking

Amerine-Tchelistcheff exchange Taber, *Judgment*, 72.

Alioto-waiter exchange Siler, *House of Mondavi*, 85.

Goldwyn anecdote Author's interview with Craig Goldwyn, December 18, 2013.

Harry Waugh praise Taber, *Judgment*, 81–82.

Balzer blind tasting David J. Hanson, "Historic Paris Wine Tastings of 1976 and Other Significant Competitions," publication of the sociology department of SUNY Potsdam, accessed December 30, 2013, www2.potsdam.edu/hansondj/Controversies /20060517115643.html#.UsGO4bQvngx.

"Solid French titles" Robert Lawrence Balzer, "A Visit to Europe Brings Chances in California Winemaking," *Los Angeles Times* magazine, December 1, 1974.

still favored sweeter generics Wine Institute, "Wine Consumption in the US," accessed September 24, 2014, www.wineinstitute.org/resources/statistics/article86.

Sales numbers Lapsley, *Bottled*, 137. These figures include imports.

Winery numbers "Number of California Wineries," the Wine Institute, accessed March 4, 2015, www.wineinstitute.org/resources/statistics/article124. The author would offer a final theory as to the growing popularity of fine wine. By the early 1970s, most beer in the United States was made by a handful of operations—and it all tasted very similar, based as it was on a watery version of the Czech pilsner style. Drinkers looking for distinction and variety in their alcoholic beverages might have been inclined to look at small, independent wineries.

Part II

An Englishman Abroad

Steven Spurrier biographical details Author's e-mail exchange with Steven Spurrier, September 2013; Steven Spurrier's "Saintsbury Oration," October 24, 2011; Taber, *Judgment*, 6–9; Frank Prial, "Briton Selling Paris Wine Interests," *New York Times*, August 3, 1988, C10.

had little in the form of a wine trade Spurrier, "Saintsbury Oration."

starting to drink less wine Panos Kakaviatos, "The Vilification of Wine in France," *Decanter*, May 24, 2010.

Chez American

Grgich offer and dialogue with Barrett Taber, *Judgment*, 127–28.

he flew to the vineyard Ibid., 115–16.

details about Waters Acitelli, *Audacity of Hops*, 41–42.

"a chef of international repute" Craig Claiborne, "Cuisine Bourgeoise Out West," *New York Times*, June 3, 1981, C1.

"good and beautiful products" Ibid.

Jim Barrett wanted to get Taber, *Judgment*, 128–29.

Grgich crushed 12,147 gallons Taber, *Judgment*, 129.

A tasting club in San Diego Ibid., 130.

Back to School

Details on L'Académie du Vin Spurrier, "Saintsbury Oration"; author exchange with Spurrier; Frank J. Prial, "Foreigners Run Unusual School," *New York Times*, December 10, 1975, 69; author's e-mail exchange with Steve Spurrier, September 2013; Taber, *Judgment*, 15.

Spurrier was no fan Taber, *Judgment*, 15.

The Year of the Wine Writer

Robert Finigan background Mitch Frank, "Wine Writer Robert Finigan Dies," *Wine Spectator*, October 3, 2011; Frank J. Prial, "Robert Finigan, an Early Wine Critic, Dies at 68," *New York Times*, October 11, 2011, A16. Interestingly enough, Finigan was at one time married to Alice Waters and at another to Alexis Lichine's daughter.

Finigan's newsletter details William Rice, "The Guiding List," *Washington Post*, November 10, 1977, E6.

"barely drinkable swill" Frank, "Wine Writer Robert Finigan Dies."

"trash" Elaine Woo, "Robert Finigan Dies at 68," *Los Angeles Times*, October 19, 2011.

"As usual, Mouton-Cadet" Robert Finigan, *Robert Finigan's Private Guide to Wines* (Walnuts and Wine, Incorporated, 1975), 53.

swelling toward ten thousand William Rice, "The Guiding List."

Alexis Bespaloff details Mary Rourke, "Alexis Bespaloff, 71; Author of Popular Wine Guidebook," *Los Angeles Times*, April 30, 2004; Frank J. Prial, "Alexis Bespaloff, 71, Witty and Wise Guide to Wine's Golden Age," *New York Times*, April 24, 2006, B7.

delivering direct descriptors Stephen Meuse, "Come Back, Alexis Bespaloff—and Bring Wine Prices With You," Boston.com, November 3, 2011, accessed January 7, 2014, www.boston.com/lifestyle/food/dishing/2011/11/come_back_alexi.html.

Prial details Eric Asimov, "Frank J. Prial, a Guide to the World of Fine Wine, Dies at 82," *New York Times*, B17; Steve Heimoff, "Frank Prial: A Tribute," SteveHeimoff.com, accessed January 8, 2014, www.steveheimoff.com/index.php/2012/11/09/frank-j-prial-a-tribute/; Pinney, *History of Wine*, 247.

Prial kept up his other reporting for the Times, and "Wine Talk" did not actually become a mainstay of the newspaper until 1977, when it was incorporated into the new Living section; it ran occasionally in the Sunday magazine as well.

"It was an instructive" Frank Prial, "Of the Two Tastings, One was Designed to Teach the Average Man," *New York Times*, July 21, 1973, 19.

Gerald Asher details From Asher's keynote address at the 2011 Symposium for Professional Wine Writers via Alder Yarrow's Vinography.com, accessed January 8, 2013, www.vinography.com/archives/2011/02/gerald_asher_on_wine_writing.html; Frank J. Prial, "At a Tasting for Fun and Profit, but Mostly Profit, They Appraised 60 Bottles," *New York Times*, March 2, 1975, 24. Asher was a frequent visitor, per Steve Spurrier's e-mail exchange with author. Bespaloff and Prial pressed Spurrier on California wines (per Taber, *Judgment*, 15).

Impact

"tied to the fact" "A Progress Report on Consumer Issues," *U.S. News & World Report*, October 27, 1975, 26. The author also wrote about this phenomenon of consumer awareness in his previous book, *The Audacity of Hops: The History of America's Craft Beer Revolution*, 34.

Charles Olken and Connoisseurs' Guide "Wine Biz Interviews Part Two Sir Charles Olken . . . aka Puff Daddy," Samantha Sans Dosage, accessed January 9, 2014, http:// sansdosage.blogspot.com/2010/02/wine-biz-interviews-part-two-sir.html.

Nick Ponomareff and California Grapevine Gordon Smith, "Grapevine Spreads Word on Top Choices in Wine," *Los Angeles Times,* November 21, 1986.

proved the most durable Thomas Pinney notes (in *History of Wine,* 246–47) other newsletters that came and went, like the *Bacchus Journal, Wine World,* and *Grand Cru,* as well as some of the more forgettable guidebooks of the era.

Nathan Chroman details Dennis McClellan, "Nathan L. Chroman Dies at 83," *Los Angeles Times,* March 20, 2012.

Hank Rubin details Jackie Burrell, "Berkeley Food Guru Hank Rubin Dies at Age 94," *San Jose Mercury News,* March 15, 2011.

Marvin Shanken and Impact "Marvin R. Shanken, BBA, '65," University of Miami School of Business Administration, accessed January 9, 2014, www.bus.miami.edu/explore -the-school/development/boards/overseers/shanken/.

wanted to dominate Ibid.

was fond of Ibid.

Parker feelings on career McCoy, *Emperor,* 25.

The Battle of Versailles

Details on the evening, including reactions Enid Nemy, "Paris Is in a Tizzy, but Then It's Not Just Another Fashion Show," *New York Times,* November 28, 1973, 50; Enid Nemy, "French Were Good, Americans Were Great," *New York Times,* November 30, 1973, 26.

French stylists considered Kerry Pieri, "American Runway Revolution: New Doc Explores a Pivotal Moment in Fashion History," *Harper's Bazaar,* February 21, 2013.

Sí, Se Puede

March details "10,000 in Protest at Gallo Winery," *New York Times,* March 2, 1975, Week in Review. The flag was the flag of the UFW.

United Farm Workers, Chavez background Roger Bruns, *Cesar Chavez and the United Farm Workers Movement* (Santa Barbara, CA: Greenwood, 2011), xiii–xvii; Cesar Chavez, *Cesar Chavez: Autobiography of La Causa* (Minneapolis: University of Minnesota Press, 2007). The UFW officially took its name in 1972, after being accepted as a full member by the AFL-CIO, but Chavez's organizing efforts started at least a decade before.

Boycotts and aftermath Bruns, *Cesar Chavez,* xv–xvi; "10,000 in Protest at Gallo Winery."

were a Communist front Patt Morrison and Mark Arax, "For the Final Time, They March for Chavez," *Los Angeles Times,* April 30, 1993; Cletus E. Daniel, "Cesar Chavez and the Unionization of California Farmworkers," *Labor Leaders in America* (Urbana: University of Illinois Press, 1987).

read aloud messages of support "10,000 in Protest at Gallo Winery."

Brown support, CALRA Robert Lindsey, "Cesar Chavez, 66, Organizer of Union for Migrant Workers, Dies," *New York Times,* April 24, 1993, A1.

the UFW virtually ran the tables Rick Tejada-Flores, "Cesar Chavez," PBS.org, accessed July 11, 2014, www.pbs.org/itvs/fightfields/cesarchavez.html.

Teamsters largely gave up Lindsey, "Cesar Chavez, 66, Organizer of Union for Migrant Workers, Dies."

never grew beyond 20 percent Ibid.

While hundreds of liquor stores "10,000 in Protest at Gallo Winery."

Sky's the Limit

Joseph Baum and his new task Greg Morabito, "Windows on the Word, New York's Sky-High Restaurant," Eater National, September 11, 2013, accessed January 13, 2014, http://ny.eater.com/archives/2013/09/wotw.php; Zachary Sachs, "The World of Windows on the World," Container List, the blog of the Milton Glaser Design Study Center, February 24, 2012, accessed January 13, 2014, http://containerlist.glaserarchives.org/index.php?id=215.

mayor Abraham Beame secretly drafted Ralph Blumenthal, "Recalling New York at the Brink of Bankruptcy," *New York Times*, December 5, 2002, B1.

did not necessarily bowl Sachs, "The World of Windows on the World"; Mimi Sheraton, "Stylish Menu Is Full of Promise That Isn't Yet Fully Realized," *New York Times*, June 24, 1976, 57.

"revealed many flaws" Ibid.

"Even New Jersey looks good" Gael Greene, "The Most Spectacular Restaurant in the World," *New York*, May 31, 1976.

Baum's effort was a hit Fred Ferretti, "Sky High Dining in 'Windows'," *New York Times*, July 16, 1976.

E. & J. Gallo had introduced some varietally McCoy, *Emperor*, 35.

out of fashion Zinfandel covered much less California acreage than other higher-end grape types—less than 9 percent of the state's wine-grape total by 1980, in fact (per Charles Lewis Sullivan, *Zinfandel: A History of a Grape and Its Wine* [Oakland: University of California Press, 2003], 117).

Sutter Home's White Zinfandel "Bob Trinchero on the First Sutter Home White Zinfandel," Dr. Vino blog, January 18, 2011, accessed January 14, 2014, www.drvino.com/2011/01/18/white-zinfandel-sutter-home-trinchero-first-1975/; David Stoneberg, "Bob Trinchero to Be Inducted Into Vintners Hall of Fame," *St. Helena Star*, February 17, 2011.

Trinchero originally called his creation Oeil de Perdrix, or "eye of the partridge," a french term sometimes used for paler wines made from red grapes. In 1975, he dropped the phrase and went with the subtitle, "White Zinfandel." Per Frank Prial, "The House Built on White Zinfandel," *New York Times*, October 28, 1998, Dining and Wine.

one and a half million cases "Bob Trinchero on the First Sutter Home White Zinfandel."

"over Americans who thought" Linda Murphy, "White Zinfandel, Now 30, Once Ruled the Wine World," *San Francisco Chronicle*, July 3, 2003. Chardonnay supplanted it in 1998.

biggest-selling fine wine varietal Ibid.

Columbia Winery and Lloyd Woodburne "Our History," Columbia Winery website, accessed January 15, 2014, www.columbiawinery.com/history-columbia-winery; Peyton Whitely, "Educator Lloyd S. Woodburne Spurred Washington Wine Industry," *Seattle Times*, July 4, 1992.

Moët & Chandon Laurie Daniel, "Domaine Chandon Turns 40," *San Jose Mercury News*, July 22, 2013. The first wine was produced in 1974.

bought an eighty-acre William Grimes, "Jess Jackson Dies at 81, a Wine Grower with a Taste for Thoroughbred Racing," *New York Times*, April 21, 2011, B11.

Conservative estimates already pegged Pinney, *History of Wine*, 243.

talked of people drinking Ibid., 241. The smart money included analysts at Wells Fargo and Bank of America drawing up forecasts.

Tales in Two Cities

Adam Strum details Author's interview with Adam Strum, January 16, 2014.

It was still a struggle Ibid.

Time *details on Gallo* "American Wine Comes of Age," *Time*, November 27, 1973; "A Brief Guide to California Wines," *Time*, November 27, 1973.

Marcia Mondavi sales Strum author interview.

Craig Goldwyn travels, newsletter Goldwyn author interview.

if a microcosm of a typical American wine selection Numerous sources, including Goldwyn, described retail wine selection in the United States in the early 1970s in these terms. Indeed, the entire nation boasted only a handful of what we would call luxury or high-end wine shops, perhaps the most prominent being Sherry-Lehmann Wine & Spirits in Manhattan. Most stores that sold wine sold mostly other alcohol, like liquor and beer. Americans, after all, then spent 10 times as much on those beverages combined as on wine (per "American Wine Comes of Age").

"Ah, Back to France!"

The JUDGMENT OF PARIS *excerpts* George Taber, "Judgment of Paris," *Time*, June 7, 1976. The author would like to extend his gratitude to George Taber not only for his wonderfully informative book of the same name but for his help in tracking down this particular article. Interestingly enough, Taber's original report ran to nearly two thousand words, or eight pages, and *Time*'s New York staff cut it to its published 362-word length. The typos, such as "Academic du Vin," were in the original (Taber, *Judgment*, 207).

Roughly four million people based on *Time* circulation estimates from the 1970s of approximately four million (per "Time," *Encyclopedia Britannica*).

Eight-Year-Olds Drinking Wine

George Taber details Author's interview with George Taber, October 9, 2014. Details also came throughout Taber's book, *Judgment of Paris*.

"probably the world's most expensive" George Taber, "Growing Gold on the Vines," *Time*, December 5, 1969.

Happy Birthday, America—Love, France

Valéry Giscard d'Estaing's visit Flora Lewis, "US-French Links Hailed by Giscard," *New York Times*, May 20, 1976, 9; Milton R. Benjamin, "The Flying Frenchman," *Newsweek*, May 31, 1976, 33. The Gerald R. Ford Presidential Library confirmed to the author that Ford served a California wine at the state dinner.

French economic and social problems Angus Deming and Elizabeth Peer, "Giscard's Soft Sell," *Newsweek*, May 17, 1976, 45.

The World Turned Upside Down

Fallout of Judgment of Paris Taber, *Judgment*, 213–16; author's interview with Taber; Frank J. Prial, "California Labels Outdo French in Blind Test," *New York Times*, June 9, 1976, 27; Frank J. Prial, "Some California Reds Score High in Tasting, But Some Caveats Must Be Weighed," *New York Times*, June 16, 1976, 39; Jack Heeger, "Book Notes Calistoga's Tie to Napa Wine Fame," *Weekly Calistogan*, September 29, 2005.

And Taber only showed Author's interview with Taber.

French publications snubbed it Author's e-mail exchange with Spurrier.

Flying off the Shelves

Jim Barrett conversation, telegram, reaction Taber, *Judgment*, 206–08; author's interview with Bo Barrett.

Warren Winiarski reaction Taber, *Judgment*, 209; author's interview with Warren Winiarski.

All eighteen hundred cases Prial, "California Labels Outdo French in Blind Test."

Retail prices Ibid.; Taber, *Judgment*, 216. These prices meant that in 2013 dollars, the top American-made wines in the United States cost around thirty dollars a bottle.

the racks and shelves of Paris Spurrier, "Saintsbury Oration."

Spurrier considered too big Author's e-mail exchange with Steven Spurrier, September 2013.

"I was tickled to death" Mondavi, *Harvests*, 185.

J'Accuse!

Steven Spurrier knew things Spurrier, "Saintsbury Oration."

France produced around one-fifth Elliott R. Morss, "The Global Wine Industry—Where Is It Going?" paper presented at the annual conference of the American Association of Wine Economists, June 2012.

the average French tippler Kakaviatos, "The Vilification of Wine in France." Converted from liters.

French reaction, including quotes Spurrier, "Saintsbury Oration"; Taber, *Judgment*, 217–19.

dogged the tasting for years afterward Taber, *Judgment*, 219–22.

The ball really started Ibid., 155–61.

Spurrier figured the rest of the judges Spurrier, "Saintsbury Oration."

Part III

Oodles of Fruit

Robert Parker Jr., Victor Morgenroth bonding, and Château Lafite Rothschild anecdote McCoy, *Emperor*, 19–20, 63. Other details about both are also taken from McCoy's *The Emperor of Wine* and William Langewiesche, "The Million-Dollar Nose," *Atlantic Monthly*, December 2000.

At least then, the two reasoned Ibid., 64.

"Although scoring systems of 0 to 100" M. A. Amerine and M. A. Joslyn, *Table Wines: The Technology of Their Production*, 2nd ed. (Berkeley: University of California Press, 1970), 711. Interestingly, Australian Dan Murphy may have come up with a one-hundred-point system around the same time as Parker and Morgenroth (Tyler Colman, "Who Invented Wine's 100-Point Scale?" *Dr. Vino*, February 14, 2012), though it's unlikely the two knew about it.

Wine Advocate excerpts, low subscription McCoy, *Emperor*, 70–71, 73. A small geographical note: The *Wine Advocate*'s offices are in Parkton, near Parker's home; the publication's post office box is in Monkton, another small community about ten miles to the southeast (as of 2014 it actually mails issues from Baltimore). This distinction has resulted in several erroneous reports pinpointing the *Wine Advocate*'s production hub in Monkton rather than Parkton.

Going Mainstream

The video of Dan Aykroyd's Julia Child impersonation is widely available online. A transcript can be found at the SNL transcripts website, accessed February 2, 2014, http://snltranscripts.jt.org/78/78hchef.phtml. Child was said to have enjoyed watching the skit (per William Porter, "Remembering Julia Child—and a Classic SNL Parody," *Denver Post*, August 15, 2012).

NBC's phenomenally successful Tom Shales, "'Saturday Night': A Show a Peacock Can Crow About," *Washington Post*, September 28, 1977, B1.

more than two dozen printings based on editions of the cookbook available through AbeBooks.com, including a twenty-seventh printing from 1976.

Wine numbers The Wine Institute, accessed March 4, 2015, www.wineinstitute.org /resources/statistics/article86.

around twenty states Hudson Cattell, *Wines of Eastern North America: From Prohibition to the Present—A History and Desk Reference* (Ithaca, NY: Cornell University Press, 2014), 91.

was producing large amounts Frank J. Prial, "Premium Surprises from New California Vineyards," *New York Times*, September 1, 1976, 22.

New Jersey wines "State's Wineries Prepare for Harvest," *New York Times*, August 27, 1976, B19. Most of the wines from New Jersey's dozen operations were working with inferior grape types; the first furtive steps toward higher-end varietals were taken in this period.

which had just started making Howard Hammell, "Sherry to Champagne, State's Wineries Produce It," *New York Times*, August 30, 1981, 11–12.

Carl Banholzer, a founder "Vintner Harvests First Commercial Wines in Indiana," New York Times News Service, November 18, 1975; Cattell, *Wines*, 275.

Llano Estacado Neil Crain and Katherine Crain, *The History of Texas Wine: From Spanish Roots to Rising Star* (Charleston, SC: History Press, 2013), 44–45.

Ste. Chappelle and Steven Symms David Bryce, "Wine Making in the USA: Idaho's Ste. Chappelle Winery," Vino in Love, accessed February 2, 2014, http://vinoinlove.com /wine-making-in-the-usa-idahos-ste-chapelle-winery/; the Idaho secretary of state database, accessed March 4, 2015, www.sos.idaho.gov/corp/index.html. Symms's Sunny Slope Fruit Company, Inc., incorporated in 1971, shares the same address as the winery.

A Surer Thing

Reported a 20 percent jump Wall Street Journal, September 2, 1976, 1.

"[V]intners are independent people" Frank J. Prial, "A Harvest of Upstate Wineries," *New York Times*, September 7, 1977, C1.

The California numbers would eventually Frank J. Prial, "The Tourists Flock to Visit Wineries," *New York Times*, July 9, 1975, 81. Winemakers readily admitted that the tastings were the real reason people took the tours.

Grape-growing land prices; "You're nowhere in San Francisco" Frank J. Prial, "Around Vineyards, It's Getting Crowded," *New York Times*, October 10, 1976.

built Stag's Leap with generous financial aid Taber, *Judgment*, 106, 112. Lottie Winiarski put in $20,000, unasked, for what became Stag's Leap.

which could quickly run into; "*Chateau Debacle*" Susan Cheever Cowley, Gerald Lubenow, and Betsy Carter, "The Grape Escape," *Newsweek*, October 17, 1977, 109.

a certain fatalistic comfort level Cowley, Lubenow, and Carter, "The Grape Escape." Some newcomers did seem to be comfortable with the idea that they might go out of business; they were in it for the lifestyle, however short.

with $420 million in net income Edwin McDowell, "The Shh-ot-Out in Soda Pop," *New York Times*, October 19, 1980, 3-1.

spooked a bit Lynn Langway, Michael Reese, Lester Sloan, David T. Friendly, and Connie Lesslie, "Alors! American Wines Come of Age," *Newsweek*, September 1, 1980, 56.

Smothers Brothers Terry Robards, "Wine Talk," *New York Times*, July 21, 1982, C11; "Remick Ridge Vineyards," Smothers Brothers website, accessed February 10, 2014, www.smothersbrothers.com/remick.html; Robert Lindsey, "Dick Smothers Turns to Vines," New York Times News Service, December 17, 1976.

Francis Ford Coppola Robards, "Wine Talk"; Suzanne Hamlin, "A Director's Vision for Celebrating Food, Wine and Film," *New York Times*, July 10, 1996, C7; "Perfecting the Rubicon," an interview with Francis Ford Coppola, Gayot.com, May 23, 2013, accessed February 10, 2014, www.gayot.com/wine/interviews/francis-ford-coppola .html; author's winter 2014 e-mail exchange with and visit to Inglenook. The information about the *Apocalypse Now* collateral is in the Gayot.com interview. The first two *Godfather* movies won ten Oscars. The Coppolas' winery eventually became Rubicon Estate as the couple acquired more of Niebaum's original land. They paid $14 million for the Inglenook name in 2011 and renamed their much larger operation that (per Victoria Moore, "The Grape Director," *Daily Telegraph*, July 2, 2011, Weekend 7).

"a wine of extremely" Robards, "Wine Talk."

Nearly one-fifth of America's counties Cattell, *Wines*, 91.

often placed an up-and-coming winery's Author's interview with Randall Grahm, October 14, 2014.

For states such as Texas Crain and Crain, *Texas Wine*, 46.

Varietal regulations Frank J. Prial, "Wine Talk," *New York Times*, January 24, 1996, C7; Richard Mendelson, *From Demon to Darling: A Legal History of Wine in America* (Berkeley: University of California Press, 2010), 143–46. The Bureau of Alcohol, Tobacco, Firearms and Explosives enacted other rules in the 1970s, though some of them were short-lived. For instance, so-called "seal wines," wines from certain designated geographic areas or vineyards, with certain amounts of grapes grown in these designations, were discontinued because the government became concerned consumers would think it was endorsing certain wines—and wine-drinking. Finally, when it came to designating geography and vineyards, the ATF in 1978 settled on American viticulture areas, which have an 85 percent grape-source requirement (per Mendelson, 145). The reader can find more on federal varietal regulations here, including those for non-higher-end grapes: www.ttb.gov/wine/grape-varieties.shtml.

The legislature of Suffolk County Prial, "Around Vineyards, It's Getting Crowded."

the state enacted a farm winery bill Frank J. Prial, "Wine Country Tour Gives Mrs. Krupsak a Look at Problems," *New York Times*, September 21, 1976, 41.

a thirty-thousand-ton grape surplus Ibid.

Like dozens of other states that would pass Cattell, *Wines*, 91–92. Pennsylvania, in 1968, was the first state east of the Mississippi to enact a farm winery law. New York's remained the most impactful, however, due to the state's output, second then only to California's.

Barreling Toward the Bull

Jack McAuliffe, New Albion, Fritz Maytag Based on the author's research, including extensive interviews with McAuliffe, for his book *The Audacity of Hops*.

Four Seasons details Craig Claiborne, "Dining in Elegant Manner," *New York Times*, October 2, 1959, 22. The article can be found on the restaurant's website, too: www.fourseasonsrestaurant.com/history-continued.php.

"perhaps the most exciting" Ibid.

"the wine trade's most glittering" Frank J. Prial, "Wine Talk," *New York Times*, May 27, 1985, C15.

a dismissive semantic catchall Author's interview with various sources. Claiborne's 1959 Four Seasons review refers to Bordeaux and Burgundy wines costing twice as much as "domestic" ones.

Warren Winiarski thought his invitation Prial, "Wine Talk."

"to the center of public relations" William Rice, "California's New York Showcase," *Washington Post*, March 27, 1977, K1.

California Barrel Tasting logistics, changes Prial, "Wine Talk."

a cadre of perhaps a dozen Author's interview with Goldwyn; author's interview with McCoy.

the approximately forty-three million Americans Allan J. Mayer, Tom Joyce, Pamela Ellis Simons, and William J. Cook, "The Graying of America," *Newsweek*, February 28, 1977, 50.

Economic impact of baby boomers Ibid.; "Baby Boom," AP US History Notes, accessed February 7, 2014, www.apstudynotes.org/us-history/topics/baby-boom/.

hit an all-time high National Center for Education Statistics, "Table 187: College Enrollment Rates for High School Graduates, By Sex, 1960–1998," accessed March 5, 2015, http://nces.ed.gov/programs/digest/d99/d99t187.asp.

more than two hundred chapters Donnel Nunes, "The Wine Merchants," *Washington Post*, October 16, 1977, 39.

dramatically drove down Scott McCartney, "The Golden Age of Flight," *Wall Street Journal*, July 22, 2010.

Adam Strum and Wine Enthusiast Author's interview with Adam Strum, January 16, 2014.

"We have a bumper crop" Langway, Reese, Sloan, Friendly, and Lesslie, "Alors! American Wines Come of Age," 56.

The baby boomers were also the advertising Shales, "'Saturday Night.'"

quickly gaining a quarter-million subscribers Margalit Fox, "Michael Batterby, Influential Food Editor, Dies at 78," *New York Times*, July 29, 2010, B15. It reached this milestone in 1980.

$40,000 McCoy, *Emperor*, 81.

saw something in the tabloid; "very unprofitable" Samir Husni, the Mr. Magazine Interview with Marvin Shanken, September 14, 2012, accessed February 10, 2014, http://mrmagazine.wordpress.com/2012/09/14/marvin-shanken-to-samir-husni-my-stomach-usually-leads-my-mind-and-other-words-of-wisdom-from-the-editor-in-chief-and-publisher-of-cigar-aficionado-wine-spectator-and-whiskey-advocate-the-mr-mag/.

after he realized more than 20 percent William Rice, "The Guiding List," *Washington Post*, November 10, 1977, E6.

Morrisey; Wine Spectator James Laube, "Bob Morrisey, *Wine Spectator* Founder, Dies," *Wine Spectator* online, March 28, 2005, accessed March 5, 2015, www.winespectator.com/webfeature/show/id/Bob-Morrisey-Wine-Spectator-Founder-Dies_2461;

Philip H. Dougherty, "Choosing the Best TV Ad Buy," *New York Times*, July 2, 1979, 4–13.

Be the Judge of It

Great Chardonnay Showdown Author's interview with Craig Goldwyn; Craig Goldwyn, "The Great Chardonnay Shootout," *Chicago Tribune* magazine, November 9, 1980. It was held at what was then Solomon's wine warehouse. The *Tribune* called it the shootout; most subsequent coverage called it a showdown or the Great Chicago Chardonnay Showdown (per Goldwyn).

To Goldwyn, what would come Goldwyn, "The Great Chardonnay Shootout."

"the finest dry white wine in the world" Goldwyn, "Chardonnay—the Finest Dry White Wine of All," *Chicago Tribune*, November 9, 1980, F1.

Grgich Hills Cellar Taber, *Judgment*, 225–29.

A decade and a half would pass Ibid., 229.

As Bo Barrett, Jim's son Author's interview with Bo Barrett. Barrett became winemaker in 1982.

appear to have outpaced inflation Craig Goldwyn, "Wine Prices Have Inflated Faster Than Most," *Chicago Tribune*, February 5, 1979, F4.

One analysis compared Ibid.

"most American consumers" Frank J. Prial, "Did Merchants Act to Bid Prices Up?," *New York Times*, June 11, 1975, 36. Prial and other wine writers speculated widely as to the causes of the Bordeaux price variations in the mid-1970s. One theory explored by Prial was that merchants, worried about their potential customers getting the wines they had bought years ago at cheaper prices, actively bid to drive up the tags. Such a conspiracy theory only added to the feeling of arbitrariness that surrounded wine prices in the 1970s.

despite dramatic drops Frank J. Prial, "Bordeaux Market in a State of Shock," *New York Times*, April 9, 1975, 54.

sometimes outpaced what they went for Frank J. Prial, "At a Wine Auction Here, Some Prices Are More Than in Neighborhood Stores," *New York Times*, May 29, 1975, 30.

Wine auctions Craig Goldwyn, "Why People Pay $18,000 for One Bottle of Wine," *Chicago Tribune*, May 21, 1979, E21; William Rice, "Vintage Spectacle," *Washington Post*, June 3, 1979, K1; Rick Gladstone, "Record Price for a Bottle of Wine," Associated Press, May 28, 1980. It appears that both Grisanti and Mara turned their epic purchases into fodder for charity.

The auctions were like gambling Rice, "Vintage Spectacle."

Some bottles at the auctions didn't Prial, "Did Merchants Act to Bid Prices Up?"

scandals in the wine world Edmund Penning-Rowsell, "An Armchair Tour of Vineyards," *Financial Times*, July 10, 1982, I–6; Michael Ruby, Jane Friedman, and Barbara Graustark, "Vin Problematique," *Newsweek*, August 30, 1976, 66.

American Viticultural Areas (AVA) The Wine Institute, "American Viticultural Areas by Date," accessed February 12, 2014, www.iwineinstitute.com/avabydate.asp; Alcohol, Tobacco Tax and Trade Bureau, "American Viticultural Area (AVA)," accessed February 12, 2014, www.ttb.gov/wine/ava.shtml. Perhaps it wasn't so curious Missouri was picked for the first AVA: the state had been one of the nation's biggest wine producers before Prohibition (per Shiller-Wine blog, June 6, 2011, http://schiller-wine.blogspot .com/2011/06/in-oldest-ava-american-viticultural.html).

In a 1979 speech Marvin Shanken, "The Stars of '79," *Wine Spectator* online, December 15, 2006, accessed March 5, 5015, www.winespectator.com/blogs/show/id/The-Stars-of-79_14546,

Beverage Testing Institute Author's interview with Craig Goldwyn; "About the Beverage Testing Institute," accessed February 12, 2014, accessed March 5, 2015, www.tastings.com/bti/about_bti.html.

Tuscany, California

The opening credits of Falcon Crest *are widely available online, with commentary.*

"Dallas with grapes" Jerry Buck, "Vintage Years," Associated Press, July 19, 1981.

Earl Hamner Jr. details Fred Rothenberg, "'Dallas' Plus 'The Waltons' Equals 'Falcon Crest,'" Associated Press, December 14, 1982.

who originally titled Buck, "Vintage Years."

While critics derided Tom Shales, "Falcon Crest: One Too Many," *Washington Post*, December 4, 1981, D2.

became a breakaway hit "CBS Wins Weekly Nielsen Ratings and First Six of Top 10," Associated Press, December 14, 1982; Rothenberg, "'Dallas' Plus 'The Waltons' Equals 'Falcon Crest.'"

Tedeschi Vineyards Kay Lynch, "Vintner in Decade-Long Pursuit to Produce Hawaiian Red Wine," UPI International, December 1, 1980.

at least thirty-six states Langway, Reese, Sloan, Friendly, and Lesslie, "Alors! American Wines Come of Age."

had doubled from 1979 through 1981 Richard T. Lyons, "For New York Winemakers, Optimism on the Vines," *New York Times*, November 23, 1981, B2.

Consumption and number of wineries The Wine Institute.

"seemed a permanent curse" "Still Bad, Still Getting Worse," *New York Times*, December 24, 1982, A24 (board editorial).

Reagan administration warned "Reagan Administration Sees Jobless Rate Peaking," Associated Press, December 9, 1982. Interestingly, Jane Wyman, who played Angela Channing on *Falcon Crest*, was Ronald Reagan's first wife.

Economic information Jason DeSena Tennert, "Remembering the Reagan Bull Market," *Wall Street Journal*, August 13, 2009, A1; "Still Bad, Still Getting Worse"; "Reagan Administration Sees Jobless Rate Peaking."

Wine Futures

who had studied at the famed Le Cordon Bleu Elizabeth Taylor, "William Rice, Our Food and Wine Columnist, Is a Foodie and Proud of It," *Chicago Tribune*, August 12, 2001.

Phyllis Richman biography Author's interview with Phyllis Richman, March 19, 2013; Phyllis Richman, "Answering Harvard's Question About My Personal Life, 52 Years Later," *Washington Post*, June 9, 2013, B04.

Richman's blind tasting nights Author's Richman interview.

$150 per bimonthly column McCoy, *The Emperor of Wine*, 82–83.

"pitch-perfect taste" Author's Richman interview.

"What a coup!" McCoy, *The Emperor of Wine*, 85.

Wine Advocate subscribers; travels; writing, tasting Ibid., 75–77.

Parker, Johnson visits Ibid., 84–85.

Finigan vs. Parker Ibid., 80; author's assessments of their respective work and background.

his first magazine piece McCoy, *The Emperor of Wine*, 85. Parker returned with a report heavy on jug wines from California because of their consistently fresh, fruity style (per McCoy, *Emperor*, 85).

"In the meantime, our notes" Phyllis Richman, "Secret Rites of Linen Bibs and Dinner Bells," *Washington Post*, May 3, 1981, L1.

The Birth of the Wine Bar

"What is a wine bar?" Jo Hawkins, "Wine Alone Doth Not a Wine Bar Make," *Washington Post*, May 24, 1981, 30.

The first American wine bar Several sources cite the London Wine Bar as the first, including Frank Prial ("New York Wine Bars: A Special Vintage," *New York Times*, September 17, 1982, C1), though the bar was known to serve English-style cask ale as well.

first post-Prohibition wine bar in New York Prial, "New York Wine Bars: A Special Vintage."

the first one in Chicago "Top 5 Wine Bars in Chicago," *Wine Life Today*, November 19, 2012, accessed March 5, 2015, http://winelifetoday.com/top-5-wine-bars-in-chicago/.

"A modern wine bar is" Prial, "New York Wine Bars: A Special Vintage."

offered some 350 wines Frank J. Prial, "A Different Kind of Bar," *New York Times*, February 4, 1979, 71.

up to 40 wines Prial, "New York Wine Bars: A Special Vintage."

approximately 100 wines William Rice, "Wine Bars: An Idea Whose Time Has Come to Washington," *Washington Post*, January 13, 1980, C1.

Some wine bars adopted Cruvinets Prial, "New York Wine Bars: A Special Vintage."

The Gong Show

Olympic Hotel sommelier Author's interview with Larry Stone, February 19, 2014.

ran the California Sommelier Academy "Outsnobbing the Wine Snobs," United Press International, November 22, 1982.

Court of Master Sommeliers The Court of Master Sommeliers website, "About CMS," accessed February 17, 2014, www.mastersommeliers.org/pages.aspx/about-cms-overview.

Stone biography, job interview Author's interview with Stone.

a would-be behavioral psychologist "About Eddie Osterland, MS," EddieOsterland .com, accessed February 20, 2014, www.eddieosterland.com/americas-first-master -sommelier/eddie-life-story.html#.UwY7qIVfQQA.

could move twice as many bottles "Outsnobbing the Wine Snobs."

Ugly Ducklings

Randall Grahm background, discovery of fine wine Author's Grahm interview; Arthur Lubow, "The Do Over," *Inc.*, July 1, 2008, accessed October 7, 2014, www.inc.com /magazine/20080701/the-do-over.html; Randall Grahm's author website, accessed October 7, 2014, www.beendoonsolong.com/author/; Eric Asimov, "His Idea Is to Get Small," *New York Times*, April 21, 2009, D1.

"were not just disappointing or mediocre" John Winthrop Haeger, *North American Pinot Noir* (Berkeley: University of California Press, 2004), 49.

would frequently describe Ibid.

dropped their Pinot Noir lines Ibid., 50.

Albert Winkler acreage amounts Nancy Sweet, "Cabernet Sauvignon at FPs," Foundation Plant Service, FPS Grape Program Newsletter, October 2008.

chose the word prosaic *to describe* Lubow, "The Do Over."

"ugly duckling grape varietals" Grahm's author website.

Bonny Doon launch; Le Cigare Volant Lubow, "The Do Over."

Le Cigare Volant breakdown W. Blake Gray, "23 Years of Le Cigare Volant," The Gray Report, May 11, 2010, accessed October 7, 2014, http://blog.wblakegray .com/2010/05/23-years-of-le-cigare-volant.html.

critics struggled for years Ibid.

Bonny Doon never produced Ibid.

only emboldened him Author's Grahm interview. To be clear: Grahm's Bonny Doon did produce wines from Cabernet Sauvignon and Chardonnay, though they were never the winery's focus.

"the end of history"; Chardonnay, Cabernet Sauvignon growth Susan Arrhenius and Leo McCloskey, "End of History of New California Grape Varieties: Winning Is Winning Forty Years After the 1976 Paris Tasting," Enologix newsletter, September 29, 2014, shared with the author over e-mail.

Grapes That Can Fight

Mike Benziger biography Dan Berger, "Bruno Benziger, Founder of Glen Ellen Winery, Dies," *Los Angeles Times*, June 11, 1989; "J. Bruno Benziger, a Vintner in California," *New York Times*, June 12, 1989, B7.

Benziger-Rector conversation Dan Berger, "A Case for the Fighting Varietals," *Sarasota Herald-Tribune*, February 10, 1999, 3E.

shipping fifty thousand cases "J. Bruno Benziger, a Vintner in California."

more than two and a half million cases Lawrence M. Fisher, "Winery Carves a Profitable Niche," *New York Times*, June 27, 1988, D1.

As many as fifteen trucks Ibid.

Glen Ellen's suggested retail price George Taber, *A Toast to Bargain Wines: How Innovators, Iconoclasts and Winemaking Revolutionaries Are Changing the Way the World Drinks* (New York: Scribner, 2011), 19.

in fact, the biggest word on the label Ibid.

required all newly bottled Louise Cook, "Liquor by the Milliliter," Associated Press, February 15, 1980. The changeover, of course, did not eliminate larger fine wine bottles from American shelves, as older stock had to transition out. Nor did it eliminate half-gallon and gallon jugs, which suddenly fell under other, metric measurements.

Europe soon followed the United States "A History of the Glass Wine Bottle," WallaFaces .com, accessed February 22, 2014, www.wallafaces.com/a-history-of-the-glass-wine -bottle/.

"a classy, attractive product" Taber, *A Toast to Bargain Wines*, 19.

served at the Reagan White House Tim Teichgraeber, "Kendall-Jackson First to Woo Obama," Decanter.com, November 11, 2008, accessed March 5, 2015, www.decanter .com/news/wine-news/485353/kendall-jackson-first-to-woo-obama. The wine also became a favorite of Barack and Michelle Obama's in their pre–White House days.

to sales of one million cases Kendall-Jackson website, "Kendall-Jackson Historical Timeline," accessed February 23, 2014, www.kj.com/timeline.

None other than generic giant E. & J. Gallo Bob Hosmon, "For Gallo, $30 Bottle of Wine Is Approaching Its Time," *Florida Sun-Sentinel*, August 6, 1992.

accounted for perhaps 70 percent William Rice, "The Latest Word Right Off the Rack," *Washington Post*, February 21, 1980, E2.

wine-making industry with a major surplus Fisher, "Winery Carves a Profitable Niche"; Frank J. Prial, "California Surplus Produces Bargains in Blended Wines," *New York Times*, August 31, 1983, C1. The acreage of Cabernet Sauvignon had increased by 1,301 from 1973 to 1983 (per Napa County crop reports).

"plenty of good wine at ridiculous prices" Fisher, "Winery Carves a Profitable Niche."

"Even if every year" Frank J. Prial, "Great Expectations," *New York Times*, December 18, 1983, 93.

"1984 may see" Ibid.

When Robert Met Robert

The news traveled fast McCoy, *Emperor*, 101–02.

"single most important" Ibid.

At the tasting Ibid.; Robert M. Parker Jr., "The California Vintners' Lavish Tasting Dinner," *Washington Post*, April 6, 1983, E1. According to Parker's count, 220 people attended that year's California Barrel Tasting.

Parker in Bordeaux McCoy, *Emperor*, 99–100; Langewiesche, "The Million-Dollar Nose"; Robert Parker, *Wine Advocate*, vol. 26, April 11, 1983.

freakishly ideal weather Parker, *Wine Advocate*, vol. 26.

"lightish" Ibid.

Bordeaux vintages The Wine Cellar Insider, "Bordeaux Vintage Chart 1959 to Today, Vintage Rankings Characteristics," accessed February 24, 2014, www.thewinecellarinsider .com/wine-topics/bordeaux-wine-buying-guide-tasting-notes-ratings/bordeaux-wine -vintage-chart/; *Wine Advocate* Vintage Guide, 1970–2012, December 2013.

Bordeaux wines 50 percent Ruby, Friedman, and Graustark, "Vin Problematique."

including First Growth giant Château Margaux The château, which carried as much as $10 million in bank loans, finally did trade in 1977 to Greek grocery magnate Andre Mentzelopoulos and his French wife, Laura. The French government blocked an earlier deal with the National Distillers & Chemical Corp. because ownership of such a First Growth château by an American firm would hurt "national prestige" (per Ruby, Friedman, and Graustark, "Vin Problematique").

abnormally abundant 1979 grape harvest Robert M. Parker Jr., "The French Shall Rise Again," *Washington Post*, October 18, 1981, G1.

Frank Prial wrote in the New York Times Frank J. Prial, "Wine Talk," *New York Times*, March 2, 1983, C14.

"too early to know" Terry Robards, "Wine Talk," *New York Times*, January 19, 1983, C15.

a seventeen and a half out of twenty Ibid.

Other reactions to the '82 Bordeaux McCoy, *Emperor*, 99.

"Phenomenal" Ibid., 102.

though he found it strange Parker, "The California Vintners' Lavish Tasting Dinner."

he had been nervous Langewiesche, "The Million-Dollar Nose."

notebook and driving through Bordeaux McCoy, *Emperor*, 90, 100.

could send bottles flying off shelves William Rice, "Clawing Their Way to the Top in Comparative Wine Tasting," *Chicago Tribune*, October 16, 1986.

"the dean of wine writers" Ibid.

Finigan-Parker meeting; Finigan recall of meeting McCoy, *Emperor*, 71–2, 102; author's interview with McCoy.

Finigan had been disappointed McCoy, *Emperor*, 103.

"A Monumental Vintage"

Wine Advocate *excerpts* Parker, *Wine Advocate*, vol. 26; Parker's report started on the front of the newsletter.

The March 30 edition McCoy, *Emperor*, 103.

"Everything in the wine" Frank J. Prial, "Wine Talk," *New York Times*, March 9, 1983, C8.

including Craig Goldwyn Author's interview with Goldwyn.

several châteaus reported Parker, *Wine Advocate*, vol. 26.

He would declare; Parker advised his readers McCoy, *Emperor*, 106.

swelled toward twenty thousand Rice, "Clawing Their Way to the Top in Comparative Wine Tasting."

writing books on Bordeaux Ibid. Simon & Schuster asked Parker to update the Bordeaux book every four years and gave him contracts for books on three other topics.

Demise of original and later Finigan guides Ibid.; Frank J. Prial, "Robert Finigan, an Early Wine Critic, Dies at 68."

"The soaring trajectory" Eric Asimov, "The Line Drawn by the '82 Bordeaux," *New York Times*, March 20, 2012, appeared on the Diner's Journal blog, accessed March 5, 2015, http://dinersjournal.blogs.nytimes.com/2012/03/20/the-line-drawn-by-the-82 -bordeaux/.

Part IV

24 Brix

"Wait until the world hears" Author's interview with Goldwyn.

Mara enjoyed a similar Author's interview with Charles Mara, March 3, 2014.

Anticipation and auction of Opus One "Wine Talk," *New York Times*, June 24, 1981, Home & Garden section.

Robert Mondavi, no publicity virgin himself Author's interview with Mara.

Robert Parker found it "not a great wine" Robert M. Parker Jr., "History in the Making, Hoopla in the Marketing," *Washington Post*, March 14, 1984, E1.

"basically a very good" Jeanne Lesem, "Costly New California Wine Arrives with French Accent," United Press International, March 20, 1984.

Frank Prial warned Frank J. Prial, "Great Expectations," *New York Times*, December 18, 1983, 93.

sold for about $20 Ibid.

"The hoopla surrounding" Parker, "History in the Making, Hoopla in the Marketing."

Napa Valley Wine Auction "Wealthy Wine Lovers in Wild Napa Valley Auction," United Press International, June 18, 1984.

California Wine Experience James Conaway, "Paying Through the Nose," *Washington Post*, December 2, 1984, 55.

A Nebuchadnezzar was named after the Babylonian king mentioned in the Bible.

boasted more collectors Frank J. Prial, "Wine Talk," *New York Times*, August 3, 1988, C10.

"Acquisitiveness, or, if you will, greed" Ibid. Details of the marathon tastings were taken from Prial's article and from the book *The Billionaire's Vinegar: The Mystery of the World's Most Expensive Bottle of Wine* by Benjamin Wallace.

a rarity even in wine-drinking households Author's interview with Adam Strum.

Accessory examples Susan Dooley, "Joy to the Host," *Washington Post*, November 28, 1983, C5; Frank J. Prial, "Wine Talk," *New York Times*, December 3, 1986, C16.

"a Rube Goldberg" Prial, "Wine Talk," December 3, 1986, C16.

balloon toward twenty million annual shoppers Author's interview with Strum. Strum believes this peak came in the 1990s, right before the rise of the World Wide Web. By the 1980s, the catalog retailed for two dollars. The *Wine Enthusiast* catalog should not be confused with *Wine Enthusiast*, the magazine, which reached about 800,000 readers by 2011 (per *Wine Enthusiast* media kit).

had rarely used premium *in the US* A LexisNexis search of newspapers, magazines, and journals from 1970 to 1980 turned up only twelve usages of the phrase "premium wine." It started appearing with much greater frequency thereafter.

helped spur these adjectival Robert M. Parker Jr., "The Price Is Right," *Washington Post,* June 1, 1983, E1.

"It appeared that, having expressed" Frank J. Prial, "A Dissenter's View of California Wines," *New York Times,* September 16, 1981, C1. A brix is a measure of the sugar level in grapes.

"In America wine has its own" Ibid.

"It still isn't clear" Frank J. Prial, "Notes From an Iconoclastic Wine Writer," *New York Times,* November 11, 1987, Home & Garden.

"The ongoing trend" Conaway, "Paying Through the Nose."

The Scorekeeper

Steven Spurrier and Château Mouton Author's interview with Spurrier; McCoy, *Emperor,* 152.

"the Parker phenomenon" Prial, "Notes From an Iconoclastic Wine Writer."

Wine Advocate statistics McCoy, *Emperor,* 144–45.

Bordeaux book Ibid., 143.

Shanken even offered Ibid., 148. Parker wrote a few articles for the *Wine Enthusiast* and consented to several exclusive interviews (per McCoy, *Emperor,* 151).

Demand for Parker Ibid., 141–51; Langewiesche, "The Million-Dollar Nose."

California Barrel Tasting statistics Frank J. Prial, "Wine Talk," *New York Times,* March 27, 1985, C15. It's debatable whether Parker's influence was felt that acutely so soon after his verdict on the 1982 Bordeaux. But attendees of the annual tasting hinted to this author that his prominence had led the owners of the Four Seasons to cancel what was becoming such a huge event to host.

wanted to know how to talk McCoy, *Emperor,* 146.

ten thousand wines a year Langewiesche, "The Million-Dollar Nose."

"A wine goes in my mouth" Ibid.

a neighbor was surprised Ibid.

Wine prices Frank J. Prial, "What Price Bordeaux?," *New York Times,* September 13, 1987; author's interview with Mark Wessels at MacArthur Beverages in Washington, DC, March 8, 2014.

"a green light to the Me Generation" Prial, "What Price Bordeaux?"

particularly at Shanken's Wine Spectator McCoy, *Emperor,* 149.

"When Parker spits, the world listens" David Shaw, *Los Angeles Times,* February 23, 1999.

Warning

San Francisco meeting Dan Berger, "Vintners Rally Against Criticism," *Los Angeles Times,* October 13, 1988; "Amer-Wine-Industry," *Businesswire,* October 6, 1988.

amid shifting views on alcohol Kim Foltz, "Alcohol on the Rocks," *Newsweek*, December 31, 1984, 52.

caught the American fine wine movement All indications from media reports are that Mondavi and others in the movement, including the Wine Institute, the trade voice for California winemakers, were reacting to the neo-Prohibitionist trend rather than staying in front of it.

"What nonsense!" Mondavi, *Harvests*, 258.

Mondavi commissioned research Ibid, 258–60.

"perpetual stream" Michael E. Hill, "Dr. Tim Johnson: Diet Books," *Washington Post*, November 13, 1983, 8.

"Fettuccine alfredo is dangerous" Langewiesche, "The Million-Dollar Nose."

Reagan address "Primary Resources: Campaign Against Drug Abuse," American Experience website at PBS.org, accessed October 1, 2014, www.pbs.org/wgbh/americanexperience /features/primary-resources/reagan-drug-campaign/.

the federal government was amassing Mendelson, *Demon to Darling*, 164.

"alcohol is a gateway drug" Ibid. The full quotation contains further dread: "While alcohol is a gateway drug that can lead to other, stronger chemical dependencies, it has its own addiction: alcoholism."

"Americans came closest" Ibid., 163.

Symposium comments "Amer-Wine-Industry."

"Anthropologists, priests, ministers"; marketing force Joanna Simon, "Crusader Defends the Grape," *Sunday Times*, February 7, 1988, Issue 8529.

sowed confusion instead; sulfites Frank J. Prial, "You Can't Tell a Wine's Sulfites, Even with Labels," *New York Times*, April 13, 1988, C1.

drove Mondavi and others mad Mondavi, *Harvests*, 258; Berger, "Vintners Rally Against Criticism."

accounted for 40 percent Hillary Chura, "Brand in Trouble," *AdAge*, May 29, 2000.

fifty-five smaller wineries Berger, "Vintners Rally Against Criticism."

"increasingly vocal anti-alcohol" Lawrence M. Fisher, "Smaller Wineries Gain in Power," *New York Times*, June 12, 1990, D1.

The French Paradox

Excerpts and segment descriptions The *60 Minutes* segment is available through YouTube, and a transcript is available through CBS, accessed March 10, 2014, www.youtube .com/watch?v=njm1LkXP2sg. The July 12, 1992, transcript is also available.

Morley Safer background Safer biography on the CBS News website, accessed March 12, 2014, www.cbsnews.com/news/morley-safer/.

60 Minutes' *popularity* "'60 Minutes' rerun No. 1 in primetime," BPI Entertainment News Wire, Dec. 30, 1992. The show then routinely reached around twenty million households. The "forty-million-plus Americans" is based on Census estimates that pegged the number of households at 94,312,000 with 2.63 residents per household.

"the same wine the French drink" Joe Pollack, "French Paradox Spurs Sales of Red Wine," *St. Louis Post-Dispatch*, August 6, 1992, 3E.

Shipments and revenues Frank J. Prial, "Mondavi on Wall Street, Wine in the Spotlight," *New York Times*, May 19, 1993, C1.

a quintiple increase "Wine Coolers: Gone and Almost Forgotten," Dr. Vino, September 2001, accessed April 11, 2015, www.drvino.com/2007/09/20/wine-coolers-gone -and-almost-forgotten.

Robert Mondavi happily drew Mondavi quotes publicist Harvey Posert in his memoir as saying that the *60 Minutes* segment sprung from talks between him, Ellison, and Safer. Safer said no winemaker had anything to do with it (per Siler, *House of Mondavi*, endnotes).

a lot of this new information was bunk Frank J. Prial, "Wine Talk," *New York Times*, December 25, 1991, 29.

Scenes from a Recovery

Larry Stone Author's interview with Stone; Kristine N. Curry, "American in Paris Wins with French Wines," *Chicago Tribune*, June 30, 1988.

Wally's Wine & Spirits David Shaw, "He Sips and Spits—and the World Listens," *Los Angeles Times*, February 23, 1999.

Steve Wallace background Mitch Frank, "Guess Executives Buy Top Los Angeles Retailer Wally's Wine & Spirits," *Wine Spectator*, June 18, 2013, accessed March 6, 2015, www.winespectator.com/webfeature/show/id/48586.

Prodigy interactive personal service launch Rachel Parker, "Online Service Targets Home User," *InfoWorld*, October 10, 1988, 46.

Napa Valley Wine Train "About Our Train," Napa Valley Wine Train website, accessed March 5, 2015, http://winetrain.com/about; Mark Magnier, "Grapes of Wrath," *Journal of Commerce*, September 11, 1989, 2B.

"an enological Billy Graham"; Mondavi announcement Frank J. Prial, "Wine Talk," *New York Times*, December 26, 1990, C10.

into two slots Phyllis C. Richman, "A Gray Area: Smoking Room," *Washington Post*, March 8, 1991, N25.

Wine Experience Frank J. Prial, "Wine Talk," *New York Times*, October 9, 1991, C12.

Sutter Home "Sutter Home Pioneers New Premium Wine Closure," PR Newswire, July 20, 1993.

did not stop critics from predicting Frank J. Prial, "Marriage of Wine and Cork: Rocky Times Ahead," *New York Times*, January 6, 1993, C1.

Andre Tchelistcheff died in Napa "Andrew Tchelistcheff, 92, Authority on Wine."

Virtual Vineyards; "as easy as a few keystrokes" "Virtual Vineyards Takes the Fear Out of Electronic Commerce," BusinessWire, September 5, 1995. Virtual Vineyards became Wine.com in 2000.

Made in America

The author covered much of the material in this chapter in his book *The Audacity of Hops*, 180–83. Craft brewing, much like fine wine–making, was also a bright spot in America's manufacturing sector.

"center of attention" Douglas Jehl, "President Begins a Lobbying Blitz for Trade Accord," *New York Times*, November 9, 1993, A1.

NAFTA debate "Ross Perot vs. Al Gore NAFTA Debate FULL! 1993," YouTube video, from a televised 1993 CNN debate, posted by yeoldbasser, December 20, 2012, accessed March 5, 2012, www.youtube.com/watch?v=5XEziSYRqhU.

more than three million Barnaby J. Feder, "A Surprise: Blue Color Jobs Rebound," *New York Times*, December 6, 1993, D1.

Details on manufacturing jobs Feder, "A Surprise: Blue-Collar Jobs Rebound."

Job growth comparisons Morton J. Marcus, "A Graphic Overview of Employment and Earnings in the 1990s," *Indiana Business Review*, fall 2002.

Job numbers Vince Bonafede, "Analysis of Wine Label Design Aesthetics and the Correlation to Price," March 2010, thesis presented to the agribusiness department of California Polytechnic State University; "California Wine Stats Profile, 2013," the Wine Institute.

Cults, Christ, and Frankenstein

Richard (Dick) Graff details Frank J. Prial, "Richard Graff, California Vintner, 60," *New York Times*, January 14, 1998.

Rodney Strong details Eric Asimov, "Rodney Strong, 78, Dancer Turned Pioneering California Vintner, Is Dead," *New York Times*, March 9, 2006, C3. Strong eventually renamed the winery after himself.

Leo McCloskey algorithm Author's interview with Leo McCloskey, October 2, 2014.

McCloskey background Ibid.; David Darlington, "The Chemistry of a 90+ Wine," *New York Times* magazine, August 7, 2005, 36; William Neuman, "The Grapes of Math," *Wired*, November 2001.

Chalone tasting Author's McCloskey interview; Darlington, "The Chemistry of a 90+ Wine."

Ridge Vineyards founding "Ridge Vineyards Is Sold," *New York Times*, January 7, 1987, C15.

Paul Draper Taber, *Judgment*, 182–3; Ridge Vineyards website, "Winemaker Profiles," accessed October 8, 2014, www.ridgewine.com/About/Winemaker%20Profiles.

Draper-Maytag Ridge Vineyards website, "York Creek," accessed October 8, 2014, www.ridgewine.com/Vineyards/York%20Creek. Maytag, who sold the Anchor Brewing Co. in 2010, remains the owner of the York Creek vineyard, Ridge's only Napa Valley grape source. Readers wanting to learn more about Maytag are directed to the author's book *The Audacity of Hops*.

"observe the separation" McCloskey e-mail to author, October 2, 2014.

McCloskey education; "things like chemistry" Darlington, "The Chemistry of a 90+ Wine."

"the critics were going to win" Ibid.

Enologix details Ibid.; Author's McCloskey interview and October 2014 e-mails; Alice Feiring, "For Better or Worse, Winemakers Go High Tech," *New York Times*, August 26, 2001, 3-4.

Vinovation Feiring, "For Better or Worse, Winemakers Go High Tech."

"emergency rescues" Ibid.

Some in the industry Author's McCloskey interview.

"Who among them"; Bonny Doon label Eric Asimov, "Vintner With Nothing to Hide Finds That Few Are Looking," *New York Times*, October 4, 2012, D4. Tartaric acid can help balance the acidity in wine; it is found naturally in grapes but sometimes has to be added if the grapes used are not particularly ripe.

Olken quotations; "superstars" Charles Olken, "The Winemaker as Heroic Figure," *Connoisseurs' Guide to California Wine*, April 3, 2014, accessed October 14, 2014, www.cgcw.com/databaseshowitem.aspx?id=80250.

"From the outside" Brian Halweil, "Alchemy in the Cellar," Edible East End, April 23, 2014, accessed October 14, 2014, www.edibleeastend.com/2014/04/23/alchemy-cellar/.

"There are even characters" Andrew Catchpole, "King of the Wine Frontier," *Telegraph*, September 22, 2001, 9.

employed more than one million National Grape & Wine Initiative, "Economic Impact Study," January 17, 2007. Accessed via California's Wine Institute.

"We've sold the math"; Dr. Frankenstein McCoy, *Emperor*, 266.

Château Lafite anecdote Darlington, "The Chemistry of a 90+ Wine."

Global Wine

sixty-five clients Feiring, "For Better or Worse, Winemakers Go High Tech." Based on number of wineries that had bought Enologix's software.

Import figures John Tagliabue, "Sobering News for Bacchus," *New York Times*, March 8, 1997, 37.

There was even talk of Peru Kevin G. Hall, "Grape Expectations," *Journal of Commerce*, November 12, 1997, 1A.

Spain was reasserting itself Cynthia Magriel Wetzler, "Consumers Discover the Wines of Spain," *New York Times*, October 25, 1998, 14WC.

overproduction at home European governments, particularly in Spain and Italy, spent—and overspent—subsidizing smaller wineries to the detriment of their overall industries, creating more wine than they had domestic consumers for (per Tagliabue, "Sobering News for Bacchus").

"There's a snobbism" Tagliabue, "Sobering News for Bacchus."

Italian, French drinking Ibid.

Sales and shipping Frank J. Prial, "Bordeaux Again Leads a High-Price Parade," *New York Times*, September 17, 1997, F10.

Prices Ibid.

"In most wine stores" Mort Hotchstein, "Retailer Highlights Wine Styles," *Wine Business Monthly*, January 2000.

"anti-wine store" Gerry Khermouch, "Less Is More: Best Cellars, in New York City, Pioneered a Unique Approach to Presenting Wine at Retail," *Beverage Dynamics*, March 1, 2007. The author met Wesson during a talk on the East End of Long Island in February 2014, where they informally discussed the American fine wine movement.

Screwed

Thierry Bouchon wake; Grahm quotation George Taber, *To Cork or Not to Cork* (New York: Scribner, 2009), 157–58; Jancis Robinson, "Mourning the Cork in New York," JancisRobinson.com, 2, 2002, www.jancisrobinson.com/articles/mourning-the-cork -in-new-york; Author's Grahm interview. This book uses the term *screwtops* rather than *screwcaps* or *screw caps* (both of which remind the author of the seals on cheaper bottles of beer); the terms, though, can be understood to be interchangeable.

Jancis Robinson eulogy Robinson, "Mourning the Cork in New York."

The trade press had gotten the message Author's Grahm interview.

If I can mobilize Ibid.

PlumpJack founding, Getty-Newsom relationship Chuck Finnie, Rachel Gordon, and Lance Williams, "Newsom's Portfolio," *San Francisco Chronicle*, February 23, 2003; "History," Plumpjack Winery website, accessed September 5, 2014, www.plumpjackwinery .com/our-story/history.

Uniqueness, significance of PlumpJack's screwtop decision Author's interview with John Conover, September 8, 2014; Frank J. Prial, "Boldly, Off with Its Head," *New York Times*, October 31, 2001, F1; "PlumpJack Winery Owners Announce First Screw Cap Closures for Luxury Wine," press release from PlumpJack republished on Just-Drinks.com, June 6, 2000, accessed March 5, 2015, www.just-drinks.com/news/plumpjack-winery -owners-announce-first-screw-cap-closures-for-luxury-wine_id75088.aspx. PlumpJack chose the popular Stelvin screwtop, developed in the 1950s and first used in France, as its closure.

Price per bottle "PlumpJack Winery Owners Announce First Screw Cap Closures for Luxury Wine."

corks failed to adequately protect Author's interview with Conover.

cork producers and suppliers were; "fed up" Author's interview with Grahm.

Reaction of production, marketing sides Conover, general manager of PlumpJack, in a YouTube promotional video about the decision, accessed September 5, 2014, www .youtube.com/watch?v=Lu9UP9fbxCI; author's interview with Conover.

"For most wine consumers" Prial, "Boldly, Off with Its Head."

one of the more profitable John Mariani, "PlumpJack by Getty, Newsom Is First-Rate Tipple," *Bloomberg*, January 20, 2006.

one estimate pegged 2013 Paul Gregutt, "Screw Caps Go Upscale," *Wine Enthusiast*, May, 14, 2013. The estimate was "about 10 percent."

as high as 80 percent Curtis Phillips, "Consistency Key in Selecting Closures," *Wine Business Monthly*, June 2014, 20. It seemed the production of a winery determined the amount of bottles capped with screwcaps vs. corks of whatever material. Wineries producing at least fifty thousand cases annually used screwcaps more than smaller wineries (Ibid., 19).

perhaps fewer than 3 percent Eric Asimov, "A Hiccup in Screw Tops' Acceptance," *New York Times*, September 26, 2007, F8.

2005 study and excerpt M. Brajkovich, N. Tibbits, G. Peron, C. Lund, S. Dykes, P. Kilmartin, and L. Nicolau, "Effect of screwcap and cork closures on SO2 levels and aromas in Sauvignon Blanc Wine," *Journal of Agricultural and Food Chemistry*, 53:10006–10011. 2005, through the University of California, Davis.

"I was guessing that the bottle" Richard Jennings, "Cork vs. Screw Cap at 14 Years: Plump-Jack Reserve Cabernet," RJonWine.com, April 9, 2011, accessed September 8, 2014, www.rjonwine.com/blindtastings/cork-vs-screw-cap-plumpjack-reserve/.

"We noticed, however" "In Pictures: Great Wines Under Cork and Screw Cap," *Forbes*, January 29, 2009.

Market share figures Daniel Sogg, "Screw Caps Gain Acceptance," *Wine Spectator*, July 31, 2007, accessed September 8, 2014, www.winespectator.com/wssaccess/show/id/40811.

biggest market for screwtop wines Based on the fact that the United States would far outpace the overall wine markets of other nations that produced or imported screwtopped wines by 2014.

Fat Bastards and Smoking Loons

Anderson-Boudinaud conversation, relationship Deborah Scoblionkov, "Duo's Wine Is Going Places," *Philadelphia Inquirer*, May 27, 2004, F01; "Our Story," Fat Bastard website, accessed September 11, 2014, www.fatbastardwine.com/our-story.php.

Sales figures, impact Scoblionkov, "Duo's Wine Is Going Places;" William Grimes, "With Rude Names, Wine Stops Minding Its Manners," *New York Times*, December 6, 2011, D1.

best-selling French-made Chardonnay Scoblionkov, "Duo's Wine Is Going Places."

Fat Bastard Living Large tour details Ibid.

acquired in California's Central Valley "Our History," Woodbridge by Robert Mondavi website, accessed September 12, 2014, www.woodbridgewines.com/Inside-Woodbridge /mondavi-history.htm.

"suburban subdivisions" Grimes, "With Rude Names, Wine Stops Minding Its Manners."

Wetzel, Sin Zin Dave McIntyre, "The Lure of Sin Zins," *Washington Post*, August 4, 2014; "Wetzel Family," Alexander Valley Vineyards website, October 9, 2014, www.avvwine .com/about.html.

Cardinal Zin, Big House McIntyre, "The Lure of Sin Zins"; Lubow, "The Do Over."

to around $27 million Chris Rauber, "Bonny Doon Sells Big House, Cardinal Zin Brands," *Silicon Valley Business Journal*, August 1, 2006.

California Polytechnic State University study Vince Bonafede, "Analysis of Wine Label Design Aesthetics and the Correlation to Price," presented to the faculty and Agribusiness Department of California Polytechnic State University, March 2010.

"We're more like" Scoblionkov, "Duo's Wine Is Going Places."

"just turned on to wine" Ibid.

Sir Robert and the Fruit Bombs

"Merci, le President!" McCoy, *Emperor*, 248.

Legion of Honor Ibid., 247–49; Charles Bremner, "Top Wine Aware Greeted by Sour Grapes," *Times (London)*, November 20, 2000. It should be noted that Parker was technically not knighted by the French president. American citizens cannot accept noble honors, and republican France doesn't really dispense them anymore; but *chevalier* translates as "knight." In 2005, Chirac promoted Parker to an "officer" in the Legion of Honor. The leaders of Spain and Italy would bestow similarly high accolades upon the critic during the decade (per "About Robert M. Parker Jr.," eRobertParker.com)

forty thousand subscribers; forty dollars annually Shaw, "When Parker Spits, the World Listens."

"vin de putes" Bremner, "Top Wine Aware Greeted by Sour Grapes."

"The 100-point wines" McCoy, *Emperor*, 262.

"waddle"; "hedonist" Langewiesche, "The Million-Dollar Nose;" McCoy, *Emperor*, 248.

In 1997, during a ten-course meal Langewiesche, "The Million-Dollar Nose."

started noticing something Author's interview with Alice Feiring, October 25, 2013.

"How could anybody" Ibid.

"I Am Not Drinking Any Fucking Merlot"

Legion of Honor ceremony Heidi B. Perlman, "Julia Child Honored for Demystifying French Cooking," Associated Press, November 19, 2000; "Legion D'Honneur for Julia Child For Popularizing French Cuisine," *New York Times*, November 20, 2000, A22. Robert Mondavi was also inducted into the Legion in 2005.

The word foodie *itself seems to have bubbled* The rise of *foodie* in the lexicon is based on a NexisLexis search for the word back to the 1970s in newspapers and magazines. Its usage appears to have become really common toward the turn of the century.

Slow Food manifesto Acitelli, *Audacity of Hops*, 166.

"Today, from Mattituck, N.Y., to Mendocino" Frank J. Prial, "There's a Genie in the Cellar," *New York Times*, May 30, 2001, F1.

it had 5,689 locations "Planet Starbucks," *Bloomberg Businessweek*, September 9, 2002, 100–10.

drew protesters waving signs Colin Moynihan, "Protest Season Opens in the East Village," *New York Times*, June 15, 2008, A28.

"They drink wine and boutique beers" "The Classes Drift Apart," *Economist*, February 4, 2012.

acquired Joshua Wesson's Best Cellars "A&P Announces Purchase of Best Cellars," Business Wire, November 15, 2007. The move was a big deal at the time—A&P, though headed for financial trouble, had been called "Wal-Mart before Wal-Mart" because of its ubiquity (per David Kansas, "A&P Heading to the Checkout Counter," *Market Beat*, December 10, 2010).

"an increased focus" "The New York Times Continues Its National Expansion With a New Section and a Significantly Enlarged National Edition," Business Wire, March 25, 2002.

started wine clubs Vadim Lavrusik, "News Organizations Seek New Revenue in Wine Clubs," NY Food Chain, September 24, 2009, accessed April 8, 2014, http://archives .jrn.columbia.edu/2009/nyfoodchain.com/2009/09/24/news-organizations-seek-new -revenue-in-wine-clubs/.

"dozens of great wine books" Geoff Last, "Read; Then Choose a Wine," *Calgary Herald*, December 15, 2002, D15.

Alder Yarrow Author's e-mail exchange with Alder Yarrow, October 2013; "About This Site," Vinography, accessed April 25, 2014, www.vinography.com/about.html.

"Excellent light style lets" Internet Archive Way Back Machine, accessed April 25, 2014, https://web.archive.org/web/20040201223815/http://www.vinography.com/.

there were at least five hundred Derrick Schneider, "As Wine Blogs Mature, What's the Impact?," *San Francisco Chronicle*, February 21, 2010.

appeared to exert Ibid.; author's conversations with various people in the industry.

"Basically, the whole wine blog world" Ibid.

made much of their love Bill Ward, "For Lidia, the Heart of Cooking Is Family," *Minneapolis Star Tribune*, October 22, 2009, 1T. Batali apparently enjoyed Michigan wines (per Lee Levitt, "Like Star-Quality Wine? Try Sipping 'Madonna' On the Shores of Lake Michigan," *Jerusalem Post*, November 22, 2009, 7).

Cooking show ratings Gary Levin, "Food Shows Whip TV Networks Into a Frenzy; Audiences Are Eating It Up," *USA Today*, December 24, 2009, 1D.

It also damaged Merlot sales Steven Cuellar, "The 'Sideways' Effect," *Wines & Vines*, January 2009. Per Cuellar's article, the negative effects on Merlot were "confined mostly to the lower-priced segment, under $10 per bottle, while the effects on Pinot Noir [were] positive across price-points, with the largest impact being on the highest price point of $20–$40 per bottle."

"I adore France" Perlman, "Julia Child Honored for Demystifying French Cooking."

A Constellation of Wines

Mike Grgich conversation Robert F. Howe, "The Fall of the House of Mondavi," CNNMoney, April 1, 2005, accessed March 5, 2015, http://money.cnn.com/magazines/business2 /business2_archive/2005/04/01/8256045/.

"cheer of liberation" William D. Murray, "Robert Mondavi Stock Offering Sparks Excitement in Napa Valley," United Press International, April 23, 1993. The falling out with Bank of America had more to do with the bank's merger with Security Pacific than with the winery.

"This is the most exciting thing" Ibid.

"prestige buys" Ibid.

Initial public offering details "Mondavi Winery Makes Initial Public Offering," Associated Press, June 10, 1993.

two non-premium brands accounted Jerry Hirsch, "Mondavi Stock Surges on Sale Speculation," *Los Angeles Times*, August 24, 2004.

"We've got to get" Frank Prial, "The Grapevine Is Whispering, It Says Mondavi," *New York Times*, September 16, 2004, C1.

"What Robert built up" Howe, "The Fall of the House of Mondavi."

"Usurping the name" Ibid.

Family fighting Ibid.; Julia Flynn Siler, "Grapes of Wrath: Inside a Napa Valley Empire, a Family Struggles with Itself," JuliaFlynnSiler.com, accessed March 31, 2014, http://juliaflynnsiler.com/articles/grapes-of-wrath-inside-a-napa-valley-empire-a-family-struggles-with-itselftwo-rival-mondavi-brothers-are-replaying-past-battles-.

"If I had to do it" Howe, "The Fall of the House of Mondavi."

"for drinkers who wanted" Ibid.

Ted Hall, a former director Carol Emert, "Outsider to Lead Mondavi," *San Francisco Chronicle*, January 16, 2004.

threatened Hall with a hostile takeover Lea Goldman, "Big Gulp," *Forbes*, January 10, 2005.

Sands; Constellation growth Ibid.; "Canandaigua Brands Inc. Announces Name Change to Constellation Brands Inc.," Business Wire, August 28, 2000.

"to sell to them all" Goldman, "Big Gulp."

Sales, profit figures Prial, "Robert Mondavi, Napa Wine Champion, Dies at 94"; Jerry Hirsch, "Mondavi Stock Surges on Sale Speculation," *Los Angeles Times*, August 24, 2004.

Deal details Howe, "The Fall of the House of Mondavi"; James Laube, "Mondavi to Join Constellation in $1 Billion Deal," *Wine Spectator* online, November 3, 2004, accessed March 5, 2015, www.winespectator.com/webfeature/show/id/Mondavi-to-Join-Constellation-in-1-Billion-Deal_2263. Robert Mondavi remained as a "brand ambassador" for the Constellation-controlled winery. Tim and Michael Mondavi fanned out to pursue their own ventures in California wine-making.

Cabernet collaboration Howe, "The Fall of the House of Mondavi"; Michelle Locke, "Calif. wine pioneer Robert Mondavi dies," *USA Today*, May 17, 2008.

Big Money

Inglenook demolition, including "Inglenook was a Picasso" and "blunder" Paul Franson, "Coppola Demolishes Barrel Building," *Wines & Vines* online, December 13, 2007, accessed March 5, 2015, www.winesandvines.com/template.cfm?section=news&content=51917; Inglenook marketing material given to the author in March 2014.

"I get calls from" Robert Lindsey, "Popularity of Wines Unleashes Growth Pains in California Valley," *New York Times*, May 30, 1981, 1–7.

Wine-making costs Frank Prial, "Big Wineries Being Acquired by Big Names," *New York Times*, December 29, 2004, C7; author's interview with Dyson DeMara, August 23, 2014.

for roughly $1 million Author's interview with Bo Barrett, March 27, 2014.

for $2,000 each Taber, *Judgment*, 291.

at least $18,000 Gerald B. White, "Cost of Establishment and Production of Vinifera Grapes in the Finger Lakes Region of New York—2010," Charles H. Dyson School of Applied Economics and Management, College of Agriculture and Life Sciences, Cornell University, July 2011.

in the Northwest The Northwest Grapes Cost-Of-Production Calculators from the Washington Association of Wine Grape Growers. The $9,000 figure was for conventionally grown grapes with certain assumed costs and yields, including two and a half tons by year three. The costs were slightly cheaper for those grown organically.

Consolidations Prial, "Big Wineries Being Acquired by Big Names."

"to better reflect" "Our Heritage," Constellation Brands website, accessed March 5, 2015, www.cbrands.com/about-us/our-heritage.

the early 2008 sale "Constellation Brands Sells Almaden, Inglenook," Australian Stock Exchange, January 24, 2008. Constellation would also sell other brands during the latter half of the first decade of the 2000s, including Columbia Winery, Covey Run, and Idaho's Ste. Chapelle, to a privately held California firm (per "Our Heritage").

eventually be worth Charles Storch, "Crown Zellerbach to be Split Up, Sold," *Chicago Tribune*, December 17, 1985.

"The old wine country adage" Prial, "Big Wineries Being Acquired by Big Names."

One in five acres Kevin Courtney, "Conaway: Napa at Mercy of 'Vineyard Elite,'" *Napa Valley Register*, April 25, 2008.

"Swarms of millionaires," other quotations in paragraph Ibid.

built housing within vineyards Kristina Shevory, "Buying Into the Vineyard Lifestyle," *New York Times*, September 5, 2008, F1.

Garage Revolutionaries and Virtual Giants

"Whether you're a CEO" "Make Your Own Wine in Napa Valley at Judd's Hill's Micro-Crush," Business Wire, July 29, 2010.

"Hawaiian nut"; other details Carey Sweet, "Judd's Hill: Try Their Wine, or Blend Your Own," SFGate.com, January 15, 2012, accessed March 5, 2015, www.sfgate.com/travel /article/Judd-s-Hill-Try-their-wine-or-blend-your-own-2515739.php.

a fairly new phenomenon The terms *garagistes* or *garage wineries* do not appear to have shown up in an American newspaper until around 2000, when Frank Prial wrote about the phenomenon in Bordeaux. Judd's Hill's reference to itself as "one of the first 'garagiste' wineries" in that July 2010 press release suggests that the American wine industry was just then beginning to think in those terms, even if the idea of small-batch wine-making was obviously much older.

Prial excerpts Frank J. Prial, "$1,000 Wines You Never Heard Of," *New York Times*, October 25, 2000, F1.

Parker's fandom Langewiesche, "The Million-Dollar Nose."

dismissed garagistes Panos Kakaviatos, "Garage Wines Face Troubled Times," *Decanter*, July 1, 2005.

"We are not garagistes" Prial, "$1,000 Wines You Never Heard Of."

Nicholas Baby coined Ibid.

the wine-making co-op or village Lawrence M. Fisher, "Wine Made the Co-op Way," *New York Times*, October 6, 2006, C1.

"Own your own vineyard" Ibid.

the Great Recession only strengthened Jessica Yadegaran, "High-end vintners get creative as economy goes south," *Contra Costa Times*, February 25, 2009, Food.

none of America's bestselling Keith Wallace, "How Wine Became Like Fast Food," *Daily Beast*, November 3, 2009, accessed March 5, 2015, www.thedailybeast.com /articles/2009/11/03/how-wine-became-like-fast-food.html.

"Those bottles may look beautiful" Ibid.

Dyson DeMara details Author's interview with Dyson DeMara.

Silver Oak Cellars "Our Story," Silver Oak Cellars website, accessed October 12, 2014, www.silveroak.com/our-story/; Lisa Ryckman, "Colorado Business Hall of Fame: Ray Duncan," *Colorado Business*, January 1, 2012.

Gary Andrus, Pine Ridge Harvey Steiman, "Gary Andrus Dies," *Wine Spectator*, February 2, 2009.

DeMara quotations, thoughts Author's interview with DeMara.

A Journey Ends

Gary Vaynerchuk and Wine Library TV Stephen Foley, "The Grape Crusader," *Independent Extra*, August 4, 2008, 2. Old videos, including the June 20, 2008 one, can be found through http://tv.winelibrary.com/.

sold out within days Foley, "The Grape Crusader."

"the first major wine critic" Ibid.

"The California wine scene" Jancis Robinson, "Robert Mondavi Dies," JancisRobinson .com, May 16, 2008, accessed March 5, 2005, www.jancisrobinson.com/articles/robert -mondavi-dies.

"the single greatest influence" Bill Daley, "Mondavi Taught Us to Find Life in Wine," *Chicago Tribune*, September 19, 2012.

he saw no need to revise Ibid.

"With other promoters of good living" Prial, "Robert Mondavi, Napa Wine Champion, Dies at 94."

"He was very successful" Daley, "Mondavi Taught Us to Find Life in Wine."

Barrett-Mondavi exchange Author's interview with Bo Barrett, March 27, 2014.

On Parkerization, Naturally

a score of 100 upon nineteen wines Julian Knight, "Wine Investors Raise a Glass to the 2009 Bordeaux," *Independent*, March 11, 2012.

"so sumptuous"; "perhaps to go back" John Lichfield, "A Vintage Year," *Independent*, October 9, 2009, 32.

Eric Asimov excerpts Eric Asimov, "Bordeaux: A Red Goes Gray," *New York Times*, May 19, 2010, D1.

"[F]ocusing on Parker's influence" Talia Baiocchi, "Robert Parker's Waning Influence on the Current Generation of Wine Drinkers," Eater National, December 13, 2012, accessed March 5, 2015, www.eater.com/2012/12/13/6508381/robert-parkers-waning-influence -on-the-current-generation-of-wine.

California alone had more; number of New York wineries "US Wine Industry—2011," US Commerce Department, prepared by Donald A. Hodgen, 2015, accessed March 5, www.ita.doc.gov/td/ocg/wwtg.htm.

amount of imported wine; 30 percent of the wine Ibid.

had sixteen thousand members Anne Valdespino, "Welcome to the Club," *Orange County Register*, April 1, 2005.

"And we all pretend" Ron Washam, "Robert Parker's Vintners Hall of Fame Speech," HoseMaster of Wine, October 4, 2012, accessed May 5, 2014, http://hosemasterofwine .blogspot.com/2012/10/robert-parkers-vintners-hall-of-fame.html. Parker was inducted in 2013, along with labor leader Cesar Chavez and critic-turned-merchant Frank Schoonmaker. The Vintners Hall of Fame confronted financial trouble in the early part of the 2010s as expenses outran revenue, and its prospects for continuing looked bleak. Moreover, and perhaps understandably, nearly half of its inductees

from 2007 to 2013 were associated with Napa Valley, prompting criticism that the hall was too narrowly focused (per Mike Dunne, "Vintners Hall of Fame Election on Hold," *Sacramento Bee*, February 25, 2014).

"Decanter is now a global" "Decanter Re-Launches Buying Guide to Include 100-Point Scale," Decanter.com, June 28, 2012, accessed May 5, 2014, www.decanter.com /news/wine-news/530102/decanter-relaunches-buying-guide-to-include-100-point -scale#W0zCCI2slSEcVKcJ.99.

Critics of other foodstuffs, especially beer The adoption of the one-hundred-point scale by beer publications such as *All About Beer* and *Beer Advocate* prompted its own counterreaction in the craft beer world, with many of the same questions and concerns raised there as in the fine wine movement.

"It never occurred to me" Baiocchi, "Robert Parker's Waning Influence on the Current Generation of Wine Drinkers."

"I've never been a fan" S. Irene Virbila, "Robert Parker Goes Toe-to-Toe with His Critics," *Los Angeles Times*, February 27, 2014.

Alice Feiring excerpts Alice Feiring, *The Battle for Wine and Love: Or How I Saved the World From Parkerization* (Boston: Houghton Mifflin Harcourt, 2008), introduction.

Parker excerpts S. Irene Virbila, "Robert Parker Goes Toe-to-Toe with His Critics."

born in France in the 1990s Peter Hellman, "Natural Wines Gain Popularity, Despite Their Funky Flavors," *New York Post*, November 26, 2013.

"no more than a tiny collection" Eric Asimov, "Wines Worth a Taste, But Not the Vitriol," *New York Times*, January 24, 2012, D6. Asimov also covers the controversy around natural wines.

"one of the major scams" Ibid.

"essentially a phony anti-California" Virbila, "Robert Parker Goes Toe-to-Toe with His Critics."

whom Parker discovered Author's interview with Pierre-Antoine Rovani, October 22, 2013.

Pierre-Antoine Rovani quotes Langewiesche, "The Million-Dollar Nose."

An "Incomprehensible" Triumph

Richard Hodgson details David Derbyshire, "So You Think You've Got a Nose for a Good Wine? Think Again . . ." *Observer*, June 23, 2013, 20.

"a who's who of the American" Ibid.

six thousand blind tastings Ibid.

showed that labels profoundly affected Adam Sage, "Cheeky Little Test Exposes Wine 'Experts' as Weak and Flat," *Times (London)*, January 14, 2002. The same academic, Frederic Brochet, also showed that some of the best Bordeaux experts could not tell the difference between a red and a white—he added coloring to the white, and no one noticed (Ibid.).

Richard Axel and Linda Buck "The Nobel Prize in Physiology or Medicine 2004," October 4, 2004, NobelPrize.org, accessed March 5, 2015, www.nobelprize.org/nobel_prizes /medicine/laureates/2004/.

Linda Bartoshuk concluded Mary Beckman, "A Matter of Taste," *Smithsonian* magazine, August 2004.

"a powerful tool" Tony Hendra, "'The Emperor of Wine': The New World Order," *New York Times*, August 7, 2005, Book Review, 6.

"I can tell you this" Tom Wark, "Robert Parker and Digging a Wine Critic's Grave," Fermentation Wine Blog, December 19, 2012, accessed May 9, 2014, http://fermentationwineblog.com/2012/12/robert-parker-and-the-grave-diggers-of-a-wine-critic/.

Craft beer details The reader is directed to the author's previous book, *The Audacity of Hops*. Also: Brewers Association, "State of Craft Beer," 2013. The breweries that stayed open during Prohibition produced products such as cola, low-alcohol "near beer," or malt extract, which was not supposed to be for homebrewing. There were no breweries comparable to the wineries sustained by orders for grape juice and sacramental wine.

had been on the decline James Temple, "Joy for Java," *Contra Costa Times*, April 4, 2005, D01.

Starbucks' entrepreneurial roll Elizabeth Lee, "No Average Joe," *Atlanta Journal-Constitution*, October 27, 2005, 1E; Beth Kowitt, "Starbucks' Grocery Gambit," CNNMoney, December 5, 2013.

Starbucks' nearly 13 percent share Rachel Tepper, "Starbucks Aims for Grocery Store Supremacy with New Signature Aisle," *Huffington Post*, April 26, 2013, accessed March 5, 2015, www.huffingtonpost.com/2013/04/26/starbucks-grocery-store-aisle_n_3157075.html.

Starbucks' bestselling retail brand Author's e-mail exchange with Starbucks representative, May 2014. French Roast description and wine comparison from representative and the company.

approximately 37 percent "Specialty Coffee Facts & Figures, Updated March 2012," Specialty Coffee Association of America.

It should also be noted in any discussion of the near-simultaneous rises of fine wine, craft beer and premium coffee that craft brewers and coffee companies, like wineries, began in the later decades of the twentieth century to luxuriate in adjective-laden descriptions of their products. That, too, seemed to be what consumers wanted.

"People don't want to drink wine" Shaw, *Los Angeles Times*, February 23, 1999.

"If you blame anyone" Ibid.

"golden age for wine drinkers" Eric Asimov, Facebook post, September 14, 2012, accessed May 19, 2014, www.facebook.com/ericasimovhowtolovewine/posts/153513694789232.

Judgment of Paris reenactment, quotes Linda Murphy, "Judgment Day: Part Deux," *San Francisco Chronicle*, June 1, 2006; Eric Asimov, "Judgment, Schmudgment," *New York Times*, June 2, 2006, Diner's Journal blog, accessed March 5, 2015, http://dinersjournal.blogs.nytimes.com/2006/06/02/judgment-schmudgment/. The same 1971 Cabernet Sauvignon from Ridge finished fifth among the reds in the original Judgment of Paris.

Epilogue: The World's Biggest Wine Country

For the run-down on what happened to whom, the author took information from sources about those individuals already cited in these endnotes.

the world's biggest wine market "The Wine Market: Developments and Trends," International Organization of Wine and Vine, May 13, 2014. While it did not spell out grape types, the OIV did note that "bottled wines and sparkling wines made up the vast majority of the world wine market."

nearly 40 percent of French men Krishnadev Calamur, "For the Win(e): US Passes France as World's Top Wine Consumer," NPR's Salt blog, May 14, 2014, accessed May

20, 2014, www.npr.org/blogs/thesalt/2014/05/14/312478455/for-the-win-e-u-s-passes
-france-as-worlds-top-wine-consumer.

Statistics on growth, consumption, retail value, grape acreage, export "California Wine Sales
Grow 3% by Volume and 5% by Value in the US in 2013," California Wine Institute, April 24, 2014; "2013 Agricultural Crop Report," Napa County Department of
Agriculture and Weights & Measures. Other reports placed the number of American
wineries at around 7,700. The California Wine Institute's statistics, however, have been
used throughout this book, and therefore the author has gone with its 2012 total of
more than 8,800; these numbers include virtual wineries. The discrepancies in winery
totals could come from the fact that the institute counts every one the government
bonded, including individual producers and experimental wineries.

Wine Advocate *deal* Edmund Lee, "*Wine Advocate*'s Robert Parker Stepping Down as
Editor," *Bloomberg*, December 10, 2012. Neither side ever disclosed the financial
terms of the deal, but there was wide speculation that it totaled $15 million. It's
interesting, too, that none of the three buyers were older than fifty, according to
Parker—decidedly younger than the baby boomer contingency that had so long sustained the *Wine Advocate*.

Lisa Perrotti-Brown "About Lisa Perrotti-Brown MW," *Wine Advocate* website, accessed
August 15, 2014, www.erobertparker.com/info/lpbrown.asp; Rebecca Gibb, "Lisa
Perrotti-Brown: Playwright to Wine Advocate Chief," Wine-Searcher.com, July 24,
2013, accessed August 15, 2014, www.wine-searcher.com/m/2013/07/lisa-perrotti
-brown-from-playwright-to-wine-advocate-editor.

"The move recognizes" Eric Asimov, "Changes at the Wine Advocate Signal a Shift in the
Market," *New York Times*, Diner's Journal, December 10, 2012.

SELECTED BIBLIOGRAPHY

The following is not intended to be a complete bibliography. It instead contains books related to fine wine that might be of interest to the reader, including ones consulted for this book.

Acitelli, Tom. *The Audacity of Hops: The History of America's Craft Beer Revolution.* Chicago: Chicago Review Press, 2013.

Amerine, Maynard A., and M. A. Joslyn. *Table Wines: The Technology of Their Production.* 2nd ed. Berkeley: University of California Press, 1970.

Balzer, Robert Lawrence. *Wines of California.* New York: Harry N. Abrams, 1978.

Bonné, Jon. *The New California Wine: A Guide to the Producers and Wines Behind a Revolution in Taste.* Berkeley: Ten Speed Press, 2013.

Bruns, Roger. *Cesar Chavez and the United Farm Workers Movement.* Santa Barbara, CA: Greenwood, 2011.

Cattell, Hudson. *Wines of Eastern North America: From Prohibition to the Present—A History and Desk Reference.* Ithaca, NY: Cornell University Press, 2014.

Child, Julia, Louisette Bertholle, and Simone Beck. *Mastering the Art of French Cooking.* New York: Alfred Knopf, 2010.

Child, Julia, with Alex Prud'Homme. *My Life in France.* New York: A. A. Knopf, 2006.

Conaway, James. *Napa: The Story of an American Eden.* New York: Mariner Books, 2002.

Crain, Neil, and Katherine Crain. *The History of Texas Wine: From Spanish Roots to Rising Star.* Charleston, SC: History Press, 2013.

Feiring, Alice. *The Battle for Love and Wine: Or How I Saved the World from Parkerization.* Boston: Mariner Books, 2009.

———. *Naked Wine: Letting Grapes Do What Comes Naturally.* Cambridge, MA: Da Capo Press, 2011.

Gallo, Ernest, and Julio Gallo, with Bruce Henderson. *Ernest & Julio: Our Story.* New York: Random House, 1994.

Haeger, John Winthrop. *North American Pinot Noir.* Berkeley: University of California Press, 2004.

Halpern, Dan, ed. *Not for Bread Alone: Writers on Food, Wine, and the Art of Eating.* New York: HarperCollins, 2009.

Hargrave, Louisa. *The Vineyard: A Memoir.* New York: Penguin Books, 2004.

Johnson, Hugh, and Jancis Robinson. *The World Atlas of Wine.* 7th ed. London: Mitchell Beazley, 2013.

Kamp, David. *The United States of Arugula: How We Became a Gourmet Nation.* New York: Broadway Books, 2006.

Kladstrup, Don, and Petie Kladstrup. *Wine & War: The French, the Nazis & the Battle for France's Greatest Treasure.* New York: Broadway Books, 2001.

Lukacs, Paul. *American Vintage: The Rise of American Wine.* New York: Houghton Mifflin, 2000.

McCoy, Elin. *The Emperor of Wine: The Rise of Robert M. Parker, Jr. and the Reign of American Taste.* New York: Ecco, 2005.

McInerney, Jay. *Bacchus and Me: Adventures in the Wine Cellar.* New York: Vintage, 2002.

———. *A Hedonist in the Cellar: Adventures in Wine.* New York: Vintage, 2007.

Mondavi, Robert, with Paul Chutkow. *Harvests of Joy: How the Good Life Became Great Business.* New York: Harcourt Brace, 1998.

Parker, Robert M., Jr. *Bordeaux: A Consumer's Guide to the World's Finest Wines.* 4th ed. New York: Simon & Schuster, 2003.

Parr, Rajat, and Jordan Mackay. *Secrets of the Sommeliers: How to Think and Drink Like the World's Top Wine Professionals.* Berkeley: Ten Speed Press, 2010.

Pinney, Thomas. *A History of Wine in America.* Vol. 2, *From Prohibition to the Present.* Berkeley: University of California Press, 2005.

Polan, Dana. *Julia Child's* The French Chef. Durham, NC: Duke University Press, 2011.

Reardon, Joan, ed. *As Always, Julia: The Letters of Julia Child and Avis DeVoto.* Boston: Houghton Mifflin Harcourt, 2010.

Rowe, Walker Elliott. *A History of Virginia Wines: From Grapes to Glass.* Charleston, SC: History Press, 2009.

Schneider, Steven J. *The International Album of Wine: Your Personal Record of Wine Labels and Tastes.* New York: Holt, Rinehart and Winston, 1977.

Schoonmaker, Frank. *Encyclopedia of Wine.* New York: Hastings House, 1965.

Siler, Julia Flynn. *The House of Mondavi: The Rise and Fall of an American Wine Dynasty.* New York: Gotham Books, 2007.

Smith, Andrew F. *Eating History: 30 Turning Points in the Making of American Cuisine.* New York: Columbia University Press, 2009.

Spitz, Bob. *Dearie: The Remarkable Life of Julia Child.* New York: A. A. Knopf, 2012.

Sullivan, Charles L. *Zinfandel: A History of a Grape and Its Wine.* Berkeley: University of California Press, 2003.

Taber, George M. *Judgment of Paris: California vs. France and the Historic 1976 Paris Tasting That Revolutionized Wine.* New York: Scribner, 2005.

———. *A Toast to Bargain Wines: How Innovators, Iconoclasts, and Winemaking Revolutionaries Are Changing the Way the World Drinks.* New York: Scribner, 2011.

———. *To Cork or Not to Cork: Tradition, Romance, Science, and the Battle for the Wine Bottle.* New York: Scribner, 2009.

Wallace, Benjamin. *The Billionaire's Vinegar: The Mystery of the World's Most Expensive Bottle of Wine.* New York: Three Rivers Press, 2009.

INDEX